Fifth Edition ————————————

D0082347

THE 500-WORD THEME

Discovery,
Organization,
Expression

————————————————————

Harry P. Kroitor
Texas A&M University

Lee J. Martin

PRENTICE HALL, Englewood Cliffs, New Jersey 07632

Library of Congress Cataloging-in-Publication Data

Kroitor, Harry P.
    The five-hundred-word theme: discovery, organization, expression/
    Harry P. Kroitor and Lee J . Martin.—5th ed.
        p.   cm.
    Includes index.
    ISBN 0–13–321357–9
    1. English language—Rhetoric.   I. Martin, Lee J.   II. Title.
III. Title: 500 word theme.
PE1408.K77   1994
808′.042—dc20   93–20440
                                                              CIP

Acquisitions editor: Alison Reeves
Editorial/production supervision, page layout,
    and interior design: Colette Conboy, Jenny Moss
Cover design: Design Solutions
Production coordinator: Herb Klein
Editorial assistant: Kara Hado

© 1994, 1984, 1979, 1974, 1968 by Prentice-Hall, Inc.
A Paramount Communications Company
Englewood Cliffs, New Jersey 07632

Printed in the United States of America
10 9 8 7 6 5 4 3 2 1

ISBN 0-13-321357-9

Prentice-Hall International (UK) Limited, *London*
Prentice-Hall of Australia Pty. Limited, *Sydney*
Prentice-Hall Canada Inc., *Toronto*
Prentice-Hall Hispanoamericana, S.A., *Mexico*
Prentice-Hall of India Private Limited, *New Delhi*
Prentice-Hall of Japan, Inc., *Tokyo*
Simon & Schuster Asia Pte. Ltd., *Singapore*
Editora Prentice-Hall do Brasil, Ltda., *Rio de Janeiro*

Contents

2 SEEING THE WHOLE PAPER 16

3 GETTING STARTED: DISCOVERY, SPECIFIC FOCUS, THESIS 47

Contents

4 MAINTAINING UNITY AND COHERENCE   86

5 UNDERSTANDING THE PARAGRAPH   113

8 RESEARCHED WRITING AND THE LONG PAPER   214

PART TWO: REVISION: MECHANICS AND STYLE   272

9 MECHANICS: GRAMMAR, PUNCTUATION, SPELLING   272

11 REVISING YOUR PAPER: SENTENCES   359

12 THE ESSAY AT WORK 389

Preface

Although this fifth edition of *The Five-Hundred-Word Theme* is more than twice the length of Lee J. Martin's original 1968 version, I have retained the basic conceptual approach of that first edition, modifying and extending material primarily to provide a clear rhetorical framework. Since Martin's death over twenty years ago, I've kept this rhetorical focus central, despite the added chapters on the researched paper and the mechanics of expression. Because Martin never intended the idea of a limited five-hundred-word essay to become proscriptive, I have now affirmed this in the book's opening unit. To support and extend the work begun with Martin continues to give me great satisfaction.

This edition still presents basic thinking approaches to writing short papers and the developmental paragraphs that comprise them. Increasingly I've emphasized that if nothing is going on "upstairs," little or nothing can happen on the blank page or computer screen. By defining the term "five-hundred-word theme" in the first chapter, I hope to encourage the view that the term increasingly has become synonymous with "short paper," and that writers aren't held to exactly five hundred words. Paradigms and picture-outlines, I suggest, are starting points only; an active mind should be able to move beyond them. More important, the paper's one logical point (thesis) should be clearly focused through one specific *controlling attitude* established in an introductory paragraph and then adequately developed in two, three, *or more* supporting paragraphs.

I have completely rewritten Chapter 1 on the traditional "modes," tying the explanations more closely to *purpose* and emphasizing the widespread practice of combining modes. I've added writing assignments, exercises, and examples designed to stimulate writer interest and raise questions for class discussion. In Chapter 2 I have extended the material on the relationship between the inductive and deductive approaches, suggesting that beginning writers may want to practice the simpler inductive pattern (Theme Pattern A) before trying the deductive one. For example, the chapter includes a new diagram to show how the "funnel effect" works in the inductive approach. I've replaced the model theme "Unleashed Danger" with "People Problems" (an essay about the human causes of highway auto accidents). The chapter's unit on outlining and the picture-outline reflect the organization of this new paper. "Unleashed Danger" remains, however, as an exercise option at the end of the chapter.

To allow more flexibility in the prewriting discovery process, I have also completely rewritten Chapter 3 ("Getting Started: Discovery, Specific Focus, Thesis"). It now includes short units (with exercises) on free association, brainstorming, clustering, free writing, and quick-question approaches. I suggest that these techniques inevitably precede and are always part of the directed discovery approach, and I have simplified and generalized the directed discovery questions. A simple tree diagram now precedes the revised diagram on logical division, and a new diagram shows how the limiting process works in both the subject and predicate areas of a thesis statement.

The original chapter on "Writing Paragraphs" remains split into two, "Understanding the Paragraph" (Chapter 5) and "Developing Paragraphs: How to Stay Focused" (Chapter 6). The reorganized material on methods of paragraph development retains the question–answer approach (still carried throughout the book) to encourage writers to develop ways of *thinking about* subjects rather than simply following set "organizational patterns." In Chapter 6 I have further emphasized the function of developmental paragraphs within the whole paper and their relation to a paper's thesis. Throughout the section I've changed writing assignments and updated examples, added new exercises, and expanded old ones.

I have extensively revised the chapter on the researched paper, providing comparative citations for MLA and APA documentation style. Though I've retained the title "Monkey Talk," the paper itself has been completely revised and updated (it follows the MLA style of internal documentation). I've updated the material on library use to include an introduction to the library computer catalog and computer databases, but I have kept the explanation of the card catalog and basic (hard copy) research sources.

I have always intended Chapter 9 ("Mechanics: Grammar, Punctuation, Spelling") to work very much like a handbook, since it provides correction symbols to represent most of the major problems encountered by beginning writers (reinforced by the symbol summary on the inside covers of the text). The chapter still begins with an independent unit on the revision process, emphasizing the larger rhetorical elements while still cautioning students about precision in grammar, punctuation, and spelling.

The basic approaches presented in the book I intend as *starting points,* not rigid patterns to be followed slavishly or indefinitely. To emphasize this point, throughout the text I've suggested alternative approaches for experimentation. The definition of exposition used includes writing with an argumentative edge to explain a main logical point. In reworking this edition, I have retained and revised the material on the function of attitude and audience in the writing process, hoping to encourage students to make their writing more personal and interesting.

Still aimed at freshman composition students, the book gives explicit thinking and writing instructions to follow. With some extension, its assumptions and methods are basically those of rhetoric as it has been known for over two thousand years: discovery and invention, arrangement and organization, and, through revision, an introduction to some of the problems of tone and style.

I'm pleased to have this continued opportunity to revise the material and to reaffirm my confidence in a book whose conciseness, directness, and clarity have won for it the support and respect of hard-working teachers at many schools and at several academic levels. To the many constructive reviewers whose suggested changes have guided my revisions I offer sincere thanks, and especially to Elizabeth Macey of Rancho Santiago College, Marc H. Goldsmith of Mitchell College, Robert Brien of Madison Area Technical College, and Elliott M. Hill of Kennesan State College. And finally, at Prentice Hall, thanks to Phil Miller for his support over many years of revision, and a special thanks to Jenny Moss, without whose diligence and support this edition could not have succeeded.

Harry P. Kroitor
Texas A&M University

To the Student

You already know how to write. Keep this thought secure as a reminder that you already have skills to develop into effective communication techniques. This book will help you develop basic writing and thinking approaches needed to create short papers that clearly make one logical point and adequately support it.

Although the writing and thinking approaches described in the early chapters are successful ways to *begin* developing your skills, eventually you will want to experiment on your own. Mastery of these basic approaches will improve your self-confidence and provide important information about the writing process. You will learn that effective writing develops out of clearly focused thinking and a specific, controlled attitude toward a chosen subject. You'll discover that readers will follow your ideas more readily if your papers have unity and coherence. And you will see that the approaches used to develop short papers apply equally to longer ones, including the researched paper.

Practicing these basic writing and thinking approaches is your starting point. In addition, you will become more aware of the importance of *attitude* and *audience* in effective writing. The attitude you have toward your subject matter and reading audience is always projected by your writing: "I'm interested," or "I don't care," or "This subject is important," or "I don't want to do this," or "I'm bored" will be reflected in the tone of your writing. Your reader will respond positively only if the attitude you project is positive. If you don't understand your reading audience or the attitude you may be projecting, the result could be a kind of "writing in a vacuum" that keeps you from sounding like a real person. Effective writing creates a bridge across which your mind connects with another and elicits a positive response: "I understand. I like what I hear."

Through these basic approaches, this book will help you strengthen your writing by practicing two skills—how to explain a main point with supporting evidence, and how to project a convincing, personal attitude of self-confidence. Part One of the book (Focus, Discovery, Organization) stresses primarily the first skill. Part Two (Revision: Mechanics and Style) shows that there's more to effective writing than following a formula. It provides, in handbook form, a review of grammar, punctuation, and spelling, and it shows you how to make papers project confidence by understanding the way words work and sentences move.

1

Writing to Improve Communication

This book is really about thinking—the kinds of thinking that motivate, launch, support, enliven, and develop the *writing process.* To be successful, thinking and writing should be self-motivating, self-questioning, and ongoing. Successful thinking and writing produce effective products—carefully chosen words, good sentences, developed paragraphs, organized essays.

To improve this process, Part One of this book (Focus, Discovery, Organization) presents some basic principles applicable to all writing. You will learn how to jump-start your mind into action—how to conquer the blank page or blank computer screen. You will learn how to get started and keep your thinking process moving, how to ask questions, probe for answers, sharpen purpose. And in the process you will learn how to write an effective *five-hundred-word theme.* Part Two (Revision—Mechanics and Style) is a compact handbook. It provides a basic guide to revision and shows you how to correct the most common problems in mechanics (grammar, punctuation, spelling). It also shows you how to make your writing more convincing by improving your word choice (diction) and *sentence* components.

WHAT IS A FIVE-HUNDRED-WORD THEME?

"Write a theme on population control." "Turn in your paper on AIDS." "Prepare for an essay exam." "Write an essay on the causes of ozone depletion." "Prepare a report on employment problems in the field of nursing." *Theme, paper, essay, report:* these words appear regularly in classroom writing assignments; *report* is common in many business situations. "What kind of writing," you may ask, "am I expected to do?" The word *theme* actually means subject or topic. The word *essay* can mean to try or to attempt (verb), but it can also refer to a short composition or paper (noun). In this book I use the words *theme* and *essay* to mean *any planned, organized short paper about a specific subject,* whether a first attempt or the final revised composition. In these short papers you will

> write from personal experience and knowledge
> write and think clearly about a specific subject that interests you
> present your views according to a clearly organized plan
> explain why you have those views

In Chapter 8 you'll learn about the long paper—a researched *report.*

FOUR BASIC KINDS OF THINKING AND WRITING

Though rarely used in isolation by professional writers, four basic kinds of thinking and writing are often defined in books. In fact, you already know much about them. If you've written a letter telling someone, perhaps minute by minute, of a personal experience—a wedding, an on-the-job disaster, a cooking casualty you endured, a fishing or hunting experience, a swimming adventure—then you were probably "telling a story." You were using *personal narration,* perhaps colored by some detailed *description* designed to *persuade* your reader that the experience was humorous or beyond your budget or exhausting or financially rewarding. More likely, you have probably *told* someone a story or a joke, or tried to *prove* a point or support an opinion you hold. You may have *argued* that listening is an important social skill or tried to *prove* that someone you know is a racist. Or you may have tried to *explain* to someone why you think censorship is wrong, or how you learned to drive. Most simply stated, you *tell, show, argue, explain*—that is, you regularly use *narration, description, argumentation,* and *exposition.* They are part of everyday communication.

    Consider, for example, the general subject of auto accidents. By remembering a specific accident you saw or experienced, you could *tell a story* moment by moment, perhaps dramatizing the events and the people involved. You might, instead, choose only to *describe* in detail the *scene* of that accident, perhaps including the condition of the car, the place of the accident, the sounds, the shouting, the screaming, the people milling about. Or, depending on your role in the event, you might choose to *persuade* your parents (or an officer) that the accident wasn't your fault. You could also choose to be less personal and, by using specific examples or illustrations, you might try to *explain* what you think *causes* most auto accidents. In fact, the *purpose* (aim) you have in mind influences the "slant" or approach to the basic kinds of writing as they appear in your papers.

These aims may include any—or *all*—of the following:

> To *inform*—to present facts or information; to describe factually
> To *persuade*—to influence a listener to *agree with* a view or to take action
> To *explain*—to express what you feel or think *about* an idea, event, or object

Decide on a purpose, and you influence the way you *think about* a subject. The resulting *attitude* will, in turn, determine the kind—or *kinds*—of writing you'll be doing. Let's summarize these four basic approaches to thinking and writing. Note how choice of *aim* determines the kind of writing and sometimes requires a combination of more than one kind.

Telling: Narration

Narration presents an orderly sequence of events in time—how you survived your first pregnancy, caught your whale-sized fish, survived your first job interview, had your worst kitchen accident, shot your first deer, rescued your pet cat from a tree, learned to ride a bicycle. Though used primarily in storytelling (fiction), narrative paragraphs often work well in exposition and argumentation to illustrate a point. Although your main aim is to inform, to present information by telling a story, indirectly you also may be expressing your personal feelings or thoughts. You are trying to get your reader to say, "I see," "I understand what's going on."

Showing: Description

Objective description presents an orderly, part-by-part word picture of something—a room, the taste of beer, the main street of a town, night sounds in August, a classroom, a guitar, an oak tree, a building, the smell of sea water, an odd shoe, a wrinkled face. This kind of writing uses language mostly to report the features or qualities of something. In this kind of description, the main aim is to *inform*—to present information factually, usually without a personal reaction to the subject. It tries to get the reader to say, "I see," "I understand," "I get the picture."

Subjective description provides an additional element: the describer's *reaction to* the subject. The August night sounds might be described as *frightening* or *romantic;* the wrinkled face might suggest *hard work* or *foolish dissipation*. In these cases the aim of the description is partly persuasive. As in argumentation (below), it tries to get the reader to say: "I see," "I understand," and "I agree." Thus, description can also combine two of the basic kinds of writing.

Persuading: Argumentation

Argumentation presents valid proof to persuade people to accept an opinion or idea and to do something, even if all they do is change their minds. Some writers consider exposition to be a form of *persuasion;* in fact, you'll find it hard to present an argument without also providing an *explanation* (exposition). If you've ever offered an argument, you probably have noticed that a basic questioning pattern suggests how formal argumentation develops and works:

> What is it? [How would you define or describe it?]
> What caused it? [How did it come about?]
> Is it desirable or undesirable? [How would you evaluate its effects?]
> What action should we take? [What should you do?]

Though argument focuses chiefly on the last two of these questions, it probably develops best when the other two are also addressed. Do we agree on what it is? Do we agree on its causes? These first two questions require the kind of explanation usually associated with exposition. But you can hardly convince listeners or readers to take action if they don't understand or agree with such explanations. The chief aim of argumentation, then, is to *persuade,* to get readers or listeners to *accept* a specific point of view or take some specific action.

Consider these two assertions:

> *Family planning can be accomplished in many ways.*
>
> *Family planning, like abortion, is wrong.*

The first statement promises only to explain what *ways* can be used; it would, incidentally, persuade the reader that the ways are *many.* The second statement is clearly argumentative; it promises to explain why family planning and abortion are in some way similar and why both are *wrong.* In the first, the chief aim is to get the reader to say, "I understand," "I agree." To these two aims the second statement adds a third: "I want to change the reader's mind."

Explaining: Exposition

Expository writing explains in a straightforward manner a process, an object, an idea, an event. It analyzes or accounts for something by presenting specific information to make the explanation clear. Suppose you wanted to explain what steps your community has taken to begin a trash recycling program. In an expository paper you would *report* what you knew about that recycling program. If, however, you wanted to *convince* a reader that your community's trash recycling program is the *most successful* one in your county, you probably would have to research the subject and document the *success.* You would have shifted into exposition with a *persuasive edge.* The kinds of support needed in these two approaches and the kinds of agreement expected from the reader are basically different.

Exposition is probably the most common kind of writing since it includes explanations of a specific point of view, or of how to follow a road map, make a cake, rebuild a motor, write a theme, or drive a car. The main purpose is to explain or to analyze or to describe. Any writing—no matter what approaches are combined—that has as its primary purpose to make a subject clear by convincingly presenting specific information we will consider expository writing. Its basic aim is to report thoughts about a specific subject. You will try to get your reader to say, "I understand," "I see your point," "Your explanation is clear." In practice the complete separation of narration, description, argumentation, and exposition is rare. Combining these approaches and giving exposition a *persuasive edge* (a *thesis* or *controlling attitude*) requires skills this book will help you develop.

COMBINING APPROACHES: THE PERSUASIVE EDGE

If you discover that you can best develop your paper's subject by *combining* several—perhaps all—of these approaches, by all means use them. Though it's possible to write a paragraph or paper using only one of the approaches, rarely does an accomplished writer use only one without introducing others. Many professional expository papers include both narration and description, and most have a *persuasive edge:* they try to get readers to agree by explaining something to them. Consider, for example, these opening sentences of a *narrative* **paragraph:**

> The accident really wasn't my fault. It happened only a few blocks from my house on the coldest day in January. It had been snowing for days and the street was covered with packed snow, deeply scored with ruts made by the cars and trucks that regularly traveled that road. Beneath the snow a sheet of ice waited for the unwary driver. I pulled out of the driveway, turning right toward Main Street. As usual, I hit the accelerator and . . .

The first sentence suggests that the writer will try to defend the no-fault idea *(argumentation)*. The paragraph also provides a sense of scene and place *(description)* as well as time and story movement *(personal narration)*. Perhaps the approach that can best stand alone is description:

> The car was a silver blue 1990 Thunderbird, equipped with power steering, power brakes, and a digital dashboard with all the electronic measuring devices. The dark-blue leather interior complemented the bucket seats and tinted windows added a definite sense of style. The whitewall tires . . .

Precise description can enhance the persuasive effect of any narrative or argument. It also has an honored place in good exposition.

To illustrate how difficult it sometimes is to separate these four basic approaches to writing, here are some student paragraphs to consider. Each three-paragraph group focuses on a single event. As you read each paragraph within a group, try to decide (1) who seems to be speaking, (2) what the student's main *aim* was in writing the paragraph, and (3) which basic approaches appear.

I

A.   I knew they would let Jeff go. He's been wild at times and he talks tough, but I know Jeff could never hurt anyone. The judge could tell that all those other people were lying, especially that district attorney. It seems as if it's always been that way—someone trying to blame Jeff for something he didn't do. The judge could see it. That's why he let my son go.

B.   Seems to me it was all time wasted—all of us taking that much time away from our jobs and families to sit on the jury, hearing all that evidence, and then that scoundrel goes free. I don't even remember exactly what was said. I was wondering if that old judge was still listening or just wishing it were all over. Then his expression changed. His eyes hardened, his forehead lines deepened, his lips tightened, unsmiling. And that little defense attorney jumped up and it was all over. The judge had to do what he thought was right, I guess, but it just keeps getting harder to convict a criminal, even when you know he's guilty. Or that's how it seems to me.

C.   Today I was forced to dismiss murder charges against the defendant in a case which had become emotionally overloaded. Considerable evidence had, in fact, been presented against the man. But that one vicious statement made by the prosecuting attorney could have—unalterably and unjustly—prejudiced the jury. I'm sure I will read in tomorrow's paper that another brutal criminal was freed on a technicality. But if I overlook what is to me an obvious breach of due process, then the whole idea of due process becomes a farce, an unimportant ritual—before the sentence but after the verdict. I have another sleepless night ahead.

WRITING ASSIGNMENT

A. Rewrite paragraph *B* of group I, using ***third-person*** point of view. Instead of using "I" or "me," supply a name (Tom, Dick, or Susan) or use a pronoun (he, she). Add any names you wish. As you eliminate ***first-person*** point of view, notice the problems you run into and the many changes you have to make. If you have trouble getting started, you might begin your rewrite with "Susan thought that . . ." or "Tom thought that . . ."

B. Which version do you prefer, the original or your own? Why?

C. Do you think the writer of paragraph *B* is presenting an *argument*? Does the writer want the reader to *agree* with a specific point of view? How can you decide? What effect is the *description* of the judge supposed to have?

D. Does each paragraph in group I comment on the same *event*? Do all three paragraphs present the same information? What causes the differences?

II

A.   At exactly 12:07 p.m. today, firemen were summoned to the residence of Michael P. Roe at 5706 Belrose Street. In the garage they extinguished a blaze apparently started when Roe knocked over a glass container of gasoline. The gas caught fire when it ran under the hot water heater, instantly spread, and Roe's pants caught fire. He apparently smothered the flames by rolling in the grass. Neighbors took Roe to St. Anne's Hospital, where he was admitted with second-degree burns of the arms and legs. Fire chief Jackson Brown estimated damage to the structure and contents of the garage at $2,000.

B.   It was sitting on the workbench in the garage and had been there for months. When I knocked it over, the glass jug full of high-test gasoline seemed to explode when it hit the floor. Paralyzed, I watched in horror as the gas spurted across the floor and under the hot water heater. In the same instant, an explosive roar and blinding smoke filled the garage. "Don't panic!" I thought. "Don't panic!" I groped my way through the choking smoke to the open door. My pant legs were on fire. I remember burning heat but no pain. Stumbling into the back yard I threw myself onto the grass and tried to beat the flames with my bare fists. Then I remembered to roll over and over to smother the flames.

C.   I had just pulled into my driveway when I heard a muffled explosion and saw black smoke billowing out of Mike's garage. Leaping out of the car, I tore across the street and to Mike's garage. The smoke was so black and thick that I couldn't see anything in the garage. The front door was open. I stepped inside and screamed: "Mike! Mike!" No answer. I ran to the back yard and found Mike lying on the grass. He stared at me without speaking. Then I saw that his pant legs were burned off at the knees. Big, ugly blisters were forming on his arms and legs.

What do you think the writer's main aim was in each of these three paragraphs? Which of the four basic approaches do you think dominates? Be prepared to explain your opinion. Is exposition present in any of the paragraphs?

These six paragraphs should show you that any event can be presented in many ways, depending on how much role-playing a writer is willing to do. Later in this book you will return to this method of expanding information and adding an *edge* to your writing. They also show that narration and description can be powerful partners—no matter what other aims a writer may have.

Depending on how much experience and information you have, choosing one—or combining several—of these four approaches could lead to a paper that rambles for too many pages. The first part of this book tries to prevent this rambling by asking you to examine some basic thinking processes and to concentrate on writing a five-hundred-word theme, a short paper of *approximately* five hundred words, about a specific, controlled (limited) subject. This short paper may have fewer or more than five hundred words, depending on the guidelines your instructor gives you.

The most important thing you will learn is how to sift through your thoughts and keep them straight. Discover and limit a subject, decide on an attitude to control that subject, create a series of clear statements about that attitude, present these statements according to a clearly organized plan—these are the important goals of the first seven chapters.

Nor should you assume that you'll forever use the four- or five-paragraph paper you begin with. Clearly, short papers may take other forms. Once you've mastered the basic approach, therefore, you will want to experiment with others. In addition, writing these short papers will teach you to communicate persuasively—more precisely, more convincingly—by developing three basic thinking skills:

> recognizing general, all-inclusive statements
> logically dividing a general subject into specific parts
> classifying many ideas into related groups

You probably already use all of these skills. What you will learn to do here is to become more conscious of these thinking processes and their function in writing.

WRITING EXERCISES

A. Choose something very specific and personal to *describe:* a favorite hat or odd outfit, a well-worn shoe or pair of jeans, an outrageous haircut or a peculiar pet, a wrinkled hand or an unusual face—anything you can keep in *actual view* as you describe the details in one long paragraph. First simply *list* all the details you want to include in your paragraph, then decide on the sequence or order of the details, and finally write the paragraph. Be prepared to explain whether your paragraph is objective or subjective *description.*

B. Closely observe something interesting or surprising that happened (to you or to someone else) at home, at work, or at school. List as many minute-by-minute details of the *event* as you can. Decide whether you will tell the story in *first person* ("I/we") or *third person* ("he/she/it/they"). Then in one long paragraph describe what happened. (Look at the sample paragraphs on page 7.) Be prepared to explain whether your paragraph uses narration, description, exposition, or a combination of these.

C. Write an *objective* description of the cartoon showing the little "flower girl" (page 9). Use specific details to clarify position, relationship, and all activity. Don't comment on what the artist is trying to communicate to you.

Drawing by Charles E. Martin; © 1961, 1989 The New Yorker Magazine.

WHY SHOULD YOU LEARN TO WRITE AND THINK MORE EFFECTIVELY?

Writing effectively isn't easy; it demands patience and discipline. Why, then, should you make the effort to learn to write and think more effectively? Because communicating is a social act, the obvious answer is *survival*. If you learn to communicate your thoughts and feelings accurately and persuasively, people will be less likely to misunderstand you. In school, you'll improve your grades; when you graduate, you'll probably get a better-paying job; with a better-paying job, you'll be able to create new opportunities for self-improvement and success. For example, effective teachers, business leaders, politicians, and other professionals are persuasive communicators. You aren't likely to have these opportunities if you can't communicate effectively. Beyond these potential rewards, however, is the pride you'll enjoy as your skills and self-image grow.

Effective ***communication*** is a three-way process involving (1) an information source (reality, books, knowledge), (2) a ***message-sender*** who processes information, and (3) a ***message-receiver*** who tries to understand the resulting end product or ***"message."*** Message-senders, however, don't always project what they *think* they are sending, as the two illustrations in this section reveal. Message-receivers can be misled by incomplete, vague, or ***all-inclusive statements*** made by message-senders:

Driving the same freeway every day. [Incomplete. Who is driving? Where?]

I have a car. [Vague. What kind of car?]

People don't dress right. [Vague. Why?]

Dogs are vicious. [All-inclusive generalization. Why?]

All people are equal. [Vague generalization. What does equal mean?]

Politicians are dishonest. [All-inclusive generalization.]

One of your most important jobs as a writer (message-sender), therefore, is to learn to think as a reader (message-receiver), asking questions, anticipating questions, providing specific supporting details to help prevent misunderstanding.

For example, as you write, be aware that many readers are offended by ***sexist language***—male-dominated allusions. Such expressions as "everyone must do *his* job" and "the doctor can treat *his* patients" should be used only when the context demands the male reference. One way to avoid the use of sexist language is to alternate references, using "doctor . . . *she*" as often as "doctor . . . *he*" (for example). Careful writers also avoid using such common nouns as *policeman, stewardess, mankind, poetess, chairman*. Alternatives include *police officer, flight attendant, humans, poet/author, chair/chairperson*. Perhaps the most widely used method of avoiding sexist language is to use plurals. (For additional information see page 262.)

Peanuts

PEANUTS reprinted by permission of UFS, Inc.

Always consider the entire ***communication situation.*** Think of your readers and ask, "Will they understand what I'm saying?" Don't let them jump to the wrong conclusion; lead them inescapably and persuasively to the ideas you have in mind. This is perhaps the most important reward of learning to write more effectively. You won't go around wondering, "Why don't people understand me?"

Having communication skills at your command will help you gain confidence in your own ability to function as an individual—to carry your own weight in a social or business situation. When you apply for a job, you will have to write a letter outlining your qualifications, and you will have to convince the person doing the hiring to give you the job. You will be doing two things: (1) *describing your qualifications with supporting **evidence,*** and (2) *projecting a convincing attitude of* *self-confidence*. Providing supporting evidence and projecting a convincing attitude: these are basic to all effective communication.

In school or on the job, a knowledge of the techniques of expository writing will greatly increase your chances for success. Writing an essay examination or a paper requires you to organize facts and apply revision techniques to strengthen your presentation and make it convincing. Almost any job requires you to write memos, letters, and reports. These will *represent* you—to your employer, to fellow workers, to prospective clients. You will want to present yourself in the best possible light.

Cultivate the ability to write logically and to recognize logical thought when you read or hear it. The techniques of expository writing require you to use all the evidence you can collect to support the ideas you want your reader to understand, or to accept, or to act on. You should be able to judge the logic of your own ideas and, if the evidence disproves them, discard or alter them. You should also become cautious about accepting *generalizations others* make, unless they support them with valid evidence. This cautious approach to ideas will help you survive—at school and on the job. It will also teach you to question politicians and other kinds of salespeople who use words to cloud rather than support issues.

EXERCISES

   A. Study the cartoon showing the little "flower girl."
      1. Decide on an appropriate caption (title) for the cartoon, using a word, a short phrase, or a very short statement.
      2. Rewrite your caption as *one* fully developed sentence to express clearly what you think is the cartoon's main point.
      3. To support this caption and sentence, write a good paragraph based on the cartoon's details. Explain what you think is *happening* to the little girl, the teacher, and the other children in the cartoon.
      4. Write another paragraph to explain why you think *one* of the following statements is true:
         a. It's important to encourage imaginative thinking.
         b. It's important to know your personal preferences.
         c. People don't have to agree in order to learn from each other.
   B. Study the "dog" cartoon.
      1. In three or four good sentences describe the problem experienced by the two "speakers" in the cartoon.
      2. Using these sentences as your starting point, write a good paragraph to show how the problem can extend to *one* of the following relationships:
         a. A teacher giving students a writing assignment.
         b. Someone *for* planned parenthood and someone *against* abortion.
         c. Someone *for* no censorship and someone *against* pornography.
         d. Freedom of the individual and the well-being of the group.
         e. Choose a relationship of your own.
   C. Explain why the following statements could be misunderstood:
      1. Accidents are caused by people.
      2. Advertisements misrepresent their products.

3. Today's television programs are full of sex and violence.
4. Parents want to have prayer as part of the school program.
5. Poverty and lack of education go hand in hand.

D. Below are the first nine paragraphs from the essay "Thinking as a Hobby" by William Golding (author of *Lord of the Flies*). (The complete essay appears on page 399.) As you read the selection, consider these questions:
1. What kind of person seems to be speaking to you?
2. Does the selection use *narration? Description?* (Where?)
3. What evidence can you find that *exposition* with a persuasive edge is also present? Write a paragraph to explain where it appears and to support your choice.
4. What is the effect of Golding's use of first person ("I")?

Thinking as a Hobby[1]

1   While I was still a boy, I came to the conclusion that there were three grades of thinking; and since I was later to claim thinking as my hobby, I came to an even stranger conclusion—namely, that I myself could not think at all.

2   I must have been an unsatisfactory child for grownups to deal with. I remember how incomprehensible they appeared to me at first, but not, of course, how I appeared to them. It was the headmaster of my grammar school who first brought the subject of thinking before me—though neither in the way, nor with the result he intended. He had some statuettes in his study. They stood on a high cupboard behind his desk. One was a lady wearing nothing but a bath towel. She seemed frozen in an eternal panic lest the bath towel slip down any farther; and since she had no arms, she was in an unfortunate position to pull the towel up again. Next to her, crouched the statuette of a leopard, ready to spring down at the top drawer of a filing cabinet labeled A–AH. My innocence interpreted this as the victim's last, despairing cry. Beyond the leopard was a naked, muscular gentleman, who sat, looking down, with his chin on his fist and his elbow on his knee. He seemed utterly miserable.

3   Some time later, I learned about these statuettes. The headmaster had placed them where they would face delinquent children, because they symbolized to him the whole of life. The naked lady was the Venus of Milo. She was Love. She was not worried about the towel. She was just busy being beautiful. The leopard was Nature, and he was being natural. The naked, muscular gentleman was not miserable. He was Rodin's Thinker, an image of pure thought. It is easy to buy small plaster models of what you think life is like.

4   I had better explain that I was a frequent visitor to the headmaster's study, because of the latest thing I had done or left undone. As we now say, I was not integrated. I was, if anything, disintegrated; and I was puzzled. Grownups never made sense. Whenever I found myself in a penal position before the headmaster's desk, with the statuettes glimmering whitely above him, I would sink my head, clasp my hands behind my back and writhe one shoe over the other.

5   The headmaster would look opaquely at me through flashing spectacles.

"What are we going to do with you?"

Well, what *were* they going to do with me? I would writhe my shoe some more and stare down at the worn rug.

[1]From William Golding, "Thinking as a Hobby," *Holiday,* August 1961.

"Look up, boy! Can't you look up?"

6   Then I would look up at the cupboard, where the naked lady was frozen in her panic and the muscular gentleman contemplated the hindquarters of the leopard in endless gloom. I had nothing to say to the headmaster. His spectacles caught the light so that you could see nothing human behind them. There was no possibility of communication.

"Don't you ever think at all?"

No, I didn't think, wasn't thinking, couldn't think—I was simply waiting in anguish for the interview to stop.

"Then you'd better learn—hadn't you?"

7   On one occasion the headmaster leaped to his feet, reached up and plonked Rodin's masterpiece on the desk before me.

"That's what a man looks like when he's really thinking."

I surveyed the gentleman without interest or comprehension.

"Go back to your class."

8   Clearly there was something missing in me. Nature had endowed the rest of the human race with a sixth sense and left me out. This must be so, I mused, on my way back to the class, since whether I had broken a window, or failed to remember Boyle's Law, or been late for school, my teachers produced me one, adult answer: "Why can't you think?"

9   As I saw the case, I had broken the window because I had tried to hit Jack Arney with a cricket ball and missed him; I could not remember Boyle's Law because I had never bothered to learn it; and I was late for school because I preferred looking over the bridge into the river. In fact, I was wicked. Were my teachers, perhaps, so good that they could not understand the depths of my depravity? Were they clear, untormented people who could direct their every action by this mysterious business of thinking? The whole thing was incomprehensible. In my earlier years, I found even the statuette of the Thinker confusing. I did not believe any of my teachers were naked, ever. Like someone born deaf, but bitterly determined to find out about sound, I watched my teachers to find out about thought.

E. Read the poem that follows, Robert Frost's "A Considerable Speck," and note the skillful combination of *personal narration* and *description*. Try to decide, also, whether he's using the example to *explain* something he believes in (as one might do in *exposition*).
  1. In a short paragraph retell the important events in the poem, following the order used by Frost. (Imagine you are telling a story.)
  2. Using as his basis the events he describes, Frost identifies two kinds of "mind" (note especially the poem's last four lines). In a short paragraph (four or five sentences), explain what you think these two kinds of mind are.
  3. To what two different things does the word *sheet* (last line) probably refer? What is it that makes the poet "glad"? Write a paragraph of four or five sentences to explain *why* (think of reasons) you might agree with the point that Frost makes in the poem's last line. If you wish, begin your paragraph with: In the last line of Frost's "A Considerable Speck," the word *sheet* refers to _____(a)_____ and _____(b)_____.

A Considerable Speck[2]

(Microscopic)

A speck that would have been beneath my sight
On any but a paper sheet so white
Set off across what I had written there.
And I had idly poised my pen in air
To stop it with a period of ink,   5
When something strange about it made me think.
This was no dust speck by my breathing blown,
But unmistakably a living mite
With inclinations it could call its own.
It paused as with suspicion of my pen,   10
And then came racing wildly on again
To where my manuscript was not yet dry;
Then paused again and either drank or smelt—
With loathing, for again it turned to fly.
It seemed too tiny to have room for feet,   15
Yet must have had a set of them complete
To express how much it didn't want to die.
It ran with terror and with cunning crept.
It faltered: I could see it hesitate;
Then in the middle of the open sheet   20
Cower down in desperation to accept
Whatever I accorded it of fate.
I have none of the tenderer-than-thou
Collectivistic regimenting love
With which the modern world is being swept.   25
But this poor microscopic item now!
Since it was nothing I knew evil of
I let it lie there till I hope it slept.
I have a mind myself and recognize
Mind when I meet with it in any guise.   30
No one can know how glad I am to find
On any sheet the least display of mind.

REVIEW TERMS

Here are some of the more important terms used in this chapter. Understanding these will make the next chapter easier.

A. Aim, all-inclusive statements, argue, argumentation, attitude, communication, communication situation, description, essay, evidence, explain, explanation, exposition, expository, first person, five-hundred-word theme, generalization, to inform, message, message-receiver, message-sender, narration, paragraph, personal narration, to persuade, persuasion, persuasive edge, prove, purpose, report, scene, sentence, sexist language, short paper, show, tell, theme, third person, writing process

B. First person, paragraph, sentence, third person

[2]From *The Poetry of Robert Frost,* edited by Edward Connery Lathem. Copyright 1942 by Robert Frost. Copyright © 1970 by Lesley Frost Ballantine. Copyright © 1969 by Henry Holt and Company, Inc. Reprinted by permission of Henry Holt and Company, Inc.

2

Seeing the Whole Paper

Faced with presenting our ideas to someone else, we hesitate. How can we get started? How much information should we include? Which ideas are most relevant to the point we're trying to communicate? Are we right? How will we be judged? Does the order of presentation guide the reader?

Many of these questions and much of the hesitation will disappear if you use systematic strategies and have a definite plan in mind. The best *approach* is one that helps you get moving. The best *plan* organizes your thoughts so that they move logically and systematically from the opening statements into the supporting *paragraphs* that follow. Every good paper has a beginning to engage the reader's attention and reach out toward the paragraphs to follow. It also has a middle part to echo and support the beginning. And it has an ending to tell readers you've arrived where you promised to take them.

ORGANIZING THE PAPER: TWO BASIC APPROACHES

Start somewhere, say something, wrap it up. This seems like a simple enough outline of the task. But it provides neither a systematic approach nor a definite plan. To write an effective paper, you should have a fairly specific idea of the product you want to create. What is it? What does it look like? What are its aims? To begin with, your product will be a short *expository* paper (about five hundred words). As you've already learned, expository writing is the straightforward explanation of a process, an object, an idea, an event. It analyzes or accounts for something by presenting specific information to support the explanation given. Your first task will be to learn about two basic approaches to expository writing and the plans they require.

Depending on your choice, the ***organization pattern*** of your paper will be ***inductive*** or ***deductive.*** *Induction* is a way of thinking in which a person observes and investigates a number of specific examples, events, objects, or situations and then *concludes* something about them. Essentially it is a *questioning process* even though the question may not be clearly formulated. In its simplest form the resulting *pattern* can be represented like this:

INDUCTIVE PATTERN

Introduction:	Leads to a question to be explored and answered
Body:	Specific example 1, plus observation and concluding statement 1
	Specific example 2, plus observation and concluding statement 2
	Specific example 3, plus observation and concluding statement 3
Conclusion:	Generalization about the observations
	Answer to the question asked (final concluding statement)

If you choose this inductive pattern, you will *"lead* your reader *into"* the paper, either by asking a question or by suggesting a line of investigation *to be followed* in the subsequent paragraphs. As you begin this kind of paper, you are saying to the reader that the results of the investigation are still unknown.

While the word "induction" means "to lead *in,*" the word "deduction" means "to lead *away from.*" In its simplest form, the paper following a deductive pattern can be represented like this:

DEDUCTIVE PATTERN

Introduction:	Leads to a thesis/assertion to be supported
Body:	Specific support 1
	Specific support 2
	Specific support 3
Conclusion:	Restatement or summary

If you choose deductive organization, you will "lead the reader away from" a ***thesis statement*** asserted somewhere in the introductory paragraph and *explained* or *supported* in the rest of the paper. This thesis statement is the result of inductive thinking. It is usually a conclusion you reached based on a preliminary exploration of some question. As you begin this kind of paper, you are saying to the reader, "This is a *conclusion* (thesis) I have reached, and here are my reasons for holding this view." Let's look at these two ways of thinking and the basic writing patterns they generate.

The Inductive Approach: Theme Pattern A

The basic diagram for inductive organization will help you visualize the whole paper by showing the logical relationship of each part of the paper to the whole. Study this diagram carefully.

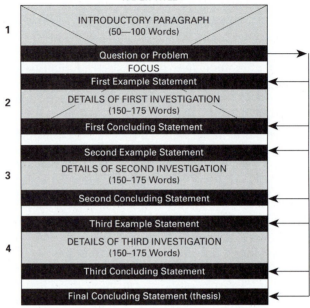

The diagram for inductive organization pictures a dynamic, creative thinking/writing process in which the mind actively works with a number of interrelated, overlapping activities:

1. Asking questions, searching for information, getting moving
2. Answering questions, organizing information, testing approaches
3. Organizing and planning a specific approach, outlining
4. Constructing and writing sentences, writing paragraphs and papers
5. Testing and revising the plan, rewriting, revising the paper

Steps 1, 2, and 3 make up the *prewriting stage,* the *discovery* or *invention process.* Whether it's done on paper or in your head, this thinking/brainstorming process precedes the establishment of a clear focus or point of view. Most of it should occur *before* you write a paper and will be discussed in detail in Chapter 3.

If you have trouble writing papers, however, this preliminary part of the process probably needs to take the form of a written paper using Theme Pattern A (Inductive Organization). Each block in the diagram represents one exploratory paragraph in the paper, the total number of paragraphs depending on how complete the investigation will be. As the diagram suggests, Theme Pattern A requires you to lead the reader to an unanswered question or problem in the introductory paragraph, to investigate or analyze a number of situations or examples, and to reach a final answer in the concluding paragraph at the end of the paper.

To answer this paper's question *reliably,* however, you would have to study far more examples than the diagram suggests. The question/problem statement at the beginning functions somewhat like a thesis statement, example statements function as topic sentences in each exploratory paragraph, and concluding statements are added throughout (specific observations). A concluding paragraph summarizes the findings of the investigation. A paper with inductive organization of this kind could be much longer than the basic short theme you will write following Theme Pattern B (Deductive Organization).

The final concluding statement is a *generalization,* a *summary* of the investigations described in the body of the paper (paragraphs two through four in the diagram). This final generalization is similar to the *thesis statement* found at the beginning of many professional papers and shown in the introductory paragraph in Theme Pattern B (see page 22). Thus, the paper using inductive organization is similar in approach to the scientific method of examining a number of specific examples to *answer a question.*

The first block in the diagram shows the ***introductory paragraph.*** The line across the bottom of this block is used to show that the final sentence of this paragraph will be a *question* suggesting the one main *problem* you will be investigating. Although this question-sentence could be placed anywhere in the first paragraph, even at the very beginning, it probably functions most effectively in the end position. This position lets you use the rest of the first paragraph to introduce the general subject of the investigation, to try to grab the reader's attention and interest, and to provide a bridge to the specific question you will be trying to answer. This approach lets you bypass the problem of immediately phrasing a thesis statement and, instead, lets you write an entire paper that explores possible answers to a question. In effect, *it becomes a thinking exercise in a written form.* You *write out* the kind of thinking that usually occurs *before* thesis statements can be phrased.

If, for example, you wanted to investigate the safety of children's toys, your question might be, "Are children's toys safe?" Or, "Are children's toys unsafe?" Or, "How safe are children's toys?" To gather information you could read articles and books in the library, or you could actually look at as many toys as possible. Suppose you were told not to use the library but to do some checking on your own. You could visit a number of toy stores, examine each toy for potential safety hazards, describe the hazards discovered in each toy (paragraphs 2, 3, and 4), and then accurately summarize your discoveries in a concluding statement (or paragraph) at the end of your report.

This final conclusion would present the *results* of your investigation and then answer the question asked at the beginning of your paper. Your last two sentences in this final paragraph could say, "Though many of the toys examined were found to be safe, at least half of them have potential safety hazards that could lead to injury. Clearly, not all toys are safe." This ***conclusion*** *accurately* states what the evidence supports. It doesn't say, for example, "Children's toys are unsafe," implying that *all* toys are unsafe. Nor does it say, "Most children's toys are unsafe." It concludes clearly that *of those toys examined, a specific number* were found to be unsafe.

Here's a simple illustration of an introductory paragraph on the subject of safety in children's toys.

```
              HOW SAFE ARE CHILDREN'S TOYS?

     Guns, dolls, cars, hammers, shovels, games, paints,
phones, and other children's toys sit on store shelves begging
to be bought. Children cry for them; parents resist buying
them. Eventually, however, the tearful child, or Santa Claus,
or a doting grandmother wins. The toys are bought, perhaps
lovingly wrapped, and carried into the home for the youngster
to play with. But in committing this act of love, how many
parents give much thought to the potential dangers hidden in
the toys bought for three-year-olds? Although some parents
certainly do, many do not. Before you buy any child a toy, an
important question should be asked: "How safe are children's
toys?"
```

Notice the basic thought pattern in this paragraph:

1. It introduces the *general* subject of the whole paper (toys).
2. It tries to get the reader's attention and interest (the *grabber*).
3. It provides a *bridge* from the *general* subject (toys) to a more specific, limited subject (potential dangers) of the paper.
4. It provides a specific focus through a question (how safe?)

In the first introductory paragraphs you write, this is the basic thought pattern you will follow. Once you gain more experience, you may want to change the position of the question-sentence, or you may decide to think your way through all the available information and use an assertive thesis statement instead of a question (the deductive approach).

As you can see, the basic inductive pattern is easy:

QUESTION
↓
APPLY THE QUESTION TO SPECIFIC SITUATIONS
↓
CONCLUSION

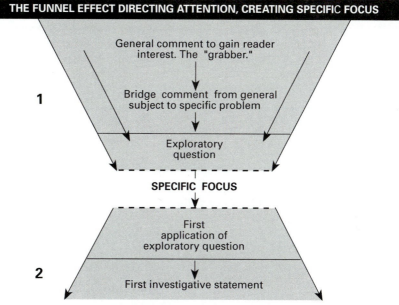

THEME PATTERN A — INDUCTIVE APPROACH

THE FUNNEL EFFECT DIRECTING ATTENTION, CREATING SPECIFIC FOCUS

1

General comment to gain reader interest. The "grabber."

Bridge comment from general subject to specific problem

Exploratory question

SPECIFIC FOCUS

2

First application of exploratory question

First investigative statement

In fact, most of the special relationship patterns used in expository writing can be seen as variations of the inductive approach. Here are examples of some of the questions you could ask:

What kind of man does a woman want for a husband? [Analysis]
What kind of woman does a man want for a wife? [Analysis]
Does alcohol damage our brain cells? [Effects?]
Why are there so many kitchen fires? [Causes?]
What is an amoeba? [Definition/Parts?]
How does an amoeba function? [Process description/Analysis]
Does violent behavior have a biological cause? [Causes?]
What makes some people violent? [Causes?]
Do television ads encourage harmful behavior? [Effects?]
How is the AIDS virus transmitted? [Process description]
How does the increasing population influence everyday life? [Effects?]

WRITING ASSIGNMENTS

    A. Following the basic four-part thought pattern representing the sample introductory paragraph on "How Safe Are Children's Toys?" write introductory paragraphs to *lead up to* three of the following questions:

        1. What dangers should we guard against when a tornado approaches?
        2. What kind of sex education should be part of the school curriculum?
        3. What kind of man should a woman look for in a husband?

    4. What kinds of restrictions should be placed on abortion?

    5. What does the word *obscene* really mean?

    6. Phrase your own question.

B. You may be asked to complete the theme "How Safe Are Children's Toys?" Be clear on whether you are to look at the toys yourself or check the library for research done on toys by the U.S. Consumer Product Safety Commission.

C. Following Theme Pattern A (Inductive Approach), complete the theme to go with one of the introductory paragraphs you wrote for the first assignment.

The Deductive Approach: Theme Pattern B

The basic diagram for deductive organization will help you visualize the whole paper by showing the logical relationship of each part of the paper to the whole. Study this basic diagram carefully.

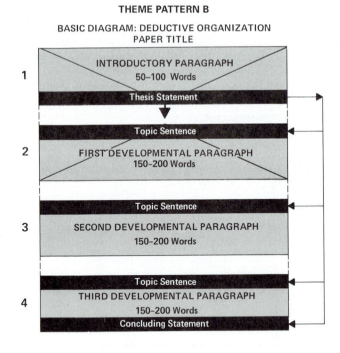

THEME PATTERN B

BASIC DIAGRAM: DEDUCTIVE ORGANIZATION
PAPER TITLE

1 INTRODUCTORY PARAGRAPH
50–100 Words
Thesis Statement

Topic Sentence
2 FIRST DEVELOPMENTAL PARAGRAPH
150-200 Words

Topic Sentence
3 SECOND DEVELOPMENTAL PARAGRAPH
150-200 Words

Topic Sentence
4 THIRD DEVELOPMENTAL PARAGRAPH
150-200 Words
Concluding Statement

BEGINNING

The chief difference between this pattern and the inductive one you have just studied is that the introductory paragraph here (50 to 100 words) does not end with a question. Instead, it leads the reader to a *thesis statement*. The relation of the thesis statement to the rest of the paper, where you place it and how you phrase it, influences the organization pattern of the paper and the way in which you present explanatory, supporting evidence. If, for example, you give the thesis statement in the beginning paragraph of the paper, as shown in the basic diagram, and then follow it with supporting evidence in each paragraph, you will be reasoning logically from a *general* assertion (thesis) to *particulars,* details that explain or illustrate it. In effect, you have already examined the particulars and reached a "conclusion," which is then represented by the thesis statement. You will learn more about thesis statements in Chapter 3. For now, consider the thesis statement as a special version of the final ***concluding statement*** of a theme using Theme Pattern A.

Because it is much easier to phrase a good thesis statement if your mind has gone through the ***question-answer approach*** represented by Theme Pattern A, you'll find it helpful to study the relationship between the two basic theme patterns and the thinking processes they represent. This relationship can be suggested by a diagram showing the two patterns side by side.

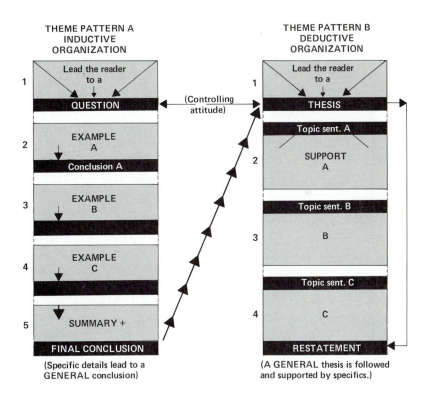

The arrows pointing from the final conclusion of Theme Pattern A to the thesis of Theme Pattern B suggest an important relationship, since you can't phrase an effective thesis unless you have gone through the thinking process suggested by Theme Pattern A—however informal and experimental that process may be. Here's the *thinking sequence* this relationship suggests:

QUESTION → ANSWER/CONCLUSION → THESIS

Using the theme on toys as an example, here's what this sequence might look like:

Question:	How safe are children's toys?
Answer/Conclusion:	Though many of the toys actually examined were found to be safe, at least half of them had potential safety hazards that could lead to injury. Clearly, not all children's toys are safe.
Thesis Statement:	Because many children's toys have potential safety hazards that could lead to injury, it is clear that not all children's toys are safe.

Whether it ends with a question, as in Theme Pattern A, or with a thesis statement, as in Theme Pattern B, your introductory paragraph is crucial. It influences the way in which you will *think about* and organize the information you have thought up or researched. And it also suggests the pattern to be followed by each developmental paragraph—a general statement in the **topic sentence** (or example statement), with supporting details in the sentences following it. Consider, for example, the following description, the beginning of a **developmental paragraph** (Theme Pattern B) with a topic sentence as the opener:

```
         Sheila is also a sharp dresser. She pays careful attention
    to color coordination, usually wearing colors that harmonize or
    contrast effectively. She never wears badly wrinkled jeans,
    usually changing them daily for a neat, fresh look. Her skirts
    and blouses look as if they've just come off the ironing board,
    and . . .
```

The ideas in this developmental paragraph move from a *general statement* in the topic sentence (the first one) to the supporting particulars of the sentences that follow. Similarly, a paper modeled on Theme Pattern B moves from the thesis assertion of the introductory paragraph to each particular supporting point of the developmental paragraphs that follow.

Placing the thesis statement at the end of the introductory paragraph has several advantages: It lets you use the first sentences of the paragraph to set the general tone of communication between your reader and yourself, to establish a kind of **common ground** or acceptance; it prevents you from confusing or misleading the reader with information placed between a first-sentence thesis statement and the first paragraph of the body; and it facilitates coherence because it positions the thesis close to the body of the paper, creating a link with the topic sentence at the beginning of the first developmental paragraph.

Here are two introductory paragraphs that lead the reader to thesis statements at the end. Consider how effectively each:

1. Introduces the general subject of the whole paper
2. Gets the reader's attention and interest

3. Provides a bridge from the general subject to a more specific, limited subject for the paper
4. Provides an anticipatory blueprint
5. Provides a specific focus (controlling attitude) through a thesis statement

---

THE UMBRELLA MAN

At least two defensible truisms apply to Americans. Both are exemplified by the multiplicity of "conspiracy" and "coverup" charges following the assassination of President John Kennedy. Fortune-seeking authors who refused to believe the simple answer--that one man could kill a President--found a ready audience in millions of Americans who were eager for a mystery. The House Select Committee on Assassinations convened for a second attempt (the first was the Warren Commission in 1964) to end these theories. The "umbrella man" conspiracy theory, one of those considered by the committee, illustrates the two truisms: that Americans love a murder mystery and that they love to make things complex.[1]

DATING AS A CONTACT SPORT

There may be no referees, whistles, or time-out, but dating is as much a game as football, baseball, or soccer. Complete with players, rules, fouls, and points, the intricate act of going out on a date requires precise execution, as does any play in many sports. The stages are well defined, including the introduction of players, pre-game warm-up, the main event, and major plays. These and other similarities qualify dating as a contact sport.

EXERCISES

After carefully studying these paragraphs, write answers to the following questions.

A. *The Umbrella Man*
  1. Is "umbrella man" the general subject of this paragraph?
  2. In what sentence is the general subject found?
  3. What is the difference between the statement of general subject and the thesis statement at the end of the paragraph?
  4. In what way does the early part of the paragraph prepare for the thesis statement? (Point to specific words or phrases.)

[1] The complete paper for "Umbrella Man" appears in Chapter 7.

     5. Does this paragraph have an anticipatory blueprint?

     6. Do you find the paragraph interesting? Why?

B. *Dating as a Contact Sport*

     1. Does the title of this paper suggest the general subject?

     2. What word in the title points to the thesis of the paragraph?

     3. What is the purpose of the word *game* in the first sentence?

     4. How does this writer try to get your attention and keep your attention?

     5. How does this paragraph anticipate the support to be presented for the thesis statement?

     6. Do you think this paragraph is as well written and developed as the "umbrella man" paragraph? Why?

Clearly, how you conceive and plan the beginning of your paper is crucial to the successful organization and development of the whole. The beginning paragraph reflects your *approach* to the subject and guides your readers by providing them with adequate clues to follow. For the first papers you write, put the thesis statement at the end of the introductory paragraph; after you have mastered this approach to Theme Pattern B, you should try others.

You will learn more about the introductory paragraph later. In your first papers following Theme Pattern B, concentrate on the main functions of this paragraph. It can serve as a kind of "map" or blueprint for the rest of the paper by suggesting the order of presentation (the organization pattern) for the ideas in the rest of the paper. This ***blueprint*** (order) may be suggested by the thesis sentence itself, or it may be implied elsewhere in the introductory paragraph.

THEME PATTERN B — DEDUCTIVE APPROACH

THE FUNNEL EFFECT DIRECTING ATTENTION, CREATING SPECIFIC FOCUS

1

General comment to gain reader interest. The "grabber."

Related comment to gain reader acceptance.

"Blueprint"
+
Thesis Statement

SPECIFIC | FOCUS

2

First Topic Sentence

First Supporting Statement

Although "The Umbrella Man" paragraph does not have an explicit blueprint, it anticipates the paper's main ideas. The phrase "two defensible truisms" in the first sentence is restated in the last sentence and spelled out: "Americans love a murder mystery" and "they love to make things complex." However, the introductory paragraph from "Dating as a Contact Sport" provides an explicit anticipatory blueprint in its next-to-last sentence: (1) introduction of the players, (2) pre-game warm-up, and (3) major plays. A reader would expect the paper to present its ideas in that *order*.

Either way the blueprint can be a valuable guide to readers as they move through the developmental paragraphs that follow. Your first paragraph, therefore, is very important: It contains a thesis statement, it establishes tone and common ground, and it provides a "blueprint" for the ideas following it.

The importance and effect of this introductory paragraph can be represented visually, as in the diagram of Theme Pattern B—Deductive Approach. The diagram shows that the introductory paragraph has a *funneling effect*. It directs reader interest and acceptance, its blueprint *controls the direction* of the whole paper, and its thesis statement creates a *specific focus* immediately echoed by the first topic sentence in the First Developmental Paragraph.

MIDDLE

In the basic diagram for Theme Pattern B, in the block representing the paper's second paragraph and labeled First Developmental Paragraph, the first sentence is the *topic sentence*. Again, this position is arbitrary. The topic sentence can come in the middle or at the end of the paragraph, or it can be implied. But for the first few papers you write, place all topic sentences, specifically stated, at the beginning of developmental paragraphs. The topic sentence is to the paragraph what the thesis statement is to the whole paper; it is the *one point* the paragraph makes. But it is even more closely related to the thesis statement; it is one reason the thesis statement is *valid*. The remainder of the paragraph, about 150 to 200 words, is *evidence* presented to establish the soundness of the topic sentence. Once you have written this paragraph, you will have one tightly reasoned unit supporting the main point of the paper. In the first papers you write, you will include two more such units; however, *there's no reason why a short paper shouldn't have more than three developmental paragraphs, or only two.*

The topic sentence in the Second Developmental Paragraph is the second "proof" of the thesis, and the material presented in the paragraph supports this second topic sentence. When you have completed this paragraph, your support of the thesis statement becomes much stronger. You have given two reasons to show that the thesis statement is valid, and you have supported each reason with logical *evidence.*

The final paragraph, the Third Developmental Paragraph, should be the strongest in support of the thesis statement. Make the most important reason—the one you think will clinch the point—the topic sentence of this paragraph. Give it strong support in the remainder of the paragraph, and you will leave readers with the understanding you want them to have. Once you have them at this point, hit them with the concluding statement as the last sentence in the whole paper.

ENDING

In the basic diagram, your paper's last sentence is also the last sentence of the Third Developmental Paragraph (as in Theme Pattern A). However, depending on your choice of organization pattern and the length and complexity of your paper, this sentence may have to be expanded into a *concluding* fourth *paragraph,* separated from the Third Developmental Paragraph.

As the diagram suggests, in your first papers the *concluding statement* will simply restate the thesis statement so that you finish by reminding the reader that this is the point you have made in the paper. Because it's better not to make the point in the exact words used at the beginning of the paper, change the wording enough so that the concluding statement will serve as an "echo" as it concludes your strongest paragraph.

Whether you are writing a simple concluding statement or a more complete concluding paragraph, don't tell the reader you are ending your paper. Such statements as "In conclusion it can be seen that . . ." or "To sum up . . ." are trite and unnecessary. Although a formal concluding paragraph is usually unnecessary, summing up is often desirable in a much longer paper or in one following Theme Pattern A. Also, certain kinds of papers may require recommendations or questions for further consideration. But in a five-hundred-word paper, the concluding statement usually does the necessary summing up, sparing you and your readers the tediousness of a concluding paragraph that often adds little to the paper.

A kind of picture-outline, the basic diagram for Theme Pattern B represents only *one* convenient pattern for writing a short paper. But it can serve as your first model. *If your subject requires variation, then alter the formula; add or delete a paragraph.* You will know how because you will have learned the basic approach and will be able to see the whole paper. But until you do learn the basic approach, follow the diagram we have just examined.

The writer of the paper "People Problems" followed the basic approach. To help you follow the pattern, the thesis statement, topic sentences, and concluding statement are highlighted.

PEOPLE PROBLEMS

1   Play with the word <u>accidents</u>, and it will explode into many meanings. Accidents in nuclear power plants evoke frightening possibilities. At home, at school, in the workplace, accidents change our lives. Motorcycles, airplanes, motorboats, tractors, cars--vehicles of all kinds--regularly are involved in accidents. On our nation's highways alone, car accidents kill thousands every year. And what are the causes? Bad brakes and blowouts? Bad weather and slippery roads? It's

easy to blame the vehicle or the road or the weather, but too often it's the drivers who are at fault. Some don't understand the effects of certain drugs, others think they're better drivers than they are, and far too many aggressively take unnecessary chances. Although mechanical failure and environmental hazards often do play major roles, most car accidents on our highways result from human error.

2   Human error causes these accidents when people don't understand the effects of mind-impairing substances. By slowing a driver's reaction time, alcohol depresses alertness, reducing the inhibitions needed for safe driving. As a result, the uninhibited drunk driver carelessly endangers himself and others. Other substances have subtler effects. Many people use sleep-inducing, over-the-counter medications and erroneously assume they can still drive safely. Although that may indeed be true for some, for many people such medications as antihistamines, some painkillers, and muscle relaxants cause drowsiness. Again this error in judgment often causes a serious highway accident. Even worse, some people use mind-impairing drugs like cocaine or crack and think it's all right to drive. Failure to understand the effects of such drugs as these can cause fatal errors in driving judgment.

3   Highway accidents also result from human error because too many people think they are better drivers than they really are. Relaxed and self-assured, they're convinced they can drive safely when tired and sleepy. Assuming that driving is just an automatic response, they insist that all-night driving is safe. They forget that fatigue will dull alertness and shut down the mind, no matter how good the driver is. Some are so self-assured that they turn their heads to talk to back-seat passengers. Many think they can drive safely while drinking coffee or eating food. But reaching for hot coffee or manipulating a hamburger takes one hand off the steering wheel and distracts the driver. A moment of inattention, a quick move to avoid scalding pain, and the car's out of control. Others, certain they're good enough to drive while reading a road map or checking a shopping list, end up in a ditch or entangled in some farm fence. And then there's the person who smugly asserts, "I've been driving for years. Why should I learn how to turn out of a skid on a slippery road?" These are the people who are sure they can't improve by taking safe-driving tests or defensive driving lessons.

4   Human error causes many accidents because too many people aggressively take unnecessary chances. These aggressive drivers take unnecessary chances when they try to pass cars in heavy, fast, oncoming traffic. What are the results? Sometimes a fatal collision, sometimes the fatal scramble for nonexistent space on the shoulder of the road. Often the urge to pass in a no-passing zone is fueled by an unthinking road-hog driving 30 mph less than the allowed speed. This frustrating situation leads to a shout of anger, a burst of speed, an oncoming truck, a fatal crash. These are the aggressive drivers who love the challenge of exceeding speed limits and then find themselves wrapped around a utility pole. Some aggressive drivers insist on taking chances by trying to round curves faster than highways were designed to allow. Because curves are banked to help cars hold the road safely up to a given speed, exceeding the posted limit can cause the car to fly off the highway. Auto accident statistics document the results: a rollover in the

```
ditch, collision with a roadside tree, a fatal meeting with the
never-absent utility pole. Taking chances on the highway
involves human judgment, human judgment provides opportunity
for human error, and human error in a fast-moving car on a
highway can kill.
```

This paper makes just one main point: most car accidents on our highways result from human error. It's stated at the end of the introductory paragraph, preceded by a *blueprint* of supporting reasons. Although these reasons answer the implied question *why* and focus attention through the use of *because,* the best thesis sentences don't actually use the words *why* or *because*. Then, to convince the reader of the validity of the main point, the middle part of the paper explains the reasons in the same blueprint order as in the introduction, one in each of the three developmental paragraphs. The topic sentence of each paragraph restates a reason. (How this writer explored the general subject of *accidents* to discover the specific focus on *reasons for car accidents on highways* is detailed in Chapter 3.)

The first topic sentence, its controlling idea highlighted, opens the second paragraph and makes the point that human error causes car accidents because people don't understand the effects of certain drugs. The rest of the paragraph establishes the validity of this topic sentence by suggesting some consequences of this lack of understanding. People don't understand that alcohol slows reaction time, depresses alertness, and reduces necessary inhibitions—that the drunk driver is dangerous. They don't understand that over-the-counter medications can cause drowsiness and that hard drugs like cocaine can cause fatal errors in judgment.

The second topic sentence, its controlling idea highlighted, opens the third paragraph and directly states that human error causes car accidents because people think they are better drivers than they really are. They convince themselves they can drive safely when tired and sleepy, forgetting that fatigue dulls alertness and shuts down the mind. They look back to talk to back-seat passengers; they drink coffee or eat food. They're certain, too, that they're good enough to drive while reading a road map and that their experience exempts them from learning how to turn out of skids and from taking defensive driving lessons.

The third topic sentence, its controlling idea highlighted, begins the fourth paragraph and presents the writer's strongest feelings: human error causes car accidents because people aggressively take unnecessary chances. Aggressive drivers who pass cars in heavy traffic can cause fatal collisions. They react to road-hogs with anger and speed, and love the challenge of exceeding posted speed limits. They insist on rounding curves faster than the posted speed limit and often end up rolling over into a ditch or colliding with a tree or a utility pole. The writer strongly presents the consequences of aggressive chance-taking. The concluding statement, highlighted at the end of the fourth paragraph, echoes the thesis by asserting that human error causes highway accidents, some of which are fatal. For emphasis, some writers choose to put even this one-sentence conclusion into a paragraph by itself (the fifth paragraph).

This is an acceptable paper. The writer has made a point and supported it with evidence based on experience and observation. One criticism that some readers might make is that it is too impersonal and doesn't do enough to grab attention and create interest. Even very serious papers sometimes cautiously use first-person "I" or *contractions* to add a personal tone, as you can see if you check the sample introductory paragraphs on pages 123, 125, and 353. Because it's not easy to do well and can become repetitious, your instructor may not let you use "I" or contractions in your first papers. This does not mean, however, that you have to be impersonal and dull, as the freshman introductory paragraph on page 352 shows. A more formal approach that boldly asserts the subject without using "I" can be seen in the introductory paragraphs on pages 126 and 355 and in the examples and exercises at the end of this chapter.

But the writer of "People Problems" tried to create interest in a number of other ways. For example, you are invited to "play with the word *accidents*" in the opening sentence—clearly an attempt to get your mind involved. Also, the writer has used four *contractions* in the opening paragraph—"it's" (twice), "don't," and "they're." Spell out all the contractions, read the sentences aloud, and notice what happens to the "sound" (tone) of the paper. The paper contains a number of strategically placed *rhetorical fragments* that complete the answers to questions (two in the first and one in the last paragraph). What effect do they have? Because not all readers (or instructors) would approve of these rhetorical fragments, use them cautiously and when you are confident that they will be well received. (Check the discussion of acceptable *rhetorical fragments* in the handbook part of this book, page 297.)

To create additional interest, this student writer has used a number of carefully *balanced* constructions: "At home, at school, in the workplace . . ." and "A shout of anger, a burst of speed, an oncoming truck, a fatal crash" are good examples. Can you find others? Note how these balanced constructions tend to increase your reading speed. Also, the writer's use of direct quotes (third paragraph) adds interest, as do the descriptive words ("entangled in some farm fence," "wrapped around a utility pole," "scalding pain," "fueled by an unthinking road-hog"). These and other constructions show that this writer has tried to maintain reader interest and create an appropriate *tone.* As suggested on pages 36, 120, and 194, and explained on pages 350–55, tone is an important quality used by a writer to gain *reader interest* and *reader acceptance* and to project the *writer's voice.* Even solid supporting statements, logically presented, may fail to get understanding and agreement from the reader if the tone is unsuitable. You will find a preliminary exercise on changing the "writer's voice" (tone) on page 127.

The organization of basic papers such as "People Problems" can be shown in another type of diagram, one that inserts the supporting points for each topic

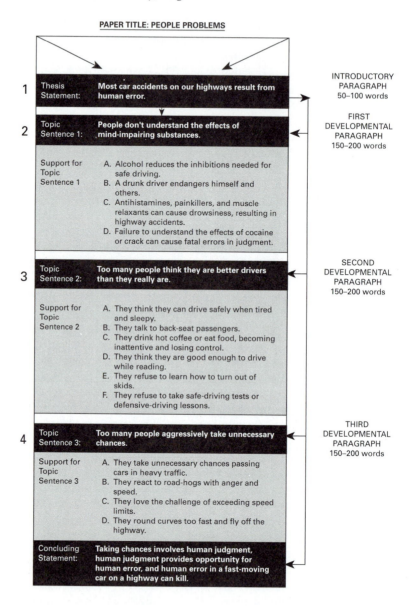

PAPER TITLE: PEOPLE PROBLEMS

1 Thesis Statement: **Most car accidents on our highways result from human error.**

INTRODUCTORY PARAGRAPH 50–100 words

2 Topic Sentence 1: **People don't understand the effects of mind-impairing substances.**

FIRST DEVELOPMENTAL PARAGRAPH 150–200 words

Support for Topic Sentence 1
A. Alcohol reduces the inhibitions needed for safe driving.
B. A drunk driver endangers himself and others.
C. Antihistamines, painkillers, and muscle relaxants can cause drowsiness, resulting in highway accidents.
D. Failure to understand the effects of cocaine or crack can cause fatal errors in judgment.

3 Topic Sentence 2: **Too many people think they are better drivers than they really are.**

SECOND DEVELOPMENTAL PARAGRAPH 150–200 words

Support for Topic Sentence 2
A. They think they can drive safely when tired and sleepy.
B. They talk to back-seat passengers.
C. They drink hot coffee or eat food, becoming inattentive and losing control.
D. They think they are good enough to drive while reading.
E. They refuse to learn how to turn out of skids.
F. They refuse to take safe-driving tests or defensive-driving lessons.

4 Topic Sentence 3: **Too many people aggressively take unnecessary chances.**

THIRD DEVELOPMENTAL PARAGRAPH 150–200 words

Support for Topic Sentence 3
A. They take unnecessary chances passing cars in heavy traffic.
B. They react to road-hogs with anger and speed.
C. They love the challenge of exceeding speed limits.
D. They round curves too fast and fly off the highway.

Concluding Statement: **Taking chances involves human judgment, human judgment provides opportunity for human error, and human error in a fast-moving car on a highway can kill.**

sentence. The result is a picture-outline to show clearly the paper's main points as well as their logical relation to each other and to the support given for each point.

With this framework of thesis statement, three basic reasons to uphold the thesis statement, support for each reason, and a concluding statement, you could have written "People Problems." This kind of picture-diagram can be used to test the validity of either the preliminary outline or the first draft of similar short papers.

OUTLINING

This section will introduce *outlining* and point out where you can find additional information on outlines and outlining as a *process*. The picture-outlines given for Theme Pattern A and Theme Pattern B in this chapter should suggest two basic approaches to all the outlines you are likely to write. And you will find examples of outlines in Chapter 3 (p. 80), Chapter 7 (199), and Chapter 8 (260–61). Study those examples after completing this section.

Outlining is a logical thinking process based on our ability to see *relationships* among things, ideas, people, places, and events. To outline is *to classify*—to sort things into groups or to see that something is part of a whole class of things. Faced with "chair" and "bed," we say (almost automatically) FURNITURE; "carrots" and "beans" belong to the class VEGETABLES; and "love," "hate," "fear," and "anger" suggest the class of items we know as EMOTIONS. This ability to see relationships and to sort items into classes or groups allows us to create *outlines*.

For longer papers, such as research papers or technical reports, the outline is a must. However, even a shorter essay—such as the five-hundred-word theme—can usually benefit from an outline. The preliminary outline helps sort related ideas into classes that represent parts of the written paper—paragraphs or sections. Once it is written down, the preliminary outline also generates new ideas during the early writing stages. This preliminary outline should be a guide to thinking and writing, not a straightjacket that puts braces on your brain. Once you have written a first draft of your paper, you can write a final outline. Again, the final outline should not be allowed to cramp your thinking. If new ideas occur as you are writing the final draft of the essay, add them; you can change the outline later. Clearly, in writing a longer research or problem-solving paper, you shouldn't need to change the outline as often, since you will have on note cards most of the ideas you are going to include in the paper. Your instructor will tell you when to turn in your outlines—preliminary and final.

The final outline you turn in with your essay or research report may be either a *topic outline* or a *sentence outline.* In the topic outline every entry is a *subject heading*—sections, paragraphs within sections, major ideas within paragraphs. In a sentence outline every entry is a complete sentence, again one for every section, paragraph, and major concept. Whether you write a topic outline or a sentence outline, you will follow this numbering system:

I. _____
  A. _____
    1. _____
    2. _____
  B. _____
    1. _____
      a. _____
        (1) _____
          (a) _____

               (b) _____

          (2) _____

       b. _____

    2. _____

 II. _____

   A. . . . etc._____

Following this pattern, let's redo the picture-outline for "People Problems" (see page 32) as a topic outline:

PEOPLE PROBLEMS

Thesis: Most car accidents on our highways result from human error.

   I. Failing to understand effects of mind-impairing substances
     A. Failing to understand effects of alcohol
     B. Failing to understand the danger of drunk driving
     C. Failing to understand effects of nonprescription drugs
     D. Failing to understand effects of cocaine
  II. Thinking they are better drivers than they really are
     A. Thinking they can drive safely when tired and sleepy
     B. Turning to talk to back-seat passengers
     C. Drinking coffee or eating
     D. Thinking they are good enough to drive while reading
     E. Refusing to learn how to turn out of skids
     F. Refusing to take driving tests and lessons
 III. Taking unnecessary chances aggressively
     A. Taking chances passing cars in heavy traffic
     B. Reacting to road-hogs with anger and speed
     C. Loving the challenge of excessive speed
     D. Rounding curves too fast

     Concluding statement: Human judgment provides opportunity for human error, and human error in a fast-moving car on a highway can kill.

Although this topic outline may be more detailed than you need, it provides a check of all the supporting details and their relationships to the three main subject headings. Here is how you would rewrite this plan as a *sentence outline:*

PEOPLE PROBLEMS

Thesis sentence: Although mechanical failure and environmental hazards often do play major roles, **most car accidents on our highways result from human error.**

   I. People don't understand the effects of mind-impairing substances.
     A. They don't understand that drinking alcohol slows a driver's reaction time.
     B. They don't understand that drunk drivers endanger themselves and others.
     C. They don't understand the effects of nonprescription drugs.
     D. They don't understand the effects of cocaine and crack.
  II. Too many people think they are better drivers than they really are.
     A. They think they can drive safely when tired and sleepy.
     B. They turn to talk to back-seat passengers.

     C. They drink coffee or eat.
     D. They think they are good enough to drive while reading a road map.
     E. They think they don't need to learn how to turn out of skids.
     F. They think they don't need to take defensive driving tests and lessons.
III. Too many people aggressively take unnecessary chances.
     A. They try to pass cars in heavy, fast, oncoming traffic.
     B. They react to road-hogs with anger and speed.
     C. They love the challenge of excessive speed.
     D. They round curves faster than highways were designed to allow.

    Concluding statement: Human judgment provides opportunity for human error, and human error in a fast-moving car on a highway can kill.

Now study the paper below and decide whether it is better than "People Problems," using, if you wish, the check sheet given on page 195.

THE PRACTICAL COLLEGE MARRIAGE

1   Can two really live as cheaply as one? As any struggling coed and her haunted husband can testify, those two had better prepare for a painful existence, but <u>practical</u>. The money that the folks were glad to send their young one must now serve two. The lessons this pair learns are the most practical in the world, though. They know before the honeymoon is over that, although they'll cry a lot, they'll learn to slice their output and savor their income. They learn to be practical about entertainment, about the care and mending of garments, and about the nourishing qualities of peanut butter.

2   Entertainment is not what it used to be. In the old days, Maria took for granted two or three movies a week and dancing at least on Saturday night. Mom and Dad didn't mind paying that little bit, as long as their college daughter kept up her grades. Now in their room—with—kitchen—privileges apartment Maria and Juan get along fine——but movies are out, and they wouldn't dream of trying to squeeze a dancing cover charge out of what little Dad sends and they can earn. For entertainment, Juan can help with the dishes, and they can walk together, hand in hand, to the library for a blissful evening of research. It's a terribly <u>practical</u> pursuit, actually.

3   The clothing situation gets serious. Neither Maria nor her Juan would dare gain weight, even if their home—cooked meals were that tempting. They dressed well in their single days, and they still do, but alas, in the very same garments that looked so much better last semester. Shoes get resoled now, instead of replaced, and the shine on Juan's "good" suit is more noticeable. It isn't as though he had to keep up with his fraternity brothers any longer. Camaraderie with that carefree group is nice to remember, but meeting with the boys is no longer practical. Maria watches fashions, but she does not buy the fads. She found out in a hurry that it is not the <u>practical</u> way to dress.

4   Their menu does not vary much, and there is no longer the balanced touch of the dormitory dietician. They watch out for

> yellow and green vegetables, of course, and a potato a day with
> some kind of protein. But the old zip is gone, and with it went
> between—class cokes and Sunday at the Garden Steakhouse with
> the rest of the business majors. They are grateful, naturally,
> to the famous scientist who developed peanut butter. Even if it
> does stick to the palate and begin to grow old too soon, Maria
> and Juan buy more peanut butter, because it's very <u>practical</u>.
> But when it's all over and the children are grown, Juan and
> Maria will look back on these days as some of the best in their
> lives, because look at the great lessons they learned.

Compare this paper with the basic diagram for a five-hundred-word paper, and you will see that this paper follows the diagram exactly but is not a slavish, mechanical, line-by-line copy of it. *Nor should it be. Translating the basic diagram into a paper truly your own requires decisions in tone, in diction, in sentence structure, in selection and organization of ideas.* What is the purpose of the opening question? How is it related to the thesis statement given at the end of the paragraph? In what ways is this first paragraph similar to the diagram representing Theme Pattern A?

Note how this writer establishes a friendly, informal tone in the first few sentences by choosing words to suggest a friendly attitude: *really, coed, haunted, folks,* and *they'll* are good examples. You don't have to write a dull, formal paper just because you are following a preplanned picture-outline. A little creative thinking will help you write a fresh, personal paper. Eventually you'll want to experiment with patterns of organization quite unlike the basic diagram you are studying here and with papers considerably longer than five hundred words. You may want to try inductive organization, and you will want to practice expanding your developmental paragraphs by fleshing out your supporting reasons, perhaps as E. B. White has done in the paragraph given on page 186.

EXERCISES

I. Analyze the following papers for organization. Answer the questions at the end of each paper to aid your analysis.

A. MISPLACED GOALS IN EDUCATION STIFLE THE INQUIRING MIND

1   Lack of encouragement of creativity in the present school system discourages a real search for knowledge. Importance continually placed on following a certain form has given students a misplaced set of values.

2   Even though following directions is important, too often students are graded solely on how well they do this. In spite of their original thoughts their grades may be low because they left too small a margin, wrote on the bottom line, or numbered the pages in the wrong corner. Following a rigid form of roman numerals, students

lose sight of the content of the material. If they have researched the subject, they might lose all credit because they have not tagged their sources properly. Professors should emphasize the thought shown in students' work rather than rigid adherence to a given form.

3   Thinking things through for themselves, students might come up with ideas other than their professor's. Grade school and high school have taught them that this is not advisable. Students who can most nearly duplicate the teacher's instruction are regarded most highly. If the instructor will "lay it on the line," then it can be easily duplicated. Such narrow goals restrict students, making them conform to the ideas already set out for them. But stepping outside the expected way of working a problem, finding a different meaning to a passage in literature, or bringing some original idea to class is too often penalized.

4   Memorization of details clutters the mind with facts that are never assimilated. World geography consists of a detailed compilation of isolated facts on individual countries. "How many square miles is Uruguay?" and "What is its population?" are asked rather than "How has its location in South America affected its economic growth?" The value of associating the past with the future is lost in history classes where twenty dates are given—students are asked to write who was president and vice-president.

5   With elementary and secondary education goals set on teaching students to follow strict forms or to reproduce an instructor's or text's words and memorize details without connecting them, it is easily understandable that students today apparently lack an inquiring mind. Any deviation from the usual they wish to do must be done outside their classwork.

6   To encourage original thought educational goals must be realigned. Importance must be placed on the entire content of the material and its broad implications. Reslanting history to increase the value, using geography in studies of modern economics and politics, looking into physics proofs rather than just formulas will help stimulate thought. A broadening of instructors' views will broaden the scope and responsibility of students. More scholastic freedom and more creative goals will reawaken the inquiring mind.

QUESTIONS FOR ANALYSIS OF PAPER A

This exercise answers its own questions so that you can understand what you are expected to do in analyzing the organization of the paragraphs.

1. What is the thesis statement of Paper *A*?

Answer: The thesis statement is the first sentence: *Lack of encouragement of creativity in the present school system discourages a real search for knowledge.*

2. How does the second paragraph support this thesis statement?

Answer: It gives and supports one reason for the validity of the thesis statement. It makes the point that students are frequently graded on how well they follow form rather than on how deeply they think.

3. What is the function of the second sentence in the introductory paragraph?

Answer: This sentence does not belong in the introductory paragraph. It should be the first sentence of the second paragraph, because it is really the topic sentence of that paragraph. All of the second paragraph is a discussion of the subject given in the second sentence of the introductory paragraph. Nowhere else in the paper is *following a certain form* discussed. The introductory paragraph should be expanded, with the thesis statement at the end. Rarely can a single sentence function effectively as a whole paragraph.

4. How does the third paragraph support the thesis statement?

Answer: It gives and supports a second reason for the validity of the thesis statement. It makes the point that too frequently students are rewarded for simply parroting the instructor's ideas and are penalized if they put forward the result of their own thinking.

5. Which sentence is the topic sentence of the third paragraph?

Answer: The last sentence in the paragraph is the topic sentence. It probably would be better placed as the first sentence.

6. a. Which sentence is the topic sentence of the fourth paragraph?
   b. What is the function of this paragraph in the paper?

Answer: (a) The first sentence in the fourth paragraph is the topic sentence. (b) The fourth paragraph gives and supports a third reason for the validity of the thesis statement. It deplores the emphasis on insignificant details.

7. What is the function of the fifth paragraph?

Answer: The fifth paragraph sums up the points that have been made in support of the thesis statement. The paper would be more effectively organized if most of the material in the fifth paragraph were part of the revised introductory paragraph and if a concluding statement were placed at the end of the fourth paragraph. (This problem in organization, especially demonstrated by the inadequacy of the introductory paragraph, is probably caused by the writer's failure to think through the subject before starting to write. She probably devised her support for the thesis statement as she wrote from paragraph to paragraph. Then when she got to the end she could see what the support was and summed it up there. It takes a skillful student to succeed at the organize-as-you-write plan. This student was not quite skillful enough.)

8. Does the sixth paragraph support the thesis statement? Does it belong in the paper? Why or why not?

Answer: The sixth paragraph does not support the thesis statement because it does not give and support a reason for the validity of the thesis. In fact, this paragraph does not belong in the paper because it introduces a second subject by attempting to explain what should be done about the situation. The subject of this paragraph could be explored and supported in another paper, not here.

9. Where should this paper end?

Answer: The paper could end with the fourth paragraph if a concluding statement were added to it.

B. EDUCATORS WHO DISCOURAGE THINKING

1   There is no doubt that today's public school students lack creative thinking ability. They find it far less trouble to develop a sort of mnemonic memorizing mind that follows but never leads. Therefore, most students prefer to memorize and leave tiresome thinking for later.

2   Classroom discussion is different. There students are often willing to shine forth orally, but never, never in writing. They would rather be asked to respond with a *T* for True and *F* for False on a simple and clearcut objective exam than be asked to think an issue through and discuss it in writing.

3   Students are inclined to drag their feet when it comes to showing their instructor, via clear and thorough essay-type discussions, that they have a full understanding of course content. But this is hardly the fault of the student, at least not in the high school that I attended. In fact, from the elementary level up to Grade 12, we were trained to memorize, and we soon learned that perfecting the practice of spouting out the outlined truths, with no time out for understanding and tying together of isolated facts, was the way to the best grades. We worked out the formula for success and we learned to like it, in the way any child learns to adapt to the security of a system.

4   If the nation is to continue to survive and even to progress, then such trends as this must be halted. Such lazy testing is developed for lazy grading, and the obvious answer is that instructors must begin to care enough to improve their methods. Instructors must be taught before they can teach; otherwise, the inquiring minds of our potential leaders will never be freed from the regimented, "fill-in-the-blank" type of nonthinking. It could even be that there is more truth in the ancient admonition: If you can't do it, teach it; if you can't teach it, teach others to teach it.

QUESTIONS FOR ANALYSIS OF PAPER B

1. The thesis statement of this paper is the last sentence of the first paragraph: *Most students prefer to . . . leave tiresome thinking for later.* The writer makes only one point in the remainder of the paper to support this thesis. What is it?

2. The second paragraph consists of only two sentences and does not give or support an idea. Could these two sentences be integrated into any other paragraph in the paper? If so, which one? If not, why not?

3. The third paragraph is the only one that can be called a developmental paragraph. What topic sentence does it develop?

4. What is the purpose of the fourth paragraph? Does it contain material that might be used in the third paragraph? Is there another subject here that might be used as a topic sentence in support of the thesis statement? What is it?

5. Since the paper gives only one reason for the validity of the thesis statement, make up two more reasons that might be supported in developmental paragraphs. (The writer of this paper can handle the language fairly well. From all indications, however, he wrote this paper without much planning. The result is that the paper does not fully support its thesis, some ideas and paragraphs are left undeveloped, and the last paragraph begins with a vague *such trends as this must be halted.*)

C. THE CASE AGAINST HIGH SCHOOL FOOTBALL

1   High school football is an outrageous waste. The game is too expensive: in dollars and cents, in hours and minutes, in morale, and in physical well-being. When gym equipment and coaching salaries grow more important than academic progress and class work waits upon athletes, when the student's sense of academic and competitive values is distorted, and fine young bodies are deliberately exposed to physical violence, then football does indeed cost too much.

2   Seldom does the total gate receipt for the season, even with the added dimes and quarters from concession stands, smooth out the balance. School administrators and their staff pay top prices for dummies, pads, cleated shoes, and face guards; their boys need and deserve the best possible protection out there on the field of danger. Turfs, sturdy bleachers, and weather-conditioned gymnasiums are theirs to maintain (with a giant slice of the school board's carefully balanced budget). And the hiring of the go-gettingest coach available is one of the greatest expenses the school faces. But all that is the simple, red-and-black side of the ledger.

3   Though not quite so obvious to the outsider as dollar cost, the existing situation makes it almost shameful for students to neglect their team in favor of class work. When there are posters to put out, tickets to sell, or athletic banquets to be arranged, students are often expected to make the time, even during a class period, if the heat is on, to back the team. They can hardly be expected to pay more attention to their Biology III notebooks than they pay to the Homecoming Game; why, it's practically a breach of faith! So they set aside the biology assignment and the Latin translation, and the three chapters in the Hardy novel due tomorrow, so they won't be late for the pep rally. After all, Miss Hopkins and those other instructors must realize (they've heard it all week over the intercom) that Coach Jamison and his boys need all the spirit that can be whipped up if they're to ring up another victory for Consolidated High.

4   However, the song that resounds across the campus for the week is not an echo of the old softie that insists "It is not that we win or lose, but how we play the game!" None of that mush for the up-to-date pigskin elevens. It's no more who we play, but who we beat. The coach shouts out his determined promises, then the bugles blare for the captain Himself, the biggest imaginable Man on Campus. So long to the fellow with the *A* average and to all the other wearers of the letter sweater, the mark of the scholar. And often the school's reputation is built on its team's winning streak, not on the number of serious students who go on to excel in their college studies. As a result, the football-centered school distorts the value of competition, substituting "beat the opposition" for "compete honorably." Still, all this is to say nothing of the deliberate exposure to physical dangers, even death, to which public schools subject their students in the glorious name of football. We'd rather not dwell on the number of boys who either don't make it at all or who are carried out between quarters to a life of lameness, of back or brain. Besides those caught in the crossfire on the gridiron, too, are those who suffer (or die) in automobile or school bus collisions en route to the Big Game.

5   There's no winner in high school football. When the count is taken of money, time, energy, and suffering spent on "the game," both teams have lost, no matter how many times the boys first downed, touched down, touched back, or kicked goal. The real score (obscured by the glaring numbers on the great electric scoreboard) reads NOTHING to NOTHING.

QUESTIONS FOR ANALYSIS OF PAPER C

1. Outline Paper *C* so that it fits the basic diagram for a five-hundred-word paper. Arrange and label your outline as follows:

Thesis Statement: ....
    Topic Sentence 1:...
        Supporting Statement A: ....
        Supporting Statement B:..
        Supporting Statement C: ....
        ....
    Topic Sentence 2: ....
        Supporting Statement A: ....
        Supporting Statement B:..
        Supporting Statement C: ....
    Topic Sentence 3:...
    ....

2. Does the introductory paragraph contain a blueprint? List these anticipatory ideas in the order in which they appear in the paragraph. Does this paragraph follow the diagram illustrating the "funnel effect" (see page 26)? Is the second paragraph clearly tied to the introductory one?

3. Examine paragraph four for unity. Does every sentence comment on the distortion of competitive values? Do you think this topic is sufficiently developed? Suggest several possible solutions to the problem.

4. What is the purpose of paragraph five? What does it replace in the basic diagram? Does it succeed? Why?

D. UNLEASHED DANGER

1   If you are a dog lover don't read this. Tend to your dogs instead: Train them, restrain them, kennel them. But don't let them run loose near my house—unless you want a bruised and battered dog, with fear in his heart and a permanent whimper in his voice. Not that I dislike dogs. Not at all. I have been known to affectionately pet puppies of all kinds. I bow to no man in my respect for all ages, sizes, and breeds of well-disciplined dogs, but I hate the havoc that unleashed dogs cause. Their habit of wet-marking their romping trails is upsetting, and the surprises they leave for bare feet on a lawn are disgusting. Far worse, however, dogs on the loose terrorize cyclists and pedestrians, create traffic hazards, and damage gardens. Clearly, their unleashed presence on streets and sidewalks is a dangerous nuisance.

2   Although barking dogs may not bite, they can scare cyclists and pedestrians half to death. I don't know which is worse, the little yappers or the big barkers. If you're riding a bicycle the yappers are mostly a nuisance, though they are threatening enough to force you to zig-zag dangerously on the street. It is a brave cyclist who can ignore the barker whose flashing teeth are nipping at the handle bars. I have seen school children panic on their bicycles when a barker leaps out at them, forcing them to turn wildly to avoid being bitten and sometimes even causing a youngster to fall onto the road. Or suppose you are walking at night and one of the yappers rushes out, snapping and snarling only inches away from your heels. I tend to freeze in my steps, cuss quite a bit, and wish I had a big stick. Or a big gun. Or a middle-sized tiger.

3   Both yappers and barkers are traffic hazards. Motorists and cyclists and pedestrians, conditioned by dog-lovers to think of these brutes as people, automatically react to protect them. Just watch a jaywalking dog saunter across a busy highway in some suburban town. Cars swerve, brakes screech, accidents occur. The unsuspecting driver thinks the dog is patiently waiting for a break in the traffic, or for a light to turn green, perhaps. Then without warning man's best friend heads across. The sickening thud of flesh against metal is a sound that will haunt any driver for weeks—if he escapes traffic in the adjoining lane as he tries unthinkingly to avoid the dog. Equally hazardous are those dogs that dart onto the road they think they own, barking at everything rolling by. Once a little yapper so worried me that I ran my car into an innocent fire hydrant. Throw together one dog, a few cyclists, and several cars and the results can be tragic. Or watch a young pedestrian trying to coax his reluctant mutt across a car-filled street. Frightening. And dangerous.

4   What makes me blow up, however, is that unleashed dogs damage gardens. If you are a gardener then you probably react as I do after some night-marauding barker with size thirteen feet has stomped through your flower bed or tomato patch. The first time I saw a three-inch-deep depression in the soft soil I reached for my shotgun, certain some wild beast had chosen my yard for a den. Just as irritating is the systematic territory marker who has chosen a corner of the front hedge and the base of the yard lamp as routine targets—with Master only feet away, half-sharply calling, "No, no Spot!" Spot isn't listening. But what really makes me irate is when I'm crossing the lawn barefooted on a Sunday morning to get the newspaper and I step into some marker's calling card. I don't think I'd actually shoot the scoundrel if I caught him, but I might make him walk barefoot on my lawn for a few days. Yappers, barkers, markers are fine as puppies, or firmly on a leash, or in a kennel; on the loose, however, they're definitely a menace.

QUESTIONS FOR ANALYSIS OF PAPER D

Paper *D* has been included to raise questions about *tone* and *audience* in the writing of expository papers. As you will discover if you check the section on tone in Chapter 10 (page 350), on the written page tone is the sound of your "voice" *as your readers hear it,* and it may not be the "voice" you intended at all. Once you freeze a word on paper, it loses much of the added power and interest you could give it if you spoke it. The issues raised by the following questions, therefore, are important.

1. List three desirable and three undesirable qualities you see in this paper. Compare your views with those of others in your class.
2. How serious do you think this writer is? What specific qualities in the paper led you to your conclusion?
3. If you removed all contractions, what effect would this create if you were *listening* to the paper?
4. List the rhetorical fragments used by this writer. Do you think they are intentional? Effective? Do professional writers use fragments? Why? (You might want to explore this by looking at a number of articles in popular magazines or newspapers.)
5. List what you consider to be the ten most *descriptive* words in the paper. Are they appropriate for this subject? Do you think they are effective? Discuss your choices with others in the class.
6. Does this paper follow the form of Theme Pattern A or Theme Pattern B? How closely? What are the main points made by this paper?

Written by a professional writer, Paper *E* differs from the basic pattern you have been analyzing. Its first two paragraphs provide important background information *against* which its real thesis is asserted. The paper's first paragraph really states a basic issue in two different ways. If you stated this issue as a question, then the second paragraph provides statistics to suggest that the answer to this question is *yes*. But the paper's title and the first sentence of paragraph 3 reveal the writer's real purpose.

As you read the paper, note how carefully the writer uses topic sentences and transitions to lead you from paragraph to paragraph.

E. THE MYTH ABOUT BLACK VIOLENCE[2]

1   The belief that blacks are more prone than whites to commit acts of violence is a central premise in the view that black males in the inner city constitute a new "under-class." When evidence of so-called black-on-black violence is combined with frustration in dealing with crack, gangs, and female-headed households, even prominent black academics are tempted to portray inner-city black culture as self-destructive and pathological.

2   At first glance, this portrait seems unassailable. Blacks constitute 13 percent of the urban population, but, according to the FBI, they are more than half of those arrested for murder, rape and and non-negligent manslaughter. This is five times the rate for whites. The victims of this violence are also far more likely to be black. Ninety-five percent of all violence against blacks is committed by blacks. Nationally, homicide is the major cause of death for younger black males as well as for black women under 40. Inner-city blacks appear to be particularly violence-prone. The homicide rate for young black males living in standard metropolitan areas is twice that for young blacks living in other locations. The figures on black teen-agers seem more ominous still. From 1977 to 1982 more than half of the juvenile arrests for the most violent crimes were among black teen-agers and the relative rate of incarceration for black as against white youth was an astounding 44 to 1.

3   The problem with drawing conclusions from this information is that its primary source—data on arrests and imprisonment—may itself be the product of racial discrimination. Our picture of black violence may reflect official attitudes and behavior, not racial differences. This alternative view is supported by national surveys of crime victims, a far more accurate source of information about crimes committed than arrest reports. Thus, according to the FBI, the proportion of blacks arrested for aggravated assault in 1987 was three times greater than the proportion of whites. But the National Crime Survey, based on victim interviews, found that the actual proportion of blacks and whites committing aggravated assault in 1987 was virtually identical: 32 per 1,000 for blacks; 31 per 1,000 for whites. The National Youth Survey involved 1,725 youths 11 to 17 years of age, whose law-violating behavior between 1976 and 1980 was determined by confidential interviews. The survey reported that, with the exception of 1976, "no significant race differences were found in any of the violent or serious offense scales."

4   The presumed link between greater violence among blacks and drug use is equally mistaken. Although accurate data on drug use is hard to come by, interviews with admitted drug users consistently show that a greater proportion of whites than blacks use hard drugs and that whites use hard drugs more frequently, including heroin and cocaine. Although race does not determine who initiates violence, fatal outcomes are far more likely when blacks are involved. The question then is not why

[2] Evan Stark, *Houston Chronicle* 19 July 1990: 11b. Stark teaches public administration at Rutgers University in Newark, N.J.

blacks are more violent than whites—they may not be—but why are the consequences of violent confrontation for blacks so much more severe?

5   Society's response to violence in the black community, particularly police protection and medical care, directly contributes to this tragic outcome. The belief that blacks are "violence prone" leads to a double standard in police response. When white and black teen-agers commit the same offense, police are seven times more likely to charge black teen-agers with a felony and courts are more likely to imprison the teen-ager. The belief that violence among inner-city blacks is normal also leads police and the courts to tolerate levels of violence among black adults that would not be accepted from other groups, particularly in and around the home. The result is that arrest and imprisonment are deemed appropriate only after violence escalates. This pattern is illustrated most dramatically with domestic violence—a major cause of death among black women under 40. The typical domestic homicide is preceded by assaults; law enforcement has failed to intervene until a serious injury or a fatality occurs. Homicides among black males, including gang offenses, often have a similar history.

6   Thus, the myth of black violence nonetheless has real and tragic consequences. The same discriminatory attitudes that lead to high arrest and imprisonment rates among black teen-agers inhibit police action to limit violent crime among black adults. What needs to be changed is racism—not black manhood, culture or families headed by women.

QUESTIONS FOR ANALYSIS OF PAPER E

Paper *E* has been included because it departs in several important ways from the basic pattern you have been studying. The following questions will help you discover these differences and compare them with this pattern.

1. **a.** The first two paragraphs of this paper provide a formal introduction. In what ways is this introduction different from those you've been studying?
   b. Is there a thesis statement anywhere in these two paragraphs?
   c. Why is the word *seems* important to the paper's development?
   d. Could the paper's title be considered a "thesis"? Where else in the paper does the title appear?
2. **a.** Restate as simple questions the statements made in the first paragraph.
   b. What word in the title challenges these two statements?
3. **a.** In the first sentence of the second paragraph, to what does "this portrait" refer? What important purpose do these two words serve?
   b. What is the function of the word *unassailable*?
4. **a.** Identify the important transition words in the first sentence of the third paragraph. Be sure to identify *all* words that point back to paragraph 2.
   b. Is this sentence a topic sentence? How does it anticipate the information presented in the third paragraph?
   c. Sentence three of the third paragraph begins with the words "this alternative view." To what two previous statements does this phrase refer?
5. The fourth paragraph begins with a topic sentence. What part of this sentence "echoes" previous information? What part of this sentence points *forward*? What main point will this paragraph make? How does this paragraph also look *forward* to the fifth one?

6. **a.** In the fifth paragraph, to what does "this tragic outcome" refer? Why is this phrase important to the development of the paper?
   b. What is the topic sentence of this paragraph? What topic does provide for development in this paragraph?
7. **a.** In the final paragraph, what two important "echoes" does the first sentence provide?
   b. How much of the second sentence provides a transition from previous information? What important part of this sentence serves as a concluding idea for the whole paper?
   c. The final paragraph serves as a conclusion to the paper. Do you think it should be expanded to provide more summary material? Do you think the last sentence should be deleted? Explain why or why not.

II. To see how well you manage a short paper, write one to fit Theme Pattern A and one to fit Theme Pattern B. Choose only *one* of the following questions as your starting point *for both papers*.
   A. Are good writing skills important?
   B. Do women have the same job rights as men?
   C. Are today's young people given enough responsibility?
   D. Should sex scenes in movies be less explicit?
   E. Has our justice system lessened discrimination against minorities?
   F. Should doctors be allowed to change genes that cause fatal diseases?
   G. Should the use of hard drugs be legalized?
   H. Is more sex education needed in our schools?
   I. What does the word *pornography* mean to most people?
   J. Should the theory of creationism be taught in public schools?

III. Using Theme Pattern A, write only introductory paragraphs for three of the questions given above in Exercise II.

IV. Practice finding reasons to support any opinions you adopt. Here are some suggestions to get your mind moving:
   A. If you could be any animal you wanted to be, which would you choose? List three or four reasons to support your choice.
   B. If you could be any person (real or imaginary) you wanted to be, whom would you choose? List four or five reasons to support your choice.
   C. Make a list of one-sentence statements to answer each of the following questions:
      1. Why is marriage like a contact sport?
      2. Why is marriage like a roller coaster?
      3. Why is a city slum like a contagious disease?
      4. What are the most dangerous hazards in and around your home?
      5. Why is it all right for a husband to do the cooking?
      6. Should people be allowed to commit suicide under any circumstances?

REVIEW TERMS

Understanding the meaning of the following terms will help you master the material in this chapter.

   A. Beginning, blueprint, to classify, common ground, concluding paragraph, concluding statement, conclusion, contractions, deductive, developmental paragraph, direction, discovery, ending, evidence, expository, focus, funneling effect, grabber, inductive, introductory paragraph, invention process, middle, organization pattern, paragraph, prewriting stage, question–answer approach, reader acceptance, reader interest, rhetorical fragments, sentence outline, thesis statement, tone, topic outline, topic sentence, valid, writer's voice

B. Contraction, first person, fragment, grammatical fragment, informal (tone), rhetorical fragment, sentence

3

Getting Started: Discovery, Specific Focus, Thesis

Writing is a creative *action,* an active *processing* through which you convert feelings, attitudes, and thoughts into words to make it possible for someone to understand you. This conversion depends on and begins with a *thinking process* that must be self-motivating, self-questioning, and ongoing. If nothing is going on in your mind, you can't expect something to happen on your computer screen or on a blank sheet of paper facing you. Sometimes the simple action of writing down *anything* or making your fingers type words—even nonsense—will help jump-start the thinking process. This conversion action will continue if you randomly *list* thoughts or quickly *describe* what you are feeling. By repeating these actions—thinking, listing, describing—you will soon be able to combine your list of ideas into sentences, then paragraphs, and finally a complete theme—the end product. As you can see, writing is a complex, ongoing, multistage process. It is also clearly one of our greatest inventions.

In this writing process, getting started also means having a purpose, a reason for writing. It means repeatedly asking yourself questions, keeping your mind moving, keeping it involved. It means finding a subject to write about and knowing why you are writing about it. It means understanding who will be reading your paper, and writing to please, inform, or persuade that reader. It means searching your mind for feelings and ideas and then converting them into relevant meaning. But to begin with, getting started means learning how to overcome the barrier of the blank page or empty computer screen. To overcome this barrier, you must first perform two very basic actions:

1. *Get moving: Do something physical.* Sit at a desk, pick up a pencil and write or type something. Using a typewriter or computer keyboard *is* doing something physical.

2. *Eliminate or ignore fear of failure or ridicule.* Don't think your ideas are not worthwhile. They are. When you first begin, assume a completely uncritical attitude toward your ideas, no matter how odd they may seem to you. Creating a sense of "free play" is crucial. If you waste time stewing about "what people will say," you will block the discovery process. Only an insensitive person would ridicule what you say; a constructive reader will find ways to help you say it better.

If you're working on a computer, getting started takes on special meaning and provides unique advantages. If, at last, you've managed to seat yourself at the computer desk, the very act of turning on the machine and calling up the word-processing program you use is a positive *action.* You are moving. Faced now with a lonely cursor on a blank screen, what should you do? Get your fingers moving—with a pen or on a keyboard—to get your mind moving. The unique advantage provided by the computer gives you freedom and power—to erase, repeat, move, or alter words, sentences, paragraphs. And all with the flick of a finger or the click of a mouse button. This chapter will help you put that freedom and power to work.

Each time you write, you tell your reader something about your experiences and ideas. You project part of your *self.* You must discover and *choose* the part you want to communicate. But which part? How do you choose? Before you begin any serious writing, therefore, you must become actively involved in a self-questioning, problem-solving process reflecting your feelings and ideas as well as your relation to the people and the world around you. This crucial part of getting started is often called *prewriting.* Though you already may be setting down ideas this early in the process, mostly you'll be trying to crank up the motor of your mind, trying to find out what to say and how to say it, trying to control and focus your subject. Then, even as you write, your mind will continue to think, to ask searching questions. The very act of writing itself should become a creative part of this *discovery process.* Later, once you have set down most of your ideas, you will critically reread, edit, and revise—several times—in the final stages of the *writing process.*

DISCOVERY: THE PREWRITING PROCESS

Today what we call *discovery* extends an approach used by ancient teachers of writing and oratory, but they called it *invention* (*inventio,* in Latin). Though they used the process mostly to discover ("invent") lines of argument to support and develop a point of view, some also used it to find *subjects* to discuss and explore. As you will see from the discussion that follows, we will stretch this discovery process even further.

Prewriting—the early stages of the overall writing process—includes such mind-involvement games as *free association* of ideas, *brainstorming* (by yourself and with others), *clustering, free writing,* the *quick-question* (reporter's) *approach,* and *directed discovery—classical invention,* reading, interviewing, observing, note-taking, researching. The success of your writing depends in great part on how actively and fully you get involved in these prewriting processes. Question. Play. Set down words—on the computer screen or on paper. Get your mind moving. Break the blank-screen or empty-page barrier. If there's little or nothing going on in your mind, you can't expect much to appear on your paper or on your computer screen.

In addition to the two basic actions already noted (getting moving, eliminating fear of failure and ridicule), all prewriting involves:

1. Asking questions, thinking, searching for information, getting motivated
2. Answering questions, taking notes, organizing information, testing approaches, setting down ideas as they occur to you
3. Planning a specific approach, classifying, outlining, controlling, focusing

For the personal, expressive paper—the basic five-hundred-word theme—the most important part of prewriting is to discover your own ideas and feelings and ways to communicate them. The prewriting stage can begin in the shower with the *free association* of ideas. It can move to your study desk and to some *brainstorming* or *clustering*. Or it can take you to the library for research to discover what professionals say about the question you're trying to answer. It can take you into the laboratory to set up experiments, to a field to grow plants, or to people for answers to a questionnaire. Discovery approaches abound.

Nor does the discovery process end with the prewriting stage. For many writers, the actual writing process itself—simply putting words on screen or paper—reactivates the discovery of ideas. As they set down words—selecting, adding, rejecting—they discover new words to fit more exactly the thoughts and feelings they're trying to communicate. And they also discover new ideas. This is one reason why writing down words during brainstorming, clustering, and free writing is important. Moreover, if you know how to type, you may improve this creative discovery by becoming more *action-oriented*—getting your fingers to make words appear on a computer screen and breaking the blank-page barrier.

Try it. To get moving, make this discovery process work for you. Allow enough time to explore, enjoy, and play with your feelings and thoughts and the words that fit them. Learn to discover your exact thoughts and attitudes before you try to set them down more formally in structured sentence form—that's what getting started is all about. Here are some free association approaches to get you moving.

FREE ASSOCIATION APPROACHES: LETTING YOUR MIND PLAY

Perhaps the most important component in the successful prewriting process is the willingness—and the ability—to let your mind "play." It is this motivated play that leads to the *free association* of ideas:

> **up**/down/high/low/sad/drag/**nag**
> **black**/white/pure/clean/refined/**sophisticated**
> **big**/large/great/superior/super/**the best**
> **eating**/food/dessert/chocolate/**dark**
> **black**/night/fear/terror/terrorists/**hijacking planes**

In its simplest form this is a game any five-year-old can play—opposites, rhymes, synonyms, and anything else that freely comes to mind. Let's look at this list. How do you get from *up* to *nag*? From *black* to *sophisticated*? From *eating* to *dark*? (Notice that I'm asking questions.) You must start with something—anything will do, provided that you set it down and play with it. Once you set it down, *up* can lead you to *down* (its opposite), and to *high* (its synonym), and to *low* (another opposite). But "feeling low" is a *drag* and that rhymes with *nag*. "What is a nag?" you might then ask. Asking a question and finding an answer at this point is important. "A nag is somebody that just keeps pushing and pushing and pushing, until. . . ." Well, you could keep right on going, couldn't you? Or *nag* might lead you to "a tired, old horse, ready for the glue factory because. . . ." *Black*, you will notice, leads first to an opposite, then to a series of synonyms, ending with *sophisticated*, which could be explored in a series of questions and definitions. Try, play, ask questions, look for answers. Fill your page; make the computer screen light up. For you, however, the game shouldn't end with a simple word or a simple answer. You'll learn to continue *asking questions* about the ideas that you have found through free association: What is *terror*? *The best* what? What makes it "the best"? Who is *sophisticated* and who is not? How do you decide? What besides chocolate is *dark*? What about *hijacking planes*? Why do hijackers do it? What effects does hijacking have on the hostages? During any free association exercise, set down some of the ideas as well as the questions you discover. These can then become the starting places for other discovery approaches. In free association, ideas are toys and words are tools, as the following prewriting approaches show.

Brainstorming

Brainstorming is the prewriting process of discovering ideas to write about by freely listing—writing down—all ideas and questions that occur to you about a chosen subject. You can brainstorm alone, or you can work with a group; either way you should take notes. Begin with a general subject and set down all ideas, no matter how odd they may seem. This free association listing process can be effective even if you are working alone on a typewriter or computer, depending on your typing skills. Every word you set down will help break the blank-page barrier, will help convince you that you *can* find something to say. Here's an example, beginning with the general subject *accidents*:

ACCIDENTS

cut finger	broken toes	bad brakes
broken nose	car wreck	driving drunk

collision	school accidents	shooting my foot
slippery	computer accidents	drug overdose
slippery road	accidents on the job	broken arm
muddy road	swimming accidents	broken dishes
kitchen accidents	cooking accidents	scattered glass
fire		

Although using a computer to list ideas provides fast, printable records, writing them down also works well. Keep listing until you run out of ideas. If, however, you do nothing further than simply list terms, you still won't have anything to write about. Again, ask questions and study your list to find relationships or patterns you can think and write about. What terms seem to be related, seem to belong within larger groups? Looking at the list of accidents, you should discover by grouping related terms (*classifying, clustering*) that this brainstorming session has really led you to a number of *general subject areas:* car accidents, personal accidents, home accidents, school accidents, hunting accidents. "Cut finger," "broken dishes," and "scattered glass" might suggest kitchen accidents at home, perhaps. "Cut finger" and "shooting my foot" could lead to more ideas about hunting accidents. "Bad brakes," "driving drunk," "collision," and "slippery road" clearly point to causes of auto accidents, suggested, perhaps, by the "car wreck" item in the list. What other relationships can you discover in the list? You now have a beginning. Your mind is moving and you have some leads to follow.

But don't stop asking questions. Continue to explore the general subject areas you have discovered: What *causes* hunting accidents? How can hunting accidents be *prevented*? What are the *effects* of auto accidents? Asking the right relevant questions could lead you to a *specific subject* suitable for a short paper.

EXERCISES

    A. Choose one of the terms from the brainstorming list (for example, "drug overdose," "fire," or "accidents on the job"); then try a *group* brainstorming session to explore the effect of beginning with a more specific term. Choose someone to set down (on screen or paper) all the ideas that the group discovers.

    B. Try a *group* brainstorming session beginning with the term "weapons."

Clustering

Clustering is the prewriting process of discovering ideas to write about by *deliberately grouping* or *classifying* related ideas into **clusters,** forming a picture-diagram of your thinking process. Unlike brainstorming, clustering expects you to keep related, connected ideas next to each other, resulting in "branches" or "clusters" of ideas. To see how this process works, write a general subject in the middle of a blank sheet of paper. Then write around it other ideas you associate

CLUSTERING: DISCOVERING IDEAS THROUGH CLASSIFICATION

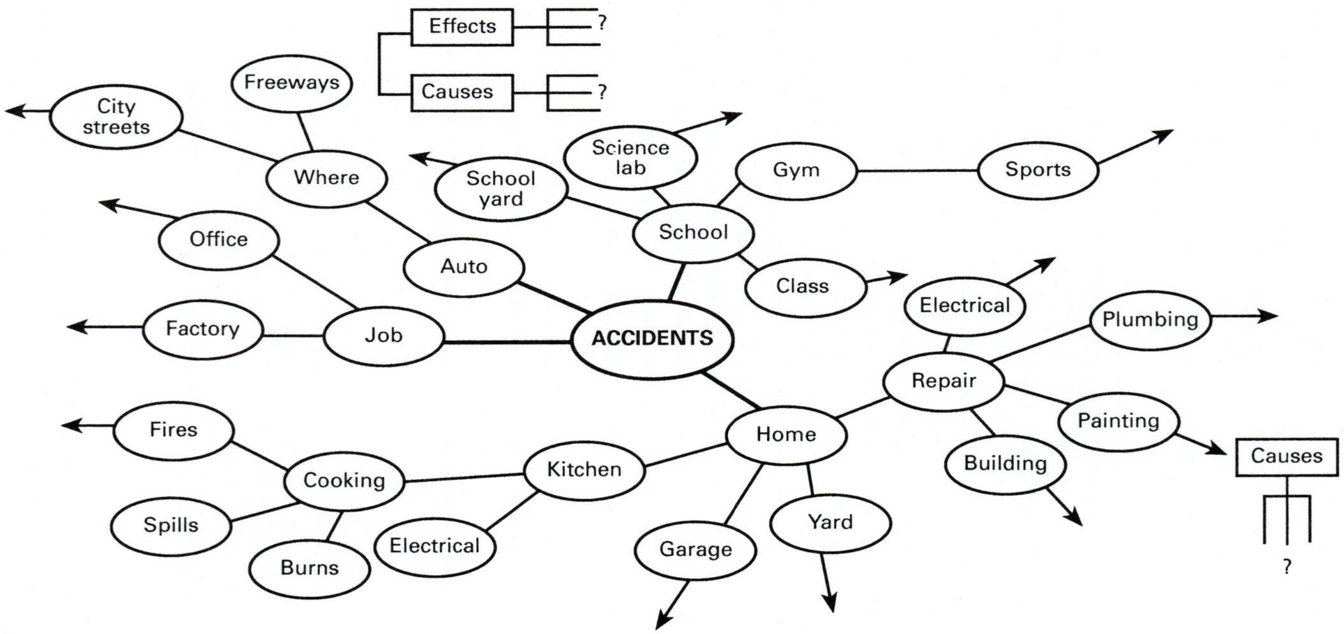

with this subject. Then use a line to connect related phrases and words to each other and to the subject. The clustering illustration on page 52 uses *accidents* (a general subject) as the starting point.

Not everyone would arrange these ideas in exactly this way, since the way in which we perceive relationships varies from person to person. The important thing is to get the mind working, to break the very real "barrier" we all face staring at a blank page or empty computer screen. Notice that four key words—*job, auto, school, home*—represent the major branches (*classes* or categories) in this cluster. If you follow the branch represented by the word *auto,* you will see that the free association process developed along these lines:

accidents / **auto** accidents / **where** do auto accidents take place? / auto accidents on **freeways** / auto accidents on **city streets** / what are the **causes** of auto accidents on freeways? / what are the **effects** of auto accidents on freeways? / . . .

This process has led finally to two questions, each with a fairly limited subject, "auto accidents on freeways," and each with its own ***controlling question,*** "What are the CAUSES. . . ?" and "What are the EFFECTS. . . ?" As this chapter develops you will discover that any effective exploration process should lead to a ***limited subject*** and a *controlling question* or ***controlling attitude.***

EXERCISES

A. Practice constructing a cluster diagram using the following ideas suggested by the central term *prewriting:* thinking, freewriting, discussing, reading, note-taking, observing, interviewing, researching, people, environment, field trips, brainstorming, clustering, talking, personal journals, books, outlining, listing, movies, illustrating, magazines. What are the major *branches* of the cluster you have constructed?

B. Create a cluster diagram for two of the following general subjects:

1. Movies	4. Cats
2. Advertisements	5. Television
3. Mammals	6. Population growth

Free Writing

Free writing (sometimes called *"looping"*) is a prewriting process that gets you to set down your ideas *without stopping,* usually only for a few minutes at a time, using sentences *(or not)* as you choose. Using a computer to practice free writing can transform your screen into a game-board; you create it, the computer stores it. Later, when you retrieve the document, you can play with it further—adding, altering, deleting with ease. In the following example the writer began with the word *movie* and kept moving:

> ```
> Movie. Movies. Movies I like. I like movies. I like movies that
> make me laugh. Stand up comics. Musicals. Horror flicks. TV
> movies. Adventure movies. Like Indiana Jones and the Last
> Crusade. Or The Abyss. Alien contact. Aliens. I like science
> fiction movies. Science fiction movies like Star Wars or the
> Star Trek series. Return of the Jedi and Darth Vader! I guess
> the Star Trek series. Especially the one about the whales. I
> wonder why? Why did I like the one about the whales? Whales.
> The whales. Saving the whales. Maybe that's why. And the
> special effects. This Star Trek movie had laughs in it too.
> When Spock was swimming in the tank with the whales. And the
> hospital scene was funny. I guess I like science fiction movies
> that have serious issues and some humor.
> ```

In free writing—using pen, typewriter, or computer—the *free association* is a little more focused, and new attitudes tend to appear as the writer develops sentence units. More important, the act of putting words together—writing, typing—actually breaks the "barrier" created by a blank page or an empty computer screen. The purpose of such an exercise isn't to write complete sentences but to keep writing until the ideas seem to *focus,* to find a direction, as the last sentence in the example indicates. Thinking back, this writer has really concluded: "I liked the science fiction movie *Star Trek IV* because it had good special effects, some serious issues, and some humor." This could serve as a *thesis sentence* for a five-hundred-word paper or even a longer essay.

Although your first attempts at free writing may not be as successful as this one, keep trying. The writer might very well have stalled on the word *movie:* "Movie. Movie. Movies. Which movies? Which movies? Movies I hate? Movies I like? Movies I like. I like. I like." If you stall, just keep putting down words. Free association plus the act of writing—moving pen across paper or making words appear on a computer screen—should soon stir up some ideas you can use.

EXERCISES

A. Try free writing for five minutes; begin with the word *afraid.* Find a recurring idea in the passage you have written, and restate it as a complete sentence.

B. Try free writing for five minutes; begin with one of the following words: *rock, cool, scared, pollution, pregnant.* After you are finished writing, draw a line below what you have written and then write a sentence that brings together the dominant controlling ideas of the writing. Try rephrasing this sentence into one that takes the form of a question. Explain why you could (or could not) use either of these sentences to develop a five-hundred-word theme.

The Quick-Question Approach

The *quick-question approach*—sometimes called the "reporter's approach"—is really a simplified version of the *directed discovery* approach of *classical invention,* which we will look at shortly. With the quick-question approach, you begin with any subject—though an event or "happening" usually works best—and then ask one or more of the following questions:

Who?	**When?**	**Why?**
What?	**Where?**	**How?**

Let's try it, beginning with one of the terms from the cluster diagram on accidents—*auto accidents:*

AUTO ACCIDENT

Who was involved in the auto accident?
Who was driving the car?
Who caused the accident? What happened to this person?
What did the person do to cause the accident?
What happened to the car?
Where did the accident take place?
Where was the person going?
Where did they take the person?
When did the accident take place?
Why did the accident occur? Who caused it?
How did it happen? What are the details?

Here the six basic questions limit free association and keep you *focused;* they control and direct your thinking. However, *you don't have to use all the ideas generated by the quick-question approach.* Assuming that you're thinking of a specific auto accident, one of these questions—or a combination of several—could serve as the basis for a five-hundred-word paper: "*Who* caused the accident and how?" "*What* exactly happened during the accident and *where* did it take place?" "*What* effect did the accident have on the driver and the car?" Once you begin to ask probing questions about a general subject, you've moved from free association to the more controlled methods of *directed discovery*—classical invention, reading, interviewing, observing, note-taking, researching. The more questions you ask, the more you'll be able to *choose, limit,* and *focus.*

EXERCISES

    A. Recall a striking event that you clearly remember. Perhaps you can recall an important turning point in your life, a sports event, a speech you gave, your first job, an accident at home or on the road. (If you can't think of a real event, try to imagine one.) Use the quick-question approach to explore your memory and list a series of detailed questions clearly related to the event. Arrange your list into groups or clusters of related questions. On the basis of these clusters, write down several possible titles for a short paper. Save this exercise for future use.

B. Use the quick-question approach to explore the subject of planned parenthood, listing a series of detailed questions clearly related to this general subject. Can you now divide the general subject into a series of more specific problem-subjects? List these specific subjects and save them for future use.

How much time you take to think, research, plan, and write will depend on the difficulty of the subject, your knowledge of the subject, and your experience with it. You'll be ready for the more controlled, *directed discovery* approaches if you let the prewriting free association techniques work for you first. Before choosing a specific idea and the writing strategy to fit it, always allow enough prewriting time—hours, perhaps days—to explore, enjoy, and play with your feelings and thoughts and the words that fit them. You may not have this much time, but you probably have more discovery time available than you are aware of—while eating, showering, shaving, combing your hair, brushing your teeth, or walking to work or to class. And especially while you're in the library. Last-minute, one-shot writing lacks this sense of play and discovery. Instead, it projects a feeling of fumbling, of false starts hastily covered up with uncomfortable words, of fuzzy thought in worn-out language. If you're a fumbler or last-minute writer, practice exploring and listing your thoughts and feelings before trying to write them down in paragraph form. That's what getting started is all about. Then continue the discovery process as you *plan, outline,* and *write* the paragraphs of your paper.

To take you past the free association approaches efficiently, this chapter also asks you to think about and to practice a number of *directed discovery* processes:

1. Discovering a *single, limited subject.*
2. Discovering the *specific point* you're going to establish *about* this limited subject *(focus, controlling attitude)*
3. Discovering how to write a *complete thesis statement*
4. Discovering *support* for the thesis statement
5. Discovering how to write a complete *purpose statement*

DIRECTED DISCOVERY:
CHOOSING, LIMITING, FOCUSING

At the beginning of a writing course, your instructor may assign a specific subject for a short paper and clearly define its purpose. But you may simply be given a general subject or sent to the library to find your own. To cut down on false starts and unnecessary fumbling, you'll need to practice discovering single, limited subjects you can discuss adequately in approximately five hundred words.

1. Discover a Single (One), Limited Subject

Suppose, after you have used the prewriting association techniques, you have chosen six possible subjects for your paper:

1. The Life of Abraham Lincoln
2. Accidents I Have Experienced
3. My College
4. My Summer Jobs
5. Civil War Battles
6. Pollution

Any of these general subjects could be used for a paper, depending on its length and the *controlling question you ask about the subject*. For the first, fifth, and sixth subjects you would probably use material you had learned in school or from your reading, or possibly from research in the library. Ideas for the others could come from your own experience and observation; you would discover the information by giving your mind time to explore and to think.

But none of the general subjects, as stated, is suitable for development in a *short* paper. Since many volumes have been written about Lincoln's life, you probably couldn't write five hundred truly significant words about the *entire* life of Lincoln. You might succeed, however, with a paper that proclaimed: "Lincoln Was Not an Abolitionist." (Though he opposed slavery, Lincoln didn't consider himself an abolitionist.) Similarly, the second subject, as it stands, can't be used for a short paper, since you probably can say very little meaningful about *all* your accidents in only a few paragraphs. You would do better if you chose one accident or, better yet, some specific aspect of one accident, and then said something significant about it. (For example: "How I Totaled My Very First Car.") The third subject presents the same problem. Free association and clustering should readily show that any college has numerous "parts"—faculty, students, dormitories and other buildings, courses, many sports, student union, and so on. But you can't write convincingly about all of these. Not in five hundred words. However, if you chose "My College" as your subject, that's exactly what you'd be expected to do. Again you would do better to choose a specific "part"—the swimming program's successes, for example.

At first glance, the fourth subject seems fairly limited—your summer jobs. But a little thought will show you that *summer jobs* is another complex subject in disguise, since it clearly consists of many events separated in time. Even a subject like "My First Job" will suddenly become complex if you apply the quick-question approach to it. (Try it and see what happens: What did you do? For whom? Where? When? Why did you take the job?) Obviously, the fifth subject is unsatisfactory too. It would be very difficult for anyone to say anything truly meaningful about *all* the battles of the Civil War in a short paper. In fact, in a short paper you couldn't write meaningfully about *all* aspects of even *one* battle. The last subject, "Pollution," will quickly explode into many clusters if you test it out: pollution of air, soil, water; noise pollution, chemical pollution; pesticides, herbicides; oceans, lakes, rivers; ozone, industrial smoke, fluorocarbons; auto exhausts—the list could go on endlessly. You need to explore your subjects further and think more exactly before you start writing; you must practice asking questions that *direct* and *focus* the subjects discovered through free association approaches.

Two words provide a key to your subject problem: *single* and *limited*. Note that *single* here doesn't mean *singular*; limited subjects can also be plural. To explain an idea, a physical object, a process, or an event in a short paper, you can "divide" a general, all-inclusive subject logically through the process of analysis.

Suppose your instructor asks you to choose one of the subjects given below and write a five-hundred-word paper on it:

Accidents	Drugs	Lifestyles	Promiscuity
Advertisements	Education	Love	Racism
Aggression	Environment	Magazines	Railroad
Ambitions	Equality	Minorities	Recreation
Animals	Expectations	Morality	Right to die
Archaeology	Family planning	Motorcycle	Riots
Books	Farm subsidies	Movies	Robots
Buildings	Feminism	Music	Roles
Cars	Flight	Neighbors	Science fiction
Censorship	Free expression	Newspaper	Sciences
Characters	Friends	Obscenity	Sexism
Cities	Games	Oil spills	Sexual behavior
Clothes	Gangs	Ozone	Slums
Clubs	Genetic engineering	People	Social coercion
Colleges	Greenhouse effect	Pests	Spacecraft
Computers	Guns	Pets	Sports
Congress	Hobbies	Police	Strikes
Courting	Hostility	Politics	Suicide
Customs	Inflation	Pollution	Televangelists
Decisions	Intolerance	Population	Television
Dehydration	Jargon	Pornography	Terrorism
Discrimination	Jets	Pregnancy	Violence
Dogs	Jobs	Prejudices	Waste
Drinking	Labor unions	Presidents	Waste disposal

Don't panic. *Choose*. Reject any notions that you have nothing to write about. You've acquired a great deal of knowledge in your lifetime (or else what have you been doing all this time?). You have had many unique experiences, you have observed people, places, events, you have formed strong opinions.

With proper limitation, you could easily write a good short paper on any of these subjects, and if you put your mind to work, you could discover many more. Few of these, for instance, would let you use much of the knowledge you've picked up in your study of literature or history or science. Using free association to make a quick mental tour of your studies, you should discover many additional general subjects—wars, battles, great men and women, novels, plays, characters in fiction, poems, chemicals, animals, test tubes, air, gas, and geese are a few. Discovery is a game; play it with a positive attitude and you will find getting started much easier than you think.

Once you have chosen a general, ***all-inclusive subject*** (or it has been assigned to you), try some brainstorming, clustering, or quick-questioning to begin the limiting process. Although you *can* write a short paper on a general subject, the odds are that it will be weak because you will not have planned carefully enough or limited your subject to one you can discuss in relatively few words and in four or five paragraphs.

Limiting is the process of "dividing" a general subject into its parts, selecting one of these, and then further limiting it until you have a single *specific* subject. Sometimes called ***tree diagraming,*** this limiting process depends on the use of questions to direct the discovery process. It should lead to a ***"tree diagram"*** similar to the one on page 61 titled "Divide All General Subjects Through Analysis." Though similar to clustering, this process is more systematic, requiring thoughtful questioning at each stage of the process. And it can bring order to the information gathered through free association or brainstorming.

Suppose you have chosen to write about *accidents*. Free association and brainstorming might very well lead to a list of items similar to these:

ACCIDENTS

bad brakes	hunting accidents	broken dishes
auto accidents	bullet wound	scattered glass
school accidents	cut finger	kitchen accidents
broken nose	drug overdose	electrical fire
broken toes	skidding	drunk driving
fire	slippery road	asleep at the wheel
car wreck	motorcycle	sports accidents
collision	bicycle	computer accidents
sideswipe	natural accidents	tackling
potholes	falling rocks	workplace accidents
speeding	bad weather	factory accidents
cooking spills	fog	traffic jam
garage accidents	jammed rifle	construction
gym accidents	explosion	repair
windshield wipers	burns	swimming accidents

Your list, of course, will be different. It probably will be shorter and may reflect your experience with specific accidents you have been involved in recently or know about. It might include more details or, perhaps, just one ***cluster*** of accidents (only "workplace accidents," for example). The important thing is to develop a personal list of items. These items usually will be fairly ***general subjects,*** and almost always a *general* subject includes other *specific*, limited, ***single subjects.*** Your free association list, through the application of many ***directed discovery questions,*** could eventually lead you to a fairly specific subject—an accident you actually experienced, or one you read about.

But you can approach your free association list or your general subject—in this case *accidents*—more systematically by ***logical analysis,*** by "tree diagraming" and the repeated, thoughtful application of a basic question:

Can this subject be divided into more specific, closely related subjects?

This basic question can be restated in many ways, and each restatement should lead to a new *arrangement* of information you already have or to new information. Each variation of the basic question should lead you to a new way of thinking about the subject of accidents. Before applying the basic question to the general subject of *accidents,* let's look at some other versions of the question, each followed by some general subjects about which the question could be asked:

> What are the "parts" of the subject? (college, bike, company, vacation)
> What are my favorites? (rock groups, magazines, games, cities)
> Which are most popular? (rock stars, politicians, TV shows, colleges)
> Can the subject be divided and then grouped into clusters? (pollution, jobs)

As these alternate questions suggest, any general subject can be "divided" through the application of specific questions. What are the "parts" of a college, a bike, a company? Even a vacation? What kinds of games, football teams, and rock groups are there from which I can choose? What clusters (classes, parts) do the subjects *pollution* and *jobs* bring to mind? Our basic question, regardless of the form it takes, should lead to a consideration of the subject's "parts."

The subject of accidents, like these general subjects, can be approached in many ways. Each approach, however, requires that you ask the question about every subject or subject "part" that you examine: Can this subject be "divided" even further? What "types" or "parts" make up the subject? Let's begin with the general subject *accidents* again, this time using a controlled version of the clustering approach to divide the subject and create a "tree diagram."

DIVIDING GENERAL SUBJECTS: TREE DIAGRAM

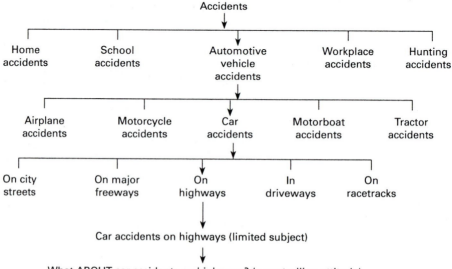

This simplified "tree diagram" represents the thinking process shown more fully in the diagram labeled "Divide All General Subjects Through Analysis."

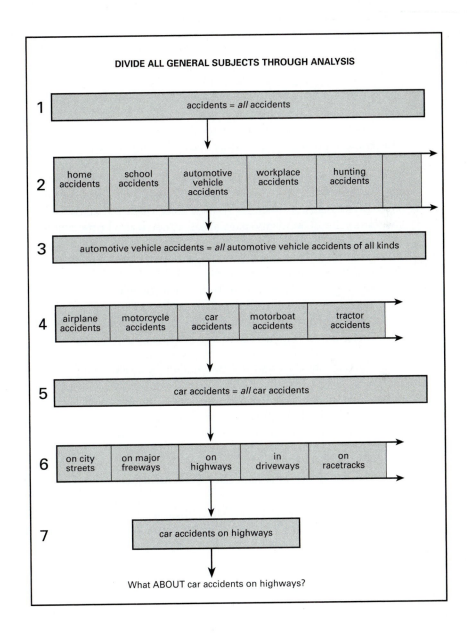

Study the diagram. Now let's follow the thinking process through all its stages:

1. Can the subject *accidents* be divided into logical parts?

Without a qualifying *modifier,* most general subjects imply *all* aspects, *everything* about the subject (rather than one aspect or some parts). *Accidents,* therefore, means "all accidents," so the answer to the question is obvious: Of course the subject can be divided.

If you look at the list of subjects on page 84, you'll see that most of them imply the modifier *all: all* advertisements (in newspapers, on television, in magazines, on billboards, on the radio, everywhere); *all* television (types of programs, program production, TV advertising, kinds of TV sets, cost of sets, cable TV, and so on); *all* aspects of education; everything about a neighborhood (physical, social, economic, linguistic).

As the cluster diagram on page 52 has shown you, an important value of the clustering approach is to identify related groups of ideas (clusters). In the tree diagram these groups appear on Level 2, where various *kinds* of accidents are named in response to the basic question, "Can this subject be divided into more specific, closely related subjects?" But the *implied* question at work here is: "What *kinds* of accidents are there?" Though some of these "kinds" appear in your free association list of accidents (page 59), they could also be missing from that list. The grouping of "kinds" represented by Level 2 limits the thinking process to a consideration of *kinds of accidents only.* You don't have to list *all* the items within *all* groups to make this limiting process work for you. And, as the tree diagram shows, the grouping provides the items from which you will choose only *one,* to limit your subject and move further "down the tree."

Once you have listed all the groups ("parts") of *accidents* that you can discover (Level 2), choose *one* that interests you and think about it.

2. Can the subject *automotive vehicle accidents* be divided into parts?

What kinds of automotive vehicles are involved in accidents? Clearly, many kinds are involved. Without listing *all* the kinds of vehicle accidents you know about (which you could do through free association), list those that interest you most (Level 4) and again choose one to think about.

3. Can the subject *car accidents* be divided into logical parts?

Clearly it can (Level 6). What kinds of car accidents are there? Where do accidents take place? As in Level 2, try to think of clusters or groups of ideas, choose one, say *on highways,* and think of its "parts."

4. Can the subject *car accidents on highways* be further divided?

Although your answer could again be *yes* if you had in mind one specific accident you had experienced, let's assume that you don't have that kind of specific information. The subject *car accidents on highways* can be "divided" only into logical subjects dealing with car accidents that have occurred on highways; it can't be divided into new subjects. At this point you probably have a *single, limited subject;* it cannot be divided into *new* related subjects. But you can ask the question "What

ABOUT car accidents on highways?" extending the questioning process to control and sharpen the *focus* by establishing a *controlling attitude*.

As this process of **logical division** suggests, almost always a general subject implies a great many *single, limited* subjects. This was the problem with the six general subjects discussed earlier in this unit. The subject *The Life of Abraham Lincoln*, for example, can be logically divided into personal background, preparation for politics, election to the presidency, Lincoln's stand on abolition and slavery, the countless problems brought on by the Civil War, his Gettysburg address, his assassination, and more. Each of these, though more limited than the general subject, can be divided still further into more specific ones: opposition to his election, tactics to gain election, the immediate results of his election, and so on.

To have unity, your paper must have one limited subject to develop in one direction. However, when you come to write a **thesis statement** you'll often be tempted to include more than one subject because *in your mind* they seem closely tied together. Here's an example:

> *Our city election is not being run properly and we must do something about it.*

Here are two thesis statements, presenting a **double subject.** The first subject condemns existing procedures and the second urges action to revise the faulty procedures. The sentence is composed of two **independent clauses** (two sentences, if you wish) joined by the **coordinating conjunction** *and*. The two parts of this **compound sentence** have equal importance because both have exactly the same grammatical construction. But you could include both parts in an acceptable thesis statement if you subordinate one part to the other and make it less important:

> *Since our city election is not being run properly, we must do something about it.*

Adding the **subordinating conjunction** *since* changes the first part of the sentence into a **dependent clause,** allowing the independent clause to carry the main statement as a single subject: We must do something about (the improper procedures in our city election). You can see now that the dependent clause that begins the sentence can be reduced to a **phrase** and incorporated into the independent clause:

We must correct improper procedures in our city election.

Improper procedures in our city election	must be corrected.
Limited Subject Area	**Predicate Area**

Each of these thesis statements has a single, limited subject: *Improper procedures in our city election.* Each also has a specific focus *(controlling attitude)*: *must correct,* and *must be corrected.* This specific focus or controlling attitude is the predicate area of your thesis statement. Discovering this attitude is the subject of the next section.

Before writing on any subject, you must practice the process of logically dividing general subjects to discover single, limited subjects. And you must avoid the temptation to include more than one subject in a thesis statement merely because they seem closely tied together in your mind. Together, these two skills will assure you of success in the crucial first step in the prewriting discovery process.

To discover a **single, limited** *subject is to choose for your paper only* **one** *subject that cannot be significantly divided further; it is the key* *to* **unity** *of thought.*

EXERCISES

A. Study the diagram that shows you how to divide the general subject *accidents* by logical analysis.
   1. Instead of *car accidents,* narrow down *airplane accidents* and *motorcycle accidents* into more limited subjects. Use the quick-question approach to help you focus these subjects more sharply.
   2. Using the diagram as a guide (don't be afraid to modify it to suit your own discovery process), create similar diagrams to "divide" three of these general subjects: *television, pollution, cities, recreation, violence, advertisements.* If you wish, you may choose other general subjects from the list on page 58.

B. Compare your response to Exercises *A-1* and *A-2* with those of other students in the class. How much variation is there? Discuss the differences and possible reasons for them.

C. Everybody talks about freedom. Here's your chance:
   1. Without any preliminary thinking or preparation, take five minutes to write four or five *sentences* about freedom. Quickly.
   2. Now take time to divide the general subject *freedom* into as many second-level "clusters" as five minutes will allow. No need to carry the logical division all the way down to Level 7. Using your second-level "clusters" as a guide, now write another four or five *sentences* about freedom.
   3. Compare your responses to Exercises *C-1* and *C-2.* List the major differences between your two comments on freedom. Comment on the value and some of the uses of logical division.

D. Test your ability to recognize general, ***all-inclusive subjects.*** Place an "X" to the left of each of the following statements that seem to you to be partly false or misleading. Be prepared to explain your answers.
   1. Dogs are vicious.
   2. Dogs chase cats.
   3. Students cheat.
   4. Today's students cheat a lot.
   5. Today's television programs are full of sex and violence.
   6. Genetic engineering is dangerous and should be banned.
   7. Planned parenthood is a sacrilegious idea.
   8. Science fiction movies tend to be shallow and uninteresting.
   9. People shouldn't have sex because it can lead to AIDS.
   10. Our schools emphasize sports far too much.

2. Discover a Specific Focus: Controlling Attitude

Having completed the process of logically dividing your general subject, you are ready to take the next step: choosing one of the single, limited subjects for further thought and analysis. Unless you are asked to read about and research a subject, always choose one you know and are really interested in. You are then more likely to write a paper about it that sounds authoritative and convincing.

Returning to the analysis of *accidents* and, finally, *car accidents on highways,* you must now discover the specific point you're going to establish *about* this one, limited subject. You will strengthen the **unity** of your paper by giving it a specific *focus* or **direction**—by deciding on a *controlling attitude.* You must discover what to say *about* your chosen limited subject. But how? The process can be stated simply:

Ask a question about the limited subject, then answer it.
Question → Answer

This is the basic *inductive approach* you have studied as Theme Pattern A (pages 18 and 20). In a paper following Theme Pattern A, you will recall, you introduce a *question* in the introductory paragraph and then *answer* it in the paragraphs that follow. The *conclusion* reached following Theme Pattern A, however, can provide the *thesis statement* for a paper following the deductive approach of Theme Pattern B. (Review the diagram on page 22). Examine any thesis statement closely, and you'll probably find an implied question behind it. Regardless of the pattern you choose to follow, therefore, *asking pointed questions is crucial to writing a controlled, effective paper.* This unit on choosing, limiting, and focusing your subject will help you learn how to ask pointed questions.

As you have already seen (page 55), one way to discover something to say about a limited subject is to use the quick-question approach journalists often use to report events: *Who? What? When? Where? Why? How?* Applied uncreatively to the subject *car accidents on highways,* these questions won't lead you far. But the quick-question approach will work if you phrase the questions thoughtfully:

Who is often involved in highway car accidents?
Why do these car accidents usually happen?
What are some of the effects of these accidents?
When do highway car accidents often occur?

Answers to questions like these will often lead you to an answer that could serve as a thesis statement for a paper. The important thing is to keep your mind moving and to continue asking questions.

These basic reporter's questions are really a simplified version of *classical invention,* a method of *directed discovery* first used by writers over two thousand years ago to find arguments to support a point they wanted to prove. They developed a systematic way of thinking *about* any subject. Their method organized discovery questions into five basic groups: *definition, comparison, relationship, circumstance,* and *evidence.* The chart titled "Directed Discovery Questions" shows how the reporter's quick questions develop within each control group.

DIRECTED DISCOVERY QUESTIONS

Definition   (Classification, Division):

How do you define X? (Where X is the subject)
What larger class (group, "cluster") of things is X in?
How is X different from other things in the class to which it belongs?
What are the parts that make up X? *How* can you "divide" X?
What steps or events comprise X? (Is X a process?)

Comparison   (Similarity, Difference, Degree):

How is X similar to Y? (Where Y is another subject)
What qualities or characteristics do X and Y have in common?
How does X contrast with Y?
How is X different from Y?
How is X better than Y? (To what degree is it better?)
What is X inferior to? *What* is X better than?

Relationship   (Cause/Effect, Consequences):

What causes X? *How* did X come about?
What are the effects of X?
What results because of X? *What* will follow because of X?
What must have preceded X? *Why* does X happen?
What must be "false" if X is "true"? *What* is "true" if X is "false"?
What is incompatible with X?

Circumstance   (Possible/Impossible, Past Fact/Future Fact):

What is possible (for X?) in a given circumstance?
What is impossible (for X?) in a given circumstance?
What happened to X in the past?
What will probably happen to X in the future?

Evidence   (Authority, Testimony, Statistics):

How do authorities evaluate X?
What do experts (authorities) on X say about it?
Who are the experts (authorities) on X and how qualified are they?
What do people in general say about X? *How* popular is X?
What facts (statistics) are available to support X?
What facts (statistics) are available to refute X?

Though some of these discovery questions are taught as paragraph "patterns" (of cause/effect, of comparison/contrast, of definition, for example), the questions clearly represent *ways of thinking about a subject*. The "developmental pattern" follows; how you think about a subject will almost automatically lead to a specific method of paragraph development, as we shall see later in this book.

You can use the directed discovery questions of classical invention to find something to say about a limited subject because asking a question will suggest a *direction* for your answer to take. If you apply the basic questions to the subject of *car accidents on highways*, you may come up with a list similar to this one:

Definition (Classification, Division):
How do you define "car accident"? What is a car accident?
What larger class of things is the subject *highway car accidents* part of?
How are highway car accidents different from other accidents?
What major events often lead up to these accidents?
What different kinds of highway car accidents are there?

Comparison (Similarity, Difference, Degree):
What similarities do many highway car accidents share in common?
What similarities do highway collisions share in common?
What is unique about some highway car accidents?
Are these car accidents worse than other kinds of accidents? How?
Why are some highway car accidents less disastrous than others?

Relationship (Cause/Effect, Consequences):
What are some of the major causes of highway car accidents?
Are some causes more common than others?
What are some of the major consequences of car accidents?
What age groups are most often involved in highway car accidents?
What effects (physical, emotional, financial) do car accidents have on their victims?

Circumstance (Past Fact/Future Fact, Possible/Impossible):
What has been done in the past to prevent highway car accidents?
What can be done in the future to prevent highway accidents?
Are present causes of car accidents similar to the causes of the past?
Will we be able to make highway car accidents impossible?

Evidence (Authority, Testimony, Statistics):
What are the statistics on the causes (or costs) of car accidents?
What do experts say about the prevention of fatalities in car accidents?
What statistics are available on alcohol as a cause of car accidents?
What kind of testing is needed to prove mechanical failure in car accidents? What authorities are consulted? What testimony is given?

Because you can apply them to any subject, using discovery questions to come up with a list similar to this one is the most important prewriting skill you can learn. By *answering* questions on your list, you should be able to discover many possible *controlling attitudes, one* of which you would then choose to write about. The *one* controlling attitude you choose will become the *predicate area* of your thesis statement, as you will soon see. And what you say about the limited subject in the predicate area is the most important part of the thesis statement, for it is here you *express your view,* the controlling attitude to be explored and supported in the rest of the paper. Because this attitude will be the key to the content of your paper, be certain you can support it and readers can't misunderstand it.

Based on the list of questions developed above for the subject *car accidents on highways,* you might choose to consider these for your paper:

> How are highway car accidents different from other accidents?
> What similarities do many highway car accidents share in common?
> Why are some highway car accidents less disastrous than others?
> What are some of the major causes of highway car accidents?
> What effects do car accidents have on their victims?
> What statistics are available on alcohol as a cause of car accidents?

The directed discovery questions have led you to explore the information and the attitudes you have about your subject. Clearly, you could approach the limited subject *car accidents on highways* in many ways. How you would write your paper would depend on the *one* question you chose to answer. Both your choice and the way you state it are important because they will help you phrase an acceptable *limited predicate area* for the subject of your thesis statement. Here are some basic guidelines to follow.

a. The predicate area must also be limited.   Even though you've gone through the process of limiting the subject of the thesis statement, you may find when you write your statement that it's still too broad to deal with. It probably needs limiting in the ***predicate area.*** Consider this thesis statement:

> *The United States is the best of all countries.*

Proving this thesis would be easy if you were planning to write several volumes, but you cannot do it in a short paper. The predicate area of this thesis, *is the best of all countries,* obligates the writer to prove that the United States is better than *any* other country. To fulfill this obligation, the writer would have to consider the economic, moral, religious, political, and social conditions in every country of the world and then contrast them to those in the United States. This is not possible in a short paper. Similarly, a statement such as

> *Lee was a greater general than Grant.*

cannot be established without considering the campaigns of each general and then comparing them. Neither is this a job for a short paper.

b. The predicate area of the thesis statement should challenge the reader with an argumentative attitude toward the subject.   If you are to establish a main point or adequately support a thesis, your paper must be partially ***argumentative.*** After all, you are challenging the reader to accept your point as a sound one. Your paper's purpose will be to support the validity of this main point, which you will support by presenting all the logical reasons and sound evidence you can muster. Your thesis statement should be the trumpet's call that sounds the challenge—you on one side, your reader on the other. You will try to get your reader to say, "I understand" *and* "I agree." Be bold about it; issue your challenge clearly and forcefully. Use no weak phrases such as "to me" or "in my opinion" in your thesis, nor anywhere else in your paper, for they leave your reader with the impression that you are merely stating an opinion and are apologetic about supporting it. Step from the crowd and challenge your reader with thesis statements like these:

> Today's young people *need more responsibility.*
> Lady MacBeth *is more masculine than feminine.*
> Like beauty, obscenity *is in the eye of the beholder.*
> Robots *improve the quality of our lives.*
> Charles Dickens *found American life bewildering.*
> An unexercised mind *grows dull.*
> Video games *encourage analytical thinking.*

Only if your thesis statement reflects a specific controlling attitude toward one, limited subject, phrased with directness and conviction, will you grab your reader's interest.

But a striking thesis statement alone will not win your reader; the thesis still has to be logically supported. Select a thesis you can believe in and support. If you don't believe what you say, neither will the reader. And *you are writing to persuade your reader.* Even a paper that tries only to define a difficult concept is partly persuasive: through the information presented it must get the reader to agree that the definition provided is logical and adequate.

c. The predicate area must say something meaningful.   A thesis statement about which there can be no controversy, about which everyone agrees, can hardly result in a paper that anyone will want to read. If, for instance, you try to write a paper using a thesis like

> *Travel by plane saves time.*

or

> *Good conservation practices help the farmer.*

you aren't going to get much of a reaction from your reader except "Ho-hum. So what?" And justifiably. For these statements are trite and too general to be truly meaningful.

d. The predicate area must say something exact about the subject.   Look at this thesis statement:

> *The study of genetic engineering is exciting.*

The predicate area consists of two words: *is exciting.* To write a paper on this thesis, you would have to control its content to fit the key word *exciting* because it would give your paper its single direction. You could write about no other emotion. But what exactly does *exciting* mean? It's hard to define and does not *lead* the reader sufficiently. What might be exciting to one person could leave another cold. And that's the problem with such a predicate area—it does not make a precise point. It is vague, not *exact.* It lets the writer say almost anything as long as it is in any way associated with the study of genetic engineering. As a result, the writer could ramble and support no specific point in the paper. To improve this statement, assert a specific controlling attitude about one problem in genetic engineering:

> To *alter the gene that causes muscular dystrophy* creates terrible dilemmas.

The subject is properly limited and the predicate area has a single direction, *creates terrible dilemmas.* Here's another thesis sentence with a vague predicate area:

> *Macbeth* is a fascinating character.

If you are assigned a paper on *Macbeth,* make an exact point about the play:

Macbeth's early recognition of guilt	increases his conflict.
One Limited Subject	**Specific, Limited Predicate**

When you can't find something to say about your limited subject, turn to the discovery questions for help. Make a game of the process. Stretch or modify questions to fit your needs. And be sure to write down every question in a form that clearly applies to your limited subject. Now you can delete those questions that least appeal to you, one by one, until you finally end up choosing the *one* you best understand. You're on your way. You are ready to write a complete thesis statement, combining the limited subject with the specific focus you've decided to use.

3. Write a Complete Thesis Statement

A good ***thesis statement*** is vital to your paper because it clearly presents the main point you are going to make and support. It controls the focus and direction of your paper. Without it your paper will probably lack unity; with it the paper will have a controlling attitude that restricts your limited subject, focusing attention on what the paper is about.

The thesis statement should be written as a sentence with an argumentative bias—the controlling attitude. Like all sentences, it has a *subject area* and a *predicate area.* As in all sentences, the subject area of the thesis statement announces *what* will be discussed (the grammatical subject of the sentence). And, as in all sentences, the predicate area says something *about* the subject. Here is a diagram showing all the elements in a thesis statement:

Complete Thesis Statement
(A Complete Sentence)

Limited Subject + Modifiers	+	Verb + Completers + Modifiers
Limited Subject Area		Limited Predicate Area
(*One* Limited Subject)		(Controlling Attitude)

You have just studied the process of dividing a general subject to discover one, limited subject you can adequately discuss in a short paper. And you have also practiced using discovery questions to determine a controlling attitude (focus) for the limited subject. Now let's put this information to work.

Any one of the questions you discovered earlier (pages 67–68) contains the basic information you need for the thesis statement. Let's choose this question as our starting point:

What are some of the major causes of car accidents on highways?

You can see that the question contains the two elements you need:

Single (One), Limited Subject	Predicate Area (Focus)
Car accidents on highways	some major causes of

Stated as a *question* only, these two elements can provide the starting point for the kind of exploratory paper represented by Theme Pattern A (page 18). Restated as an *answer* to the question, these two elements provide the starting point for a paper following Theme Pattern B (page 22), in which the answer to the question becomes the thesis statement to be supported or proved.

Here you are looking for a way to phrase the two elements as a thesis statement. What this usually means is exploring and limiting the second element, which will become the predicate area of the thesis statement. Your subject is probably limited enough (unless you're willing to research in detail all the facts relevant to one specific accident you know about). Notice, too, that choosing only *one* question from those you have discovered has also partly limited the controlling attitude of the predicate area. Your choice has eliminated consideration of such options as *definition, effects, consequences* (of car accidents on highways), and many other matters as well. Now, since the question asks *what are some of the major causes,* you need to consider some possible answers. Focus on the word *causes* and check the list of items you got on page 50 through free association and brainstorming.

Your list of possible causes of highway car accidents could include (among others) these:

bad brakes	collision	sideswipe
potholes	speeding	bad windshield wipers
skidding	slippery road	falling rocks
bad weather	heavy fog	sleeping driver
drunk driving	drug use	traffic jam
bad tires	engine failure	icy road
bad road sign	tire blowout	horsing around

If you classify these items (group them into "clusters"), you should discover three basic kinds of major causes: *mechanical, human,* and *environmental.* These provide three fairly general answers to the question:

> *Mechanical failure* causes highway car accidents.
> *Human error* causes highway car accidents.
> *Environmental hazards* cause highway car accidents.

You could combine these three general answers into a single thesis statement:

> *Car accidents on highways are caused by mechanical failure, human error, and environmental hazards.*

You already know, however, that the three general "clusters" of major causes represent a great many details. A short paper that tried to discuss all these details could do little more than list the items. Though such a short paper would be superficial, it might very well serve as a first attempt at a five-hundred-word theme. But to do justice to all three areas you would have to write a very long paper. To gain better control of your short paper, you should probably restrict the predicate area of the thesis statement by choosing *one* of the three types of major causes:

> *One major cause of car accidents on highways is human error.*

You could restate this to make the subject and predicate areas more effective:

> *Many car accidents on our highways result from people's mistakes.*

If you wanted to let your reader know that you have thought about other major causes (which you will not be discussing), you could refer to them in an opening dependent clause preceding the actual thesis statement:

> *Although environmental hazards and mechanical failure also play a major role,* many car accidents on our highways result from people's mistakes.

These sentences differ only in emphasis; in all of them the limited subject area and limited predicate area remain essentially the same.

Limited Subject Area	**Limited Predicate Area**
(*One* Limited Subject)	(Controlling Attitude)
(many) car accidents (on our highways)	result from people's mistakes
car accidents (+ modifiers)	[causes]

If you play with the relationship between these two elements, you could easily improve your thesis:

> *Many car accidents on our nation's highways* result from foolish human behavior. *[cause = foolish behavior]*

> *Among the major causes of accidents on our nation's highways is the* irresponsible behavior of many drivers. *[cause = irresponsible behavior]*

Let's review this process of limiting and controlling both the subject area and the predicate area of a thesis statement by looking at some diagrams. Here is a basic diagram to represent the general process of limiting and controlling the subject and predicate areas that frame a thesis statement:

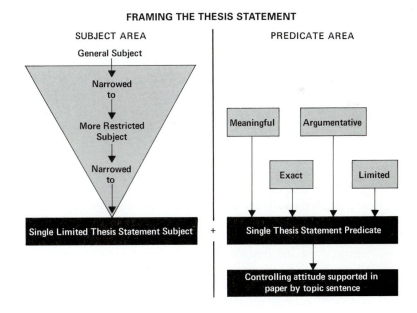

FRAMING THE THESIS STATEMENT

The left half of the diagram shows that a general subject must be narrowed to a more restricted subject, which is further narrowed to become the *single, limited thesis statement subject*. The right half of the diagram shows that the *single thesis statement predicate* must be limited also, as well as exact, meaningful and, if possible, argumentative. The predicate is the part of the thesis statement that provides the *controlling attitude* to be supported by all the topic sentences in the paper. Beginning with the general subject of *accidents,* a second diagram (page 75) illustrates how the thinking process developed through logical division (analysis).

This diagram on controlling subject and predicate through logical division shows how important the skill of *asking questions* becomes in the limiting and controlling process, first in the subject area, and then in the predicate area. As suggested by the left half of the diagram, here are the most important *directed discovery* questions asked about the subject:

> What types of accidents are there? (= can the subject *accidents* be divided?)
> What type of accident should I write about? (= which "cluster" should I choose?)
> What types of automotive vehicles are there? (= can the "cluster" *automotive vehicles* be further divided?)
> What type of vehicle do I want to write about?
> Can I write about ALL car accidents?
> Where do car accidents occur?
> What ABOUT car accidents on highways?

The final question—*What ABOUT car accidents on highways?*—extended the questioning and limiting process to the predicate area—the right half of the diagram. What are the *costs* of these accidents? What *causes* accidents on the highways? What *effects* do they have on people? How might they be *prevented?* Because free association and brainstorming had already provided some of the many *causes* of highway accidents, you were able to phrase a final question, *What are the major causes of car accidents on highways?* One answer to this question appears in the thesis shown at the bottom of the diagram: "The major causes of car accidents on highways are mechanical, human, and environmental." To make this thesis more specific, in the final step you chose to discuss only the *human causes,* which became the *controlling attitude* of the more limited thesis statement in its various forms:

> Car accidents on highways are *caused by people.*
> *People cause* car accidents on highways.
> Many car accidents on our highways are *caused by human error.*

Finally, a more complete diagram (page 76) represents the many blocks and "clusters" of information called up by the questioning process we have just reviewed.

From only one general subject, *accidents,* the questioning process led to dozens of increasingly limited subjects and controlling attitude choices. But the resulting thesis statement, *Many car accidents on highways are caused by human error,* could be made more effective, as you have seen:

> Many car accidents on our highways *result from people's mistakes.*
> Many car accidents on our nation's highways *are the result of foolish human behavior.*
> Among the *major causes* of car accidents on our nation's highways *is the irresponsible behavior of many drivers.*

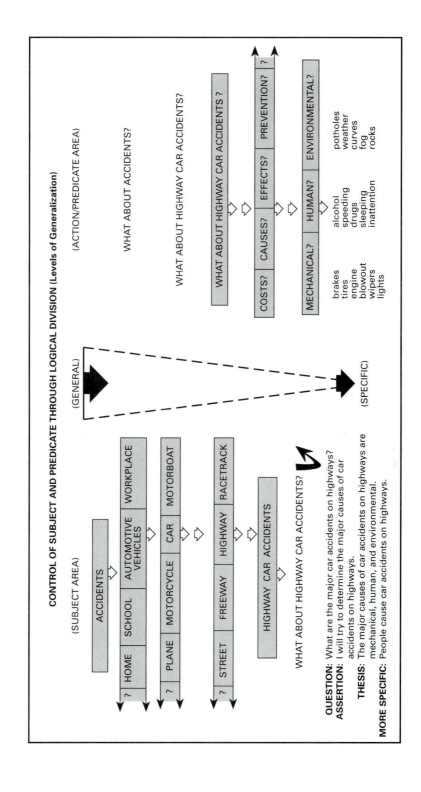

CONTROL OF SUBJECT AND PREDICATE THROUGH LOGICAL DIVISION (Levels of Generalization)

(SUBJECT AREA)

(ACTION/PREDICATE AREA)

(GENERAL)

(SPECIFIC)

WHAT ABOUT ACCIDENTS?

WHAT ABOUT HIGHWAY CAR ACCIDENTS?

WHAT ABOUT HIGHWAY CAR ACCIDENTS ?

| COSTS? | CAUSES? | EFFECTS? | PREVENTION? | ? |

| MECHANICAL? | HUMAN? | ENVIRONMENTAL? |

brakes	alcohol	potholes
tires	speeding	weather
engine	drugs	curves
blowout	sleeping	fog
wipers	inattention	rocks
lights		

ACCIDENTS

| HOME | SCHOOL | AUTOMOTIVE VEHICLES | WORKPLACE |

| PLANE | MOTORCYCLE | CAR | MOTORBOAT |

| STREET | FREEWAY | HIGHWAY | RACETRACK |

HIGHWAY CAR ACCIDENTS

WHAT ABOUT HIGHWAY CAR ACCIDENTS?

QUESTION: What are the major car accidents on highways?
ASSERTION: I will try to determine the major causes of car accidents on highways.
THESIS: The major causes of car accidents on highways are mechanical, human, and environmental.
MORE SPECIFIC: People cause car accidents on highways.

INFORMATION CALLED UP BY THE QUESTIONING PROCESS

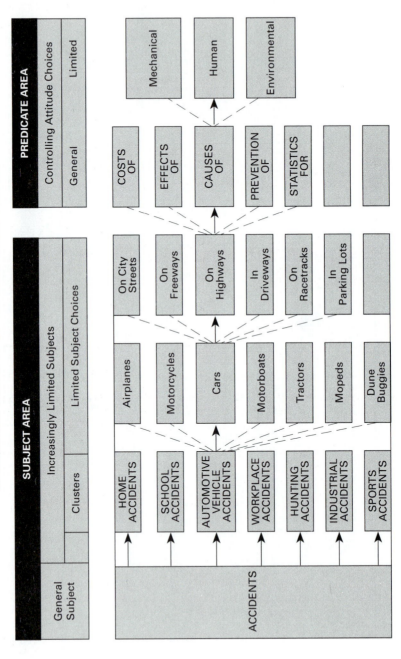

And, because a complex sentence beginning with a dependent clause will usually let you lead up to the controlling idea of your thesis paragraph, you could use the thesis sentence that refers to the other major causes of car accidents:

> *Although environmental hazards and mechanical failure also play a major role, many car accidents on our highways* result from human error.

The dependent clause of this thesis sentence lets you lead up to your controlling attitude by first referring to the other major causes, usually in the first few sentences of your introductory paragraph, as suggested in Chapter 2 in the diagram of Theme Pattern B showing the *"funnel effect"* (p. 26).

In summary, then, a good thesis statement has the following qualities:

1. It can be understood as the answer to an implied question.
2. It is really a conclusion, a generalization.
3. It is based on personal experiences, observations, or research.
4. It can be supported with some kind of evidence.
5. It projects a very specific controlling attitude.
6. It has a complete subject and a complete predicate.
7. Its subject and predicate are limited, exact, and meaningful.

EXERCISES

A. Here are some thesis statements. Decide if they are suitable for development in a short paper by examining their subject and predicate areas; list reasons for accepting or rejecting each thesis area.
1. My trip to Dallas was the most educational vacation I've taken.
2. The politician's speech was boring and full of clichés.
3. Social fraternities encourage community responsibility.
4. Video games are intriguing.
5. Body contact sports can sometimes be dangerous.
6. Young women don't drive as well as men do.
7. Young men don't drive as well as women do.
8. Human error is a major cause of accidents.
9. Skiing is more fun than any other sport I have tried.
10. A college training benefits the individual and provides responsible citizens for the community.
11. A college degree in business administration benefits the individual and provides responsible citizens for the community.
12. The cafeteria food isn't even fit for hogs.
13. Community service shapes the character of participants.
14. Helping the city's community programs shapes the character of participants.
15. Although a college degree in business administration benefits the community, its chief purpose is to provide job opportunities for the individual.

B. Rewrite in acceptable form those thesis statements in Exercise *A* that you consider unsuitable for development in a short paper.

    C. Using the discovery methods you have studied, break down the following subjects to make each a single, limited subject.
       1. Movies
       2. Rock groups
       3. Shakespeare's *Julius Caesar* (or any play you have read)
       4. Terrorists
       5. Newspapers
       6. Weapons
    D. Think about the limited subjects you devise in Exercise *C* and invent a specific controlling attitude for each.
    E. Combine the limited subjects and limited predicates of Exercises *C* and *D* into acceptable thesis statements. Restate the theses as questions.
    F. Examine the three cartoons on pages 9, 10, and 350. Devise at least two thesis statements for each cartoon, capturing the basic underlying idea as you interpret it. Be prepared to defend both subject and predicate areas of your statements.

---

4. Discover Support for the Thesis Statement

So far, the discovery prewriting process has taken you through three learning experiences: You've practiced how to find a single, limited subject; you've learned how to state a specific point about the limited subject; and you've practiced analyzing and writing complete thesis statements. You have two more skills to learn: how to discover ***support*** for the thesis statement, and how to write a complete ***purpose statement.***

    Once you have written a good thesis statement, you must find logical reasons to support the controlling attitude it contains. Suppose, for instance, you've decided to use this thesis statement:

    Many car accidents on our highways result from human error.

To find support for the controlling attitude of the predicate area, begin by asking the question *Why?: Why* (do car accidents on highways) *result from human error?* The answer to that *why* question will provide and control the reasons that make up your support: *They result from human error because.* . . . Focusing on *human causes* of car accidents on highways, you have already used free association techniques and directed discovery questions to provide you with a working list of answers to the question: *drunk driving, speeding, drug use, sleeping driver, horsing around, inattention.* Further questioning about these and other causes could lead to additional information about *human error* as a *cause* of highway car accidents: *ignoring bad eyesight, playing the radio too loudly while driving, talking on the car telephone, reading a road map while driving, eating food while driving, reaching to the car floor to pick up something, denying that one is over-tired,* and so on. You are trying to complete the statement *car accidents on highways result from human error because.* . . . The word *because* directs your search for ***evidence*** to support the controlling attitude you have asserted in the predicate area of the thesis statement. Searching for *reasons* to support this attitude, you might develop a list similar to the following:

Many car accidents on highways result from human error because:

1. People don't understand that drinking alcohol reduces the inhibitions needed for safe driving.
2. People don't understand that using cocaine or crack can cause fatal errors in driving judgment.
3. People don't understand that using antihistamines, painkillers, and muscle relaxants causes drowsiness and leads to accidents.
4. People think they are good enough to drive safely even though they are tired and sleepy.
5. People love the challenge of exceeding highway speed limits.
6. People think that exceeding highway speed limits is smart.
7. People think that showing off a fast car by speeding is all right.
8. People think they can drive safely while drinking coffee or eating food.
9. People think they are good enough to drive while reading a road map.
10. People say they can drive all night without resting or taking a break.
11. People take chances when they aggressively react to road-hogs with anger and speed.
12. People forget that playing the car radio too loudly shuts out warning sirens of approaching vehicles.
13. People aggressively take unnecessary chances by angrily passing cars when oncoming traffic is too heavy or too fast.
14. People let the air pressure in their tires get too low.
15. They aggressively round curves faster than the road was designed to allow.
16. People think they won't need to know how to turn out of a skid.
17. People think they are better drivers than they really are.
18. People aggressively take unnecessary chances.
19. People disregard driving and car maintenance laws.
20. People don't understand the effects of mind-impairing substances.
21. People don't understand that drunk drivers endanger themselves and others.
22. People think they are too good to take safe-driving tests or defensive-driving lessons.
23. They think they're good enough to turn their heads and talk to back-seat passengers.

Inspect this list and you'll see that some of the reasons may be grouped into "clusters" because they are related. Called **classification,** this process of grouping related ideas is a key to sorting and managing information. It is the reverse process of *logical division,* used early in this chapter to discover limited, manageable "parts" of general subject areas. Now, at the other end of the process, you use classification to sort your ideas systematically. You'll soon discover that some of the reasons you have listed at random may have to be left out and others may have to be modified to get the grouping that best points to your thesis statement. Also, after you begin the actual writing of the paper, new reasons probably will occur to you and some of your attitudes may change. Don't hesitate to add the new reasons to your list or make other changes you think are needed. The following *sentence outline* is one way to arrange your reasons:

Many car accidents on highways result from human error because:

I. **People don't understand the effects of mind-impairing substances.** [20]
    A. They don't understand that drinking alcohol reduces the inhibitions needed for safe driving. [1]
    B. They don't understand that drunk drivers endanger themselves and others. [21]
    C. They don't understand that using antihistamines, painkillers, and muscle relaxants causes drowsiness and leads to accidents. [3]
    D. They don't understand that using cocaine or crack can cause fatal errors in driving judgment. [2]

II. **People think they are better drivers than they really are.** [17]
    A. They think they are good enough to drive safely even though they are tired and sleepy. [4]
    B. They think they're good enough to turn their heads and talk to back-seat passengers. [23]
    C. They think they can drive safely while drinking coffee or eating food. [8]
    D. They think they're good enough to drive while reading a road map. [9]
    E. They think they won't need to know how to turn out of a skid. [16]
    F. They think they are too good to take safe-driving tests or defensive-driving lessons. [22]

III. **People aggressively take unnecessary chances.** [18]
    A. People aggressively take unnecessary chances by angrily passing cars when oncoming traffic is too heavy or too fast. [13]
    B. People take chances when they aggressively react to road-hogs with anger and speed. [11]
    C. People love the challenge of exceeding highway speed limits. [5]
    D. They aggressively round curves faster than the road was designed to allow. [15]

First, note that this outline follows the basic structure of outlines introduced in Chapter 2 (pages 33–34). Then study how this arrangement uses classification to group together related ideas. Because statements 17, 18, and 20 really define "clusters" of ideas, they provide the statements that determine the three groups in the outline. Even without them, however, you can see that statements 1, 21, 3, and 2 clearly concern the *effects of mind-impairing substances* [20]: alcohol, medications, and drugs. The second "cluster," represented by statement 17, explains that *people think they are better drivers than they really are.* Though everyone may not agree that statements 4, 8, 9, 16, and 23, belong here, they logically relate to a driver's self-perception. The third "cluster" of ideas includes the kind of aggressive, emotional response that leads to taking chances. It is represented by statement 18, and logically supports the idea that *people aggressively take unnecessary chances:* angrily passing cars in heavy oncoming traffic [13], aggressively reacting to road-hogs with anger and speed [11], loving the challenge of exceeding highway speed limits [5], and rounding curves too fast [15]. You could argue, perhaps, that some of the statements omitted from the outline can be fitted into the three groups, or that a fourth "cluster" might be established. Since you are in the driver's seat, you choose the "clusters" and decide what to include and what to omit. The important thing is to come up with a logical arrangement that will get your reader to understand your supporting reasons and to agree with them.

The thinking process you have just studied clearly has two basic steps:

1. Discover reasons to support your thesis statement
2. Classify related reasons into major controlling categories

Classifying your reasons into major ***controlling categories*** should suggest topic sentences for *developmental paragraphs* in a short paper, or *section* headings for a long paper. But whether your paper is short or long, classification is the process that gives you the information needed to write a good *purpose statement*, a kind of blueprint, anticipating the whole paper and guiding the reader systematically through it.

5. Write a Complete Purpose Statement

You have your supporting reasons, and you have classified them into logical subject categories representing your three developmental paragraphs. Now you can write a *purpose statement*. Your instructor may ask you to turn in a purpose statement for each paper you write, since a carefully worded statement will help you see the main components of your paper. A good purpose statement includes all of the following:

A single, limited subject
A specific controlling attitude
The word *because* (stated or implied)
All the supporting reasons (major subject categories)

Although the purpose statement usually does not become part of the paper proper, it does contain all the main ideas that will appear in your introductory paragraph. A purpose statement for a short paper using the material arranged above from the thesis on *car accident causes on highways* might turn out like this:

```
In this paper I will support the thesis that many car accidents
on our nation's highways result from human error because (1)
people don't understand the effects of mind-impairing
substances, (2) people think they are better drivers than they
really are, and (3) people take unnecessary chances.
```

Suppose all the students in your class wrote a paper based on the sentence outline given above for causes of car accidents on highways. Why would each paper still be unique?

This chapter has emphasized the following thinking and writing skills:

Prewriting thinking: free association, brainstorming, clustering, classification
How to discover a single, limited subject
How to discover a specific controlling attitude: directed discovery questions
How to write a complete thesis statement, containing a limited subject area and a limited predicate area
How to discover supporting reasons for the thesis statement
How to classify supporting reasons into subject categories
How to write a complete purpose statement and plan a blueprint for the whole paper

---

EXERCISES

A. Use logical analysis and clustering to divide three of the following general subjects into limited subjects suitable for development in a short paper. For each general subject you choose, devise a diagram similar to the ones on pages 60 or 61.
1. Weapons
2. TV programs
3. Movies
4. Population
5. Music
6. The newspaper
7. The government (in the United States)
8. Advertisements
If you have trouble with this exercise, try some brainstorming and clustering first; then devise your diagram.

B. Choose three limited subjects from those you discovered in Exercise *A* and write a limited, specific thesis statement for each. If you have trouble with the controlling attitude of these statements, check the *quick-question approach* on page 55 and the *directed discovery questions* on page 67.

C. Classify the following items into related groups. Which single term in the list names them all? Which four general terms in the list represent the basic groups? Write your answer in the form of a *tree diagram* (as shown on page 60).

1. cows	7. animals	13. dogs	19. crocodiles
2. snakes	8. horses	14. mammals	20. fish
3. birds	9. tuna	15. salmon	21. monkeys
4. humans	10. gorillas	16. whales	22. robins
5. swordfish	11. ducks	17. eagles	23. sharks
6. sparrows	12. reptiles	18. trout	24. dinosaurs

D. Most groups of items can be classified in more than one way, depending on (1) the basic nature of the items themselves, and (2) the aims of the person doing the classifying (the "controlling principle"). For example, the same group of objects could be grouped according to (a) shape, (b) color, (c) size, (d) material, or (e) weight.
Group all of the following items into several major classes, arranged and simply listed according to a single, clear, controlling principle you choose. After you have completed the classification, devise a second and a third controlling principle and

reclassify the items. Name each controlling principle and clearly label each class of items you have grouped together.

peach cobbler	grilled steak	carrot cake
fried chicken	baked beans	boiled carrots
boiled spinach	french fries	grilled hamburger
roast beef	fudge brownies	roast turkey
baked potato	cherry pie	fried onion rings
mashed potatoes	meat loaf	apple turnovers

E. 1. Apply the *directed discovery questions* from page 67 to three of the following subjects. Use the subjects exactly as given. For each subject you choose, list as many *exploratory questions* as you can.
   a. Love (or terror, or hate)
   b. A pregnant woman
   c. A drunk driver
   d. Death (or sleep)
   e. A movie (name a specific movie)
   f. A traffic jam
   g. Political power

  2. From each of the three subjects you selected above choose one exploratory question for further analysis.
   a. Could these three exploratory questions serve as the starting points for good short papers following Theme Pattern A? (See page 18 in Chapter 2.) Explain why or why not. If necessary, rewrite these questions to make them more specific.
   b. Try to rephrase these three exploratory questions as thesis statements that would work well using Theme Pattern B. (See page 22 in Chapter 2.) What problems must you solve before you can write these thesis statements? Explain the relationship between the exploratory questions and the thesis statements.

F. Choose one exploratory question and one thesis statement from *E-2* above. Write an introductory paragraph for each, using the "funnel effect" approach explained in Chapter 2 (see pages 20 and 26).

G. You may not have agreed with the paper about football in Chapter 2 (p. 40). Copy the following diagram and fill it in, taking the opposite view. Start with a thesis statement that says something like *Football is the best thing that ever happened to our school,* and give your reasons. Make your reasons and your support for the reasons as strong as you possibly can. Don't forget to put your most persuasive reason last.

Thesis Statement: _____
       (The thesis statement is valid because . . .)
  Reason 1: _____
      (Reason 1 is valid because . . .)
    Reason A: _____
    Reason B: _____
    Reason C: _____
      (The thesis statement is valid because . . .)
  Reason 2: _____
      (Reason 2 is valid because . . .)
    Reason A: _____
    Reason B: _____
    Reason C: _____
      (The thesis statement is valid because . . .)

Reason 3: _____
           (Reason 3 is valid because . . .)
   Reason A: _____
   Reason B: _____
   Reason C: _____
Concluding Statement: _____

H. Write a five-hundred-word paper based on one of the paragraphs you developed in Exercise *F*.

I. 1. The following article by Norman Martin presents information from Jeffery Johnson's book *The Endangered Black Male*. After reading the article carefully, list in a series of simple sentences at least six ideas ("facts") that *interest* you. Choose three of your sentences and rephrase them as *questions* beginning with either *why*, or *how*, or *where*, or *when*, or *what*.

        Choose one of your questions for speculation. Try to answer your question by providing a list three or four statements.

2. Write a five-hundred-word paper based on the answer(s) you came up with in the first part of this exercise.

3. In what important ways does this newspaper article differ from the basic five-hundred-word paper?

Black Men Put Atop New Endangered List[1]

NEW YORK — America's black males have taken the lead on the endangered species list, said a noted author on the topic Monday.

"When Americans realized the bald eagle, which used to top the list, was facing extinction, they swiftly enacted preservation measures to ensure its survival," said Jeffery Johnson, author of *The Endangered Black Male*.

"And six months ago, it was announced the eagle is no longer near extinction," he said. "The species is guaranteed new life, but there is a 'new bald eagle' in America—black males," Johnson told National Urban League delegates during a seminar on black men in crisis.

America's black males need these same preservation measures the eagle received because this nation is rapidly losing its young black males to homicide, prison and drugs, he said.

"If we can save a bird, we can definitely save a man," Johnson said.

National studies illustrate just how grim the problem is:

■ An African-American male has a 1-in-21 chance of being murdered before his 25th birthday.

■ One of four black men in their 20s is either in jail, in prison, on probation or on parole.

■ Black males are the only group that can expect to live shorter lives in 1990 than they did in 1980.

■ Homicide is the No. 1 cause of death for African-American males, and their murder rate is 8 times that of white males. In Houston, within the first six months of 1990, more black males were killed than any other demographic group.

And the list goes on.

In fact, black males rank at the bottom in almost every socioeconomic category, from unemployment and infant mortality rates to drugs and high school dropout rates.

"Preserving the American black male is my mission in life, because it's my life at stake," Johnson said. "If a brother gets killed for no good reason, any time of any day a bullet could come my way."

But Johnson isn't alone in his mission. In New York last week, 200 scholars,

[1]Norma Martin, "Black Men Put Atop New Endangered List," *Houston Chronicle*, July 31, 1990: p. 5A. Reprinted with permission.

ministers and community workers gathered to exchange research and ideas on the problems of black men and to create the National Coalition of African American Men.

The NAACP, at its national convention two weeks ago, conducted a major panel discussion with numerous speakers to address the plight of black men.

Black men suffer from image and self-esteem problems, said Johnson. "Too many of them look in the mirror and see something they don't like—themselves."

Darlene Powell-Hopson, a Connecticut child clinical psychologist, said the negative self-perceptions start at an early age.

"I often see black male children who have been sent to me because they are acting out, inattentive, rebellious and troublemakers in school," Powell-Hopson said.

She said many of these young boys carry the label of troublemakers and underachievers throughout their educational career, and it becomes a self-fulfilling prophecy.

All the groups and the panel of experts at Monday's discussion agree on one thing: The solution to the problem rests in the hands of black men themselves.

"We have to restore the black male to full dignity," said Johnson, "There's nothing wrong with being a strong black man."

REVIEW TERMS

The skills and strategies you have learned in this chapter are reflected in the terms listed below. Test your understanding of them and you'll improve your mastery of fundamental stages in the thinking and writing process.

A. All-inclusive subject, argumentative, brainstorming, classes, classical invention, classification, classifying, clustering, clusters, controlling attitude, controlling categories, controlling question, directed discovery, directed discovery questions, direction, discovery, double subject, evidence, focus, free association, free writing, funnel effect, general subject, limited subject, logical analysis, logical division, looping, prewriting, purpose statement, quick-question approach, sentence outline, single subject, support, thesis statement, tree diagram, tree diagraming, unity

B. Compound sentence, coordinating conjunction, dependent clause, independent clause, limited predicate area, modifier, phrase, predicate area, subordinating conjunction

4

Maintaining Unity and Coherence

This chapter will help you improve the focus and direction of your paper and of every paragraph you write. Discovering a single, limited subject and a specific controlling attitude for thesis statements and topic sentences is an important first step. And presenting clearly related supporting evidence or reasons also helps. But *writing to explore or support a sharp argumentative focus or direction* requires additional skills.

Suppose you are asked for directions to the *nearest* hospital. Telling about several hospitals will only confuse because of the unnecessary information. And even if you concentrate your directions on how to get to one hospital only, the person could still miss the destination if your instructions aren't *orderly* or sufficiently illuminated with *signals* that point and guide. Good communication uses both processes—concentrating on a *single,* limited subject *(unity)* and providing clear ***directional signals (coherence)***.

A short paper works toward clarifying a single point or idea (limited subject) by making every statement in the paper support the controlling attitude toward this single idea. The aim is to convince readers that this one idea is valid. To achieve this goal, the paper must have unity, singleness of purpose: *one* subject, *one* controlling attitude, *one* tone. At the same time, while every sentence and every paragraph contributes to this single aim, all of the paper's parts must hold together to guide readers and keep their attention as they move from part to part. Coherence devices hold sentence to sentence and paragraph to paragraph, guiding both writer and readers from thought to thought in support of the thesis statement. Unity can be called the "togetherness" of all the ideas in the paper's parts, the sense that all the ideas presented are logically related to one another. Coherence is the resulting overall effect provided through directional signals; it is the easy, natural movement of ideas from part to part, reinforcing and emphasizing the paper's unity. Trying to move through a paper with inadequate coherence signals can be as frustrating as trying to drive behind a car that gives no directional signals.

UNITY

In communication, unity means oneness. *One subject, one controlling attitude, one tone.* In all your writing—sentences, paragraphs, short and long papers—you will work for this oneness.

The key to unity is to keep focused on your aim—on the argumentative controlling attitude toward your single, limited subject. Whether it appears as an exploratory question or a thesis, this controlling attitude is a ***pointer;*** it provides the *focus* and ***logical direction*** for all the paper's ideas. Like a compass, unity provides direction. By following a specific compass direction, you can move steadily south or east or north or west—or in any marked direction between these main points. But if you don't follow only *one* point on the compass, you will never reach your chosen destination. Exactly the same is true of writing: Move in a single logical direction (your specific controlling attitude) and stick to it. Unity in writing is consistently maintaining the *single* (one), specific logical direction you head for at the beginning of your paper (or paragraph). If you don't, your work is likely to project a split personality and seem to run in several directions at the same time.

Through its specific controlling attitude, the thesis statement provides the one logical direction to be followed throughout an *entire paper,* whether it is a short paper (like the five-hundred-word theme) or a long research paper. Similarly, through its specific controlling attitude, the topic sentence provides the single logical direction each developmental paragraph follows in support of the thesis. Look again at the introductory paragraph of "People Problems" (page 28). It provides a subject focus and blueprint, designed to establish *direction* and a sense of *unity* for the paper. First, it gradually limits the general subject of *accidents* to *most car accidents on our highways.* Then, in the form of a question, it provides a bridge statement to *causes* of these accidents. Finally, it sets aside such causes as mechanical failure and environmental hazards and, through its thesis statement, provides the entire paper's controlling attitude: [accidents] *result from human error.*

Study the sentence outline on page 80 to see how this controlling attitude gives direction to the thought of the paper. To provide unity, each developmental paragraph of the paper echoes this controlling attitude:

Most accidents on our highways	(Limited subject area)
result from human error	(Limited predicate area = controlling attitude)

[because]
↓ | |
1. People don't understand the effects of mind-impairing substances.
  ↓ |
2. People think they are better drivers than they really are.
  ↓
3. People aggressively take unnecessary chances.

To make this connection clear, the topic sentence of each developmental paragraph echoes the paper's controlling attitude and establishes the *direction* for each developmental paragraph:

1. *Human error causes these accidents when people* ***don't understand the effects of mind-impairing substances.***
2. *Highway accidents also result from human error because too many people* ***think they are better drivers than they really are.***
3. *Human error causes many accidents because too many people aggressively* ***take unnecessary chances.***

If you deviate from directly supporting the controlling attitude of the thesis statement or of a topic sentence clearly tied to the thesis statement, you violate the principle of unity. A good thesis or topic sentence, therefore, provides two fundamental keys to unity:

1. A single (one), limited subject area
2. A specific, limited predicate area (controlling attitude)

Later, Chapter 10 discusses ***tone*** as a third key to unity (pp. 350–55); it isn't listed here because it is really part of controlling attitude. You can see why it is so important to think through your idea before you begin and to use great care in phrasing both the thesis statement and the topic sentences of your papers.

Remembering the two fundamental keys to unity, let's look at the following paragraph:

European castles still standing prove that life in those great damp structures was far from comfortable. Cold, wet drafts blew through the long corridors, and heating such a barn was difficult and expensive. Although many bedrooms had fireplaces in them, the beds still had to be heavily curtained in winter before the occupants could keep from freezing to death. Walls were draped with tapestries and curtains to keep the cold winds out of other rooms. Five hundred years ago, it might have been easy for a lord to retain a hundred carpenters to build enough heavy oak pieces to furnish his manor, but today such an undertaking would cost thousands of dollars. For instance, just installing wall-to-wall carpeting in one of the gigantic rooms would make a dent in a multimillionaire's bank roll. And think of the staff that would have to be maintained if a castle were to be lived in today. There would be the kitchen help, a whole battalion of housekeepers, several moat cleaners, and an army of groundskeepers.

At first reading, this paragraph may seem to be fairly good, since it does say a number of interesting things about old castles. But if you study it more closely, you'll see that it lacks unity: It does not move in a single logical direction even though it discusses only old European castles (a fairly good single, limited subject). The paragraph does not fulfill *both* requirements for unity: although it has a single, limited subject, it does not focus on only *one* specific, limited predicate (controlling attitude). Because it introduces three—perhaps four—unrelated controlling attitudes, the paragraph actually moves in three different logical directions. The student writer points out that these old castles

were *uncomfortable*
were *cold*
were *expensive to heat*
were *costly to furnish*
were *difficult to staff*

Clearly, the writer can't seem to decide whether to talk about the lack of *comfort,* the *cold,* the *cost* of heating and furnishing, or the problems of *staffing*. This student hasn't decided what to say *about* the castles; the paragraph lacks a specific controlling attitude. Consequently, the paragraph fails to make *one* point only. It violates the principle of unity. A unified paragraph could be written on any one of the four ideas.

Though written tongue-in-cheek, the following paragraph concentrates on only one specific controlling attitude, the *cost* of castle-keeping:

> At today's prices, maintaining a castle in the way the feudal lords of the Middle Ages did would be impossible even for the Really Rich. Any castle worth mentioning needed a big enough staff of domestics to at least keep the chewed-on bones shoveled up off the mead hall floor while the fulltime silversmith hammered out the amulets for next week's dragon slayers. Then there would have to be thatch put on the gardener's hut while he replanted the rosemary and thyme, and scullery jacks and jills to turn the pig on the spit in the galley. Servants stood by in platoons to weld the knights into their armor and to let down the drawbridge and grind it up again if the Danes tried sneaking through. Add knights and embroidered squires waiting permission to Crusade, and pink and pretty ladies-in-waiting standing by to deliver the next sonnet to Milady's courtly lover. Add the cost for all this to the expense of feeding the Poor Porters, the cellarful of emaciated unknowns, and the fishes in the moat. The monthly expense of the noble family's entourage would be enough to eat the heart out of any modern multimillionaire's paycheck.

This paragraph also has a single, specific subject—old medieval castles. But in addition, it focuses on only one controlling attitude—a multimillionaire today *could not afford* the upkeep of a medieval castle—and it sticks to this specific focus from start to finish. It has unity of purpose: *one* subject, *one* controlling attitude, *one* tone. It has unity of tone throughout, established mainly by the use of exaggeration and some special effects: *chewed-on bones, dragon slayers, scullery jacks and jills, embroidered squires, pink and pretty ladies-in-waiting, Poor Porters, emaciated unknowns.* The controlling attitude toward the subject remains consistent; the writer concentrates on cost and always maintains the tongue-in-cheek, humorous feeling. Together, this oneness of subject and controlling attitude give the paragraph a strong sense of unity. In your writing, you too must strive for unity of purpose: one subject, one controlling attitude, one tone.

Here is another developmental paragraph for analysis. Read through it carefully to see if it maintains complete unity:

```
        Egypt was civilized long before there was any written
history of the country. Egypt has an area of 386,000 square
miles. Ancient Egyptians knew so much about embalming that some
of their mummies are preserved for us to view in museums. The
people of the world are concerned about saving these treasures,
and others, now that the course of the Nile River is to be
altered in the next decade. The Egyptians carried on commerce
with neighboring nations. They studied and were successful with
military strategy. For a time they lived under a system of
government—controlled production. There is a wide area of
fertile farmland along the Nile River. The early Egyptians
built great halls and temples whose ruins still stand. Without
modern machinery, they built the great pyramids near Cairo.
Tourists come in great numbers each year to visit them. Long
before the birth of Christ, Egyptians knew how to turn
wastelands into arable fields. They encouraged the arts and
held great meetings where learned men gathered. They were
always a religious people, holding to their beliefs in many
gods until about 1400 B.C. when Aton, the single god who
represented the life—giving power of the sun, was established
as the Egyptian deity. In 1945, Egypt gained charter membership
in the United Nations.
```

Clearly this paragraph doesn't maintain unity but races from idea to idea, each only loosely associated with Egypt. To analyze this paragraph, look first at the opening sentence. According to the basic diagram for the five-hundred-word paper in Chapter 2, this sentence is the topic sentence for the paragraph. That is, it specifically announces the subject the paragraph is going to be concerned with. It gives the paragraph its single direction.

The opening sentence is: *Egypt was civilized long before there was any written history of the country.* If the remainder of the paragraph is to support the subject of this topic sentence and no other, the sentence must contain a word or phrase that can be called the *pointer* (the controlling attitude). It points to the single direction the remainder of the paragraph must follow to be unified. The topic sentence about Egypt has such a pointer. The word *civilized* controls the direction the paragraph will follow. If any sentence does not prove that Egypt was civilized, it does not belong in the paragraph and must be deleted.

For purposes of analysis, here are the remaining sentences of the paragraph, listed and numbered (some of them have been condensed or paraphrased):

1. Egypt has an area of 386,000 square miles.
2. Ancient Egyptians knew so much about embalming that some of their mummies are preserved for us to view in museums.
3. It is these treasures that the world is concerned about saving.
4. Early Egyptians carried on commerce with neighboring nations.
5. They studied and were successful with military strategy.
6. They lived under a system of government-controlled production.
7. A wide area of fertile farmland edges the Nile.
8. The Egyptians built great halls and temples whose ruins still stand.
9. Without modern machinery, they built the great pyramids near Cairo.
10. Tourists come in great numbers each year to view Egypt's ruins.
11. Long before the birth of Christ, Egyptians knew how to turn wastelands into arable fields.
12. They encouraged the arts and held great meetings where learned men gathered.
13. They were always a religious people.
14. In 1945, Egypt gained charter membership in the United Nations.

These sentences need to be analyzed one at a time to see if they support the pointer word, *civilized,* in the topic sentence. Sentence 1, since it tells about the land area of Egypt, has nothing to do with Egypt's being *civilized*. It does not support the topic sentence. Delete it. Sentence 2, which tells about the Egyptians' knowledge of embalming, does support the idea that Egypt was civilized, so it may remain in the paragraph. Sentence 3 says that the world is concerned about saving Egyptian treasures, but because it discusses the present world's concern and not Egypt's past, it must be eliminated if the paragraph is to follow a single direction. Sentence 4, about Egypt's commerce with neighboring nations, can stay because it does explain Egypt's past civilization, as can 5 and 6, about the early Egyptians' knowledge of military strategy and control of production. Sentence 7 must be left out; the fact that there is fertile farmland in Egypt does not prove that Egypt was civilized. But that the Egyptians built great halls, temples, and pyramids— Sentences 8 and 9—does prove their civilization, so they stay. The number of tourists who visit Egypt does not prove that Egypt was civilized because tourists often visit places that have not been civilized. So Sentence 10 must go. Sentence 11, which tells about the Egyptians' farming abilities, does indicate that ancient Egyptians were civilized, and this sentence can be retained. Any nation that cultivates the arts and holds conferences of learned men would be said to have a fairly high level of civilization. Sentence 12, then, should stay in the paragraph. Sentence 13, about the Egyptians' religious feelings, does not necessarily establish their civilization, for uncivilized peoples also have deep religious inclinations, and the sentence must be deleted. That Egypt gained charter membership in the United Nations has nothing to do with Egypt's past civilization. It is concerned with the present only, and so Sentence 14 will have to be left out.

Eliminating those sentences not supporting the topic sentence with its pointer leaves these:

2. The ancient Egyptians knew so much about embalming that some of their mummies are preserved for us to view in museums.
4. Early Egyptians carried on commerce with neighboring nations.
5. They studied, and were successful with military strategy.
6. They lived under a system of government-controlled production.
8. The Egyptians built great halls and temples whose ruins still stand.
9. Without modern machinery they built the great pyramids near Cairo.
11. Long before the birth of Christ, Egyptians knew how to turn wastelands into arable fields.
12. They encouraged the arts and held great meetings where learned men gathered.

The remaining sentences can be put together into a unified paragraph, but it is neither well-developed nor readable.

```
     Egypt was civilized long before there was any written
history of the country. These ancient people knew so much about
embalming that some of their mummies are preserved for us to
view in museums. These people carried on commerce with
neighboring nations. They studied, and were successful with,
military strategy. They lived under a system of
government-controlled production. The Egyptians built great
halls and temples whose ruins still stand. Without modern
machinery, they built the great pyramids near Cairo. Long
before the birth of Christ, Egyptians knew how to turn
wastelands into arable fields. They encouraged the arts and
held great meetings where learned men gathered.
```

Now, with all the material that does not directly support the topic sentence deleted, the paragraph is at least unified. All the sentences remaining now support the idea that ancient Egypt was civilized. Repetition of *Egyptians* and *they* helps hold the paragraph together.

Here is one more paragraph to analyze for unity.

> The composition student, in one year alone, sees enough waste to permanently destroy his sense of well-being. He sacrifices fifty minutes a day, five days a week, thirty-six weeks of the otherwise useful year. If his scooter is missing, or if Maria wasn't home when he called last night, or if breakfast was burned, it's hard for him to keep his mind on paper writing. No matter how full of vitality he is when he marches into the classroom, the essay writer droops away, physically exhausted, when the final bell rings. One of those "dedicated" instructors can turn a potential writer into a nervous, quaking mouse with her constant shoulder-tapping, headshaking, and advice-giving. Even the most enthusiastic student is ready to give up when listening always to reprimands about spelling and where to put the semicolon. Writing is bad enough, but writing under such a dictator who denies the classroom citizen basic freedoms is unbearable. Writing materials are wasted, too. High school students have to buy ball point pens for one class, cartridge pens for another, and compasses and drawing pencils for others. It's sometimes pretty difficult to figure out how the Public Education System can call itself "free." Some of the required notebooks fall apart when one semester is about half through, adding to the sense of waste.

The topic sentence of this paragraph is, as expected, the first sentence: *The composition student, in one year alone, sees enough waste to permanently destroy his sense of well-being.* The pointer here is the word *waste.* Any sentence that doesn't show the waste a composition student sees does not belong. This paragraph can also be analyzed by considering each sentence separately to determine if it follows the direction the pointer indicates. This time the sentences that do not follow this logical direction, that is, that do not support the idea of waste in composition, are crossed out.

1. He sacrifices fifty minutes a day, five days a week, thirty-six weeks of the otherwise useful year.
2. ~~If his scooter is missing, or if Maria wasn't at home when he called last night, or if breakfast was burned, it's hard for him to keep his mind on paper writing.~~
3. No matter how full of vitality he is when he marches into the classroom, the essay writer droops away, physically exhausted, when the final bell rings.
4. ~~One of these "dedicated" instructors can turn a potential writer into a nervous, quaking mouse with her constant shoulder-tapping, headshaking, and advice-giving.~~
5. ~~Even the most enthusiastic student is ready to give up when listening always to reprimands about spelling and where to put the semicolon.~~
6. ~~Writing is bad enough, but writing under such a dictator who denies the classroom citizen basic freedoms is unbearable.~~
7. Writing materials are wasted, too.

 8. ~~High school students have to buy ball point pens for one class, cartridge pens for another, and compasses and drawing pencils for others.~~
 9. ~~It's sometimes pretty difficult to figure out how the Public Education System can call itself "free."~~
 10. Some of the required notebooks fall apart when one semester is about half through, adding to the sense of waste.

This analysis indicates that only four sentences out of the whole paragraph follow the direction indicated by the pointer.

 1. He sacrifices fifty minutes a day, five days a week, thirty-six weeks of the otherwise useful year.
 3. No matter how full of vitality he is when he marches into the classroom, the essay writer droops away, physically exhausted, when the final bell rings.
 7. Writing materials are wasted, too.
 10. Some of the required notebooks fall apart when one semester is about half through, adding to the sense of waste.

Put in their simplest form, these four sentences say that the composition student who writes in class *wastes* time, vitality, and materials.

At this point, you may conclude that a paragraph is simply a short paper, as indeed it is. The methods of development are the same for both. Both have a single, central thought to be explored and developed. For the paper, that central thought is in the thesis statement; in the paragraph, it is in the topic sentence. As in the thesis statement, the predicate area of the topic sentence contains the pointer word or phrase, the controlling attitude that is the key to the content of the paragraph, and, consequently, to the single direction of the paragraph.

Look again, for instance, at the paragraph about the composition student and waste. It leads off with a topic sentence: *The composition student, in one year alone, sees enough waste to permanently destroy his sense of well-being.* In its predicate area, the single word *waste* is the pointer. The rest of the paragraph answers the question, *Why does the student see waste?* It gives three reasons: The student sees waste because he wastes (1) his time, (2) his vitality, and (3) his writing materials. The paragraph will be unified as long as it develops only these three reasons.

A unified paragraph can be illustrated by this diagram.

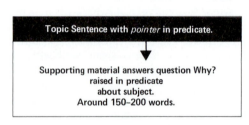

EXERCISES

  A. Pick out the pointer in each of the following topic sentences.
     1. We are a frustrated generation.
     2. Vague words can be misleading.
     3. History has shown that these rulers were cruel bigots.
     4. Reasoning from analogy proves nothing.
     5. The small car has enjoyed remarkable popularity.
     6. Reason opposes passion.
     7. Marriage demands cooperation between partners.
     8. Video games demand alertness.
     9. Good cooks need only a few simple rules.
    10. The computer has changed the writing process.
  B. For each of the following paragraphs, first write down the pointer in the topic sentence, and then list by number the sentences that support the pointer.

1.

(1) The family predicted that Jodie would some day make a fine veterinarian. (2) He had always shown a real tenderness toward animals. (3) Stray dogs and cats seemed to collect around the farm. (4) Once a beautiful trained Collie showed up and never left again, but that wasn't as surprising as the pair of sleek Siamese cats that moved in. (5) Those cats killed every rat in the barn inside of a week. (6) Animals all loved Jodie, too. (7) Folks used to drive out from town on Sundays to look at the whole families of painted buntings that ate with Jodie's chickens. (8) He kept Rhode Island Reds, mostly. (9) They say the bunting is rare in this part of the state. (10) Jodie was the quickest kid for learning things. (11) His teachers, every one, had nothing but praise for him. (12) He was never content to play until he had all of his homework done. (13) And he never missed a Sunday but once, going to church all through grammar school.

2.

(1) Elmer Dugan studied the coffee table. (2) There was something embarrassing about it, he realized. (3) The bowl of slightly melted Christmas candy should have been cleaned and refilled weeks ago. (4) Beside the candy jar sat an ashtray running over with bobby pins, bits of rickrack, and three spools of yellow thread. (5) Next to the ashtray was the current issue of Wild <u>and</u> <u>Free</u> magazine, the trashy literature his wife and her good friend next door read and traded constantly. (6) John Thompson was getting a little nervous. (7) Elmer hoped that John and his loud-mouthed wife would get bored enough to leave soon. (8) But they didn't, and Elmer's gaze wandered to the second tier of the coffee table. (9) Adele Thompson was raving on about her eight-year-old's ballet

accomplishments. (10) She could go on forever, and Mary kept
encouraging the chatter. (11) Elmer counted eight magazines on
the second shelf of the coffee table, and one darning egg. (12)
He supposed the darning egg had its rights, but why couldn't
Mary keep it on the thirty-nine-dollar, three-legged, Early
American rockmaple sewing stand she had insisted he buy for her
last Christmas? (13) What he saw next, and couldn't believe,
was a small, dead, and dried scorpion that Mary had reported
killing three weeks ago. (14) The phone rang, a wrong number,
and Adele Thompson started in on one of her favorite and most
boring of all topics, the community and its telephone manners.

3.

(1) It was plain to the doctor that his day was going to
be dreary. (2) Already twelve patients waited in the outer
office. (3) The happy Tiller teenager giggled over a comic book
as she rolled up her sleeve for her shot. (4) It was a joy to
chat for a moment now and then with a happy, healthy, and
well-adjusted kid. (5) It didn't improve the day, either, to be
haunted by the difficult tonsillectomy facing him Monday
morning. (6) By mid-afternoon poor old Mrs. Clark would come
begging for another bottle of sugar pills to pull her through
another half-dozen "heart attacks." (7) The Everson infant
needed surgery, but there was no convincing his backward
parents, and the telephone jangled constantly. (8) Both the
Mumford twins were down with a dangerous relapse. (9) Not that
he had really hoped to fish tomorrow, but already a cold mist
was falling. (10) By morning his little world would be iced
over. (11) At least Nurse Hearne wouldn't be around to annoy
him. (12) Never again. (13) He had gladly let her go when she
demanded a sizeable pay raise and an extra half-day off. (14)
He meditated for the length of one cigarette, coughed, and
studied the frayed edge of his office carpet. (15) Craig Adams'
test had come back positive, of course, and young Mrs. Adams
would go into hysterics. (16) It would take until closing time
to calm her. (17) And the town drunk, in for another Cure, was
at this moment passing out in the waiting room.

C. Read this paragraph by E. B. White.

It is a miracle that New York works at all. The whole thing is implausible. Every
time the residents brush their teeth, millions of gallons of water must be drawn from
the Catskills and the hills of Westchester. When a young man in Manhattan writes a
letter to his girl in Brooklyn, the love message gets blown to her through a pneumatic
tube — pfft — just like that. The subterranean system of telephone cables, power lines,
steam pipes, gas mains and sewer pipes is reason enough to abandon the island to the
gods and the weevils. Every time an incision is made in the pavement, the noisy
surgeons expose ganglia that are tangled beyond belief. By rights New York should
have destroyed itself long ago, from panic or fire or rioting or failure of some vital
supply line in its circulatory system or from some deep labyrinthine short circuit.
Long ago the city should have experienced an insoluble traffic-snarl at some
impossible bottleneck. It should have been wiped out by a plague starting in its slums
or carried in by ships' rats. It should have been overwhelmed by the sea that licks at

it on every side. The workers in its myriad cells should have succumbed to nerves, from the fearful pall of smoke-fog that drifts over every few days from Jersey, blotting out all light at noon, and leaving the high offices suspended, men groping and depressed, and the sense of world's end. It should have been touched in the head by the August heat and gone off its rocker.[1]

This paragraph maintains unity through its tight organization. To determine its organization, answer the following questions.

1. What is the topic sentence of the paragraph? State the limited subject area and the predicate area. What is the controlling attitude? What is the pointer?
2. Two principal reasons are given in support of the topic sentence and its pointer. What are they?
3. These two reasons also have supporting details to establish their validity. Write down the two principal reasons supporting the topic sentence, one at the head of one column and one at the head of another. Then, making two columns, list the supporting details for each of the two reasons.
4. a. List some of the words or phrases that seem to give the paragraph a relaxed, half-serious feeling.
    b. Does the writer maintain this feeling throughout the paragraph? How?
    c. On the basis of your answer to Question 2, what would you conclude about the author's attitude toward New York?
    d. On the basis of the pointer you found in the topic sentence and the feeling you examined in *a* and *b,* what else could you conclude about the author's attitude toward New York?
5. On the basis of your answers to Question 4, is unity of subject matter and support the only kind of unity in this paragraph? Be prepared to explain and support your answer. (If you have trouble with Questions 4 and 5, recheck the comments on page 90.)

COHERENCE

Unity is a matter of *logical direction;* coherence is a matter of **interlocking connection.** As you have seen, in any paragraph or paper, unity is the logical thought relationship established between sentences and paragraphs, resulting from choosing one subject, one controlling attitude, one tone. Coherence is the effect of interlocking connection provided by directional *signals* of many kinds, designed to guide the reader in the one direction established through unity. The key to coherence is the word *interlocking.* Through **interlocking devices,** the writer ties sentence to sentence and paragraph to paragraph. The result is coherence.

Consider, for instance, these two sentences taken out of context:

Mr. and Mrs. Vitek thought that under the circumstances there was only one course to take. The young man on my left saw several alternatives.

---

[1]Excerpt from pp. 24–25 of *Here Is New York* by E. B. White. Copyright © 1949 by E. B. White. Reprinted by permission of HarperCollins Publishers Inc.

These two sentences are on the same subject, but the second sentence appears at first glance to be on another subject because of the mention of the unnamed *young man*. Readers must pause to get their bearings when they reach the second sentence because of this apparent change in subject. They are momentarily confused. Yet note that the addition of one word, *but*, before the first word in the second sentence avoids this confusion:

> *Mr. and Mrs. Vitek thought that under the circumstances there was only one course to take. But the young man on my left saw several alternatives.*

Now, readers can go easily from the first sentence to the second with no pause, with no confusion. The two sentences are drawn together by the one word *but*. The use of such a transition word is one method of achieving coherence. But there are more. Some of these interlocking devices that serve as signals are grammatical, some are rhetorical, and some are mechanical. Let's look at the most important ones.

1. COHERENCE THROUGH CONSISTENT POINT OF VIEW

Point of view is the position in time and place from which writers view their subject. It is most often a grammatical problem, though it can also be a matter of physical perspective, as you will see shortly. Considered grammatically, point of view involves two basic elements:

1. The grammatical subject of each sentence (person)
2. The verb (tense as a time indicator)

```
      A year spent teaching in the "shacks" adjacent to the city
schools provides a unique education to any teacher. The
classroom temperature gets awfully cold sometimes. You cannot
imagine how hard it is to teach when it is forty-six degrees
inside the building. Field mice race over the student lockers
just as the teacher begins an important assignment. As summer
approaches with its rising temperatures and increased noise
level, the teacher has decided that she would gladly trade her
unique experience for anyone's traditional classroom. The water
fountain is so far away that it occupies a good part of the
class time for teacher and students to get a drink.
```

This paragraph has unity. In the first sentence, *unique education* is the controlling attitude (pointer), and the remainder of the paragraph shows how the teacher gets this education from teaching in the shacks. But it is not coherent. The writer doesn't guide the reader smoothly from sentence to sentence because the **grammatical signals** are at fault, causing point of view to *shift* from sentence to sentence. You can see the shift by picking out the subject of each sentence following the topic sentence. The subject of the second sentence is *temperature*. The subject of the third sentence is *you*. The fourth uses *field mice;* the fifth, *teacher;* and the sixth, *water fountain*. Therein lies the trouble with coherence in the paragraph. Because the paragraph obviously concerns a teacher and her experiences, each sentence should be about the teacher. A simple revision of this paragraph, using *teacher* (or its equivalent) as the subject of each sentence, greatly improves coherence.

        A year spent teaching in the "shacks" adjacent to the city schools provides a unique education to any teacher. She learns to adjust to a temperature of forty-six degrees inside her classroom, a condition that persists although all the radiators are working at full capacity. She learns to cope with the problem of field mice racing over the student lockers just as she begins an important assignment. As summer approaches with its rising temperatures and increased noise level, the teacher has decided she would gladly trade her unique experience for anyone's traditional classroom. She learns to control her thirst and teaches this lesson to her students, since the water fountain is so far away it is almost impossible to get a drink.

Now the ***grammatical subject*** of all the sentences after the topic sentence is *teacher* (or its ***pronoun*** substitute, *she*), and as a result the point of view is consistent. Note that when you make the subject the same throughout, you also make other changes almost automatically, improving the whole paragraph.

But another kind of grammatical shift is possible. Suppose, for example, the writer became careless with verbs in the revised version and shifted the tenses unknowingly. The result could look something like this:

        A year spent teaching in the "shacks" adjacent to the city schools provides a unique education to any teacher. She learns to adjust to a temperature of forty-six degrees inside her classroom, a condition that persisted although all the radiators were working at full capacity. She learned to cope with the problem of field mice racing over the student lockers just as she begins an important assignment. As summer approached with its rising temperatures and increased noise level, the teacher has decided she would gladly trade her unique experience for anyone's traditional classroom. She learns to control her thirst and teaches this lesson to her students, since the water fountain was so far away it is almost impossible to get a drink.

In this version, even though the grammatical subject remains consistent (high-lighted), the time indicators (underscored verbs) shift from present to past for no logical reason. The result is again a lack of coherence because of a grammatical shift in point of view. The sentences don't interlock properly, do they?

2. COHERENCE THROUGH PRONOUN REFERENCE

You should be able to see from the above discussion of the grammatical subjects in a paragraph that coherence through *pronoun reference* is closely related to point of view. Repeating the same noun too often in a paragraph, especially if repetition isn't needed for clarity, will usually bore the reader. With care, you can use a series of pronouns to do the job; the result is a series of interlocking, pointed grammatical signals clearly referring to an *antecedent* noun and providing logical continuity. The result is coherence through pronoun reference. Study the way in which the pronouns in the following student paragraph create this interlocking effect of coherence.

> The specialized languages Herbert uses in the Dune series also serve to make characters more realistic. A dialect is a tangible tie between characters in the same group. The four-novel series involves several dozen major and over fifty minor characters. The words a character uses place him in the reader's mind with the right associations. Near the end of the third book, for example, a character named Duncan Idaho appears. Although his name was familiar to me, I couldn't remember if he was friend or foe, much less why he was important to the story. However, when he made a hand signal that only the ruling house's chief swordmaster used, he was immediately recognized both by his old student and by me. Similarly, people using unusual syntax are identified as Fremen from the deepest part of the desert. In the first book, offworlders refer to the young duke as Paul Atreides; Fremen called him Paul Maud'Dib. The reader immediately draws lines of association from a character's use of language, eliminating much of the need for distracting explanations of that character's home-place.

Note the number of times the pronouns *he* and *his* have been circled and tied to the *proper* antecedent noun. Any pronoun may be used to achieve this interlocking effect (*he, she, they, we, you,* or any other form). This method is a simple means of maintaining coherence. It is closely related to consistency in the point of view and to the next coherence technique, repetition of key words.

3. COHERENCE THROUGH REPETITION OF KEY WORDS

Now look at the *Dune* paragraph for coherence gained through repetition of a special kind. Notice the **key words** connected by lines.

The specialized languages Herbert uses in the <u>Dune</u> series also serve to make characters more realistic. A dialect is a tangible tie between characters in the same group. The four-novel series involves several dozen major and over fifty minor characters. The words a character uses place him in the reader's mind with the right associations. Near the end of the third book, for example, a character named Duncan Idaho appears. Although his name was familiar to me, I couldn't remember if he was friend or foe, much less why he was important to the story. However, when he made a hand signal that only the ruling house's chief swordmaster used, he was immediately recognized both by his old student and by me. Similarly, people using unusual syntax are identified as Fremen from the deepest part of the desert. In the first book, offworlers refer to the young duke as Paul Atreides; Fremen called him Paul Maud'Dib. The reader immediately draws lines of association from a character's use of language, eliminating much of the need for distracting explanations of that character's home-place.

Note the obvious interlocking effect in this paragraph. Two key words, *characters* and *character,* appear in the paragraph seven times. This repetition of key words would probably not be noticed on a first reading, if the words were not marked as they are here, and that is the way it should be. But this method of achieving coherence, when the paragraph is analyzed, emerges as an important way of holding the paragraph together.

The author of the above paragraph is an effective student writer who uses this method of achieving coherence well. Use caution, however, to prevent the method itself from becoming obvious and obtrusive. In the following example, a student has used repetition of key words to achieve coherence.

It is necessary for college students to receive a balanced education. This balanced education will help them decide what their goals are and how to achieve them. If students fail in their first endeavors, this balanced education will also help them by giving them the background necessary to start in another field of work. With a balanced education, students have a better opportunity to succeed. Without a balanced education, students' options for success are more limited.

In this example, the student writer has repeated *balanced education* five times and *students* four times in an attempt at coherence. Instead, the writer has succeeded only in annoying the reader with the unnecessary repetition of two words. Here's a more successful version, in which key nouns still remain but pronouns take over part of the job:

> College students need a balanced education to help them
> decide on their goals and how to achieve them. If their first
> job efforts fail, it will also help them by giving them the
> background needed to start in another field. With it, they have
> a better chance to succeed; without it, their options are
> limited.

4. COHERENCE THROUGH SPATIAL ORDER OF SENTENCES

In using a *spatial order* to achieve coherence, a writer explains or describes objects as they are *arranged in space*. What this means is that the physical perspective or position from which the writer views these objects moves in an orderly, logical manner, giving the reader clear directional signals to follow from place to place. It is the nongrammatical aspect of point of view. (See Section 1, above.) The trick is to choose a specific position as your starting point and then direct the reader to follow your eye as it moves in an orderly pattern from the chosen point. For example, to describe a room, you might choose a position in a doorway as your starting point. You would begin by guiding the reader to the wall to your right as you describe it, then direct attention to the wall opposite you as you describe it, then describe the wall on your left, and finally take the reader into the center of the room as you describe what it contains. You could just as easily reverse this order, of course. The result is that you will impose an *order* on your descriptions, creating an interlocking effect and giving your descriptive paragraph greater coherence. Try following the description in this paragraph.

> The main characteristic of the little farm we had walked
> over was disorder. The winding, narrow road was bumpy and
> rough, and weeds grew rank and tall on each side of it. Near
> the barn stood a battered, unpainted tractor, plow, and rake.
> On the other side of the road, weeds sapping lifegiving
> substances from the soil were also growing among the small,
> withered cotton plants. The house needed paint and repairs. The
> steps and porch were rickety, and several of their boards were
> broken. The fence around the pasture was badly in need of
> repairs. The broken window panes in the house had pieces of tin
> and boards over them. On one side of the road lay bundles of
> grain decaying from long exposure to wind, rain, and sunshine.
> The wire was broken in many places, and the wooden posts,
> rotted at the ground, were supported by the rusty wire. The
> yard was littered with rubbish--tin cans, broken bottles, and
> paper. The barn lacked paint; its roof sagged and some shingles
> needed to be replaced. In the pasture, diseased with weeds and
> underbrush, grazed thin, bony cattle, revealing their need for
> more and better food and shelter.

This paragraph has unity because the pointer in the topic sentence is *disorder,* and all the details in the paragraph indicate the disorder on the little farm. But it lacks coherence because the description of the disorder is presented to the reader at random; the writer has not taken a position from which to describe the disorder.

The resulting paragraph is itself disordered, as an analysis will quickly disclose. Sentence two, immediately following the topic sentence, tells of the road and the weeds on each side of it. Sentence three talks about the barn. The fourth sentence goes back to the road again. The fifth jumps to the house, the sixth to the porch, and the seventh to the pasture. The eighth returns to the house and the ninth to the road. The tenth describes the fence around the pasture; the eleventh, the yard around the house; the twelfth, the barn; and the thirteenth the pasture and cattle. But if the writer rearranges the sentences so that they present the objects on the farm as one would see them from a position of walking up the farm road to the house, the paragraph will be more coherent.

> The main characteristic of the little farm we had walked over was disorder. The winding, narrow road was bumpy and rough, and weeds grew rank and tall on each side of it. On one side of the road lay bundles of grain decaying from long exposure to wind, rain, and sunshine. On the other side, among the small, withered cotton plants, weeds sapped the soil. The fence around the pasture was badly in need of repair. The wire was broken in many places, and the wooden posts, rotted at the ground, were supported by the rusty wire. In the pasture, diseased with weeds and underbrush, grazed thin, bony cattle, revealing their need for more and better food and shelter. Near the barn stood a battered, unpainted tractor, plow, and rake. The barn itself lacked paint; its roof sagged and some of the shingles needed to be replaced. The house, too, needed paint and repairs. The steps and porch were rickety, and several of their boards were broken. The broken window panes were mended with tin and boards. The yard was littered with rubbish--in cans, broken bottles, and paper.

The paragraph now has a logical spatial order; it takes the reader from the road to either side of the road, to the pasture, and to the barn and house. Having decided on the spatial order, the writer gives the reader clear directional *signals: each side, on one side, on the other side, around the pasture, in the pasture, near the barn, the barn itself.* These signals are similar to those given by the transition words discussed in Section 7.

5. COHERENCE THROUGH CHRONOLOGICAL ORDER OF SENTENCES

Chronological order means simply the order in which events happen. This order is seen most often in narrative—writing that tells a story—and narrative is often a part of expository writing, particularly in illustrating a point. Narrative is not necessary, however, to the use of chronological order. For instance, a chronological order may be superimposed on the *revised* paragraph about the teacher, and the coherence of the paragraph becomes even stronger. Look at this further revision.

```
        A year spent teaching in the "shacks" adjacent to the city
schools provides a unique education to any teacher. In the
fall, the teacher learns to cope with the problem of field mice
racing over the student lockers just as she begins an important
assignment. In the winter, she learns to adjust to a
temperature of forty-six degrees, a condition that persists
inside the classroom although all the radiators are working at
full capacity. In the spring, she learns to control her thirst
and teaches this lesson to her students, since a trip to the
water fountain occupies a good part of the class time. In
summer, with its rising temperatures and increased noise level,
she has decided that she would gladly trade the unique setting
for anyone's traditional classroom.
```

This version, as indicated by the highlighted phrases, takes the teacher through the seasons in chronological order during the school year. Imposing the chronological order resulted in effective coherence. Note here that there is not just one coherence device used in a paragraph but that methods are combined within any one paragraph.

6. COHERENCE THROUGH RELATED SENTENCE PATTERNS

Holding a paragraph together by repetition of sentence patterns within the paragraph is a relatively difficult means of achieving coherence because it requires even more care in designing sentences, but it is an effective means. Look at this paragraph.

> (1) To be genuinely civilized means to be able to walk straight and to live honorably without the props and crutches of one or another of the childish dreams which have so far supported men. (2) That such a life is likely to be ecstatically happy I will not claim. (3) But that it can be lived in quiet content, accepting resignedly what cannot be helped, not expecting the impossible, and thankful for small mercies, this I would maintain. (4) That it will be difficult for men in general to learn this lesson I do not deny. (5) But that it will be impossible I will not admit since so many have learned it already.[2]

Following the first sentence, the four remaining ones are cast in the same form and arranged in pairs, the second and third sentences constituting one pair, and the fourth and fifth sentences another. Look at the second sentence in the paragraph. It starts with a dependent clause, *That such a life is likely to be ecstatically happy,* and

---

[2]W. T. Stace, "Man Against Darkness," *The Atlantic Monthly.* Reprinted by permission.

then finishes with a short independent clause, *I will not claim*. The third sentence starts with a *but*, which ties it to the second sentence, and continues with exactly the same structure as that of the second sentence: *that it can be lived in quiet content . . . this I would maintain*. The first pair of sentences, joined together with *but*, is complete. The fourth sentence starts out exactly as the others, *That it will be difficult for men in general to learn this lesson*, and finishes with the identical short independent structure as the others, *I do not deny*. The fifth sentence begins with a *but*, which ties it to the fourth. Then comes the same type of dependent clause that has started the last three sentences, *that it will be impossible*, followed by the independent clause, *I will not admit*.

Such related sentence patterns are called **balance**, which can consist of **parallel structure, contrasting ideas** (antithesis), or both. Parallel structure is a matter of grammar and arrangement of words, so that successive words, **phrases, clauses**, or sentences form very nearly the same patterns; contrast results when ideas logically oppose one another. Here are some simple illustrations:

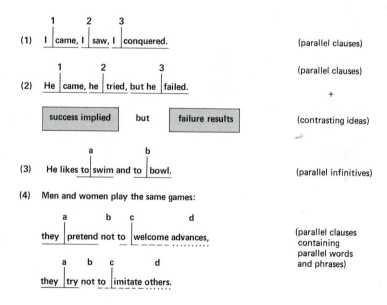

Balance is only one of many sentence patterns that can be used to add coherence. The author of the sample paragraph uses both types of balance to gain coherence, as illustrated in the following diagram.

(1) To be genuinely civilized means to be able to walk straight and to live honorably without the props and crutches of one or another of the childish dreams which have so far supported men.

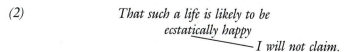

But

(3)   *that it can be lived in quiet*
                                                          content . . .
                                                                           —— *this I would maintain.*

(4)   *That it will be difficult for men in*
                                                          general to learn this lesson
                                                                           —— *I do not deny.*

But

(5)   *that it will be impossible*
                                                                           —— *I will not admit*
                                                          since so many have learned it already.

Both the four ***dependent clauses*** and the four ***independent clauses*** following them are examples of parallel structure. The *but* that begins the third and fifth sentences introduces contrasting ideas that force the reader to weigh them against the ideas of the preceding sentences. These balanced patterns force the ideas into a closer relationship; they give the paragraph coherence by creating an interlocking effect.

7. COHERENCE THROUGH TRANSITION WORDS

Probably the easiest, and most abused, method of pulling together the ideas in a passage is through the use of ***transition words.*** Transition words or phrases serve as signals to interlock sentences. They direct the reader from the thought of one sentence to that of another to indicate the relationship between the two sentences. An example of the way transition words work appeared earlier.

> *Mr. and Mrs. Vitek thought that under the circumstances there was only
> one course to take.* But *the young man on my left saw several alternatives.*

The word that interlocks the two sentences is *but,* which serves as a signal to the reader. The reader immediately expects a *contrast* to the thought of the previous sentence and proceeds without a pause *to see what that contrast is.* This word

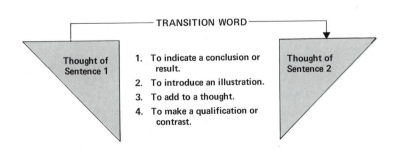

provides a *transition* between the two sentences and shows their relationship: contrast.

The English language has many transition words to express any relationship between two sentences. The diagram on page 108 illustrates some uses of transition words. To use these transition words effectively, consider each situation carefully, keeping in mind three general guidelines.

1. Use transition words sparingly.   The overuse of these words weakens writing style. Look at these sentences, for example:

> *James went to the resort planning to stay three weeks,* but *he became disgusted after the first day.* Consequently, *he packed and went home.*

The weakness in this example results from the string of three independent clauses joined together in thought by transition words. It is much better to delete at least one transition word and change one of the independent clauses to dependent.

> *James planned to stay three weeks at the resort, but after one day he became so disgusted that he packed and went home.*

Here, the *consequently* has been dropped from the last sentence and the whole has been made into a dependent clause, *that he packed and went home.* This revision is an acceptable sentence; but why not add some meaningful details, and make a good sentence out of it:

> *Although James had planned a leisurely three weeks' stay at the resort, doing what he pleased when he pleased, he found himself caught up in so many planned activities—all arranged by a loud-mouthed, back-slapping "entertainment" leader—that he packed his bags and left in disgust after one day.*

2. Use transition words to indicate logical relationships.   Consider this example:

> *The College of Veterinary Medicine at State University is the only one in Florida. Therefore, it is an excellent school.*

In this example, the transition word *therefore* is not followed by a logical conclusion drawn from the evidence presented in the first sentence.

Just because State University has the only college of veterinary medicine in Florida, it does not necessarily follow that the college is excellent. This revision is much better:

> *State University's College of Veterinary Medicine, the only one in Florida, is an excellent school.*

To Indicate a Conclusion or Result	Examples
therefore as a result consequently accordingly in other words to sum up thus then hence	1. *Therefore,* his action can be justified by valid explanation. 2. *As a result,* hollow, vain aristocracies have been established on American campuses. 3. *Consequently,* the number of qualified voters remains small.

To Introduce an Illustration	Examples
thus for example for instance to illustrate namely	1. *For example,* suppose I ask myself, ''Will socialization ever come about?'' 2. *For instance,* sophisticates can easily ridicule popular notions of government. 3. *Namely,* those who complain the loudest are often themselves the most guilty.

To Add a Thought	Examples
second in the second place next likewise moreover again in addition finally similarly further in fact and	1. *Similarly,* the German university can profit by adopting the American practice of letting the student do most of the talking. 2. *Second,* human happiness feeds itself on a multitude of minor illusions. 3. Then *again* we work *and* strive because of the illusions connected with fame. 4. *Moreover,* the child assumes an attitude that he knows is false. 5. Effective leaders are effective communicators. *And* leadership positions demand higher salaries.

To Make a Qualification or Contrast	Examples
on the other hand nevertheless still on the contrary by contrast however but or nor	1. He was not, *however,* completely qualified for the task he had undertaken. 2. The Dobu, *by contrast,* are portrayed as virtually a society of paranoids. 3. *Nevertheless,* these theories do contain real insights into the nature of value judgments. 4. *On the contrary,* one should not blindly assume that our birthrate will continue to climb.

Or consider this sentence:

Zeba was healthy and robust, and *she was born in Cincinnati in 1916.*

The two parts of this sentence, *Zeba was healthy and robust,* and *she was born in Cincinnati in 1916,* aren't sufficiently related to be joined by a transition word. Apparently, the intent of this sentence is to comment on Zeba's health for her age, because her birth year is given. The place of her birth has nothing to do with any idea expressed in the sentence. The thought can be conveyed much better with a sentence such as this one:

At seventy-four, Zeba was healthy and robust.

3. Use relative and demonstrative words accurately. Remember that certain adjectives and pronouns, when used accurately, create the interlocking effect of coherence. *These* important transition words include the following:

Relative pronouns:	who, which, what, that
Personal pronouns:	he, she, it, they, them, you
Demonstrative pronouns/adjectives:	this, that, these, those.

These aren't the only ones, of course, *that* tie sentence parts and sentences together, but *they* probably are the most important. Use *them* with care, making certain *their* ties are unmistakably clear. Check the italicized words in *these* sentences; can *you* readily follow *their* ties? You will find additional information about pronouns and their antecedents on page 284.

Although each of the means of gaining coherence is considered separately in this chapter, this doesn't mean that only one of them may be used in a given paragraph. To achieve the coherence they want in their writing, experienced writers may use several, even all, of them in any one paragraph.

EXERCISES

A. Examine this paragraph to see if its coherence can be improved.

1   One of the fastest-growing fields of study is wildlife ecology. The growth
2   is reflected in the increasing college enrollment in agriculture and forestry.
3   Student interest in conservation is the dominant force behind the new

4 popularity of these and such related fields as range science, oceanography, and
5 marine sciences. In the last decade college-bound students have become
6 increasingly aware of the great need for professionals trained in the management
7 and conservation of natural resources. Reports from the Carnegie Commission
8 on Higher Education suggest that the job market for ecology-minded graduates
9 will continue to grow into the next decade.

ANALYSIS

1. Examine first the subjects of the sentences. The subject of the first sentence (line 1) is *one*. In the second it is *growth* (line 1), in the third it is *interest* (line 3), in the fourth, *students* (line 5), and in the fifth, *reports* (line 7). This examination shows that the student should maintain a more consistent point of view to give the paragraph coherence.

2. Examine the paragraph for evidence of other methods of maintaining coherence. There is some repetition of key words: *growth* (line 1) and *grow* (line 9) echo *growing* (line 1), *fields* (line 4) repeats *fields* (line 1), *students* (line 5) repeats *student* (line 3), *conservation* appears in lines 3 and 7, *increasingly* (line 6) echoes *increasing* (line 2), and *ecology* appears in lines 1 and 8. Despite these echoes, the paragraph lacks coherence because the ideas have no clear **direction,** there are no transition words, there is no pronoun reference, and there are no related sentence patterns. Obviously, the coherence of this paragraph can be improved. Consider this revision.

1   The marked **increase** in the number of **students** enrolled in the field of
2 wildlife ecology has caused it to become one of the fastest-growing **professions.**
3 **This increase** also reflects the growing need for **professionals** trained in the
4 management and conservation of natural resources. Moreover, in the last decade
5 **college-bound students** have become increasingly aware of this need. Thus, the
6 resulting **student interest** in conservation has also become the dominant force
7 behind the new popularity of such related fields as range science, oceanography,
8 and marine sciences. Furthermore, reports from the Carnegie Commission on
9 Higher Education suggest that the job market for ecology-minded **profession-**
10 **als** will continue to grow into the next decade.

Note the number of methods used to achieve coherence in this version. The most important change is in **direction:** There is a more logical movement from sentence to sentence, partly because the ideas have been rearranged and partly because sentence subjects are repeated. The subject of the first two sentences, for example, is *increase* (lines 1 and 3), while the subject of sentence four, *student interest* (line 6), echoes the subject of the third sentence, *college-bound students* (line 5). Moreover, the paragraph contains a number of transition words—*also* (line 3), *moreover* (line 4), *thus* (line 5), *also* (line 6), and *furthermore* (line 8). Two modifiers (*this* in lines 3 and 5) and a pronoun reference (*it* in line 2) also add to the coherence. The paragraph repeats all the key words in the original version, but this time they appear in an order that improves the coherence. Note particularly the following sequence: *students* (line 1), *professions* (line 2), *professionals* (line 3), *students* (line 5), *student interest* (line 6), and *professionals* (line 9). A similar repetition is seen in the use of *increase* and *growing,* and *ecology, need,* and *conservation.* Of 113 words in the paragraph, 30, or 26.5 percent, are key words repeated to maintain coherence. This is not an unusually high percentage. Explain why this version of the paragraph would (or would not) work as a developmental paragraph in a paper. How could you improve it?

B. In the following paragraphs, find the coherence devices and be able to point them out, using the line numbers to identify them.

1.

> 1   Giants can be benevolent, like Prometheus, or savage, like the Cyclops.
> 2   Some have been regarded as friends of the human race; others, such as the
> 3   Philistine, Goliath, were its sworn enemy. Whether friend or foe, passive or
> 4   violent, giants have always fascinated their human brethren. One giant
> 5   interested Americans for over thirty years. He was known as the Cardiff Giant,
> 6   and he was a hoax. That much was plain to anyone who looked at it in an
> 7   objective frame of mind. He was twelve feet tall, four feet wide, and of solid
> 8   gypsum. It was conveniently discovered only a few feet underground, right on
> 9   the spot where Stubby Newell planned to dig a well. And P. T. Barnum came
> 10   out with his own "Cardiff Giant" after the hoax proved profitable. Even when
> 11   giants started multiplying across the country and newspaper reporters began
> 12   proclaiming the fossil a fraud, up to 3,000 people a day paid a dollar to view the
> 13   relic. Oddly enough, support for the hoax came from two factions usually in
> 14   disagreement—religion and science.

2.

> 1   Many critics of our society have said that we lack standards. This has been
> 2   said so often by preachers and by the makers of commencement addresses that
> 3   we have almost stopped asking what, if anything, it means to say that our society
> 4   "lacks standards." But that we do lack standards for welfare and standards for
> 5   education is obvious. Welfare turns into vulgar materialism because we have no
> 6   standard by which to measure it. Education fails because it also refuses to face
> 7   the responsibility of saying of what education consists. Both tend to become
> 8   merely what people seem to want.[3]

3.

> 1   Studies serve for delight, for ornament, and for ability. Their chief use for
> 2   delight, is in privateness and retiring; for ornament, is in discourse; and for
> 3   ability, is in the judgment and disposition of business. For expert men can
> 4   execute, and perhaps judge of particulars, one by one; but the general counsels,
> 5   and the plots and marshalling of affairs, come best from those that are learned.
> 6   To spend too much time in studies is sloth; to use them too much for ornament
> 7   is affectation; to make judgment wholly by their rules, is the humour of a
> 8   scholar. They perfect nature, and are perfected by experience: for natural abilities
> 9   are like natural plants, that need pruning by study; and studies themselves do
> 10   give forth directions too much at large, except they be bounded in by experience.
> 11   Crafty men contemn studies, simple men admire them, and wise men use them;
> 12   for they teach not their own use; but that is a wisdom without them, and above
> 13   them, won by observation. Read not to contradict and confute; nor to believe
> 14   and take for granted; nor to find talk and discourse; but to weigh and consider.
> 15   Some books are to be tasted, others to be swallowed, and some few to be

[3]Joseph Wood Krutch, "Life, Liberty, and the Pursuit of Welfare," *Saturday Evening Post*, July 15, 1961. Copyright 1961 by The Curtis Publishing Company.

16 chewed, and digested; that is, some books are to be read only in parts; others to
17 be read, but not curiously; and some few to be read wholly, and with diligence
18 and attention. . . .[4]

REVIEW TERMS

The strategies and skills you have learned in this chapter are reflected in the terms listed below; test your understanding of them to prove your mastery of unity and coherence.

A. Balance, chronological order, coherence, contrasting ideas, directional signals, independent clauses, interlocking connection, interlocking devices, key words, logical direction, parallel structure, pointer, point of view, spatial order, tone, transition words, unity

B. Antecedent, clause, demonstrative adjectives, demonstrative pronouns, dependent clauses, grammatical signals, grammatical subject, personal pronouns, phrases, pronoun, pronoun reference, relative pronouns

---

[4]Francis Bacon, "Of Studies." Many editions.

5

Understanding the Paragraph

Discovery, organization, style. These are the three main subjects of this book—if style is understood to include mechanics as well as rhetorical techniques. In Chapter 1 you learned to recognize all-inclusive statements and the value of communicating without misunderstanding. In Chapter 2 you studied two basic approaches to organizing the whole paper, Theme Pattern A (Inductive Organization) and Theme Pattern B (Deductive Organization). You learned the difference between these two approaches, their parts, and the relationship of the parts to the whole paper. You also studied the special relationship between these two approaches: **Question → Answer/Conclusion → Thesis.** In Chapter 3 you learned about discovering and limiting a general subject and about writing a pointed, complete thesis statement. You learned how to ask questions and how to get started. The chapter you just finished showed you how to give your paper unity and coherence through the techniques of single logical direction and interlocking connection. In this chapter you will look more closely at the nature and function of paragraphs; in the next one you'll study methods of paragraph development.

IN SEARCH OF THE PARAGRAPH

The chapter on organization showed the paragraph to be the basic building block in writing, in both inductive and deductive patterns. One way to define the paragraph is to describe it as a series of logically connected sentences presenting relevant ideas on a single subject. This is what thesis statements, topic sentences, unity, and coherence are all about. However, although this definition fits most writing, it doesn't explain the paragraph variations professional writers often use.

It is the definition of what many books call a "standard paragraph." *It is an accepted convention.*

But good writers often create a ***paragraph of convenience;*** that is, they see the paragraph as a *convenience*—for the writer as well as the reader. Occasionally writers will contrive a one-sentence paragraph merely to make an important idea stand out. Some writers create a series of short, related paragraphs to emphasize ideas, or events, or movement. Experienced writers know that a long paragraph will probably drive away the average reader. No one enjoys reading a page with no paragraph breaks. And so writers often break paragraphs that normally would function as standard building blocks. But doesn't this destroy continuity and fragment unity? Not necessarily.

In writing, the techniques of single direction and interlocking connection (unity and coherence) suggest a fundamental thought process that usually functions whether or not the boundaries of a standard paragraph are observed. Any good sentence—and especially a thesis sentence or a topic sentence—presents to the reader a promise or commitment to be kept. Consider, for example, these two sentences:

Pollution is a serious problem we all face.

Violence provides no answer to personal problems.

Most readers would not normally *expect* to find these two sentences next to each other in a paragraph, since the second can't be readily associated with the first. Most readers would *expect* the first sentence to be followed by one commenting on how we all face the problem of serious pollution. The *expectation* created by the second sentence is that it will be followed by some comment on the uselessness of violence. We *expect* logical connections.

Meaningful, rational thought processes *naturally* include this logical continuity or ***chain of meaning,*** no matter where the writer puts paragraph breaks. For example, a five-sentence paragraph on "Subject A" might be represented by this diagram:

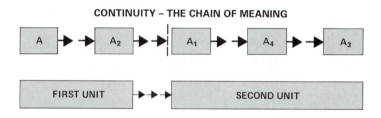

CONTINUITY – THE CHAIN OF MEANING

What the diagram tries to show is that if **A** is the sentence about pollution, then the first thoughts following it are *likely* to be about pollution, though perhaps not in the best order. Break this series anywhere you wish, and the resulting two units (paragraphs of convenience) still say something about "Subject A." This process of logical association lets a writer use paragraph breaks for convenience—to keep the reader's eye interested, to emphasize the main ideas in one unit of an argument, to create a pleasing effect on the page, and so on. Check any newspaper and you'll find that paragraph units of this kind will contain a number of related statements, even though they may not fit the definition of a standard paragraph.

Like the sentence, the paragraph is a *convention*. And most native speakers can spot both, even if they can't define them. Probably because of the way the brain first learned and stored language, speakers and listeners can tell where sentence and paragraph breaks occur. They anticipate certain patterns and logical connections.

You can test this idea for yourself by trying to decide where the sentence breaks occur in this paragraph you are now reading the breaks occur once the logical connection seems complete also you tend to hear the basic sentence patterns you first learned a noun-subject is usually followed shortly by a verb-predicate which is usually followed by a completer well aren't the sentence breaks easy to find paragraph breaks may be a little harder to spot because they represent longer units and broader logical connections in fact paragraphs do tend to have the kind of unity you learned about in the last chapter once you spot the sentence breaks you can then decide if the sentences belong together in a paragraph unit you can then signal the reader that a new paragraph unit is beginning by providing an indention the indention is simply a visual clue that makes it easier for the reader to find the paragraph breaks.

The two paragraphs you have just read discuss two ideas, sentence breaks and paragraph breaks. The word "breaks" links the two ideas in a way that makes it seem logical for the two to appear next to each other. Within each there is logical connection; between the two there is a broader logical connection. Together they seem to form a two-paragraph unit. They could be A_1 and A_2, or A_3 and A_4 in the diagram illustrating continuity in the chain of meaning.

Clearly, you can think of the paragraph in a number of ways:

1. As a group of logically connected sentences
2. As a block or division of a longer piece—an essay, a theme
3. As an extended sentence about one subject
4. As a convenient visual break to emphasize information

In the carefully organized papers you are asked to write, however, avoid breaking paragraphs merely for convenience. Build each paragraph unit so that it sticks to *one* limited subject presented in a series of sentences with a logical, coherent sequence. Save the paragraph of convenience for other kinds of writing—the best examples probably are newspaper reports and popular magazine articles.

In Chapter 2 you studied several kinds of paragraphs—introductory, developmental, concluding. In the rest of this chapter you will learn more about how to make introductory paragraphs work for you, how to be specific in developmental paragraphs, and how to write better concluding paragraphs. First you will practice writing the introductory paragraph using the funnel effect (as it appears in Theme Pattern A and Theme Pattern B). Then you'll be introduced to some other lead-in techniques. You will also learn how to make developmental paragraphs more *specific* and how to use *facts* as supporting evidence.

INTRODUCTORY PARAGRAPHS

Have you ever thought about how much information you've received by the time you've read through the first sentences of a writer's introductory pitch? Do you hear someone talking? Someone who seems aware of you as an audience? What is the writer's attitude toward his or her audience and subject—bold or hesitant, quiet or loud, formal or informal, serious or playful, expository or argumentative? Do you get a sense of order and direction? How specifically does the writer state the subject? Although you will concentrate mostly on two major purposes of the introductory paragraph of the short essay—the five-hundred-word theme is one example—you should be aware of some of the other problems and possibilities.

An essay's opening paragraph is supposed to *introduce:* Quite *independent of the essay's title,* the introductory paragraph leads readers into the subject and points them in a specific direction. Although both the leading and the pointing can be done in many ways, in all of the first essays you write, concentrate primarily on these two purposes:

1. In an opening statement introduce the general subject of the paper.
2. In the last sentence of the paragraph specifically introduce the *question* to be investigated or the *thesis* to be supported in the developmental paragraphs.

Depending on an essay's length and its writer's personal preference, the length of the introductory paragraph can vary greatly. In the short essays you will write at first, the introductory paragraph need be only about fifty to one hundred words, long enough to introduce the general subject and establish the specific dimension to be discussed. An essay longer than five hundred words might require a longer introduction, perhaps reviewing the background. The short essay, however, doesn't give you time for lengthy exploration of the subject or its background. State your subject as efficiently as possible. Then you can use the allotted space to best advantage, in investigating the proposed question or in developing and supporting a thesis.

An introductory paragraph starts with a broad, *general* statement introducing the subject of the essay, and then it qualifies this subject statement by narrowing it to the specific thesis statement (or the question to be answered). This thought pattern can be seen in the following diagram, a simplified version of the one illustrating the "funnel effect" (page 26).

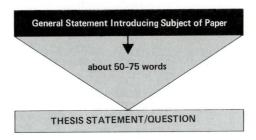

Here's an example of an introductory paragraph that follows this pattern.

> Some walls are concrete, others are imaginary. The concrete variety can be solid--brick, cement, rock. Run into one of these and you feel it. But you can also feel imaginary walls--intangible boundaries separating people. Of these the most important are those we use to guard our private spaces-- our baths, our bedrooms, our minds.

This paragraph starts with a general statement about walls and in just forty-nine additional words connects it with a specific thesis statement to be established in the remainder of the paper: the most important walls are those that guard our private spaces. Clearly, the importance of privacy will be supported in the developmental paragraphs.

This next paragraph creates the same funnel effect using only sixty-two words:

> At home, at school, and in the workplace, accidents change our lives. Nuclear accidents suggest frightening possibilities. Motorcycles, airplanes, trains, and cars--vehicles of all kinds--regularly are involved in accidents. But car accidents may be the biggest killer. And though we like to blame the car or the road or the weather, too often it's the driver who causes car accidents.

Here's an introductory paragraph designed to follow Theme Pattern A. Although it follows the "funnel effect," its last sentence ends with a *question* rather than a thesis statement (as you learned in Chapter 2). Just over one hundred words, it is a little longer than most introductory paragraphs you will first write; it explores, it anticipates, it leads. Does it have all the qualities you would expect in an introductory paragraph?

HOW SAFE ARE CHILDREN'S TOYS?

Guns, dolls, cars, hammers, shovels, games, paints, phones, and other children's toys sit on store shelves begging to be bought. Children cry for them; parents resist buying them. Eventually, however, the tearful child, or Santa Claus, or a doting grandmother wins. The toys are bought, perhaps lovingly wrapped, and carried into the home for the youngster to play with. But in committing this act of love, how many parents give some thought to the potential dangers hidden in the toys? Although some parents certainly do, many do not. Before buying any child a toy, an important question to ask is, "How safe are children's toys?"

Here's an even longer introductory paragraph—over 150 words—designed for a seven-hundred-word essay following Theme Pattern B. After introducing the general subject ("giants"), this paragraph zeroes in on "one giant," the Cardiff Giant hoax, and ends with an assertion that is the essay's thesis.

THE CARDIFF GIANT

Giants can be benevolent, like Prometheus, or savage, like the Cyclops. Some giants have been regarded as friends of the human race; others, such as the Philistine, Goliath, were its sworn enemy. Whether friend or foe, passive or violent, giants have always fascinated their human brethren. One giant interested Americans for over thirty years. He was known as the Cardiff Giant, and he was a hoax. That much was plain to anyone who looked at it in an objective frame of mind. The Giant was twelve feet tall, four feet wide, and of solid gypsum. It was conveniently discovered only a few feet underground, right on the spot where Stubby Newel planned to dig a well. And P. T. Barnum came out with his own "Cardiff Giant" after the hoax proved profitable. Even when giants started multiplying across the country, and newspaper reporters began proclaiming the fossil a fraud, up to 3,000 people a day paid a dollar to view the relic. Oddly enough, support for the hoax came from two factions usually in disagreement—religion and science.

Here, finally, are the first two introductory paragraphs from a newspaper article. (The complete article appears on page 419.)

> A lot of people talk about overpopulation; a comparative handful does anything about it. And that handful has not as yet accomplished much. Despite the best efforts of numerous international organizations and various government initiatives, world population still continues to surge at the rate of about 2 million a week.
>
> How do you slow down, let alone stop, the relentless increase of humanity? The best idea I've heard in a long time is to do it with money. To be precise, bank accounts. One for every woman in the world.[1]

This professional writer uses two short paragraphs to funnel down to his startling thesis. In addition, to echo and emphasize the thesis, he adds two rhetorical fragments. A more formal version would maintain the funnel effect, combine the two paragraphs, and probably connect the fragments into a completed sentence: "To be precise, do it with bank accounts, one for every woman in the world."

Although you will follow this basic pattern—the funnel effect—at first, eventually you will want to try other kinds of introductory paragraphs and to practice ways of making readers receptive to your ideas. You will remember from Chapter 2 that the diagram on the funnel effect suggests that the introductory paragraph should try to gain reader interest and acceptance before stating the thesis. You also learned from Chapter 2 that the end position for the thesis statement (and for the question-sentence in Theme Pattern A) is quite arbitrary. You could put it at the beginning or omit it entirely, letting readers determine for themselves the one logical point supported by the evidence presented in the essay. Whether you are presenting a question to be investigated (Theme Pattern A) or a thesis to be supported (Theme Pattern B), the opening paragraph clearly does more than merely introduce the limited subject. It should also establish the right tone, common ground with the reader, and a "blueprint" for the main points of the whole essay.

Here, then, is a more complete summary of the basic purposes to keep in mind as you write introductory paragraphs:

1. In an opening statement introduce the general subject of the essay.
2. Somewhere in the paragraph provide a *bridge* (transition) to lead the reader to one *specific* "part" of the general subject.
3. Anticipate the main divisions of your essay by stating the major points to be discussed (the blueprint).
4. Try to get the reader's attention, create interest *(emotional* and *psychological appeal)*.
5. Try to get the reader to respect and accept you and your views *(ethical appeal,* as discussed in the next section).

[1]Noel Perrin, "We Can Pay Young Women Not to Get Pregnant," *Houston Chronicle* 30 July 1990: 11A. Perrin teaches environmental studies at Dartmouth College in Hanover, N.H.

6. In the last sentence of the paragraph, specifically introduce the *thesis* to be supported (or the *question* to be investigated) in the developmental paragraphs.

The first and last of these purposes are the most important. Together, they make sure that the introductory paragraph *introduces* and *points*. If you fail in these two, no amount of clever effects with the others is likely to save your introductory paragraph. The second purpose simply reminds you to lead the reader from the general subject to the limited one by providing a "bridge" or transition. Success here will improve the coherence of the opening paragraph. The third reminds you that the order of the main points in the introductory paragraph is usually the order they will follow in the developmental paragraphs. Providing this "blueprint" will give the reader a greater sense of direction as the essay unfolds. Creating *emotional appeal* and *ethical appeal* (purposes four and five) takes practice, but when they succeed, these appeals give you a chance to be convincingly creative. First let's look at ethical appeal.

Using Ethical Appeal: Projecting a Self-Image

To make your essays more successful, always keep your reader/audience in mind. Because clear, well-supported logic often isn't enough to get a reader to say "I understand" *and* "I agree," professional writers use emotional (psychological) and ethical appeal. While emotional appeal is used to grab a reader's attention and create interest, ethical appeal is used to project a favorable self-image. You can give your ideas an added push by projecting an unmistakable, positive image of yourself and your character. When you have achieved this, you are using ***ethical appeal.*** Even such basic things as sloppiness, bad spelling, and questionable grammar can project a negative self-image. How you dress tells people something about you; how your paper looks also tells people something about you. Think about it.

Derived from the word ***ethos,*** the term *ethical appeal* is used to describe the appeal used in writing (and speaking) that comes from the apparent, projected *character* of the writer. To gain audience trust and to get them to believe what is said, the writer (or speaker) tries to create the *impression* that the writer is fair, or good, or intelligent, or sympathetic, or honest—or all of these. The writer may not actually possess these qualities, but if the work *appears* to have them then it could still convince the audience to accept the writer as a person and the ideas as presented. Ethical appeal works best when the writer really possesses the qualities projected by the work.

When you write, therefore, you should really *believe* what you are saying. If you are insincere or dishonest, your words will probably betray you, however careful you may be with ethical appeal. Here, then, are a number of well-known ways to get the reader to accept and to believe you:

1. Use unemotional, calm, unprejudiced language. (You want to appear reasonable and fair, not one-sided and inflexible.)

2. Try to establish a common ground of understanding with the reader. (Begin by emphasizing ideas or views that you *share*.)

3. If the reader clearly opposes your views, be sure to acknowledge the reader's merits. (Praise the opposition with restraint.)
4. Admit that your argument isn't perfect. (Try to point out *some* weakness in your argument.)
5. Make the reader aware of your qualifications. (Indirectly you should be able to make the reader see that you are intelligent, that you know your subject, that you have experience.)

On the basis of what you write and say, the reader will get a definite impression of the kind of person you are. This impression may very well convince the reader that your views are to be rejected (negative ethical appeal). You should begin to think about the kind of *ethical appeal* your class essays project to your teacher. What might a reader assume about careless spelling, dirty final copy, and late work? You can see, therefore, that *positive ethical appeal* can be crucial to the success of any essay you write.

The words you use reveal your prejudices more than you think. Suppose, for example, you want to convince an audience of teenage readers that using cocaine is dangerous. Consider the effects of these two opening paragraphs.

```
                            A.

     Young people are sadly mistaken if they think using
cocaine is a fun-ride to freedom. A person is really stupid to
think that the only payment is the cost of the coke. Anyone who
has any sense at all knows that coke is really dangerous
because the stuff is illegal, it creates in the addicted user a
severe dependence, and it turns users into bums who become
dropouts from society and from life.
```

Now compare Paragraph *A* and *B:*

```
                            B.

     Using cocaine is not an easy way to freedom. The user
always pays more than just the cost of the drug. Repeated use
of cocaine is dangerous because it is illegal, it creates in
the user a severe dependence, and it turns users away from
active participation in the community and in life.
```

Paragraph *B* tries to tone down the prejudiced judgments of the first version by removing such negative words as *sadly mistaken, fun-ride, really stupid, coke, really* [dangerous], *has any sense at all, stuff, addicted, bums, dropouts*. On the other hand, the first version might very well catch the favorable attention of a group of mothers who have seen their children arrested, expelled from school, and sent to jail. A calm tone is best if you want to appear *objective*.

Suppose Paragraph B started this way:

C.

    I'm told that cocaine frees the user from all inhibitions,
and I'm sure that is true. I'm told that legalizing the use of
alcohol is not the cause of its abuse, that the same argument
would hold for cocaine, and I'm sure that is true. I'm told,
also, that the occasional, moderate use of cocaine isn't really
harmful, and that may also be true. But just because there is
sincerity and some truth in all these statements does not mean
that using cocaine is not dangerous. [Now add Paragraph B to this
one and study the result.]

The writer of Paragraph *C* is trying to be personal, trying to establish a common ground of understanding with readers; he says he agrees with a number of opposing arguments. By saying that these arguments are "true" and "sincere," he is praising the opposition and giving up part of his own argument (using cocaine is *dangerous*). Even with the toned-down language of Paragraph *B* following it, Paragraph *C* would probably not convince too many readers. Try to decide why.

The writer of these three paragraphs could add one more ingredient to try to convince readers that he and his views are acceptable. He could mention or "project" his qualifications—personal experience, research, special skill. Study the following illustrations and try to decide what you would probably assume about the writer of each. Be prepared to support your opinion.

1. In the last issues of *Science* and *Science News* I read that medical authorities dispute the harmful effects of *Nicotiana glauca*. And the most recent issue of my *Christian Science Monitor* described corroborating research information.

2. Yesterday, both *Business Week* and *U.S. News and World Report* contained articles linking the use of marijuana to cocaine users. A recent issue of *The Wall Street Journal* echoes this view.

3. The last issues of *Time* and *Newsweek* both contained real good articles about cocaine use. The articles point out that experts disagree about the harmful effects of cocaine. Recently I saw a newspaper article that said the same thing.

4. Many people disagree about the harmful effects of using marijuana and cocaine. All the students I've talked to also disagree, and so do some of the so-called authorities.

With which writers are you more likely to agree? Why? Is the credibility of writers simply a matter of the kind of authority they use to support their views? What effect is produced by the kind of language used by each writer? What we assume, accurately or not, about each writer is based on what they *seem* to reveal about themselves; it is tied to the *ethical appeal* they seem to project.

Now, take another look at Paragraph *C,* above, and try to add two or three sentences to the beginning to improve the writer's credibility, the ethical appeal. To get additional ideas, study the following four introductory paragraphs from "In Favor of Capital Punishment," written by a professional writer.

D. In Favor of Capital Punishment

A passing remark of mine in the *Mid-Century* magazine has brought me a number of letters and a sheaf of pamphlets against capital punishment. The letters, sad and reproachful, offer me the choice of pleading ignorance or being proved insensitive. I am asked whether I know that there exists a worldwide movement for the abolition of capital punishment which has everywhere enlisted able men of every profession, including the law. I am told that the death penalty is not only inhuman but also unscientific, for rapists and murderers are really sick people who should be cured, not killed. I am invited to use my imagination and acknowledge the unbearable horror of every form of execution.

I am indeed aware that the movement for abolition is widespread and articulate, especially in England. It is headed there by my old friend and publisher, Mr. Victor Gollancz, and it numbers such well-known writers as Arthur Koestler, C. H. Rolph, James Avery Joyce and Sir John Barry. Abroad as at home the profession of psychiatry tends to support the cure principle, and many liberal newspapers, such as the *Observer,* are committed to abolition. In the United States there are at least twenty-five state leagues working to the same end, plus a national league and several church councils, notably the Quaker and the Episcopal.

The assemblage of so much talent and enlightened goodwill behind a single proposal must give pause to anyone who supports the other side, and in the attempt to make clear my views, which are now close to unpopular, I start out by granting that my conclusion is arguable; that is, I am still open to conviction, *provided* some fallacies and frivolities in the abolitionist argument are first disposed of and the difficulties not ignored but overcome. I should be glad to see this happen, not only because there is pleasure in the spectacle of an airtight case, but also because I am not more sanguinary than my neighbor and I should welcome the discovery of safeguards—for society *and* the criminal—other than killing. But I say it again, these safeguards must really meet, not evade or postpone, the difficulties I am about to describe. Let me add before I begin that I shall probably not answer any more letters on this arousing subject. If this printed exposition does not do justice to my cause, it is not likely that I can do better in the hurry of private correspondence.

I readily concede at the outset that present ways of dealing out capital punishment are as revolting as Mr. Koestler says in his harrowing volume, *Hanged by the Neck.* Like many of our prisons, our modes of execution should change. But this objection to barbarity does not mean that capital punishment—or rather, judicial homicide—should not go on. The illicit jump we find here, on the threshold of the inquiry, is characteristic of the abolitionist and must be disallowed at every point. Let us bear in mind the possibility of devising a painless, sudden and dignified death, and see whether its administration is justifiable.[2]

---

[2]Jacques Barzun, "In Favor of Capital Punishment." Reprinted from *The American Scholar,* Vol. 31, No. 2, Spring 1962. Copyright 1962 by the United Chapter of Phi Beta Kappa. Reprinted by permission.

These four paragraphs comprise only the *introduction* to a much longer essay that maintains the same ethical appeal throughout. In what ways does the writer reveal himself? His age, education, knowledge? Is he well known? Make a list of the words the writer uses that you probably wouldn't because they aren't in your active vocabulary. What kind of "voice" do these words convey? Point out at least three specific ways in which the writer tries to get on common ground with the readers who oppose his views.

Clearly, an introduction as long as this one would be out of place in a short essay. But the methods it uses to project the right ethical appeal could be applied to a one- or two-paragraph introduction in a much shorter essay. And there is no reason why you can't use some of its techniques in the one-paragraph introduction diagrammed for the five-hundred-word theme.

Remember, good writing demands *honesty* as well as supporting facts. If you assume that "anything goes" in order to convince your readers, you're likely to lose them when they spot insincerity because you overwork ethical appeal. Ethical appeal works best when writers really possess the qualities they try to project in their work (intelligence, fairness, objectivity, for example), when they really believe what they are saying.

Creating Reader Interest

A final point: Introductory paragraphs should also try to get the reader's interest. Usually this means trying to get the reader involved psychologically or emotionally. If you compare the following opening paragraphs with the diagram for the introductory paragraph, you will discover changes in the pattern as well as other techniques of creating reader interest.

E.

The bad news a manager gets from her staff could well be the most useful news she gets all year. Unfortunately, bosses tend to hear rosy reports and projections or none at all. And it's not surprising: Who wants to be the one to tell the chief her brilliant new marketing plan is a flop?

What managers need from subordinates is "effective backtalk," writes Warren Bennis, PhD, professor of business administration at the University of Southern California, in his book *On Becoming a Leader*. Movie mogul Samuel Goldwyn showed an understanding of this concept at some gut level, says Bennis, when, after six box-office flops, he brought together his staff and said, "I want you to tell me what's wrong with me and MGM. Even if it means losing your job."

Goldwyn, like too many other corporate leaders, obviously liked his yes-men, but he was smart enough to realize he needed to know the truth. There are two types of effective back talk, and in this instance he put his finger on both: Managers need criticism of their department or company as well as of themselves.[3]

[3]First appeared in *Working Woman*, April 1990. Written by Elyse T. Tanouye. Reprinted with permission of *Working Woman* Magazine. Copyright © 1990 by Working Woman, Inc.

Many writers use a ***provocative question*** to get started and to arouse the curiosity and interest of the reader. In example *E* the author uses several words to project a friendly, almost informal tone: *rosy, it's, flop.* She ends her short first paragraph with a challenging question that echoes the title and anticipates the real thesis of this article—how to get people to communicate honestly to the manager. This thesis appears as the very short, one-sentence last paragraph of an eight-paragraph introduction:

> *The manager who recognizes these communication blockers can* work to free the information flow from below.

Notice how this writer uses the second and third paragraphs of her introduction to establish a sense of authority (she quotes from a professional work) and create interest (the reference to "movie mogul" Sam Goldwyn). The second paragraph maintains the friendly tone with *movie mogul, gut level, box-office flops.* The third paragraph ends on a serious note ("two effective kinds of back talk") that also anticipates the thesis.

If your subject is important and current, sometimes you can state it in aggressive language designed to grab readers forcefully and get them involved quickly. Example *F,* even more clearly aimed at an audience of working women than example *E,* probably would catch both women and men—though not necessarily for the same reasons.

F.

By now the classic corporate good old boy—the cigar-chomping, backslapping type who said, with no shame, that women belong in the kitchen—is a nearly extinct species. Changing social mores, not to mention antidiscrimination laws, have made his blatant brand of sexism unacceptable.

The rising young male executive these days is a more enlightened breed: He was educated at a good coed school and talks proudly about his wife, the corporate lawyer. Of course, he would say, women should have the same opportunities as men, and he would think himself quite sincere.

That's why it comes as something of a shock when this man—who could be your peer, your subordinate or your boss—shows signs of some distinctly archaic attitudes. In the daily department meetings, he directs his conversation only to the men. Or he makes "kidding" remarks about your wardrobe or love life in front of a (male) vice president. Sometimes he'll flash you a patronizing smirk after you've made an important point.

Hardly worthy of an EEOC investigation—but that's what makes his behavior so insidious and why, in many ways, the New Old Boy is a more formidable obstacle than the old-style sexist pig. You can go for months working very well with him—until he feels threatened. Then he will use any weapon in his arsenal to fight back. That includes finding ways to tap into a lingering sexism and using it against you. "His methods are so subtle that some women may wonder if the behavior is intentional or if they are being overly sensitive," says Joyce Russell, PhD, an associate professor of management at the University of Tennessee in Knoxville. In fact, many women executives won't give a name to the problem for fear of being thought petty or paranoid.[4]

Although there's little doubt that example *F* quickly grabs attention with its first paragraph, some of its wording endangers the ethical appeal: *cigar-chomping, backslapping, blatant, smirk, old-style sexist pig*. Do you think the writers have succeeded in this example?

There are, of course, many other ways of introducing the subject and pointing the way for the reader. You can begin by logically dividing the subject into its parts and then telling your reader which you will emphasize. You let the reader follow your thinking process: *Flight? Flight of birds, flight of planes, flight of animals, flight of men, flight from freedom, flight to avoid punishment, flight from responsibility*. Or you can present an explanation or justification of your essay, particularly if it is one based on personal observation. Some writers lead up to a thesis statement by beginning the introductory paragraph with a relevant quotation or incident, a striking illustration, or an anecdote. Others begin by stating a view which they will oppose, creating interest through contrast.

G.

> The philosopher Diogenes lived in a tub in the market place. He owned the clothes on his back and a wooden cup; one morning, when he saw a man drinking out of his hands, he threw away the cup. Alexander the Great came to Athens, and went down to the market place to see Diogenes; as he was about to leave he asked, "Is there anything I can do for you?" "Yes," said Diogenes, "you can get out of my light."
>
> At different times, and in different places, this story has meant different things . . .[5]

H.

> Swaminathan Asokan dreams of water. It gushes out of a giant tap and fills bucket after bucket. But then he wakes up—to a nightmare. For at Asokan's house in Madras, India's fourth largest city, there is no water. The tap has long been dry. So he must get up in the dark of night and, laden with plastic pails, take a five-minute walk down the street to a public tap. Since the water flows only between 4 a.m. and 6 a.m., Asokan, 34, a white-collar worker at a finance company, tries to be there by 3:30 a.m. to get a good place in line. His reward: five buckets that must last the entire day.
>
> Compared with many of his countrymen, Asokan is fortunate. At least 8,000 Indian villages have no local water supply at all. Their residents must hike long distances to the nearest well or river. In many parts of the country, water is contaminated by sewage and industrial waste, exposing those who drink to disease.

[4]First appeared in *Working Woman*, April 1990. Written by Annetta Miller and Pamela Kruger. Reprinted with permission of *Working Woman* Magazine. Copyright © 1990 by Working Woman, Inc.
[5]From *A Sad Heart at the Supermarket* by Randall Jarrell. Copyright 1955 by Street & Smith Publications; copyright 1962 by Randall Jarrell. Reprinted by permission of Mrs. Randall Jarrell.

The sad state of India's water supply is just one sign of what could become a global disaster. From the slums of Mexico to the overburdened farms of China, human populations are outstripping the limited stock of fresh water. Mankind is poisoning and exhausting the precious fluid that sustains all life.[6]

Example *G* uses an *interesting **anecdote*** about a Greek philosopher to catch the reader and, in a general way, anticipate the rest of the essay. Example *H* uses a serious two-paragraph *narrative illustration* to prepare the reader for the article's thesis, which is presented boldly in the short third paragraph: *Mankind is poisoning and exhausting the precious fluid that sustains all life.* It is a "global disaster" that this writer is concerned about. These paragraphs, like the rest of the article, use specific factual details to establish a strong ethical appeal.

Introductions that take more than one paragraph give the writer a chance to make both an emotional and an ethical appeal. They can be fun to create and they're always a challenge. However, a careless writer runs the risk of using appeals that fall flat: They can sound insincere and exaggerated, especially if the writer's main method of catching readers is to entertain them. Before experimenting with emotional and ethical appeals, therefore, you should master the method of straightforward logical appeal (in *one* paragraph), as diagrammed at the beginning of this discussion of introductory paragraphs. You must conceive and state your thesis clearly if your additional efforts are to succeed. Turn back to page 41 and check the student theme on "Unleashed Danger" for emotional and ethical appeals. Do you think the appeals succeed? Or, you can study the examples of introductory paragraphs given on pages 351–55 in the section on tone; these also go beyond simple logical appeal.

EXERCISES

    A. By now you have probably written introductory paragraphs for several themes (see pages 77 or 81). Rewrite two of your introductory paragraphs, paying special attention to reader interest and reader acceptance, assuming that the reader is
      1. A group of parents *and* teachers
      2. Your best friend
    B. List the kinds of changes you made in Exercise *A,* including examples of words, sentences, and information. Be prepared to comment on the changes you needed to make most to alter the tone of your original paragraphs.

---

[6]Eugene Linden, "The Last Drops," *Time* 20 August 1990: 58. Copyright 1990 Time Inc. Reprinted by permission. (The complete essay appears on page 410.)

DEVELOPMENTAL PARAGRAPHS

Because they present the evidence you have to support your thesis statement, developmental paragraphs are the meat of your paper. They are the "standard paragraph" discussed earlier in this chapter. Again, a diagram explains the developmental paragraph.

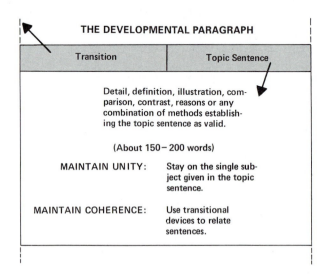

In this diagram, the space representing the first sentence in the paragraph is divided. The first part, labeled *Transition,* indicates that a word, phrase, clause, or sentence would normally be used in this position to provide the ***interlocking connection*** between this paragraph and the preceding one. The second part, the topic sentence, leads the reader *into* the paragraph. For example, look at this opening sentence:

> *I am arguing,* then, *that there are* two readers *distinguishable in every literary experience.* . . .

Then is a transition word that suggests a summing up and a continuation of the thought of the preceding paragraph. The *two readers* in the last part of the sentence are to be explained in the remainder of the paragraph.

Here's another opening sentence:

> *I have given the impression that the Farm was remote, but this is not strictly true.*

The first part of this beginning sentence points *back* to the preceding paragraph. The last points *forward* to the remainder of the paragraph by announcing its topic.

Here's another example:

Closely associated with this distinction *between author and speaker,* there is another and less familiar distinction *to be made.* . . .

This distinction in the first part of the sentence is *obviously* the subject of the preceding paragraph. *Another and less familiar distinction* is the controlling attitude pointing to the subject of *this* paragraph. Here's a final example:

Although fraternity expenses *are less hindrance to affluent members, the society* interferes *indiscriminately* with the studies *of its members.* . . .

Here *expenses* refers to the subject of the preceding paragraph; *interferes with the studies* is the controlling attitude pointing to the subject of the paragraph the sentence introduces.

These opening sentences all demonstrate transitional techniques needed for the reader's easy progress from the main point of one paragraph to the main point of the next. They provide the interlocking connection or coherence you studied in Chapter 4, and they apply to Theme Pattern A as well as Theme Pattern B. Use these techniques to give your whole paper coherence and apply them *within* each developmental paragraph as well, regardless of the method of development—whether you use factual detail, specific examples, comparison or contrast, reasons or causes, definition, or a combination of methods.

Equally important, you may already have discovered that most developmental methods are effective only if the information presented is factual or, if not, when the information is acceptable for other reasons. For example, your reader will probably respect your supporting evidence *if you are careful to distinguish between personal opinion and fact,* and *if your statements are specific rather than general.* Before examining specific methods of paragraph development, let's look at these two related problems so often found in the supporting evidence of developmental paragraphs.

Supporting Evidence: Fact, Opinion, Judgment, Inference

If you are to get your reader to say, "I understand," "I agree," you will need to learn not to use opinion, judgment, or inference as fact. Your *evidence,* the specific details presented to support your thesis statement (or a topic sentence in a paragraph), must consist of *facts* or clearly qualified *opinions, judgments,* or *inferences.* You will also need to know how to recognize some of the more important *fallacies* in reasoning.

FACTS

A *fact* is a verifiable statement, an accurate *report* of happenings, or accurate comments about persons, objects, or ideas. It is something everyone will *agree* to. For instance, the following sentences are all facts. All are verifiable.

1. Yesterday a car wreck occurred on Interstate 75 about three miles south of the city limits. (This statement is easily verifiable by the police or the newspapers. Anyone will accept the validity of either source.)
2. The Weather Bureau reported that 3.00 inches of rain fell on the city yesterday. (Here the question of fact is not whether 3.00 inches of rain fell but whether the Weather Bureau *reported* it. Again, this fact is easily checked in the newspaper or at the Bureau.)
3. There are sidewalks on each side of the street. (Anyone who questions this statement can check it simply by looking at the street. Probably, no one would want to question it.)
4. In 1982 the population of Texas was only 14,228,383. (Easily verified by the government census reports in official documents.)
5. Juan Rodriguez told me that he saw a leopard change its spots. (Here again the question is not whether Juan Rodriguez *saw* a leopard change its spots but whether he *told* me he saw it happen. As long as Juan will admit that he told it, the statement is verifiable. If he will not, the question must then be resolved by the reliability and reputation of the two people involved.)

OPINIONS

An *opinion* is a conclusion or conviction formed about any matter. An opinion is stronger than a mere impression but less strong than positive knowledge. It is usually based on evidence of some kind, as are most conclusions and personal convictions. Though an opinion may be thought out, it is open to dispute because the evidence can be logically sound or logically fallacious. An opinion is not a clearly proved matter. It is more likely to be a strong *feeling* based on selective impressions. To be convincing, opinion should be based on factual evidence, and the person expressing the opinion should be able to support it with fact and sound logic. If you should say, for example, "We lost the football game to the referee," you would probably be voicing an *opinion* based on a few, selective, momentary impressions. Didn't the team fumble or make any mistakes? Was it only one crucial bad call by the referee that sent the team to defeat? Are you really an objective, professional authority? Your opinion might be convincing, however, if you have such a reputation for experience with the subject and knowledge of it that you are recognized as an authority. You would then try to project credibility by using ethical appeal. But without either detailed facts or authority, an opinion may not be very convincing in any discussion.

JUDGMENTS

Many writers use the word *judgment* to mean any *opinion*. As used in this book, however, a judgment is an opinion expressing a person's *approval* or *disapproval* of objects, happenings, persons, or ideas. It's a limited form of opinion, also usually based on evidence of some kind, and also open to dispute because evidence can be logically sound or logically fallacious. Or evidence for the judgment can be simply inadequate, resulting in a hasty generalization.

For instance, suppose your family bought a house from a real estate agent named Jessie Washington and that before you made the down payment he promised to put a new roof on the house. When no workmen appeared to start work on the roof and you asked Washington when he was going to order the roof put on, he denied making any such promise. Your first reaction would probably be "Jessie Washington is a crook," and you might make this statement to your friends. But wait. Even though Washington has wronged you, to call him a crook is to say that he has been a crook and always will be a crook in business dealings. On the basis of this one example only, such a judgment is hardly justified. About all you can say is that in this situation you think he dealt with you unethically.

Or suppose you bought a Waumpum car two years ago and have now driven it for 75,000 miles with only a few minor repairs. You might well say, "The Waumpum is an excellent car." Yet the fact may be that yours is the only Waumpum to go over 50,000 miles without a major overhaul. Again, on the basis of experience with one car of one model, such a judgment is not justified. This judgment is clearly an all-inclusive, faulty generalization.

INFERENCES

To infer is to conclude something on the basis of observed evidence or experience. An *inference* is a conclusion, a projected guess about the unknown based on the known; it is a statement based on evidence. Again, this evidence can be logically sound or logically fallacious, it may be adequate or inadequate and, therefore, the statement isn't necessarily valid.

Imagine yourself in a situation such as this one: You observe a woman you have seen many times before, and you turn to your friend and say, "There goes that wealthy woman I see all over town." Your friend says, "Really? How do you know she is wealthy?" "Well," you reply, "she wears obviously expensive clothes, she drives a large, late model car, and she lives in a house that anyone would call a mansion." "That doesn't prove anything," says the friend. "She may just be deep in debt." Your friend would be right; you have not proved your point. You did, however, draw an *inference* about the woman: To *infer* is to *conclude*.

But an inference is not necessarily a valid conclusion because there are usually *other* conclusions you could just as logically derive from the evidence. For instance, suppose in the middle of a classroom lecture the student sitting next to you suddenly bangs his book closed, grimaces, rises, and stomps out of the room, slamming the door behind him. You might say to yourself, "Something the professor said made him angry." But again you might be wrong. The student may have had a sudden and uncontrollable stomach cramp from something he ate for lunch and had to leave the room at once. What other possible inferences could you draw on the basis of this evidence only? To be accurate and factual, how could you describe *and* comment on the episode?

Even when you have more than one piece of evidence on which to base a conclusion, the inference you draw can be all-inclusive and therefore faulty. The diagram on the next page provides a good example.

What this diagram shows is that on the basis of four rather limited experiences the student has made a general, hasty inference: "Today's teachers are dull and boring." Then, on the basis of this questionable conclusion and the same

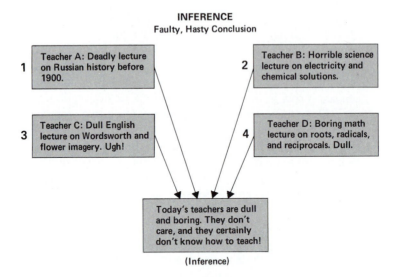

INFERENCE
Faulty, Hasty Conclusion

1 Teacher A: Deadly lecture on Russian history before 1900.

2 Teacher B: Horrible science lecture on electricity and chemical solutions.

3 Teacher C: Dull English lecture on Wordsworth and flower imagery. Ugh!

4 Teacher D: Boring math lecture on roots, radicals, and reciprocals. Dull.

Today's teachers are dull and boring. They don't care, and they certainly don't know how to teach!

(Inference)

evidence, he generalizes further: "They don't care" and "they certainly don't know how to teach." If the four experiences were fresh in the student's mind, he might *feel* quite justified in reaching his conclusions. But the evidence, clearly, does not support him. Did he consider *all* the lectures he has heard? Are the four teachers representative of *all* teachers? The student's final inference would be more valid and more acceptable if he said, simply, "The four lectures I heard today were dull and boring." Then he might add, "*Some* teachers don't *seem* to care, and they don't *seem* to know how to teach effectively." At least these inferences don't suffer from a fault most of us have—making faulty, all-inclusive generalizations. We jump to conclusions because we have a tendency to emphasize *similarities* and ignore *differences* in the experiences we've had. (See also the fallacy of "faulty generalization" under "Fallacies.")

Opinions, judgments, and inferences should not be stated *positively as if* they were valid conclusions or absolute truth. With care, you'll learn to avoid them and stick to specific, factual details when presenting supporting evidence. Or, if you decide to use opinions, judgments, or inferences as evidence, you'll learn to qualify the conclusions you reach. You will be accurate and specific. "Jessie Washington is a crook" will become "Jessie Washington behaved unethically." And "The Waumpum is an excellent car" will become "*My* Waumpum is an excellent car." Similarly, the inference "There goes that wealthy woman" will become "There goes the woman with the expensive clothes and the late model car." These revised statements are now more accurate and more specific. And they are also more convincing. Your reader is now more likely to say, "I understand," "I agree." As you can see, being specific and factual requires careful thinking and precise writing. Test your understanding of the material in this unit by doing the exercises at the end of this chapter.

Fallacies

Making supporting evidence logical and convincing, however, requires more than pointed accuracy in using facts, opinions, judgments, and inferences. It also requires some basic knowledge of *fallacies* and how they color the thinking and writing process. You can think of a fallacy in two basic ways: (1) as a statement that is false or clearly at odds with known *facts;* and (2) as an error in the reasoning process, a failure to follow the rules of logical inference. Fallacies of the first kind have problems in subject *matter* or content; they may lack facts, substituting emotional appeal for real content, or the facts may be distorted, or the information may simply be erroneous. Therefore, fallacies of matter can be corrected only if the truth (i.e., the facts) is known or can be determined. Statements like "The earth is flat" or "The earth is the center of the universe" are obvious examples of *fallacies of matter.* These fallacies of matter, however, don't usually appear in a clear-cut form; they are frequently tied to emotional arguments that further cloud the issues: "Everyone believes the earth is flat; therefore, it must be flat."

In fallacies of the second kind, conclusions don't follow logically from the previous statements; these *fallacies in reasoning* are misleading or deceptive and can be detected because the links in the chain of reasoning don't fit together, or because there are too few facts presented, or because assertions are made without proof. From the discussion of facts, judgments, opinions, and inferences you should already be able to see some of the reasons for *fallacies of matter* and *fallacies in reasoning.*

But it isn't easy to group all questionable thinking into just these two types. You will consider these obstacles to clear thinking under three main headings: **Emotional Argument** (fallacies of matter), **Faulty Reasoning** (fallacies in reasoning), and **Misuse of Language** (misleading language). However, try to discover problems in *subject matter* in those fallacies described as "faulty reasoning" (fallacies in the reasoning process).

EMOTIONAL ARGUMENT

1. *Attacking the person:*   In Latin, this fallacy is the *argumentum ad hominem,* which means that the attack is against the *person* rather than against the arguments presented. The point to remember is that whether a person is "right" or "wrong" does not depend on that person's personality or occupation. For example: "The senator's proposed legislation on health care should not be approved. How reliable can a man be who has been divorced and who has had extramarital affairs?" This fallacy can take the form of simple *name-calling,* as when a person is called a communist, or fascist, or left-wing radical, or liar.

2. *Appeal to the people:*   This is an unwarranted appeal for public support, not on the merits of an issue but because "we are all Americans," or "we are friends and neighbors," or "we all belong to the same church." This fallacy includes the all-too-familiar appeals to God, motherhood, home, and country. One form of this kind of appeal is sometimes called the "bandwagon appeal," asking somebody to do something because "everybody's doing it." Many advertisers rely heavily on this kind of appeal; in effect, they are asking people to "support their product by buying it." Because unwarranted appeals for group unity or public support can result in mob action, this kind of emotional appeal can be dangerous.

3. *Appeal to authority:*   Although ethical appeal can be enhanced by appealing to professional authority, such an appeal proves nothing. Because a certain person believes something (Einstein, the Pope, the U.S. president) does not necessarily mean it is true or desirable. Celebrities—movie stars, athletes, TV personalities, columnists—aren't necessarily good judges of clothes, foods, cosmetics, and other consumer products. The appeal to authorities is reliable when their views have been examined to determine (a) whether their views are based on *verifiable fact* rather than personal feeling, and (b) whether they are recognized authorities in the subject under consideration.

4. *Appeal to force or fear:*   This emotional appeal is essentially a threat—usually against a person's social, economic, or political status. For example, someone's boss may insinuate that the person may "lose his job" or be "reported to the authorities" for his *beliefs*. When an argument is attacked as "dangerous," the implied threat makes it an appeal to force. In these instances the aim is to *destroy* the argument rather than *solve* it.

5. *Red herring fallacy:*   The argument shifts ground, confuses or obscures the issues. This emotional trick gets its name from a hunting trick—dragging a strange scent across the trail to throw the dogs off the trail. In rhetoric, the red herring fallacy occurs when someone introduces a false issue or a totally irrelevant one, leading the argument away from the main point under discussion. Example: "I don't think men and women should receive the same pay for similar work. Women want equality and yet they ask for special treatment socially—expecting men to open doors for them, pay for the dinner date, and so on. They want to be equal and still be special." The red herring here is the introduction of the *social issue,* which has nothing to do with equal pay and equal job opportunities.

FAULTY REASONING

1. *Faulty (hasty) generalization:*   A general conclusion based on a few selected instances is a faulty generalization. It is an inference based on too little evidence. "Students cheat," "Teachers give too much homework," and "Haste makes waste" are all examples. You've already seen this problem in the form of *all-inclusive* generalizations. Generalizations hold true only for specific circumstances. Even important generalizations, such as "Thou shalt not kill" and "Thou shalt not lie," are not reliable for *all* situations. (See also "Inferences," in a preceding section.)

2. *Post hoc fallacy:*   This reasoning error appears when a person argues that because "B" follows "A," therefore "A" must be the *cause* of "B." For example: "Unemployment has declined again; as a result, the stock market has declined again"; "I walked under a ladder just before my exam. I failed my exam. The ladder caused the failure because a ladder is bad luck"; "I've been President for only six months and already the economy has improved." The full name of this kind of reasoning is the *post hoc ergo propter hoc* fallacy, which means, "after this, therefore because of this." It is really a form of hasty generalization.

3. *Talking in circles:*   Usually called **begging the question** or *circular reasoning,* this fallacy occurs when part of what is to be proved is assumed to be true: "Jack is a good man. Why? Because he is virtuous"; "We all know that minorities commit most big-city burglaries. Since Miami is a big city, the burglaries there must be committed by minority groups"; "You should buy the new Chevrolet because it's the best car on the market. Why is it the best car? Because Chevrolet makes it."

4. *Either–or fallacy:*   This fallacy is usually the result of oversimplification; it is often an attempt to prevent a logical choice by belittling or minimizing an important difference. Sometimes called the "black-or-white fallacy," it is a favorite of extremists, who ignore the many possibilities between two extreme positions. When someone

says, "You have only two choices, either 'A' or 'B' "—they are oversimplifying the alternatives, trying to make things simply black or white. For example: "Kelly's work has been unsatisfactory. Either he lacks the ability, or he is loafing on the job." When the choice is truly between only two available alternatives (life or death, a member or a non-member), then the reasoning will not be questioned.

5. *Argument from ignorance:*   This fallacy occurs when someone argues that something must be true because nobody has proved it false. Example: "The god Jupiter must exist because nobody has proved he does not exist"; "There must be human beings elsewhere in our Milky Way galaxy because nobody has proved they don't exist." This is *shifting the burden of proof*—assuming an assertion is true simply because it has not been disproved. Consider these arguments as *assertions* that require proof.

6. *Argument from analogy:*   To say that "A" shares similarities with "B" does not prove anything. "Death is like an unending sleep" may be poetic, but it actually misrepresents the truth. An analogy is a *comparison,* usually used to clarify or illustrate; it should not be used to "prove" a genuine relationship. The fact that two things being compared are alike in *some* ways isn't enough to prove that they are the "same." Although analogies can be useful, the *unexamined analogy* can lead to trouble in an argument. (For example, see the two illustrations on pages 181–82.)

MISUSE OF LANGUAGE

1. *Misuse of metaphor:*   While analogy usually is based on a number of resemblances, metaphor uses only a very limited number of similarities. People are called "lions," "cats," "sheep," "tigers," "wolves," "mice," "angels," and "monsters," usually on the basis of only one or two characteristics. Such metaphors are often confusing and misleading. Calling a woman a "cat," for example, may cause us to attribute to her many characteristics that she does not really have—sharp claws, a lashing tail, slit eyes, long fur, and whiskers.

2. *Confusing the abstract and the concrete:*   This fallacy is really a failure to distinguish between abstract and concrete words. Because people have a tendency to assume that abstract words refer to concrete entities, a writer can speak of "justice," "liberty," "freedom," "love," and "democracy" as if these words referred to concrete things. Unlike the word "chair," the word "freedom" has no concrete entity to which it can be linked. Here are some examples of this fallacy (called *hypostatization*): "Nature cares for all creatures, large and small"; "The State can do no wrong"; "Democracy guards human liberty"; "Science makes Progress."

3. *Equivocation:*   When a person deliberately or mistakenly uses the same word with different meanings in the same context, the resulting fallacy is called *equivocation.* This kind of argument looks good because use of the same word or expression throughout often disguises differences in meaning. Here, for example, are two people who seem to agree: *A* says, "I believe in free enterprise. The government should prohibit all cartels and monopolies and conspiracies by one part of an industry against other parts." *B* says, "I believe in free enterprise, too. The steel industry, auto industry, and the railroads should not be regulated by laws and government regulations." The problem is that *A* believes in *maximum competition* and *B* believes in the *absence of regulating laws.* The only real link between *A* and *B* is the term "free enterprise." Also called *semantic ambiguity,* this problem arises from the fact that almost all words are potentially ambiguous because almost all words have more than one meaning: "Anyone who puts productive machines out of commission is committing sabotage. Therefore, any person who goes on strike is committing sabotage, since that person is shutting down his machine, and that puts it out of commission."

EXERCISES

A. Identify the following statements as fact, opinion, judgment, or inference.
1. My history teacher has asked me a question in class every day for the past two weeks.
2. Don't take that history course—it's tough.
3. The referee penalized our team much more than seventy-five yards in that game with State University.
4. We lost that game to the referee.
5. We might have won that game with State University if we hadn't received so many penalties.
6. That referee was no good.
7. Since Congressman Stayaway missed several more House roll calls than Congressman Faithful, clearly Faithful has a better record in Congress.
8. Termites have damaged the floor joists in that house.
9. I studied everything and went to class every time, but I still didn't pass because the instructor doesn't like me.
10. That's the worst instructor I ever had.

B. The first statement in this group is fact and the others are based on it. Identify them as judgment or inference.
1. There is a six-foot fence around their house.
2. They don't want people to visit them.
3. Their house looks like a prison.
4. They want privacy in their home.
5. There must be something wrong with those people.
6. Those people are crazy.
7. They must have something to hide.
8. I don't like that house because it has a high fence.

C. List the inferences that might be drawn from these sets of circumstances.
1. He was weaving as he walked along. He staggered several times. He suddenly sat down on the curb and held his head in his hands.
2. The man ran from the store in great haste. He jumped in his car and sped away. The store's owner ran out on the curb and shouted something after him.
3. After dinner she went straight to her room, took out paper and pen, and spent busy hours writing her English paper. She received a failing grade on it.
4. Everyone must be convinced by now that cigarette smoking does contribute to the high incidence of lung cancer. Yet the rate of cigarette consumption in the United States increases each year.
5. While the population of the United States has been increasing, church attendance has been decreasing.

D. Select from each of the lists you have written for Exercise C the inference you think is likely to be the most valid, and indicate your reasons for thinking so.

E. Be prepared to discuss both the evidence and the conclusions in each of the following examples.
1. *Larry:* It's safer taking a long trip than driving into Houston to shop.
   Teresa: What? You've gotta be kidding.
   Larry: No, I'm right. You know that half of all auto accidents occur within five miles of home.
2. A recent article in *The New York Times* presented verified statistics showing that test scores on the Scholastic Aptitude Test are going down in the United States. The article concludes that students are not as well educated as they used to be.
3. Figures from the American Medical Society on Alcoholism show that more than 80 percent of alcoholics studied had a blood relative who also was an alcoholic.

The AMSA concludes that an inherited biochemical deficiency could be the reason why some people become alcoholics while others do not.

F. Test yourself on fallacies—problems in thinking. Using the fourteen fallacies discussed in this unit, identify the errors of thinking in the following examples. Be prepared to *explain* the errors, showing clearly that you understand the problem. Write explanations for 5, 9, 11, and 12.

1. Since the eruption of the volcanoes, the weather patterns have changed.
2. We can recognize that basketball players must be given special consideration in their grades, or we can let the university slip to last place in the college basketball race.
3. Here in the United States you are either a Democrat or a Republican.
4. If you work for a living, then you are in business. What helps business, therefore, helps you.
5. Apartment dwellers are inconsiderate. Late last night the tenants in the apartment next to mine played their stereo at full blast, and this morning some idiot on a motorcycle nearly ran me down in the parking lot.
6. As far as I'm concerned, the government is responsible for this country's economic problems.
7. It's clear to me that the very basis of American family life is threatened by those who advocate abortion.
8. I think we should all support the Christian Socialist Party in Africa. It's clear that the Pope does.
9. Everybody knows that teenagers are responsible for the majority of big-city car accidents. In a city the size of Philadelphia, it's logical, therefore, to expect that most car accidents involve teenagers.
10. People must be capable of moving objects by using telepathy, since nobody has shown that it's impossible to do.
11. All members of the PTA (Parent–Teachers Association) should support the local school board's decision to remove from our school libraries all books that offend our well-established moral standards. After all, if there were a flu epidemic we'd expect our health authorities to use their power to wipe it out. Pornography is worse than any disease, since it infects the morals and minds of our young people, not just their bodies. We should all applaud the school board's prompt action in eliminating this moral disease.
12. I think labor unions should be exempt from antitrust laws. Labor endures the hardships of layoff, loss of pay during strikes, the danger of high-risk jobs, and the antagonism of professional workers. With all their problems, they don't need the added hardship of government restrictions.
13. Politicians are dishonest, people lie, marriages end in divorce. What hope is there for the future?
14. You ought to watch the CBS evening news on TV. Everybody I know does.
15. Shortly after we elected the new President, our economy took a dive.

DISTINGUISHING BETWEEN THE SPECIFIC AND THE GENERAL

As you can see from the section you've just finished, developmental paragraphs require special care if they are to fulfill the expectations you create in an introductory paragraph. So far you've been asked to apply these basic techniques:

1. Use detailed *facts* to support all assertions.
2. Use detailed *facts* to qualify or support *opinions* and *judgments*.
3. Qualify *inferences* accurately to make them convincing and valid.
4. Recognize and correct *fallacies* in the reasoning process.

To these you will add a fifth skill before studying methods of paragraph development in Chapter 6:

5. Use *specific* rather than *general* ideas to develop your supporting evidence.

You must be specific no matter what method your developmental paragraph uses. Definition, illustration, comparison, contrast, reasons—all of these must be *specific* if your developmental paragraphs are to be convincing. Let's begin by distinguishing between the specific and the general.

The *general* includes *all* of a class, type, or group. For example, *people, men, women, boys, students, athletes* mean ALL people, men, women, boys, students, athletes. You probably recognize these as *all-inclusive terms;* they lead to such all-inclusive generalizations as "People can't be trusted," "Men are better drivers than women," "Students don't like to work." (See *fallacies of matter* in the section on fallacies.) If they are not to be misleading, they must be qualified by a modifier or an explanation or, perhaps, a specific name *(some people, a few men, Americans, some high school students, track stars at our high school)*. The general is so common in speech and writing that most of us often must add, "What I meant was. . . ." Learning to be specific will help get rid of all those "What I meant" qualifiers.

To change a ***general*** statement to a more ***specific*** one requires thought and some awareness of ***levels of generalization.*** For example, consider the following statements:

Young people don't dress right.

Students are careless about their clothes.

College students are too casual in dress.

Freshman girls wear jeans to class.

Hazel came to class barefooted, wearing jeans.

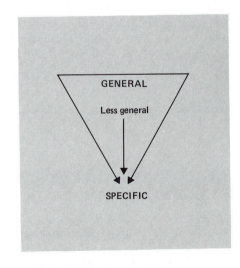

You have already seen this process at work in limiting both the subject and predicate areas of thesis statements. Here you can see it at work in making all supporting statements specific. The subject area of the original statement, *young people,* has become increasingly specific, until *Hazel* represents the specific illustration to be used. Similarly, *don't dress right* has been transformed into *barefooted, wearing jeans,* which isn't necessarily judgmental.

To make your supporting statements specific, you need to examine all the individual words carefully, choosing the exact, specific word that applies. For example, *structure* is a general word because there are many types of structures. The *specific,* on the other hand, refers to a *particular* in a class, type, or group. A building, a bridge, a television transmitting antenna, or a radar tower are each a particular of the general class, *structure.* Therefore, *building* is more specific than *structure* because it is only one member of the whole class. In the same way, *box* is more specific than *container* because a box is only one type of container. *Horse* is more specific than *vertebrate; boat,* more specific than *vehicle; meat,* more specific than *food;* and *furniture,* more specific than *household goods.*

But all these terms can be made yet more specific. *Building,* even though it is a type of structure, is still a general term that can be divided into types. A house, a service station, a garage, or a greenhouse can all be called buildings and are, therefore, more specific than *building.* Again, a filly is a type of a horse, a wooden crate is a type of box, a chair is a type of furniture, beef is a type of meat, and a kayak is a type of boat. These terms can be made still more specific by reference to building material, color, location, shape, or size. For instance, *brick house* is more specific than *house,* and *red brick house* is still more specific. *The red brick house on Lincoln Street* will specify even further by pointing to a particular house.

Similarly, beef is a type of meat, steak is one type of beef, sirloin steak is a type of steak, and grilled steak is one type of sirloin steak. And the sirloin can be made more specific by describing its appearance: *grilled sirloin steak, charred on the outside, raw within.*

To be convincing, your supporting information should project this type of specific detail. Your reader isn't likely to misunderstand an illustration like *grilled sirloin steak, charred on the outside, raw within.* Test your understanding of the general and the specific by doing the following exercises.

EXERCISES

    A. Select from the following groups the most specific in each group.
        1. (a) dog (b) mammal (c) large bird dog (d) setter (e) canine
        2. (a) a great boy (b) a witty and charming boy (c) a boy with a top-notch personality (d) a wonderful boy to know.
        3. (a) Margaret and Tony served a large quantity of food. (b) Their table literally groaned with an abundance of viands. (c) They served a quantity of foods suitable for the Thanksgiving season and tempting to the most jaded palate. (d) In the center of their table was a large baked turkey surrounded by dishes of cranberry

sauce, sweet potatoes, giblet gravy, rolls, and pumpkin pie. (e) Their cuisine was liberally illustrated by the delicious and nourishing products of culinary art distributed on the table in great number.

Answers: In Group 1, *setter* is the most specific term, because it names the type of dog involved. In this group, *mammal* is the most general term, followed by *canine, dog,* and *large bird dog*. If you picked *witty and charming boy* in Group 2, you were correct. In fact, of the choices here, this is the only one that gives any specific information about the boy. Group 3 is easy. Answer (d) is the only one in this group that tells specifically what food was on the table.

B. Select the most specific from each of these groups.
   1. (a) mosquito (b) blood-sucking insect (c) creature (d) invertebrate insect with two wings
   2. (a) man (b) person (c) individual (d) student (e) one
   3. (a) a building with an established place in the history of one of our largest states (b) a historical shrine revered by Texans (c) an old stone mission where, in 1836, Santa Anna's 4,000 Mexican troops, after a thirteen-day siege, defeated and slaughtered Colonel Travis' Texas garrison of 180 men (d) a rambling structure, once a church, where Texas history was made (e) an old mission where the Mexican forces massacred the defending Texans.
   4. (a) He wore a battered brown derby, a new light-orange sport jacket, red slacks, frayed white spats, and black shoes. (b) He was extremely oddly dressed. (c) His hat and his spats were certainly from another era, but his coat and slacks were modern, although their colors were so loud they hurt the eyes of the onlooker. (d) No piece of his clothing matched any other piece. (e) He wore an old derby, a coat that clashed sharply with the color of his slacks, spats, and shoes.
   5. (a) The book ends with a scene of mounting interest and excitement that leaves readers sitting on the edge of their chairs. (b) The ending of the book is simply magnificent in the gripping realism of its final scene. (c) At the end of the book, after Jack's followers, now complete savages, have set fire to the island and have hunted Ralph down to kill him, the reader understands with almost unbearable clarity the cruelty inherent in all mankind. (d) At the end of the book, after a series of highly interesting scenes, the reader is brought face to face with certain facts about modern life.

CONCLUDING PARAGRAPHS

You learned in Chapter 2 that a conclusion in a short essay such as the five-hundred-word theme could be a single strong sentence placed at the end of the final developmental paragraph. This kind of concluding statement should avoid using the exact words of the thesis. Rather, through a careful change in wording it should provide an "echo" of the beginning. It should remind the reader that the paper's main point has been made. This kind of conclusion is the simplest you will use.

But you will want to try other conclusions, including several sentences placed at the end of the final developmental paragraph, as well as concluding paragraphs that stand alone to restate the essay's central point and, often, the major support for that point. Recall, for example, this concluding paragraph from "The Case Against High School Football" (see page 40).

```
        There's no winner in high school football. When the count
is taken of money, time, energy, and suffering spent on "the
game," both teams have lost, no matter how many times the boys
first downed, touched down, touched back, or kicked goal. The
real score (obscured by the glaring numbers on the great
electric scoreboard) reads NOTHING to NOTHING.
```

This short student essay began with these two sentences:

High school football is an outrageous waste. The game is too expensive: in dollars and cents, in hours and minutes, in morale, and in physical well-being.

Note how the concluding paragraph "echoes" the essay's main supporting points—wasted "money, time, energy, and suffering." It does this without simply repeating the exact words of the thesis. Adding the "nothing to nothing" score idea provides emphasis through the "no winner" concept.

Here are the thesis statement and the concluding paragraph from another student essay:

```
                MOUSE, THE WONDER COUNSELOR

      . . . Sometimes the job seemed impossible, but no matter
how much I taught the girls, I regained tenfold what I gave. In
some specific matters, kids have been my best teachers. [End of
thesis paragraph]

      My summers with the kids at Camp Rocky Point did indeed
teach me much. I now own fourteen painted rocks, two pairs of
torn sneakers, innumerable lopsided keychains, and have a
definite dislike for powdered eggs and a scar on my left knee.
From the kids, however, I gained much more. Through their
optimism, flexibility, trust, and almost unconditional love,
they taught me how to face each day and grow.
```

From rocks, sneakers, and powdered eggs (none of which appears in the essay itself), the concluding paragraph moves to the restatement of the essay's main four supporting points. These serve as "echoes" to remind the reader that the writer has fulfilled the promise of the introductory paragraph—the kids have been the best teachers.

Finally, here's the concluding paragraph from "The Umbrella Man" (you'll find the complete essay in Chapter 7, page 210):

```
        The Umbrella Man will soon be forgotten because the
mystery is solved and the complex plot dispelled, but it is
only one of many theories and conjectures surrounding the
Kennedy assassination. The House Select Committee on
Assassination soon released its verdict, and it echoed the
Warren Commission--that one man, acting alone, killed President
Kennedy. If you are one who loves a murder mystery and won't
accept simple explanations, I hope you remember the Umbrella
Man before you believe another conspiracy story.
```

This concluding paragraph echoes the thesis sentence:

```
        The "umbrella man" conspiracy theory, one of those
considered by the committee, illustrates two truisms: that
Americans love a murder mystery and that they love to make
things complex.
```

The concluding paragraph reminds the reader that the "two truisms" have indeed been illustrated, adding a caution for easy believers to remember. All three of these examples are from essays following Theme Pattern B, Deductive Organization.

If, however, you were following Theme Pattern A, Inductive Organization, your concluding paragraph would be a **summary** of the investigations designed to answer the question posed in the introductory paragraph. For example, the first paragraph of the essay on children's toys (see Chapter 2, page 20) ends with the question, "How safe are children's toys?" The concluding paragraph would summarize the findings and answer this question, perhaps with a final sentence like this one:

```
    . . . Though many of the toys actually examined were found
to be safe, at least half of them had potential safety hazards
that could lead to injury. Clearly, not all children's toys are
safe.
```

Depending on how many toys you had examined (or research findings you had consulted), the length of this concluding paragraph would vary.

Longer essays, whether they follow Theme Pattern A or Theme Pattern B, will usually require the independent concluding paragraph. You will see one example of this in Chapter 8 ("Researched Writing and the Long Paper"). In theses, dissertations, and books, the conclusion can be a whole chapter. In reports, proposals, and other documents written for business and industry, both the introduction and conclusion are usually formal, independent units consisting of one or more paragraphs. The concluding units of such documents summarize the findings, restate the main issues, and often make recommendations. Unlike many academic essays, these documents also use headings to indicate these units. "Objectives" (purpose, aim), "Method of Investigation," "Scope of Investigation," and similar headings often appear within the introductions. The final unit may contain such headings as "Summary," "Conclusion," and "Recommendations," suggesting the kinds of information included.

The concluding paragraph is sometimes as important as the introductory one. It is the last chance to make certain that you've clearly communicated to the reader the meaning intended. It is the last chance to emphasize the main point of the thesis statement. It is also your last chance to hold the reader's attention right through the last word of the essay. Even in the simplest kind of essay—the five-hundred-word theme is a good example—the concluding sentence should not become merely a convenient way of stopping. Therefore, consider these possibilities for the concluding paragraph:

1. Summary: If your supporting development is complex or contains many points, (especially in a long essay), use the concluding paragraph to add coherence by bringing together the main points of the essay. Used with care in the concluding paragraph, certain transition words can be helpful and effective: "Clearly, then," "To sum up, then," "What are we to conclude, then?" or "What, then, are we to think?"

2. A striking comment: If possible, leave your readers with an idea they're likely to remember. The concluding paragraph from "The Case Against High School Football" (which you have just reviewed) ends with an effective, attention-getting comment: "The real score (obscured by the glaring numbers on the great electric scoreboard) reads NOTHING to NOTHING."

3. A final supporting point: You may save for the concluding paragraph an especially convincing piece of evidence or argument. It should be brief and forceful to be effective. Here, for example, are the last two sentences of an argument by Adlai Stevenson for world peace and stability: "Faith, knowledge, and peace— these will be the cornerstones of such a world. And, of these, none will avail if peace is lacking, if an atom split in anger turns out to be mankind's last reality" (from "Faith, Knowledge, and Peace," 1956).

4. Echo the introductory paragraph: The thesis (or the question) of the introductory paragraph can be restated, usually in a slightly different wording. This is what the writer of "People Problems" (see Chapter 2) tries to do in the concluding sentence of the last developmental paragraph: "Taking chances on the highway involves human judgment, human judgment provides opportunity for human error, and human error in a fast-moving car on the highway can kill."

Regardless of the length and kind of essay, the purpose of a conclusion (whether one paragraph or many) is to end the essay and give the reader a sense of completeness. In effect, you will have followed a fairly basic approach to writing:

1. Tell the reader what you are going to write about (introductory paragraph, thesis, question).
2. Write about it (body, developmental paragraphs, supporting evidence, details).
3. Tell the reader you have presented what you promised (conclusion, concluding paragraph, summary).

REVIEW TERMS

The following terms point to information discussed in the present chapter on the paragraph. Be sure you understand them before tackling the chapter on methods of paragraph development.

Anecdote, argument from analogy, argument from ignorance, argumentum ad hominem, appeal to authority, appeal to force or fear, appeal to the people, attacking the person, begging the question, chain of meaning, either-or fallacy, ethical appeal, ethos, equivocation, facts, fallacies in reasoning, fallacies of matter, faulty (hasty) generalization, general, hypostatization, to infer, inference, interlocking connection, judgments, levels of generalization, misuse of metaphor, opinions, paragraph of convenience, post hoc fallacy, provocative question, red herring fallacy, specific

6

Developing Paragraphs: How to Stay Focused

As the term *developmental paragraphs* implies, the paragraphs of the main body of an essay amplify the main points that *explain* or *support* the thesis statement (or question) of the introductory paragraph. This chapter examines some common methods of *developing supporting paragraphs.* From these methods you will learn how to keep your ideas focused on the thesis of your five-hundred-word theme. By using a *topic sentence* with a *pointer* and one or more of the methods of development, you will learn how to present your ideas logically in a specific direction to support your thesis.

You learned in Chapter 3 that a thesis statement can be understood as an implied question, suggesting an important relationship between Theme Pattern A and Theme Pattern B. You learned from the *quick-question* and *directed discovery* approaches that asking questions can generate thesis statements. If you learn to use the question approaches presented in this chapter, you can win an added thinking and writing bonus. You'll refine and extend the discovery skills emphasized in "Getting Started" (see page 47), and here you'll find new ways to discover for those thesis statements the kind of supporting ideas that fit into developmental paragraphs. A quick review of Chapter 3 at this point will help you understand the material in this chapter. Here we will use the same question approaches you studied in Chapter 3 to suggest the most important kinds of developmental paragraphs. Study the questions on page 153 to see the relationship between *thinking patterns* and *methods of paragraph development.*

Before looking at specific kinds of developmental paragraphs, however, you will consider a problem that affects them all: the need for specific details and facts. Without specifics, any paragraph can *sound* good and still fall flat on its logical face.

Though not one of the specific *kinds* of paragraph development, using specific details and facts also grows out of the *question–answer approach.*

USE SPECIFIC DETAILS / FACTS

Question: What are the facts? What are the specific details?

Whether you define, illustrate, analyze, compare, contrast, supply reasons, or give examples, your developmental paragraph must be factual and must use specific details. As you've already learned, it's not enough merely to *assert* an opinion, a judgment, or an inference. These must be qualified and supported with factual details. Merely to assert that "Men are better drivers than women," or "People can't be trusted," won't convince your reader. To avoid such comments as "VAGUE," "UNSUPPORTED," and "GENERAL," you need to ask, "What are the facts?" or "What are the specific details?" And you must ask these questions for every developmental paragraph you write.

Begin by studying these two student paragraphs and the discussion that follows each. Here's the first.

```
       People who buy foreign economy cars are not getting what
they think they are paying for. Foreign cars are not really any
more economical to operate than are American compacts. Those
who talk about how good foreign cars are simply don't know what
they are talking about. They should spend more time studying
the durability record of American cars than just thinking about
gas mileage. Many small foreign cars are worn out after 50,000
miles and have to be replaced. American cars will run much
longer than this. So foreign cars are not good buys.
```

This paragraph was written by a student who had been assigned a paper to write in class at the beginning of the semester. After completing this paragraph and making several attempts to continue writing the paper, the student appealed to the instructor for help: "What can I say next?" The instructor explained that the ideas of the paragraph were GENERAL and UNDEVELOPED, that the student needed to use SPECIFIC DETAILS to support the ideas and convince the reader. Consider, for instance, the general statement that foreign cars aren't more economical to operate than American compacts. What detailed facts could the student present to make this statement more than just an assertion? Without the specific details, foreign car drivers may not agree.

Here's the second paragraph.

> The adoption of a National Health Insurance Program (NHIP) will seriously damage our system of free enterprise and private medical practice. It would ruin many pharmaceutical companies and cause unemployment for thousands of workers. The control of medicine would pass from the doctors to the government. Our system of medicine has been working for nearly 200 years. Why destroy it now with NHIP? Why take control from the skilled hands of our doctors and give it to the untrained technicians of socialized medicine? This can't be allowed in the United States. NHIP must not be allowed to destroy our democratic system.

Feeling quite strongly about the subject, this student has let the discussion get out of hand. By itself, strong personal belief in something is not enough to convince others. And no matter how readers personally feel about a national health program, they certainly must recognize this paragraph as ranting, fanatic *opinion* unsupported by factual evidence. Logically, the paragraph is impossible. It equates free enterprise, private medicine, and democracy. These are not interdependent, as can be easily shown, and one does not necessarily collapse when one of the others does. How, for instance, can a national health program ruin *pharmaceutical companies* and cause unemployment? Must the practitioners in a national health program necessarily be "untrained technicians"? Are a national health program and socialized medicine the same thing, as this paragraph asserts? How can a national health program *destroy our democratic system?* How will it damage *free enterprise?* Because all these questions are unanswered, we must conclude that this student needs to support opinions with detailed, specific evidence.

To make these two paragraphs acceptable, their writers must apply the basic skills discussed in Chapter 5. Here they are again:

1. Use detailed *facts* to support all assertions.
2. Use detailed *facts* to qualify or support *opinions* and *judgments*.
3. Qualify *inferences* accurately to make them convincing and valid.
4. Recognize and correct *fallacies* in the reasoning process.
5. Use *specific* rather than *general* ideas to develop supporting evidence.

Here, then, is an example of a paragraph developed through use of details taken from the work of a successful writer. It answers a question that asks for supporting facts: "What are the responsibilities of Freeman Halverson?"

> Freeman Halverson is tall, fast on his feet and works hard. On his slender shoulders are laid many of the responsibilities of the little community. He is postmaster, storekeeper, driver of the school bus. He is chairman of the community study group, head of the newly organized conservation unit, president of the state

alfalfa seed growers' association, editor of the Hub News. He is on the citizens' advisory board of the state agricultural college. He leads the Lonepine band. At times he trains the girls' chorus. And then toward the evening he plays the clarinet at home in the family ensemble.[1]

This paragraph supports the pointer in the topic sentence, *responsibilities,* by detailing the duties Freeman Halverson carries in the community. When readers finish the paragraph, they can only agree with the author that Halverson does, indeed, carry many of the responsibilities of the community.

The following description of "the global electronic machine," also by a professional writer, uses specific details to emphasize the *worldwide scope* of the modern communication network:

> The world's biggest machine is much bigger than a nuclear aircraft carrier, a C5A Cargo Jetliner or even a continuous process automobile manufacturing plant. The world's biggest machine has become so big that it is invisible. It contains hundreds of millions of tons of coaxial cable buried under ground and beneath the oceans. It includes electronic switches and exchange equipment with enough gold and silver to fully stock a Tiffany's. Parts of the machine are invisible because they are flying in space—orbiting in circles a tenth of the way out toward the moon. Over a hundred of these space communications devices are relaying billions of messages around and across the earth every year. The machine parts are now so numerous no one can even count them. Billions of telephones, television sets, facsimile devices, telexes, computers, and radios are linked to this massive network. Each year it grows by leaps and bounds as fiber optic cables, new electronic switches and new "ports" are added to accommodate more users around the world.[2]

The paragraph develops in a way that makes its *pointer,* "world's biggest machine," convincing. In a subsequent paragraph the same author extends his description as he defines the "global electronic village":

> The Global Electronic Village is becoming a true reality. Soon people in remote Tuvalu and Niue in the South Pacific will be able to call Chicago and Toulouse or Chiang Mai, Thailand. In the last twenty years since the moon landing the number of people able to see global television events has expanded sixfold from 500 million to 3.0 billion people. Our ability to share information and knowledge is today creating global trade and culture. Tomorrow it will begin to form a global brain—a global consciousness. (120)

The writer has used the specific details in these two paragraphs to convince readers of the worldwide scope and importance of the global network provided by our electronic machines—computers, television, telephones, and related devices.

---

[1]From Baker Brownell, *The Human Community* (Harper & Row, 1950). Reprinted by permission.

[2]Joseph N. Pelton, "Future Talk: Coping with Our Electronic Technologies." In *The Future: Opportunity Not Destiny*. Ed. Howard F. Didsbury, Jr., 1989, pp. 119–120. World Future Society, 7910 Woodmount Ave., Suite 450, Bethesda, MD 20814.

Although descriptions often provide needed details, these specifics also can take many other forms—for example, reasons, or causes, or effects. In the following developmental paragraph, the writer is developing a point she has already made: the "health of older women in Latin America is largely a product of their experience and culture" and is influenced by their "subordinate social and economic status."[3] Notice how her developmental paragraph focuses on the idea of *status:*

> This low status is evident from the moment of birth when the midwife, on seeing the gender of the child, often quotes parents a bargain price for having helped to deliver a girl. Although not as extreme in Latin America as in some other parts of the developing world, girl babies may be neglected and young girls are routinely last in line when food is distributed. This practice is so widespread that a common proverb in this region captures it: "Cuando la comida es poca, a la niña no le toca"—When food is scarce, young girls get none.[4]

Here are some students' paragraphs developed through the use of supporting detail. Examine them carefully, for they will serve as models for writing developmental paragraphs. The first paragraph answers the question, "In what ways is the catcher similar to the quarterback?"

```
    The catcher is the "quarterback" of baseball. In effect,
he runs the team. He is the only man who sees every player on
the field and observes every move that takes place. He calls
the pitches by giving signals to the pitcher. Sometimes he
directs much of the defensive play by stationing the players in
key spots and by directing the moves against the opposition. He
is the one player on the team who can never for a moment relax,
whether his team is in the field or at bat. He must know wind
directions in every ball park, and he must study the opposing
batteries, the mental condition of his own pitcher, and the
spacing of his fielders. And he must watch runners on base,
keeping track of the tactical situation and seeing that the
rest of the team knows it also.
```

This paragraph uses the details of the catcher's job to establish the point that the catcher "runs" the baseball team. The writer includes enough specific details to make the point of the topic sentence quite clear. Here is another example paragraph; it answers the question, "Why couldn't the table be used?"

---

[3]Lee Sennott-Miller, "Growing Old in Latin America," *World Health* April–May 1990: 13.
[4]Sennott-Miller 13.

> **We could not use the table he showed us.** The wood was rough and saw-marked, and the finish was dull and spotty. The top was marked with several cigarette burns, although a label on the bottom promised that it was fireproof. Stains and scuffs also marred the top. The construction was poor; the joints were ill-fitted, and one leg was held on by a wire. The metal cap on one of the legs, provided originally to protect the carpet, was missing, and the drawer, which had no handle, could not be opened more than three inches. Furthermore, the table was too long for practical use and too wide to be easily moved through the door.

In this paragraph the writer uses abundant detail to support the *controlling attitude* of the topic sentence: The table was beyond use.

Here is a paragraph written by a student in business administration with previous business experience, which provides the specific details. What question does it try to answer?

> **Few people know the significant criteria that a financial manager must consider in devising a company's financial plan.** He must keep abreast of the general level of business activity to determine the company's needs for assets and funds. To operate efficiently he must interpret and use money and capital markets to the fullest extent. He must know the effects on tax rates and whether an increase or decrease in the tax rates will raise or lower the desirability of indebtedness. He must cope with seasonal and cyclical variations in business activity. To as great a degree as possible, he must know the nature and effects of competitors. He must use regulations and customs to the best practical extent. He must know the credit standing of his company and strive to keep it as high as possible.

Written by an expert bowler, a student who gave bowling lessons at the student union lanes, the next paragraph provides convincing, specific details. It answers the question, "Why is consistency the real secret for a bowler?"

> **Although the experts all claim that proper form is the most important aspect of good bowling, consistency is the real secret for a bowler.** The bowler may push the ball away too fast, but if she does it the same way every time, her game will

> not suffer. She may backswing too high or too low, but if the
> ball reaches the identical spot in the backswing arc in each
> delivery, the high score compiled for each game will not reveal
> the weakness. She may take more or fewer steps than the
> recommended four, as long as she takes the same number in each
> approach. The bowler may even commit the unpardonable sin of
> releasing the ball while on the wrong foot, provided she can do
> it exactly the same way every time. In other words, the bowler
> can do everything "wrong" and still be an expert bowler, if she
> will do it "wrong" consistently.

This paragraph makes its point about consistency being the secret of good bowling by detailing the things a bowler may consistently do wrong but still bowl well.

This paragraph, written by a young high school teacher who had returned to college after teaching for a year on a temporary certificate, persuades through the use of specific details to answer the question, "What many jobs is the teacher responsible for?"

> Although many people think the work of a public school
> teacher is easy, the school teacher actually has the
> responsibility of many jobs. Before school opens in the fall,
> the teacher must attend meetings every day, sometimes for as
> long as a week, in preparation for the fall semester. During
> the semester, the teacher has official meetings, such as those
> for the faculty and the PTA, that he must attend. He is
> expected to sponsor clubs, coach athletics, and help promote
> such fund-raising activities as carnivals. He has monitorial
> duties to perform when he is not in class. But, of course, his
> primary job is teaching. He must teach about five classes a day
> and sometimes conduct an additional study hall. In preparation
> for instructing his classes, the teacher spends about five to
> six hours a week preparing materials and reading to supplement
> textbooks. Still he must spend some of his "off" hours at
> school helping individual students having personal problems or
> difficulty learning the material. Furthermore, he must grade
> papers, evaluate the students' progress, make reports of
> various kinds, and even interview the parents of his students.
> But this is not all. To keep up with new teaching methods and
> programs the teacher himself must often go to school in the
> summer and attend conventions. And occasionally he must take
> part in such community affairs as luncheons and civic
> organizations.

After reading this paragraph with its detailing of teachers' duties, aren't you ready to agree with the point stated in the topic sentence?

EXERCISES

If you have trouble finding details for this assignment, you should check the "discovery exercises" on pages 82–83.

A. List as many details as you can to support three of these statements:
   1. Each new job provides new opportunities (or demands) (or roles).
   2. A young woman (or man) can't get along without a car.
   3. Language influences the success of its users.
   4. Humans exhibit territorial behavior in many ways.
   5. The use of hard drugs should (or should not) be legalized.
   6. The dating game can be a nuisance (or joy) (or disaster).
   7. I hate cleaning my apartment (or house).
   8. Racial tensions in the United States recently have (or have not) increased.

B. Rewrite one of these paragraphs and supply appropriate, specific detail at the italicized points. Freely add and change material that is there.
   1. He stared at the carnival booth as if hypnotized. From it issued *highly amplified sounds* that almost overcame him with their intensity. Its *many* shelves were stacked with a *variety of flashy goods. Some men stood* at the booth's counter intently concentrating on looping hoops over a *stick some feet away.* A *few boys* chased each other through the *people* standing at the booth.
   2. They entertained the *group of visitors* as best they could on such short notice. First, there was a *lunch outdoors,* followed by a long walk through *interesting gardens* of the city. After resting, the visitors were taken to a *local museum* where they were shown *relics of bygone days,* and in the evening they saw a *stage show of their choice.* At the end of the planned activities, the host took the entire group to his home, where they were joined by *friends of the hosts* for a *party to climax the delightful visit.*
   3. *A manufacturing firm nearby* went all out to advertise their products and to establish goodwill in the community at the same time. They ran a contest in the spring that offered a *costly grand prize* for the best slogan in praise of their products. In the winter, they offered an all-expenses-paid trip *to the South* for the merchant who arranged the ideal display of the firm's products. For the consumer who could think up original ideas for putting the firm's merchandise to use, *there was a reward.* The community showed its appreciation *in many ways.*
   4. The bride-to-be found it difficult to display all her lovely gifts in her parents' *small* home. Relatives from out of town had sent *lightweight but expensive knicknacks.* All these had arrived early and seemed to get choice spots in the living room. *Gifts of bedding and kitchenware* from nearby kinfolk covered the dining table and took all the space *on other furniture* in the dining room. Chums in her own age group had sent the bride more *"upbeat" gifts,* and these took over the TV room and what shelf space *there was in the house. Her gift from the groom's parents,* the one she treasured most highly of all, because of its resale value, the bride kept in her purse and brought out for frequent praise from *interested parties.*

C. Using one of the lists you made in Exercise *A,* write a paragraph developed through the use of detail. If you have trouble getting started, check again the exercises beginning on page 82.

METHODS OF PARAGRAPH DEVELOPMENT

As you work with specific kinds of paragraph development, study the following chart. It provides a list of key questions to fit each approach. Also, you'll see, separated at the top of the chart, the basic question that applies to all developmental paragraphs.

QUESTION	PATTERN
What Are the Facts or Details?	Item By Item, Part By Part
How do you define "X"?	Essential definition
To what group of things does "X" seem to belong?	Classification, sorting, grouping
What parts can "X" be divided into?	Analysis/part-by-part description/division
What steps or events comprise "X"?	Analysis/step-by-step description/process
What other words mean about the same as "X"? What are its synonyms?	Synonyms for the primary word
What are some examples or illustrations of "X"?	Exemplification, illustration, specific instances
What causes "X"?	List of causes
What are the effects of "X"?	List of effects
What is "X" similar to?	Comparison/point-by-point analogy
What is "X" better than?	Point-by-point comparison
To what is "X" inferior?	
Why does "X" happen?	List of reasons, causes
How did "X" happen?	Narration/story/chronology/sequence of events
What is "X" different from?	Contrast/point by point

These questions should tell you that how you *think about* a subject—how you approach it through the *discovery process*—will almost automatically lead to a specific method of paragraph development or a *combination* of methods. In fact, the pattern of the developmental paragraph is limited only by your imagination and willingness to try new combinations or new methods: a question/answer pattern, a topic-illustration-restatement pattern, an assertion followed by statistics (facts), a concept followed by images or word pictures. *Thinking patterns precede and determine the pattern of the written paragraph.*

PARAGRAPH DEVELOPMENT BY USE OF DEFINITION

Questions: What is "X"? How do you define "X"?
To what group of things does "X" belong?
What "parts" can "X" be divided into?
What steps or events comprise "X"?
What other words mean the same as "X"?
How does "X" work? How does "X" function?
What are some examples or illustrations of "X"?

Most *expository writing* can be considered a form of *definition*. To *explain* something you have to describe it, or tell what kind of thing it is, or enumerate its parts, or show how it works. That is why developing paragraphs by using definition can turn on the answer to many implied questions. In this section, therefore, you will find under the single heading of "Definition" some half-dozen methods of developing paragraphs: *defining, classifying, analyzing, providing synonyms, using examples or illustrations, describing a process, enumerating.*

Before studying the different ways of using **definition by classification** to develop paragraphs, read through this definition of *democracy* written by the well-known historian Carl Becker. Examine how he uses definition to develop specific supporting details.

> **In this antithesis there are, however, certain implications, always tacitly understood, which give a more precise meaning to the term democracy.** Peisistratus, for example, was supported by a majority of the people, but his government was never regarded as a democracy for all that. Caesar's power derived from a popular mandate, conveyed through established republican forms, but this did not make his government any less a dictatorship. Napoleon called his government a democratic empire, but no one, least of all Napoleon himself, doubted that he had destroyed the last vestiges of the democratic republic. Since the Greeks first used the term, the essential test of democratic government has always been this: the source of political authority must be and remain in the people and not in the ruler. A democratic government has always meant one in which the citizens, or a sufficient number of them to represent more or less effectively the common will, freely act from time to time, and according to established forms, to appoint or recall the magistrates and to enact or revoke the laws by which the community is governed. This I take to be the meaning which history has impressed upon the term democracy as a form of government.[5]

This paragraph starts with a conventional topic sentence using *implications* as the pointer to give the paragraph unity. It explores these implications chronologically by use of examples starting with the Greeks (Peisistratus) and ending with France's Napoleonic Empire. When the paragraph comes to a statement of the principal implication, which is Becker's one-sentence definition of democracy, it maintains coherence by reference to the Greeks, mentioned early in the paragraph. After the

[5]Carl Becker, *Modern Democracy.* Copyright 1954 by Yale University Press. Used by permission.

one-sentence definition, . . . *the source of political authority must be and remain in the people and not in the ruler,* the paragraph explains in more detail what this definition means. In the final sentence, the paragraph declares that this is the meaning of democracy that Mr. Becker is to use throughout his book, and the reader need have no misunderstanding of what he means when he uses the word.

As Becker has done in his paragraph, you must also often define the terms you use in writing if there is any chance that your reader may assume a different meaning from the one you intend. Many a verbal argument has ended with: "It has become obvious that we are not defining our terms in the same way, and I won't accept your definitions." This usually ends the argument, because without acceptable definitions there is no real communication. One group talks about one thing and the other group is arguing another, although they seem to be talking about the same subject. Throughout one presidential campaign, for instance, there was a running argument over whether the United States is a republic or a democracy, but nowhere in the campaign were these two terms satisfactorily defined, nor was the distinction between the two made clear. Consequently, the argument carried little weight with the voting public. So make the meaning of the terms you use in writing clear to the reader. Defining terms will not necessarily make the reader agree with you, but without adequate definitions, you run the risk of being completely misunderstood.

When you decide a term needs defining, you will not want to copy verbatim the dictionary definition and use it in your paper with a phrase like "Webster defines socialism as . . ." Such a practice defeats your purpose, which is to make clear the exact meaning *you* are attaching to a word. You can devise your own definitions, using one *or more* of the basic methods described in this section. And remember, to define is to explain; expository writing most often succeeds by using one or more of the methods of definition.

Definition By Classification

Questions: How do you define "X"?
　　　　　　　To what group of things does "X" belong?

Nearly everybody *classifies,* sorting things into groups *(clusters).* To classify effectively, you must be able to see *shared relationships.* Suppose, for example, that you have a large laundry basket full of many mixed *items:* several sheets, many towels, dozens of socks, dozens of shirts and skirts, pantyhose, t-shirts, underwear, Levi's, and more. To place each of the items into its proper *class* or group is to classify it—an easy matter because you've done it so often. In fact, you are so familiar with some of the things around you that seeing only a *single member* of the entire group prompts you to think of it as a member of its class. You think of someone as "an 'F' student," "a doctor," "a woman," "a man," and (on occasion) "an animal." You automatically think of things as being part of a group or class. You know that socks go with socks (in the same drawer, hopefully), chicken and beef are *meats,* and cabbage—you're sure—will be found in the produce section among the *vegetables.* You look for the results of the basketball game in the newspaper's *sports section,* and if you're looking for a used car at a bargain price, you'll probably turn to the *want ad section* and check the listings under *used cars.* Whether you are faced with *many* items that must be sorted into their proper classes or only *one* item that must be defined as a member of some larger class, you are **classifying.** In this section you will learn how to extend this skill and apply it to paragraph development.

You can, therefore, *define* an item by classifying it. Sometimes called the ***Aristotelian*** method, definition by classification is giving the ***essential definition*** most often found in dictionaries. The method of giving an essential definition is quite simple, involving only two steps:

1. Place the item to be defined in its family (genus, class).
2. Differentiate the item from all others in its family.

As essential definition explains what makes a thing what it is and also distinguishes it from all other things. It explains a thing's fundamental nature. For instance, if you wanted to define the relatively simple word *bridge* (to indicate that you do not mean the card game or a part of the nose or of a pair of spectacles or an arch to raise the strings of a musical instrument or a raised platform on a ship or a transition in music), you would first place the word in its *family:*

>   *A bridge is a structure.*

You have already seen that *structure* is a general term including many specific structures, a bridge being one of them. The second step, then, is to differentiate *bridge* from all other structures—buildings, houses, towers, and so forth. This can be done by naming its function:

>   *A bridge is a structure carrying a roadway over a depression or obstacle.*

Examine these definitions by classification:

Word	Family	Differentiation
Bird	vertebrate	covered with feathers and having wings.
Insect	invertebrate	having head, thorax, and abdomen, three pairs of legs, and one or two pairs of wings.
Chair	seat	having four legs and a back, for one person.
House	building	serving as living quarters for one or more families.

In defining by classification, there are three missteps to guard against.

1. Look at this definition of *net* from Samuel Johnson's dictionary:

A net is any reticulated fabric, decussated at regular intervals, with interstices at the intersections.

Since you know what a net is, you can probably make out what this definition says. But suppose you don't know what a net is. Could you possibly make sense from this definition without looking up several words in the dictionary? Therefore, when you see the need to define a word, follow this rule:

Don't use words that might not be clear to the reader (that are obscure, ambiguous, or figurative).

Suppose you read this definition: *A democracy is a government in which the citizens are sovereign.* This is a perfectly good definition as long as you know what the word *sovereign* means. The writer could have avoided the use of this word by spelling out its meaning: *A democracy is a government in which the citizens hold supreme power by periodically electing, either directly or indirectly, their representation in the government.*

2. Consider this definition: *A democracy has a democratic form of government.* Here no defining has taken place, because the definition offered leaves readers at the same place they started. The writer has used a form of the defined word in the definition itself. This definition has the same trouble: *A good man is one who performs good deeds.* The word that is being defined here is *good*, but this word has also been used in the definition of it, so nothing has been clearly defined. Stick to this rule, also:

Don't use any form of the defined word in the definition of the word.

3. Look at this definition: *Democracy is when the citizens are sovereign.* You have probably been told throughout your school career that you can't define by saying that something "is when . . ." Logically, you cannot make the adverbial construction (showing condition), *when the citizens are sovereign,* equal to the noun, *democracy;* but the use of the verb *is* says that they are. In defining, then, you must also remember this rule:

The word defined must always be equal to the definition.

That is, wherever the defined word is used, you should be able to substitute your definition in its place. You can say, for instance, *The government of the United States is a democracy,* but when you try to substitute for the word the definition of democracy just considered, complete nonsense results: *The government of the United States is when the citizens are sovereign.* So a good definition of democracy is needed, one that can be substituted wherever the word itself is used. Here is a definition that will work: *Democracy is a form of government in which the citizens are sovereign.* Now we can substitute this definition for the word *democracy* in the sentence, *The government of the United States is a democracy: The government of the United States* **is a form of government in which the citizens are sovereign.** Note that placing the word in its family and then applying differentiation corrects this misstep.

Here's a famous paragraph that classifies to develop an idea. In "Civil Disobedience," Henry Thoreau writes about excessive governmental control, asserting, "That government is best which governs least." In developing the idea that citizens should be "men first and subjects afterward," he says:

> The mass of men serve the state thus, not as men mainly, but as machines, with their bodies. They are the standing army, and the militia, jailers, constables, *posse comitatus,* etc. In most cases there is no free exercise whatever of the judgment or of the moral sense; but they put themselves on the level with wood and earth and stones; and wooden men can perhaps be manufactured that will serve the purpose as well. Such command no more respect than men of straw or a lump of dirt. They have the same sort of worth only as horses and dogs. Yet such as these even are commonly esteemed good citizens. Others—as most legislators, politicians, lawyers, ministers, and office-holders—serve the state chiefly with their head; and as they rarely make any moral distinctions, they are as likely to serve the devil, without *intending* it, as God. A very few—as heroes, patriots, martyrs, reformers in the great sense, and *men*—serve the state with their consciences also, and so necessarily resist it for the most part; and they are commonly treated as enemies by it. A wise man will only be useful as a man, and will not submit to be "clay," and "stop a hole to keep the wind away . . ."

You can also use classification to get you moving—into a paragraph or into a complete essay. The student who wrote "Plant People" uses logical analysis (division) in the introductory paragraph to establish the members (classes) of a large group ("plant people"). The basic classes established in the thesis of this paragraph then become the organizational basis *(blueprint)* for the whole essay. Each subsequent two-paragraph unit then develops through *definition by classification*. For example, in paragraphs four and five "plant freaks" are those *plant people* who are "not average or typical" because they talk and sing to their plants.

PLANT PEOPLE

1   As growing house plants has become increasingly popular, the modern American home has become a greenhouse peopled by growers. Almost any home boasts a variety of hanging, climbing, or potted plants, with growers to match them. Plant people are a diverse lot, with no common background to distinguish them. Male or female, married or single, rich or poor; housewives, executives, taxi drivers, secretaries—all are susceptible to

the plant bug. However, the careful botanical eye can sort these plant people into three distinct classes: the Simple Plant Growers, the Plant Freaks, and the People Who Don't Want to Grow Plants, But Want to Have Them Around the House Anyway.

2   The Simple Plant Growers (SPGs) are average, typical Americans who--simply--enjoy seeing things grow. For them, growing plants is a rewarding hobby, a means of brightening the home naturally. The SPGs are admirers of Mother Nature who feel a closeness to the earth. Many of them are farmers at heart who have simply been trapped in the city. SPGs often have backyard gardens as well as house plants and would rather grow their vegetables than buy them at the store. You know the type.

3   Mrs. G. Thumb (no relation to the Jolly Green Giant) is an SPG. Her house is alive with healthy, attractive green plants. Various types of ferns hang from strategically placed baskets, and African violets reach toward a fluorescent light above a north window. Begonias, pepperomias, bromeliads, and potted strawberry plants inhabit various corners, window sills, and alcoves. An avocado tree graces the livingroom. Mrs. Thumb grows herbs in the kitchen window and tomatoes, carrots, and corn in a small backyard garden. Plants enrich her life and beautify her home, Mrs. Thumb feels, and she is fascinated with working with them. She has many plants and they are an important part of her life. But Mrs. Thumb is not a Plant Freak.

4   Plant Freaks (PFs) are a strange bunch, not average or typical by any stretch of the imagination. PFs, like SPGs, appreciate and care for their plants, but they go about it differently. They talk to their plants, they sing to their plants, they give them funny little nicknames, and they stroke them lovingly. PFs never hurt their plants' feelings and never leave them unattended for more than a few minutes at a time. PFs love their plants dearly.

5   Mr. Igor E. Gore is a retired mortician's assistant. He is also a Plant Freak. Ferdinand (the Boston Fern) is his favorite, but Boris (the benjamina) and Phyllis (the philodendron) are also close friends. Phyllis is the best-behaved, reaching out and upward in any light. Boris tends to sulk and droop, apparently offended by Ferdinand's special place in Igor's affections. Still, Igor tucks them all in at night, checking for temperature, humidity, and voracious night crawler. But it is only Ferdinand who gets the bedtime story. Igor is certain he can't sleep without one.

6   Finally, there are the People Who Don't Want to Grow Plants, But Want to Have Them Around the House Anyway (PWDWGPs). This species of plant people doesn't like to mess around with plants; they have a deep-rooted fear of soiling their hands or being invaded by spider mites. Learning how to relate to green things and how to care for them doesn't appeal to them in the least. They simply want to own them, perhaps because it's fashionable or they saw a picture in House and Garden. PWDWGPs are getting back to nature to keep up with the Joneses, or perhaps the neighbors across the street.

7   Mrs. Ino Water III is a locally recognized PWDWGP. As expected, she doesn't want to grow plants, but she wants to have them around the house anyway. She and her husband live in a luxurious plant-filled penthouse in a place called Garden Towers. Mrs. Water III loves to tell her friends that she is "particularly fond of those darling little plants with the

> ruffledy leaves and the purplish flowers." But she owns dozens
> of other plants, including some with "prickly ridges" that
> sometimes "get little green warts that turn into flowers." It's
> such a chore, she complains. "You see, the plants keep dying,
> and new replacements have to be bought regularly. What a
> nuisance."
>
> 8   Although plants mean different things to different people,
> almost anyone can find a special kind of personal fulfillment
> through them. The Simple Plant Growers derive pleasure and
> enrichment from growing and nurturing their plants. The Plant
> Freaks have companions to talk to, living things to relate to.
> And the PWDWGPs have found a disposable status symbol. Plant
> fever is soon expected to reach epidemic proportions. Hopefully
> those with SPG blood in them will be hardest hit.

Although this paper is about twice the length of a five-hundred-word essay, its organization pattern is basically the same. Its method of development is primarily through definition—by defining through classification of each of the members of a larger group. Draw a picture-outline of this essay, showing introductory paragraph and thesis statement, developmental paragraphs with topic sentences, and concluding paragraph with restatement. Note that the essay has *three* developmental units, each with two paragraphs. What is the relationship between the paragraphs of each two-paragraph unit?

Definition By Synonyms

Question: What other words mean about the same as "X"?

You can readily define a difficult word by using *synonyms*—other words meaning the same thing. But this method works only if the synonyms are easier to understand than the original word. For instance, if you aren't certain that your readers will know what *prevaricating* means, you can define it by saying it means *lying* or *fibbing*. Or you can say that to *limit* is to *confine, qualify, restrict* or *define*. Or you can define *bad* as meaning *bath* in German but *evil, wicked,* or *naughty* in English. To use synonyms successfully in a definition, however, you must understand and observe three limitations:

1. Synonyms are useful in definition only when they are closer to the reader's experience than is the word defined.
2. Usually synonyms are not definitions but only approximations. They may best be used to clarify other kinds of definitions.
3. Even fairly close synonyms can have unlike connotations, affecting both tone and meaning.

The third of these limitations needs explanation. You can understand the problem if you examine the following groups of words, assuming that the first word in each group is the definition target for the synonyms that follow. Consider the problem in terms of *sender* and *receiver,* pointing out some of the misunderstanding in tone and meaning that the chosen synonyms could create.

1. *Friendly:* sociable, jovial, genial, approachable, chummy, companionable, affectionate, harmonious
2. *House:* home, dwelling, abode, residence, pad, domicile, address, living quarters, place
3. *Corpulent:* plump, heavy-set, fat, chubby, overweight, bulky, obese, stocky, paunchy
4. *Disapprove:* condemn, denounce, criticize, blame, dislike, censure, hate, resent, oppose
5. *Saving* (modifier): sparing, thrifty, tight, frugal, economical, careful, penny-pinching, scrimping, parsimonious, budget-minded

You should see at once that a *friendly* person isn't necessarily *chummy,* and someone who is merely *approachable* isn't very friendly. The *place* you live in may not be your *home,* which could be an apartment rather than a *house.* The *heavy-set* person probably doesn't mind being called *overweight,* but would probably resent being called *fat.* And a *saving* person who is *thrifty* and *sparing* isn't necessarily *tight* and *penny-pinching.* In developing any paragraph, then, choose synonyms with great care to illuminate your meaning and prevent misunderstanding.

Definition by Specific Example

Questions: What is an example of "X"?
What examples show that "X" is true?

An example is a specific fact, incident, item, or quality that is representative of all in a group. It is used to clarify, illustrate, or explain a more general term or idea. Used in this way examples *define* the term. Here are some *examples:*

Cars—Buicks, Chevrolets, Toyotas, Datsuns, Volkswagens, Oldsmobiles— have brought with them great advantages and great problems.

*I've found that students at my college are very **inconsiderate.** Last week someone stole my bicycle, for two weekends now the loud stereo next door has robbed me of sleep, my roommate uses my clothes and books without asking, and I can't count the number of times I've nearly been run over by cars.* (Caution: Can a limited number of specific examples establish a general principle or really prove anything?)

***Red** is the color of blood, tomatoes, beets, maraschino cherries, pimentos, and most ripe apples. **Green**—that's the color of live grass, spinach, lettuce, most leaves, lima beans, and cucumbers.*

*Today's colleges must satisfy the needs of increasing numbers of **students with special educational goals:** computer-oriented students, working wives in increasing numbers, engineers and managers interested in foreign*

employment, older students trying to upgrade and update their skills,
teachers returning for specialized training or refresher courses.

Defining through example will help you clarify for the reader many of the general
terms you may have to use. Often, a single, well-chosen example can illuminate a
general term:

> *Today's colleges must satisfy the needs of increasing numbers of **students***
> ***with special educational goals.** Perhaps the most striking example is*
> *today's computer-oriented student. Students in technical writing turn to*
> *the computer to learn word processing. Accounting majors and prospective*
> *managers learn to use the computer in business. Science majors*
> *increasingly turn to the computer for analysis in the research lab. And*
> *students in nearly every major are learning to use computer data banks*
> *for information retrieval and library research.*

You should be able to tell from these *examples* that paragraph development through
defining examples overlaps with other methods—use of specific details, use of
narrative illustration, and enumeration, for example. As you will see shortly,
examples and illustrations needn't be restricted to the definition of terms *within* a
paragraph. They can also be used as a basic method of developing a whole
paragraph, or even a whole paper.

Definition by Enumeration

Question: What members ("parts") make up the term being defined?

In defining words that name general classes of objects, you can sometimes simply
list the members of the class represented by that word. For example, you can define
decathlon by listing the athletic events included.

> *The decathlon is an athletic event in which each contestant competes in the*
> *100-meter, 400-meter, and 1500-meter runs, the 110-meter high hurdles,*
> *the javelin and discus throws, shot put, pole vault, high jump, and broad*
> *jump.*

Or you can define the Pentateuch by listing the books of the Bible that compose it.

> *The Pentateuch is Genesis, Exodus, Leviticus, Numbers, and*
> *Deuteronomy.*

Though some classes are too large to enumerate, often you can list enough
members of the class to make the definition understandable. For instance, to list all

the seasonings would take more space than the definition is worth and would make tedious reading. But some of the seasonings can be listed and the effect is the same as if they were all listed.

> *Salt, pepper, thyme, oregano, marjoram, are* **common** *seasonings. Fruits* **such as** *lemons, oranges and grapefruit are citrus fruits.*

Note that the definition admits the listing is not complete. And, again, you must be sure that the reader will be more familiar with the members of the class than with the name of the class itself.

Definition by Function: Operational Definition

Questions: What steps or events comprise "X"?
How does "X" work or function?
What stages comprise the process "X"?

The *operational definition* concentrates on *function* by describing *how* something operates or how something is done. To define an effect, for example, you could define how it "works."

> **Acceleration:** *When you step on the gas pedal of your car, the effect you feel is acceleration.*

> **Frictional electricity:** *When you walk on a rug, the rubbing of the shoes on the rug builds up a negative charge in you so that when you touch a metallic object a small spark is discharged and you feel a shock.*

Seen in this way, the operational definition describes the effect being defined; it describes *how* the effect "works" or functions.

This same *operational definition* can be applied to concepts.

> **Prejudice:** *A prejudice is a judgment or opinion about a person, race, religion, nation, or any particular group or object without careful consideration of facts. To feel antagonism at first meeting toward students from a rival college without actually knowing the students is to be prejudiced toward them.*

A dictionary definition of *prejudice* (following the Aristotelian method described above under Definition by Classification) might read as follows: *Prejudice is a judgment or opinion that is preconceived and usually unfavorable.* What the operational definition above does is to show how prejudice operates. The same method can be applied to a word like *claustrophobia,* which a dictionary might define as *morbid fear of enclosed or confined places.* To this you could *add* an operational definition, which could read as follows:

> *Persons who, when confined in a small, enclosed space such as an elevator, experience a rapid quickening of heartbeat, acute agitation, and a desperate desire to leave the enclosed space are suffering from a mental disturbance known as claustrophobia.*

Again, the operational definition shows how claustrophobia operates (or functions). Because it describes what happens, the resulting operational definition is a short ***process explanation*** suitable for inclusion in a developmental paragraph. And because the various "steps" and "stages" of the operational definition are the result of logical division, this method should be compared with paragraph development through ***logical analysis*** (see page 167).

The Extended Definition

Questions: What is "X"?
How do you define "X"?
To what group of things does "X" belong?
What parts can "X" be divided into?
What steps, stages, or events comprise "X"?
What other words mean about the same as "X"?
What are some examples of "X"?

Because the ***extended definition*** uses a combination of methods, all the lead questions on definition can be applied. Although an extended definition is often only a paragraph, clearly it can be much longer, using a combination of definition methods to explain the term to be defined and starting with a definition by classification. The diagram of the paragraph developed by an extended definition shows that one or all of the methods can be used.

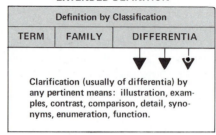

To see how this diagram works, apply it to the following student paragraph on jargon. The first sentence of the paragraph gives the term, *jargon,* names the family or class to which the term belongs, a *special vocabulary,* and presents the differentia, *understandable only to the users*. The student then extends the definition by presenting a series of short examples to explain why jargon is usually *understandable only to the users*.

Jargon is a special vocabulary understandable only to the users. In Elmstown, one has only to pay a visit to Joe's Wagon Diner, at Tenth and Canal, to hear examples of its use. Table orders are taken by the waiters and given to the kitchen in such a manner that one hears expressions like, "One-eyed jacks up, no hog," meaning an order of two eggs fried on one side and no bacon; or "One brown with dogs, add straight," meaning an order of hash brown potatoes with sausage, and coffee without cream or sugar; or "Cream it with hens," meaning creamed eggs on toast; or "Dunk one all the way," meaning doughnut and coffee with cream and sugar.

In the examples that follow, the topic sentences also appear highlighted to remind you that each developmental paragraph is considered part of an essay. More important, each paragraph represents one supporting point to show the validity of a thesis statement. In the paragraph on jargon, for example, "Jargon is a special vocabulary understandable only to the users" might point back to this thesis: "Using jargon can *create interesting problems in communication.*" As you read each developmental paragraph, try to phrase a thesis statement that it reflects.

Here are three more example paragraphs of extended definitions. Notice that the topic sentence (highlighted in each paragraph) is a definition by classification.

A "turista" is any human being who finds himself in strange surroundings that he is not able to appreciate. The word is usually employed to describe middle-aged persons who have just started traveling. It is a fit description for a woman who upon arriving at the Grand Canyon rushes to the gift shop to buy postcards before she has had a look at the sight she has traveled to see. The word, although it has a feminine ending, is applied to the male traveler who goes to the Louvre and stares at female forms in the flesh and not at the Venus de Milo. The "turista" is constantly comparing his present surroundings with the heaven-on-earth where he lives, making all listeners wonder why he had not remained in that choice place. He is a steak-and-potato man and is constantly griping about the food. He refuses to eat reindeer meat in Norway, but longs for it as he is eating lasagna in Italy, proving to uninterested listeners that he has been to Norway. The word is never applied to anyone except Americans, meaning anyone from the United States, and is used by persons in foreign countries to show their dislike for individuals who spend their money ostentatiously while traveling.

> Elephant jokes, popular some time ago, are humorous devices consisting of two lines—a question and an answer—in which an elephant is pointlessly involved. An example of this joke would be "What was the elephant doing on the expressway?" and the answer, "About three miles an hour." Or, with a risque twist, "How do you make an elephant fly?" Answer, "First, you get an eight-foot zipper." Often these jokes are presented in a series, each joke related to the last. A short example would be, "How do you tell an elephant from a blue-bird?" Answer, "Elephants live in trees." Question, "How did the elephant get flat feet?" Answer, "From jumping out of trees." Question, "Why do elephants jump out of trees?" Answer, "How else could they get down?"
>
> A thunderstorm is a weather disturbance having lightning and, consequently, thunder within it. There need not be rain falling, but without lightning it is merely a rain shower and not a thunderstorm. Thundershowers come in three types—air mass thunderstorms, frontal thunderstorms, and thunderstorms caused by unstable air over mountains. Air mass thunderstorms are common along the Gulf Coast in the afternoon during the summer. Frontal thunderstorms occur in the fall, winter, and spring along and ahead of cold fronts. Since there are no mountains in this area, the third type of thunderstorm never occurs here. Sometimes towering to heights of 50,000 or 60,000 feet, thunderstorms can be quite severe, bringing rain and hail and sometimes spawning tornadoes.

EXERCISES

A. Study the following statements to determine which are acceptable definitions. Mark acceptable definitions with a <u>C</u> and unacceptable ones with a <u>U</u>. Indicate specifically what is wrong with those you have marked with a <u>U</u>.

1. Lapidation is when you throw stones at someone.
2. A lanyard is a rope used in firing certain types of cannon.
3. A blue-collar worker is a member of the blue-collar class.
4. Malapropism is a form of cacozelia, sometimes referred to as acyrologia.
5. English is where expository writing is learned.
6. Asyndeton is the opposite of polysyndeton.
7. Tabasco is the trade name of a sauce made from red pepper.
8. Pentameter is a line of verse consisting of five metrical feet.
9. Second childhood means senility or dotage.
10. Freedom of speech is an element basic to any democracy.

B. Choose one of the following items for definition:

Congestion	Ideal wife (or husband)
Televangelists	Promiscuity
Population control	Racism
Free speech	Punk rock
Obscenity	Soul brother/sister
Stand-up comics	Panic (or fear, or hate)

1. First, write a series of short definitions of the chosen item (two or three sentences for each definition)—one definition for each of the following methods:
   Classification: To what group of things does the item belong?
   Synonyms: What other words have about the same meaning as the item?
   Examples: What are some typical representatives of the item?
   Operational: How does the item function (operate, work)?
2. After you have completed these shorter definitions, combine them into a coherent *extended definition.* You may expand or modify your short definitions a little to make them work in a single extended definition.

C. Write a brief explanation (two or three sentences) to show how all of the following might be used in a definition of one of the items listed above in *B:*
   1. *Analysis:* Into what "parts" can the item be divided?
   2. *Comparison:* To what other things is the item similar?
   3. *Exclusion:* How is the item different from all others in its class?
   4. *Analogy/metaphor:* In what limited ways is the item similar to something more familiar and easier to understand?

D. Write a short operational definition of one of the following. Begin (or conclude) your definition with an Aristotelian definition:
   1. Acrophobia   3. Fiction
   2. Smiling   4. AIDS

PARAGRAPH DEVELOPMENT THROUGH LOGICAL ANALYSIS

Questions: What parts can "X" be divided into?
               What kinds (of "X") are there?
               What steps, stages, or events make up process "X"?

Let's begin by rephrasing the guide questions to provide specific examples:

What "parts" can Miami be divided into?
What "parts" can *Macbeth* be divided into?
What "kinds" of pollution are there?
What "kinds" of love are there?
What stages comprise the process of cell division?
What steps make up the process of changing a tire?

These questions all have one thing in common: they assume that a *larger* item can be "divided" into *smaller,* constituent parts. The larger item can be a substance, a situation, or a process. The questions all represent a thinking process through which we can logically *divide* something, *separating* it into its components. They also suggest that definition, classification, and analysis are the results of related yet different thinking processes.

A definition is an explanatory statement about a term. It can relate that term to a larger **class** of things, or to a larger idea or concept (as in the ***Aristotelian definition***). In Chapter 3 you learned that analysis is the *logical division* of a concept or an individual member of a class into its "parts." The starting point for logical analysis is a complex concept or whole that can be explained if it is "broken down" into components. The starting point for classification, you will remember, is a significant number of individual members of a class; the "parts" are already there. Classification, then, is in a way the reverse of analysis. *Analysis divides the whole into parts, classification sorts the parts into groups.* Here's an illustration to help clarify these similarities and differences:

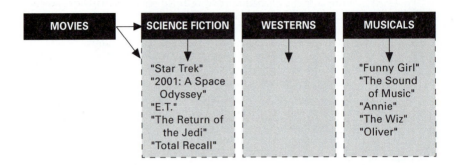

Analysis makes it possible for you to write about a general subject like "Movies" by dividing the whole class (movies) into subclasses (science fiction films, westerns, musicals, thrillers, war films, comedies, dramas, etc.). The subclasses can also be divided, giving the individual members that make up the whole class and its subclasses. Using analysis and the question approach you learned in Chapter 3, you might approach the general subject of "movies" in this way:

> What kinds of movies are there?
> What kinds of science fiction movies are there?
> What examples of movies can I think of?
> To what class of movies do *Annie, E.T., Born on the Fourth of July,* and *Butch Cassidy and the Sundance Kid* belong? *Aladdin? Friday the 13th? Rocky? Lethal Weapon? Total Recall?*

If you answer the first question by listing all the movie titles you can think of, you are "dividing" the subject through analysis. If you group these titles into different classes, you are classifying them. The question asking for examples points to one method of defining—science fiction movies: for *example,* 1, 2, 3, 4; musicals: for *example,* 1, 2, 3, 4. Clearly, a complete separation of these three thinking processes is extremely difficult.

The following selection shows how a professional writer uses logical division to explain the basic nature of *matter* (a large, complex item):

> The international competition has spurred remarkable progress in the effort to understand nature's mysteries. Says theoretical physicist Steven Weinberg of the University of Texas at Austin: "Before, we had a zoo of particles, but no one knew

why they were the way they were. Now we have a simple picture." That picture, known as the Standard Model, is based on a set of theories that attempt to describe the nature of matter and energy as simply as possible. The model holds that nearly all the matter we know of, from garter snakes to galaxies, is composed of just four particles: two quarks, which make up the protons and neutrons in atomic nuclei; electrons, which surround the nuclei; and neutrinos, which are fast-moving, virtually massless objects that are shot out of nuclear reactions. These particles of matter are, in turn, acted upon by four forces: the strong nuclear force, which binds quarks together in atomic nuclei; the weak nuclear force, which triggers some forms of radioactive decay; electromagnetism, which builds atoms into molecules and molecules into macroscopic matter; and gravity. An entirely separate set of particles—the bosons—are the agents that transmit these forces back and forth between particles, people and planets.

The basic "family" of particles is supplemented by two more exotic families, each of which has a parallel structure: two quarks, a type of electron and a type of neutrino. These two extra families are all but extinct in the modern universe, but they apparently existed in the searing heat of the Big Bang, and only accelerators can re-create them. In fact, all of the quarks in all of the families have been found or re-created—except for the one called the top, which is believed to be the heaviest of all (its mass is at least 90 times that of a proton). Because it would complete the set and thus vindicate decades of theory building, the top quark has become the object of an intensive international search. And because the top is so massive, it will take the energy of the most powerful accelerators to produce it.[6]

Here's an example of an introductory paragraph that uses analysis to anticipate the entire essay:

> So you want to know about City Community College? Although the name is fictitious, the school is not. Its students are real, its instructors are real, its administrators are real. Its buildings are equally real: the large, domed building that houses the registrar and the president; the long, low building with a glass north wall; the small cluster of student dorms; the computer center; the odd-looking science building and its neighboring engineering complex. Some argue that CCC is its people; others argue that CCC is its physical plant; I'm convinced that CCC works because of the quality of its people and the surroundings they work in.

Process Explanation (Analysis)

Questions: What steps, stages, or events comprise "X"?
How does "X" work? How do you do "X"?
How do you make (build) "X"?

[6]Michael D. Lemonick, "The Ultimate Quest," *Time* 16 April 1990: 51. Copyright 1990 Time Inc. Reprinted by permission.

Definition by function (operational definition) is a technique for describing a process—for analyzing the steps, stages, or events in a process. It also applies to longer papers (especially technical reports) in which the writer's main purpose is to define *function*—how something works. If you look for it, you'll find the method at work in a surprising number of explanations. For example, consider these subjects:

Tasting. (→ How the taste buds work)
Drilling an oil well. (→ How to drill an oil well)
Operating a dishwasher. (→ How to operate a dishwasher)
Cell division. (→ How living cells divide)
Riding a bicycle. (→ How to ride a bicycle)
Changing a car tire. (→ How to change a car tire)
The piston gas engine. (→ How the piston gas engine works)
Assembling a model airplane. (→ How to assemble a model airplane)

As stated, all these subjects require a process explanation—how something functions or how something is performed or operated. The term *process explanation* is used here to describe two types of processes: (1) describing how to do something (i.e., giving a set of directions), and (2) describing how something works (as in *cell division* and *piston gas engine*). Though related, each type requires its own writing approach. Can you see why?

A little thought should tell you that all these longer *process explanations* require a far more systematic, step-by-step approach than the simple operational definition. All require:

1. A systematic description of *all* components and parts involved
2. A step-by-step description of how *all* these parts operate in relation to one another.

Effective process explanation requires careful planning and ordering of descriptive details. Transition words, therefore, play a crucial role in ordering the information. In space: *above, below, nearby, far from, parallel to, under, over, next to.* In time: *first, second, finally, next, after, later, at the same time, while, as soon as, now.* The parts, events, steps, or stages must be immediately clear to the reader.

In the theme "Do the Hustle," the student uses process explanation, systematically providing a step-by-step description of how to *do* something. You should be able to outline the major stages in the operation (the paragraphs) as well as the individual steps within each stage (details within each paragraph).

```
                          DO THE HUSTLE

     The vibrating beat of a Bruce Springsteen tape rolls over
the parking lot as you deposit your car and walk up the
sidewalk to Sports Club's front door. After flashing your brand
```

new, full-front driver's license picture at the bouncer guarding the entrance, you proceed as calmly and maturely as you possibly can while trying to ignore your racing heart and quickening pulse.

Upon successful entry into the Club, you are now prepared to begin the challenging "girl entices boy" hustling procedure. The first step involves looking nonchalantly for a table toward the center of the room near the dance floor. (This is where all the action supposedly occurs.) As you walk slowly and deliberately toward the table you just selected, suck in your stomach and think sexy. Be extremely careful threading your way through the crowd and try to avoid tripping over chair legs. It ruins your sophisticated, "I've been here before" image.

Once you get to the table, sit down gracefully and take several deep breaths. You deserve them. When the barmaid comes to take your drink order, play it safe and order a coke. This way when you are approached, you'll be able to talk coherently and, hopefully, half-way intelligently. Besides, a coke is cheaper. After ordering your drink, survey the entire situation. Select one or two men that appear interesting and in full command of themselves and their surroundings. (Note: Be sure to select someone who doesn't have a girl hanging on his arm.) Now that you've found someone to hustle, you're ready to establish eye contact. Let your eyes wander slowly around the room several times before allowing them to linger on him. Count to five and look away. Repeat this procedure several times. If he's the right one, he'll notice you flirting and return the look. If he doesn't, forget him and proceed to your second choice.

The next step in the hustling process is up to him. At this stage in the game, you've done everything possible without making the initial move yourself. When you notice him headed in your direction, smile captivatingly, try looking mysterious (guys love to figure girls out) and hope that you've made the guy believe it was his own idea to approach you. If everything goes according to plan, he will ask to sit down at your table or ask you to dance. Don't giggle, appear overeager, or look bored because he may turn away. Let him ask the first question when he is seated and be prepared to answer him honestly. Avoid boring him with the typical rundown of your life story because chances are he isn't curious and he won't listen. As a successful hustler, you should be able to probe him without seeming like Dick Tracy incognito. If he asks you to dance, don't worry about making conversation; he can't hear you over the Bruce Springsteen tape anyway.

If you've followed the above procedure carefully, you'll have absolutely no trouble finding someone to spend a few pleasant hours with in the Sports Club or anywhere else. However, just in case you lack confidence in your capabilities, take a girl friend along. She can always keep you company, and you can use her to discourage any unplanned advances. From here on, you're on your own. Good luck, and happy hustling.

Although explaining how to "do the hustle" is much simpler than explaining how the piston gas engine works, its basic approach is similar. A paper on the piston gas engine, however, would be much longer, would require several schematic diagrams, would necessarily use some technical language to describe all the parts, and would likely number and explain each step in the piston's operation. If you've ever tried to assemble from a set of instructions even the simplest garbage cart or household appliance, you know how important a clearly written process explanation can be.

Look at this process explanation for planting a juniper shrub:

HOW TO PLANT A SIX-FOOT JUNIPER SHRUB

Before beginning the planting process, be sure you have everything you need. In addition to the juniper, you should have some good mulch or peat moss and, if your garden soil is hard or clay-like, some good potting soil. Also, collect all the digging tools you'll need, including a sharp-edged spade for digging, and a small garden fork for soil mixing. Select a sunny spot for the shrub, and be sure it fits your overall landscaping aims. Once you've assembled shrub, tools, mulch, and soil, you can begin the actual planting.

First, dig a hole at least 6" larger in diameter than the root-ball of the juniper shrub and at least 10" deeper than the ball height. If the garden soil is hard and clay-like, do not use the removed soil to backfill the bottom of the hole you have dug. Instead, mix the potting soil and mulch, using it to firmly pack the hole bottom just enough to raise the top of the root-ball to garden-soil level. Set the shrub in the hole and begin backfilling with a fifty-fifty mixture of the removed garden soil and mulch. Press this soil and the root-ball firmly, keeping the root-ball top at garden-soil level. Loosen the soil around the hole, outwards, for 12" and to a depth of 2". Thoroughly work more mulch into this loosened soil, press firmly, and remove any excess soil not used in backfilling. Water slowly and thoroughly, being certain that the water saturates the entire root area in the hole.

Try rewriting this paragraph as a series of numbered instructions. Begin each statement with a verb (*buy* the juniper, mulch, and potting soil; *assemble* the garden tools. . . .). How many different "steps" does it take to complete your process explanation?

Here, finally is a process description by a professional writer. Step by step, Konrad Lorenz explains how Siamese fighting fish mate. In a preceding paragraph he has described how the male leads the female to the bubble nest he has built. The topic sentence of the paragraph which follows it has several mutually reenforcing **pointers:** *love-play, minuet,* and *trance dance:*

> In this way the female is enticed under the bubble nest and now follows the wonderful love-play which resembles, in delicate grace, a minuet, but in general style,

the trance dance of a Balinese temple dancer. In this love dance, by age-old law, the male must always exhibit his magnificent broadside to his partner, but the female must remain constantly at right angles to him. The male must never obtain so much as a glimpse of her flanks, otherwise he will immediately become angry and unchivalrous; for, standing broadsides means, in these fishes as in many others, aggressive masculinity and elicits instantaneously in every male a complete change of mood: hottest love is transformed to wildest hate. Since the male will not now leave the nest, he moves in circles round the female and she follows his every movement by keeping her head always turned towards him; the love-dance is thus executed in a small circle, exactly under the middle of the nest. Now the colours become more glowing, more frantic the movements, ever smaller the circles, until the bodies touch. Then, suddenly, the male slings his body tightly round the female, gently turns her on her back and, quivering, both fulfil the great act of reproduction. Ova and semen are discharged simultaneously.

The female remains, for a few seconds, as though benumbed, but the male has important things to attend to at once. The minute, glass-clear eggs are considerably heavier than water and sink at once to the ground. Now the posture of the bodies in spawning is such that the sinking eggs are bound to drift past the downward directed head of the male and thus catch his attention. He gently releases the female, glides downwards in pursuit of the eggs and gathers them up, one after the other, in his mouth. Turning upwards again, he blows the eggs into the nest. They now miraculously float instead of sinking. This sudden and amazing change of density is caused by a coating of buoyant spittle in which the male has enveloped every egg while carrying it in his mouth. He has to hurry in this work, for not only would he soon be unable to find the tiny, transparent globules in the mud, but, if he should delay a second longer, the female would wake from her trance and, also swimming after the eggs, would likewise proceed to engulf them. From these actions, it would appear, at first sight, that the female has the same intentions as her mate. But if we wait to see her packing the eggs in the nest, we will wait in vain, for these eggs will disappear, irrevocably swallowed. So the male knows very well why he is hurrying, and he knows too, why he no longer allows the female near the nest when, after ten to twenty matings, all her eggs have been safely stored between the air bubbles.[7]

PARAGRAPH DEVELOPMENT BY USE OF ILLUSTRATIVE EXAMPLE

Questions: What examples of "X" are there?
                What illustrations of "X" are there?

An *illustration* is an *example* or a "for instance" used to clarify or explain something. Unlike *definition by specific example,* here the ***illustrative example*** does not merely define a term within a paragraph. It does much more: it develops a complete paragraph in support of a topic sentence. The illustrative example can consist of events, objects, pictures, charts—almost anything that clarifies and develops a topic. We will look at only two kinds, ***illustration by specific example*** and ***narrative illustration;*** the first of these is essentially a simple list of items, the

[7]Konrad Z. Lorenz, *King Solomon's Ring* (New York: Thomas Y. Crowell Co., 1952) 30–31.

second is usually a series of events, "instances," or even anecdotes. Both are used to explain and develop a topic sentence tied to the thesis of the whole essay.

Illustration By Specific Examples

Using specific illustrations to explain and clarify complex concepts is common. This opening paragraph of an essay taken from *The Future: Opportunity Not Destiny* uses a simple list of specific items to support its topic sentence:

> In many ways the development of mankind can be described and at least partially explained in terms of technological innovation. The invention of the wheel, the pulley, and the lever allowed man to magnify his natural physical abilities and laid the groundwork for the development of formal civilization. Gunpowder forever ended feudalism as a social institution. The printing press threw open the doors of literacy to the average person, and the steam engine moved western society from an agricultural to an industrial one. Even in our century, the development of radio and television has affected virtually every aspect of our lives from religion, to politics, to business, to the conduct of international affairs.[8]

The author supports the idea that human development is tied to "technological innovation," an idea which he then uses to assert that we are all "citizens of the information age." He then argues that all citizens don't have equal access to information in this new age.

If you check the examples given on page 148 to illustrate the use of specific details, you'll see that two concepts, "the world's biggest machine" and "global electronic village," are the pointers explained through a series of illustrations that develop two paragraphs.

Illustration Through Narrative Examples

Although a *narrative illustration* is also an example, it does more than define a term within a paragraph (definition by specific example). It develops a complete paragraph in support of a topic sentence. As a narrative, it tells a story—usually a chronological account of what happened in a certain situation that would support the *pointer* of the topic sentence. Illustrations can be either real or hypothetical. You can use an account of some event you actually know about, or you can, in effect, "make up" one, provided the reader understands that the illustration is hypothetical. Usually the hypothetical illustration starts with something like "Suppose such-and-such a thing happened, what would be the result?" "Suppose time travel were possible?" "Suppose we developed a computer that could really think creatively?" Then the writer goes on to supply a narrative of what would happen in the situation.

[8]T. M. Grunder, "Manifesto for an Information Age." In *The Future: Opportunity Not Destiny*. Ed. Howard F. Didsbury, Jr., 1989, p. 111. World Future Society, 7910 Woodmount Ave., Suite 450, Bethesda, MD 20814.

You can develop paragraphs using two kinds of narrative illustrations—short and extended. A collection of short illustrations, all supporting the topic sentence, may be used as a paragraph. Usually, the narrative in a ***short illustration*** is quite brief. Or an ***extended illustration,*** a single, relatively long narrative, may constitute the paragraph. Of course, any combination of extended and short illustrations may be used to support the topic sentence.

The paragraph developed by the use of illustration can be represented by this diagram:

> **TOPIC SENTENCE**
>
> A narrative or a number of nar-
> ratives, in any combination, that
> specifically illustrate the validity
> of the topic sentence.

Here are some examples of student paragraphs using illustration. The first paragraph uses a series of short illustrations in support of the topic sentence controlling attitude, *record of courage.*

> American history is a record of courage. During the
> Revolution, Paul Revere, a Boston silversmith, rode his horse
> through the night to warn the Massachusetts colonists that the
> British were coming. Daniel Boone, Kentucky trailblazer and
> Indian fighter; Davy Crockett, hero of the Battle of the Alamo;
> and Lewis and Clark, leaders of the trail expedition to Oregon,
> all did their share in shaping the growth of a young country
> struggling against unknown obstacles. In more recent times,
> Charles Lindbergh, who by making the first nonstop flight from
> New York to Paris established the importance of air power to
> our country; General Douglas MacArthur, victorious against the
> Japanese after early defeat; and John F. Kennedy, who nearly
> lost his life as a PT boat commander in World War II but lived
> to become President of the United States, all displayed the
> personal bravery so apparent in American history.

To support its topic sentence, that paragraph used seven short illustrations, arranged chronologically in American history. The next paragraph is an example of one extended illustration.

> Poor communication between the administration and staff
> results in misunderstandings among the employees of the
> Chemist's Laboratory. Recently, for instance, the department
> head told a graduate student employee, a good worker who had
> been carefully trained by another administrator in the same
> department, to go home and change out of Bermuda shorts or to
> consider himself fired. The incident, which occurred while
> several women employees were present, embarrassed the student
> so deeply that he determined not to work for such a man. The
> student resigned, and the department lost a well-trained and
> efficient worker because neither administrator had taken the
> responsibility of telling the employee what dress was
> acceptable for work.

Here is another example of the use of a series of short illustrations.

> Many people in show business have become famous because of
> a gimmick. In the thirties, for example, such entertainers as
> Helen Kane with her "boo-boop-a-doop," and Joe Penner with
> "Wanna buy a duck?" rose to national prominence. George Burns,
> the comedian, has used a cigar to establish his stage identity.
> In the fifties, Elvis Presley achieved adulation and stardom as
> a rock-and-roll singer by wiggling his hips and charming the
> teenage world by his wild gyrations. Dolly Parton's oversized
> blonde wig and ample bosom have taken her to the top in country
> and western entertainment. In the world of rock music, Kiss
> made bizarre makeup and costuming popular, while The Who was
> among the first groups to smash their instruments on stage.

The following selection comes from Konrad Lorenz's chapter, "Laughing at Animals," in *King Solomon's Ring,* and is only a small part of a long series of narrative illustrations designed to show the humorous side of the author's animal experiences. The two anecdotes included here describe the antics of Koka, the author's yellow-crested cockatoo. The two pointers are *serious fright* and *cockatoo-tricks:*

On another occasion, the frolics of this bird gave me quite a serious fright. My father, by that time an old man, used to take his siesta at the foot of a terrace on the south-west side of our house. For medical reasons, I was never quite happy to think of him exposed to the glaring mid-day sun, but he would let nobody break him of his old habit. One day, at his siesta time, I heard him, from his accustomed place, swearing like a trooper, and as I raced round the corner of the house, I saw the old gentleman swaying up the drive in a cramped position, bending forwards, his arms tightly folded about his waist. "In heaven's name, are you ill?" "No," came the embittered response, "I am not ill, but that confounded creature has bitten all the buttons off my trousers while I was fast asleep!" And that is what had happened. Eye-witnesses at the scene of the crime discovered, laid out in buttons, the whole outline of the old professor: here the arms, there the waistcoat, and here, unmistakably, the buttons off his trousers.

One of the nicest cockatoo-tricks which, in fanciful inventiveness, equalled the experiments of monkey or human children, arose from the ardent love of the bird for my mother who, so long as she stayed in the garden in summertime, knitted without stopping. The cockatoo seemed to understand exactly how the soft skeins worked and what the wool was for. He always seized the free end of the wool with his beak and then flew lustily into the air, unravelling the ball behind him. Like a paper kite with a long tail, he climbed high and then flew in regular circles round the great lime tree which stood in front of our house. Once, when nobody was there to stop him he encircled the tree, right up to its summit, with brightly coloured woollen strands which it was impossible to disentangle from the widespreading foliage. Our visitors used to stand in mute astonishment before this tree, and were unable to understand how and why it had been thus decorated.[9]

In this final sample, the author uses narrative illustrations to point to the subject of an entire essay. She uses a narrative approach in the first two paragraphs of a four-paragraph introduction to lead the reader to the essay's thesis—that "today's typical marriage is a dual-career affair" "marked by demands for fairness and parity" (in the fourth paragraph):

1   Meet Kendall Crolius, 36, an account director at the J. Walter Thompson advertising agency in Manhattan. Every day, Monday through Friday, she awakens at 6:00 a.m., prepares for work and, if two-year-old Trevor stirs, snatches a few minutes of "quality time." At 7:10 she walks to the train station near her Connecticut home; by 8:30 she is in her Lexington Avenue office. During the next nine hours, she juggles the demands of clients and researchers, creative teams and media people. But no matter how hectic it gets, Crolius usually manages to catch the 5:18 train. When she reaches home, Trevor is waiting for her. By 10:30, she is asleep.

2   Meet Stephen Stout, 38, an actor currently understudying in the Broadway hit *The Heidi Chronicles*. Each day he gets up at 7:15 a.m. If it is not a matinee day, Stout spends the next ten hours with his two-year-old son, playing and running errands. At 5:15 he leaves his suburban home to catch a Manhattan-bound train, allowing ample time to meet his 7:30 call at the Plymouth Theater. On the nights that Stout does not appear onstage, he heads for home at 9:40, after the second act is safely under way. When he walks through his front door at 11:15, he is greeted by silence; both his wife and son are asleep.

3   Stout and Crolius are happily married, though they spend only a few minutes together on a standard workday. Both agree it is not an ideal arrangement. But this is the most compatible meshing of schedules in their eight-year marriage—and it beats the 18 months they spent on opposite coasts when Stout was pursuing television work in Los Angeles. "This is as good as it gets," says Crolius. "We're both working—and we're both living in the same city."

4   Welcome aboard Marriage Flight 1990, and fasten your seat belts: it's going to be a bumpy ride. Today's typical marriage is a dual-career affair. That means two sets

[9]Lorenz 46–47.

of job demands, two paychecks, two egos—and a multitude of competing claims on both spouses' time, attention and energy. The two-job flight path is marked by demands for fairness and parity that require some mobility, a dose of originality and a high degree of flexibility.[10]

EXERCISES

A. List a number of ways in which *logical analysis* is similar to *process explanation*. Illustrate your answer by using one of these items:
1. Cell division
2. Rage
3. Tying a shoelace
4. Scrambling an egg

B. Write a process explanation for one of the items in *A* above.

C. List a number of ways in which definition through specific examples is related to classification and analysis. Use an item from *A*, above, to illustrate your answer. Be prepared to discuss your answer in class.

D. Using the want ad section of your local newspaper as your source, list six major *classes* of ads. Then under each class list four or five items as examples of *class members*. Are all class members identical? Note the differences and be prepared to characterize them. What do the words "classified ads" mean? Define the term "classified ads" by:
1. Using examples
2. Using analysis
3. Using enumeration
What differences in *emphasis* distinguish each of these three methods?

E. Select two of these topic sentences and write two separate paragraphs. In one use a series of short illustrations to support the topic sentence. In the other use an extended illustration.
1. Many rock music groups use the same gimmicks.
2. Country music has distinctive qualities.
3. Shakespeare's Macbeth is a henpecked wimp.
4. Today I met the robots in my kitchen.

PARAGRAPH DEVELOPMENT BY COMPARISON, ANALOGY, OR CONTRAST

Questions: What is "X" similar to?
What is "X" better than?
To what is "X" inferior?
What is "X" different from?
Are "X" and "Y" similar?
In what ways are "X" and "Y" similar? Unlike?

---

[10]Jill Smolowe, "When Jobs Clash," *Time* 3 September 1990: 82. (The complete essay appears on page 405.)

Let's make these questions specific:

What is water skiing similar to?
What does water skiing remind you of?
How is water skiing different from snow skiing?
Are water skiing and snow skiing similar?
In what ways are water skiing and snow skiing similar?
What are the major differences between water skiing and snow skiing?

These questions should remind you that how you **think about** a subject will decide the developmental **pattern** you will use. The questions start you thinking in a certain way; the writing pattern then reflects your thinking. Recall the question approach you learned with Theme Pattern A in Chapter 2, and you'll see that all these questions do not suggest *exactly* the same approach to the comparisons. The first two questions are *open questions;* following Theme Pattern A they could lead into an essay showing that water skiing is similar to several (perhaps many) things. The fourth question, though it limits the comparison to the two kinds of skiing, is still an "open" question, since it allows for a yes or no answer and the development of either. Also, if you compare the basic requirements for comparison with the method used in *analysis,* above, you'll see that *comparison, contrast,* and *analogy* (a special kind of comparison) all depend on analysis (logical division) if they are to be effective. You can't compare "X" and "Y"—whether things, events, processes, concepts, people, or chemicals—until you have first considered each of them **part by part** or **point by point.**

To summarize: Comparison, analogy, and contrast, as developmental methods, are similar because they require a point-by-point *logical division* of items for the method to work.

Comparison: The method of comparison is to indicate similarities between two or more things, events, processes, ideas, places, or people for the purpose of clarifying or explaining one item in terms of the others. ("X" is similar to "A" in points 1, 2, 3, 4, etc. Or, "X" is similar to "A," and "B," "C," "D," . . .)

Patricia looks like Lisa in many ways. (1, 2, 3, 4, . . .)
Patricia and Lisa have similar personalities.
Patricia reminds me of Lisa, and Maria, and Sarah.
Football and soccer are similar in a number of ways.
Fear and terror are similar.
School is like a game of basketball.

Analogy: The method of analogy is to indicate a *limited* resemblance or *similarity* between things basically unlike. Analogy can be considered an extended comparison in the form of illustration or argument. Because it deals with similarity and comparison, analogy is a simile or metaphor continued through one or more paragraphs. It often assumes that if two things resemble each other in some specific ways they will probably be similar in other ways. Analogy is frequently used to illustrate, explain, or clarify difficult or abstract concepts (love, fear, hope, success, life, time); in this form it is a figure of speech used to make the abstract concrete:

> *Fear is an iceberg lodged in my heart. (Metaphor)*

> It is cold.
> It is numbing.
> It is deep, below the surface.
> It is gigantic, shutting out all other things.
> It moves slowly, blindly, thoughtlessly.
> It eventually melts away.

Here are some additional statements to suggest development through analogy:

> Death is like sleep. (Simile)
> Money is a worldwide religion. (Metaphor)
> Time is a series of birthday celebrations. (Metaphor)
> Truth is an oyster. (Metaphor)
> Success is like wine. (Simile)

Contrast: The method of contrast is to indicate differences between two or more things, events, processes, ideas, places, or people for the purpose of clarifying or explaining one item in terms of the others. ("X" is different from "A" in points 1, 2, 3, 4, etc.)

> Unlike death, sleep is . . .
> Water skiing and snow skiing are unalike. (1, 2, 3, 4, . . .)
> Patricia and Lisa have opposite personalities. (1, 2, 3, 4, . . .)
> A car and an airplane have almost nothing in common.
> General Grant was everything that General Lee was not.

As you shall see in the extended illustrations that follow, it is usually more effective to compare or contrast point-by-point than to take the whole of the first item of comparison and then the whole of the other item. For instance, if you were comparing two cars, it would be better to compare, say, the performance of one to the performance of the other, next their economy, and finally their appearance, rather than to describe these three points for one car and then describe them for the other.

Here is a diagram of the paragraph developed by comparison or contrast.

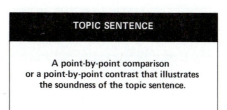

In the examples that follow, the topic sentences appear highlighted to remind you that each developmental paragraph is considered part of an essay. More important, each paragraph represents one supporting point to show the validity of a thesis statement. For example, "School is like a game of basketball" could point back to this thesis: "With all its various activities and studies, school reminds me of *carefully structured games.* " As you read each example, try to phrase a thesis statement that is reflected in the developmental paragraph.

The following student paragraph makes a point-by-point comparison between school and a *game of basketball:*

> School is like a game of basketball. In both, the time is short, and the student uses all his resources in the class as the player does in the game. The student has a background of knowledge that enables him to meet the challenges in class; the player relies on ability he has acquired previously. The student begins on registration day a period in which he matches wits with his opponent, the professor. The first whistle of the basketball game starts the player matching his wits with the opposing team. The student relaxes over the weekends, taking this time to catch his breath; time out in the basketball game allows the player to catch his breath. The student can slow down the class, if he is tired, by turning it into a bull session. The basketball player can also slow down the game. Each is aware that he runs the risk of being punished, as the professor can give a pop quiz, or the referee can call a foul. Each participant is striving for a measure of his ability, a grade for the student and a score for the player. At the end of the term, the student looks anxiously at the bulletin board just outside the classroom for the final verdict. The player's eyes scan the scoreboard for the outcome of his efforts. The result is the same. If the student makes a good grade or the player has the high score, both are pleased with their efforts. If either loses—but that is too horrible to think about.

And here is a paragraph written by a student who was very fond of her new foreign car. She planned her paragraph around a point-by-point comparison of two things that are basically unlike. Therefore, the comparison is through *analogy.*

> The proud owners of American automobiles look with scorn
> at my little foreign car and with contempt call it a beetle.
> Well, I suppose it is almost a beetle. Nature carefully
> designed oval-shaped, low bodies for beetles to decrease air
> resistance, and my tiny horseless carriage is as smooth, oval,
> and low as any real beetle. Most beetles are actually poor
> flyers and indeed, some, like my car, never fly. A true member
> of the beetle family is powerful but slow; my small auto cannot
> go over sixty miles per hour, but it can climb steep curving
> roads well in spite of ice, rain, or standing water. Bugs take
> in energy-giving food anteriorly, and my bug-car has its
> gasoline tank near its nose also. Real beetles have posterior
> air intake tubes just like my little foreign car, although the
> real beetles have more of them. Normally I dislike bugs, but I
> am so fond of my beetle-like Volkswagen that I may grow to like
> all beetles.

This paragraph compares first the appearance of the two objects, next the performance of the two, and finally the position of fuel and air intake openings.

Here's a developmental paragraph from a student essay titled "False Economic Analogies." The essay's thesis, stated in the last sentence of the introductory paragraph, cautions against the uncritical use of analogies: "Before allowing these analogies to influence our views, we should examine them critically and judge them for accuracy, validity, and usefulness." This first developmental paragraph challenges argument from analogy as inaccurate and misleading.

> Mobil Oil once ran a series of advertisements supporting
> the free enterprise system. These advertisements usually
> consisted of a short story, resembling a fable, whose moral was
> directly applied to economic conditions. One story told about a
> pie shop whose owner had no competition and who sold small pies
> at a fairly high price. However, one day a new pie shop opened
> across the street and sold larger pies at a lower price. The
> first pie maker responded by making even larger pies and
> selling them at an even lower price. Fierce competition
> developed over who could make the largest pies at the best
> price, and all the customers benefited. The moral proclaimed
> that free trade promoted competition which helped consumers,
> and it connected this moral with the real-world economy.
> Although the story sounds true and helps explain the free trade
> process, it is still a blatant case of oversimplification by
> analogy. Some local and isolated cases of free trade may fit
> this analogy. However, using this analogy to describe
> competition at the national level in a complex economy falls
> short of giving a true picture of actual conditions. National
> economies involve thousands of complex details that this simple
> analogy must ignore. Therefore, although this story is amusing
> and clever, we must be wary of allowing it to blind us to the
> true complexity of free trade on a national scale.

Although this paragraph is not developed through the use of analogy (it is really an example, an illustration), it explains how the method of *comparative analogy* works and points to basic problems in such an approach. (See "Fallacies," *Argument from Analogy*.)

This next paragraph is developed by use of contrast. Note that again the *point-by-point* plan is used, but here in contrasting rather than in comparing.

> The modern kitchen is different from the old-style type.
> It even looks different. The charm of the old kitchen lay in
> its design, from the wallpaper to the curtains to the
> tablecloth; but the modern kitchen has no designs, only shiny
> chrome and brilliant color. There's a different atmosphere,
> too. Grandma's kitchen was a place to talk things over, to have
> a hot drink and relax while savoring the odor of bread baking
> in the oven, to leisurely plan and put loving thought into
> every meal prepared there. But the modern kitchen is
> constructed for speed, for the fastest and easiest way to get
> the food on the table and the dishes washed so that the cook
> can go on to other activities. The modern kitchen seems to have
> a different role to play in our lives. Instead of being a
> center of family life, it has become a laundry, dining room,
> and office for the increasingly complicated job of the
> homemaker.

This paragraph compares the old and the new kitchen on three points: their appearance, their atmosphere, and their roles in family life.

The next paragraph, a comparison, was written by a disgruntled married student.

> Special words have been used to sympathize with the
> "golfer's widow," but no terms directly apply to the amateur
> mechanic's wife, who is no better off. Both are often left
> stranded for hours with no cars while the laundry waits to be
> washed and the pantry to be filled. The golfer cannot stand the
> thought of his friends putting on the green without him, and
> the auto maniac insists on being present after each exciting
> mechanical failure. Either situation may leave the wife
> floundering in a welter of broken social engagements. Although
> it is worse in some ways to break appointments for lack of
> transportation or an escort, the mechanic's wife and the
> golfer's wife are placed at further social disadvantages by
> knowing that, come spring, when afternoon picnics and cook-outs
> are enticing, the amateur mechanic wants to polish his car as
> well as those of his buddies, and the golfer wants to join his
> cronies on the golf course. Both leave their wives to wonder
> how the myth of "family companionship" persists.

As with most methods of paragraph development, an entire paper could be written using the methods of comparison and contrast, as in "A Pesty Roommate," the freshman paper given below. Read the paper carefully and check it for the following:

1. How does the introductory paragraph provide the general basis for comparison and contrast?
2. What kind of tone is set in the opening paragraph? How?
3. What two points about each roommate are being compared? What two are being contrasted?
4. Are the four developmental paragraphs adequately detailed?
5. What important transitions are provided between paragraphs?
6. How could you improve the concluding paragraph?

A PESTY ROOMMATE

At the beginning of school, two hastily scrawled signs were left on my dorm door as a warning of things to come. One sign said, "Avoid objects that move hurriedly in the dark" and the other read, "Beware of Annoying Pests." Unfortunately, I wasn't aware that these signs were left by a far wiser and more experienced person than myself: the room's previous occupant. The meaning of these puzzling warnings became more apparent to me after meeting my two new, yet different, roommates, one of whom proved to be a strange creature.

I met my first roommate "A" when she arrived with her entire family in a station wagon crammed with all her personal possessions. She managed to step gracefully out of the car, after being sandwiched between her big brother and the door for hours, without a wrinkle in her beautifully coordinated pantsuit. In contrast, roommate "B" scurried in late one evening from a still unknown origin carrying everything she owned on her back and wearing a dirty brown coat. I soon noticed she did everything in that brown coat from eating dinner to sleeping.

As time progressed, I discovered roommate "A" differed greatly from roommate "B" not only in personal appearance, but in personal cleanliness as well. Roommate "A" often spent hours in the bathroom plucking her eyebrows, shaving her legs, and washing her hair. On the other hand, roommate "B" seemed to have a phobia concerning water because I rarely saw her go near it. One day, however, a little excitement did occur in the bathroom. I discovered roommate "A" sitting in the sink hollering, "Kill that bug, please kill that bug" while roommate "B" looking slightly offended stared at her with an open mouth. While attempting to kill the bug. I learned roommate "B" does not like the smell of Raid as I watched her crawl down the hall. She did not return to the room until the smell of bug spray had completely disappeared.

Although obvious distinctions did exist between my two roommates, several similarities were also evident. For example, both roommates regularly depleted my food supply. I was constantly finding one or the other nibbling at my homemade "goodies" and grinning mischievously. Once I became so angry at

```
their chronic snitching, I hid my food. The minute I left the
room, however, Roommate "B" flung up her food-detecting
antennas and led roommate "A" right to it.
     Furthermore, both roommate "A" and "B" frequently borrowed
my clothes. Roommate "A" at least demonstrated some
thoughtfulness and consideration by asking me if she could
borrow my favorite shirt, etc. before doing so. Roommate "B"
never asked; instead she repeatedly bugged me by running
rampant through everything I owned with her messy feet. An
additional comparison between the two was that both roommate
"A" and "B" were free to come and go as they pleased. Neither
ever told me where she was going, when she would return, or
whom she was going out with.
     In spite of its annoyances, my first semester of dorm
living provided me with useful knowledge and insight. Armed
with this new enlightenment, I was able to decide that I
preferred roommate "A"'s company more than roommate "B"'s.
Perhaps I enjoyed "A" more because I discovered it is easier to
speak intelligently with a freshman biology major than with a
filthy cockroach.
```

Were you surprised by the ending of this paper? If you were, recheck it for the clues provided to guide you.

EXERCISES

A. Select two of these topic sentences. Write one paragraph using comparison (or analogy) as a method of development and another using the method of contrast.
  1. Zeba reminds me of three other girls I know.
  2. Women and men share similar goals in life.
  3. Women and men share similar personality traits.
  4. Death is like (or unlike) sleep.
  5. Like some animals, humans are aggressively territorial.
  6. Planned parenthood and abortion can represent two entirely different attitudes.
B. 1. Assume that the topic sentences in *A* point back to thesis statements. Write thesis statements which these topic sentences could support.
  2. List the things you would have to do to expand one of the paragraphs in *A* into a complete essay.
  3. Expand one of your answers in *A* or *B-1* into a five-paragraph paper.
C. Devise a point-by-point outline to illustrate the structure of the paper you wrote for *B-3*.

PARAGRAPH DEVELOPMENT BY REASONS, CAUSES, OR CONSEQUENCES

Questions: Why does "X" happen?
               What causes "X"?

> Why is "X" true or desirable?
> Why is "X" untrue or undesirable?
> What are the causes of effect "X"?
> What are the consequences (results, effects) of "X"?

Let's look at these questions more closely to see why they are related and can be considered as one basic method of paragraph development.

Why does it snow rather than rain? This can be rephrased as: What *causes* it to snow? Why should dogs be kept on leashes? Reconsidered, this becomes: What *reasons* can be given to support the assertion (or argument) that dogs should be kept on leashes? What will happen if women get complete, equal rights with men? This question has been repeatedly stated in other forms: What are the *consequences* of granting women equal rights? If women are granted equal rights under an Equal Rights Amendment, what are some of the *consequences*? Why is honesty (or lower income tax, peace, or education) desirable? What *reasons* can be given to support the assertion (argument) that lower income tax (or peace, or education) is desirable?

> **Assertions** need to be supported with reasons (evidence).
> **Effects** result from certain causes.
> **Consequences** follow certain happenings or events.

You have already seen the use of *reasons* in paragraph development in the section on maintaining unity (Chapter 4). Recall that example paragraphs in the section gave two or more reasons for the validity of the topic sentence and then supported those reasons. This developmental pattern is also the one suggested in "Seeing the Whole Paper" (Chapter 2), where reasons—in the form of topic sentences—support the thesis statement of the whole paper (highway accidents "result from human error"). Reviewing those sections in Chapters 2 and 4 will help you understand this section. Because a paragraph is like a short paper, you can use the same method of development within the paragraph.

In one of the exercises in Chapter 4 you were asked to analyze a paragraph by E. B. White. He developed this paragraph by using reasons. Have another look at it.

> It is a miracle that New York works at all. *The whole thing is implausible.* Every time the residents brush their teeth, millions of gallons of water must be drawn from the Catskills and the hills of Westchester. When a young man in Manhattan writes a letter to his girl in Brooklyn, the love message gets blown to her through a pneumatic tube—pfft—just like that. The subterranean system of telephone cables, power lines, steam pipes, gas mains and sewer pipes is reason enough to abandon the island to the gods and the weevils. Every time an incision is made in the pavement, the noisy surgeons expose ganglia that are tangled beyond belief. By rights *New York should have destroyed itself long ago,* from panic or fire or rioting or failure of some vital supply line in its circulatory system or from some deep labyrinthine short circuit. Long ago the city should have experienced an insoluble traffic snarl at some impossible bottleneck. It should have perished of hunger when food lines failed for a few days. It should have

been wiped out by a plague starting in its slums or carried in by ships' rats. It should have been overwhelmed by the sea that licks at it on every side. The workers in its myriad cells should have succumbed to nerves, from the fearful pall of smoke-fog that drifts over every few days from Jersey, blotting out all light at noon, and leaving the high offices suspended, men groping and depressed, and the sense of world's end. It should have been touched in the head by the August heat and gone off its rocker.[11]

The topic sentence of this paragraph is the first sentence. Its pointer (controlling attitude) is *miracle*. The two reasons that support this topic sentence are italicized in the paragraph. In its simplest outline form, the paragraph appears like this:

Topic Sentence: *It is a miracle that New York works at all.*
Main Reason 1:   *The whole thing is implausible.*
Main Reason 2:   *New York should have destroyed itself long ago.*

This outline as it stands could be assembled into a paragraph.

It is a miracle that New York works at all. The whole thing is implausible for a number of reasons. There is so much congestion that New York should have destroyed itself long ago.

But you have learned that this is not a good paragraph because it does not supply details as supporting reasons. White did it like this:

Topic Sentence: It is a miracle that New York works at all.
   Main Reason 1:   The whole thing is implausible.
      Supporting Reason 1:   Water must come from a distance.
      Supporting Reason 2:   Mail is carried through tubes.
      Supporting Reason 3:   Subterranean lines, cables, and pipes are hopelessly tangled.
   Main Reason 2:   New York should have destroyed itself,
      Supporting Reason 1:   From insoluble traffic snarls.
      Supporting Reason 2:   From hunger through failure of food lines.
      Supporting Reason 3:   From plague through slums or rats.
      Supporting Reason 4:   From the sea.
      Supporting Reason 5:   From workers' nerves.
      Supporting Reason 6:   From insanity.

A paragraph from the section on comparison and contrast may also be used to illustrate paragraph development through reasons. Look at it again.

> The modern kitchen is different from the old-style type. It even looks different. The charm of the old kitchen lay in its design, from the wallpaper to the curtains to the tablecloth; but the modern kitchen has no designs, only shiny chrome and brilliant color. There's a different atmosphere, too. Grandma's kitchen was a place to talk things over, to have a hot drink and relax while savoring the odor of bread baking in the oven, to leisurely plan and put loving thought into every meal prepared there. But the modern kitchen is constructed for speed, for the fastest and easiest way to get the food on the table and the dishes washed so that the cook can go on to other activities. The modern kitchen seems to have a different role to play in our lives. Instead of being a center of family life, it has become a laundry, dining room, and office for the increasingly complicated job of the homemaker.

The topic sentence is the first sentence in the paragraph. The pointer is *different,* and the paragraph lists three reasons for the difference.

EXERCISES

A. Using one of the following topic sentences (or questions) as your starting point, write an outline for a paragraph to be developed by reasons, causes, or consequences. You may oppose the view of the sentence/question if you choose.

Your outline should include *at least* two main reasons (causes or consequences) plus any additional ones you may need to develop the paragraph adequately. Each main reason must also have at least two supporting reasons. Follow this outline form:

Topic Sentence:
> *Main Reason 1:*
>> *Supporting Reason 1:*
>> *Supporting Reason 2:*
> *Main Reason 2:*
>> *Supporting Reason 1:*
>> *Supporting Reason 2:*
> *Main Reason 3:*
>> *Supporting Reason 1:*
>> *Supporting Reason 2:*

1. What are some of the consequences of too much sexual freedom?
2. Why is it important to develop good social habits early?
3. A motorcycle doesn't have to be a weapon of destruction.
4. Interracial marriage is destructive.
5. Do hand calculators destroy problem-solving ability?

6. Rapid population growth is a major cause of pollution.
7. The home computer will become an essential household appliance.

B. From the outline composed for Exercise *A,* write a good developmental paragraph.

METHODS OF DEVELOPMENT IN COMBINATION

Writers don't ordinarily develop paragraphs or essays by using only one of the methods you have just studied. They combine methods, choosing those most suited to the subject and to the topic sentences. Although experienced writers don't usually decide deliberately to develop a paragraph or paper by any specific method, they do use methods. As you have seen, a method of development isn't an arbitrary pattern *imposed* on subject matter. Rather, the subject matter *demands* a certain method. For example, the topic sentences in Exercise *A* on page 188 seems to demand *reasons, causes, effects.* Those in Exercise *A* on page 185 seem to demand *comparisons.* Those in Exercise *E* on page 178 seem to demand *illustrations.* And, because of their modifiers or difficulty, the topics listed on page 166 seem to invite *definitions.* How a limited subject and controlling attitude are stated will usually point to one or more methods of development. For example, study the following subjects and rephrase them as questions:

Managers.
A manager guides employees.
A good manager.
A good manager motivates, informs, and inspires.
All corporations probably have both good and bad managers.
Though good and bad managers share some similarities, they differ markedly.

Although these are all about managers, clearly *how* they are conceived and *how* they are phrased dictates the method of development. Ask the right questions, get the *subject* and *controlling attitude* specific and clear in your mind, and the method of development will logically follow.

To illustrate how professional writers combine methods, let's look at several examples. The first consists of two *definition* paragraphs:

1   Lasers—there are several varieties—are rather surprisingly simple devices
2   which generate highly disciplined and coherent light rays. To appreciate their
3   impact one must first realize that until a few years ago an important dividing line
4   cut across the electromagnetic frequency spectrum just above the upper limits of
5   the microwave region. Below this divide there were transistors and electron
6   tubes which could generate the coherent signals necessary for communications
7   or computers or any of the other tasks of modern electronics. Above it, in the
8   infrared and optical regions, there were only incoherent thermal sources—the
9   sun, light bulbs, arc lamps, flames. The electromagnetic radiation from these

10   sources is highly undisciplined, containing waves traveling in all possible
11   directions and made up of a scrambled mixture of all possible frequencies.
12   The development of the laser as a coherent light source means that this
13   division is now gone. Note that most lasers emit considerably less total power
14   than, say, a hundred-watt bulb. But the light bulb, which is incoherent, emits its
15   energy into so many frequencies and directions that the amount emitted into any
16   single specific frequency and direction is minute. By contrast, the laser, which is
17   coherent, emits all of its energy at a single frequency and in a single direction and
18   in some cases does so in a single brief but extremely intense burst. Within its
19   single frequency and direction, therefore, the laser is incomparably brighter
20   than, say, the sun or any other thermal light source.[12]

These two paragraphs are definition paragraphs. They attempt to define lasers in nonscientific terms so that an ordinary reader can understand. Several methods of development are used in the definition. Note that the first sentence is a simple definition by classification. From lines 2 through 7, the author uses explanation of background reinforced by reason. In lines 8 and 9, he defines *incoherent thermal sources* by enumeration. The last part of line 10 starts a definition by classification of the word *undisciplined* as applied to electromagnetic radiation. Lines 12 through 20 offer contrast as a method of development. Note that *incoherent* and *coherent light sources* are defined in this contrast. The last sentence is a conclusion, as shown by the transition word *therefore*.

Now look at this introductory section of a long essay to see how many different methods of development you can find:

1   The human use of communications contains the key to the future of our species.
The linking of our optical and electronic technologies in new and different ways is not
only the key to a new golden age, but a high-risk gamble as well. Our new telepower
technologies can make us or break us.

2   The "global electronic machine" is where it all starts. This machine is far bigger
than a nuclear aircraft carrier, a C5A cargo jetliner, or even a continuous-process
automobile-manufacturing plant. It contains hundreds of millions of tons of coaxial
cable buried underground and beneath the oceans. It includes electronic switches and
exchange equipment with enough gold and silver to fully stock a large jewelry store.
Parts of the machine are invisible because they are flying in space — orbiting in circles
a tenth of the way to the moon. Over a hundred of these space communications
devices are relaying billions of messages around the world every year. The parts of the
global electronic machine are now so numerous that no one can count them. Billions
of telephones, television sets, facsimile devices, telexes, computers, and radios are
linked to this massive network. Each year, the colossal machine grows by leaps and
bounds as fiber-optic cables, new electronic switches, and new "ports" are added to
accommodate more users around the world.

3   The machine is making the global village a reality. Soon, people in remote
Tuvalu and Niue in the South Pacific will be able to call Chicago, Toulouse, or Chiang
Mai, Thailand. In the 20 years since the moon landing, the number of people able to
see global events on television has expanded sixfold from 500 million to 3 billion

[12]Anthony E. Siegman, "The Laser: Astounding Beam of Light," *Stanford Today,* Autumn 1964. Reprinted by permission of *Stanford Today,* Leland Stanford Junior University, Stanford, California.

people. Our ability to share information and knowledge is today creating global trade and culture. Tomorrow, it will begin to form a global brain—a global consciousness.

4   The power of the global electronic machine is already awesome. Just one satellite, the INTEL-SAT VI, can send 200 simultaneous television channels—enough to send all episodes of *Dallas* and *Dynasty* ever made all at once. It could also transmit about a thousand 300-page books in the span of one second. In short, the global electronic machine, this multitrillion-dollar universal linkage, is very fast and very smart.

5   The many dimensions of our growing telepower will bring us both good and bad changes. On the debit side, it will bring us tele-war, technology-based terrorism, technological unemployment, and information overload. Yet, this telepower will also bring hope for high-quality schooling, nutritional advice, and medical services through tele-education and tele-health techniques.

6   Well into the twenty-first century, there can even be hope for the building of a true global consciousness and ultimately for the emergence of a "global brain." Eventually, we may even see the evolution of a new human species.[13]

EXERCISES

A. Throughout this chapter you have written many paragraphs. Choose any three and rewrite them to change the tone to fit any of the following (use a different one for each paragraph): *formal, informal, personal, impersonal, critical, emotional, more argumentative, humorous, absurd*. You may want to discuss these tags before you begin this exercise.

B. Choose one of the six paragraphs involved in Exercise *A* and rewrite it to improve reader interest and reader acceptance (assume you are writing to a close personal friend). (If you have trouble with this assignment, reread pages 120–124.)

C. 1. Think about each word in the following list and decide whether your feeling about the word is "favorable" or "unfavorable." Place a plus (+) beside those you respond favorably to, and a minus (−) beside those you respond unfavorably to. Those that don't fit either class or that fit *both*, label "neutral" (0).

crash	shout	eye	scold
rush	sit	fire	listen
cool	honest	foolish	cheer
talk	fair	hand	brag
walk	crush	careful	agree
quiet	say	clash	define
slap	frigid	stoop	jeer
wise	warm	silly	assure
run	stand	trip	beg

2. a. Be prepared to discuss your classification.
   b. What can you conclude about words and a person's feelings?

---

[13]Joseph N. Pelton, "Telepower: The Emerging Global Brain," *The Futurist*, September–October 1989: 9–10. Reprinted with permission by the World Future Society, 7910 Woodmount Ave., Suite 450, Bethesda, MD 20814. (The complete essay appears on page 421.)

    c. Compare your list with others in the class. Why are there differences?

    d. Try to spot the "feeling" words in the paragraphs you write for *A* and *B*, above.

D. Now that you have worked Exercise *C*, turn back to page 41 to paper *D* "Unleashed Danger." Make a list of all words that imply a "judgment" to you (for example, *restrain, fear, nuisance, damage, scare, affectionately*). After you have completed this list of "tone" words (you should be able to find several dozen), classify the words in the same way you did in Exercise *C*, above, but use only two classes, "favorable" (+) and "unfavorable" (−).

    1. Which "tone" words appear more frequently, (+) or (−)?

    2. Compare your list with others in the class. Why are there differences?

    3. On the basis of your classification, what do you think the person "speaking" in the theme feels about dogs? Do you think the *writer* of the theme and this "speaker" are in agreement? Explain.

    4. Your instructor may ask you to repeat this exercise using the theme on "A Pesty Roommate" (page 184).

REVIEW TERMS

Nearly all of the following terms point to information in the present chapter on developing paragraphs. Test your understanding of them before moving on to the next chapter.

Analogy, Aristotelian definition, causes, comparative analogy, comparison, consequences, contrast, definition by classification, definition by enumeration, definition by function, definition by specific example, definition by synonyms, essential definition, extended definition, extended illustration, illustration by specific example, illustrative example, logical analysis, logical division, methods of paragraph development, narrative illustration, operational definition, process explanation, question−answer approach, reasons, short illustration, supporting paragraphs

7

Putting the Parts Together: The Whole Paper

The writing techniques you have learned apply to *all* writing—to individual paragraphs, to short papers, to long papers. The basic techniques remain the same:

Discovering a subject
Focusing through controlling attitude
Providing specific supporting evidence
Maintaining unity of subject and tone
Using suitable developmental patterns

First, review the organization of the short paper in a new basic diagram (page 194), a slightly different version because your knowledge of the writing process has greatly increased. Your first papers should follow this basic organizational pattern, unless your instructor tells you to follow **Theme Pattern A** instead. Or, you may be asked first to write your ideas in the form of **Theme Pattern A** and then to rewrite the paper using **Theme Pattern B.**

Since you are better prepared now than when you wrote your first paper at the end of Chapter 2, your writing should reflect what you've learned in the meantime. Also, you now have a better idea of what your instructor looks for when reading papers. Before writing any new themes, therefore, reconsider the basic qualities of an effective paper:

1. **Content.** Do you have a meaningful, limited subject, developed logically and supported adequately?
2. **Organization.** Do you have a controlled thesis statement in the introduction, clear support in the topic sentences of each developmental paragraph, specific, detailed support for each topic sentence, and a conclusion that echoes the thesis statement without simply repeating it?

3. **Tone.** Do you capture reader interest and gain reader acceptance? What kind of "voice" have you projected? (Read your paper aloud and listen.) Remember, the kind of "voice" readers hear as they go through your paper will influence their interest, acceptance, and judgment.
4. **Mechanics.** Does your paper contain unacceptable spelling, punctuation, and grammar, faulty sentence structure (for instance, fragments that don't work), lack of unity and coherence, or faulty diction (including worn-out expressions, listless verbs, the "who-which-that disease")?

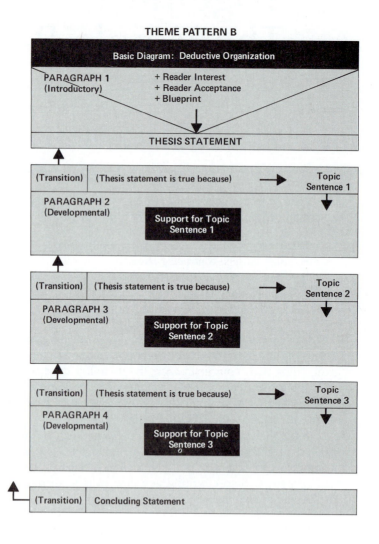

Keep in mind that weakness in any *one* of these major basic areas will negatively influence *any* reader, not just a composition instructor. You can, for example, have good content and organization, but if the mechanics of your paper or report are poor, the result could be disappointing. Similarly, mechanics can be perfect and organization good, but if the paper lacks ideas of consequence or is dull, the result may be the same. Usually the dull paper that is good in all other respects has a problem in *tone*. That is, it may have no *reader interest*, or it may lack *ethical appeal* (getting the reader to accept the writer and his views). Or it may have an informal tone where a more formal one is better suited to the subject or the reader. Or it may sound insincere because the words are far too fancy for the subject. You'll learn more about tone in Chapter 10 (see page 350). Meanwhile, if tone becomes a problem, study pages 116–27 on introductory paragraphs.

The "Simplified Check Sheet for the Whole Paper" summarizes these four basic areas a composition instructor usually evaluates: *thought, organization, tone,* and *mechanics*. Note that within each of these four areas the check sheet also lists some of the specific details to help you revise your own work. *Before* you turn in the final draft of your papers, use this check sheet to note those elements that need revision. If you are working on a computer, be sure to save your unrevised draft

SIMPLIFIED CHECK SHEET FOR THE WHOLE PAPER

PAPER TITLE: WRITER'S NAME: READER'S NAME:	Excellent	Good	Acceptable	Weak	Poor
A. THOUGHT					
1. Does the paper have a meaningful subject?					
2. Is the subject limited?					
3. Is there a clear controlling attitude?					
4. Do developmental paragraphs give specific factual support?					
5. Is the support adequate?					
6. Does the whole paper have unity of thought?					
B. ORGANIZATION					
7. Is there a clear beginning, middle, and ending?					
8. Is the thesis statement adequate?					
9. Do all topic sentences support the thesis?					
10. Is there a "blueprint" to order the ideas?					
11. Does the whole paper have coherence?					
12. Does each paragraph have unity and coherence?					
C. TONE (The Writer's "Voice")					
13. Does the paper create reader interest?					
14. Does the paper try to get reader acceptance?					
15. Is there successful ethical appeal?					
16. Does the tone fit the subject and the reader?					
D. MECHANICS					
17. Good word choice: strong verbs, care with adverbs?					
18. Spelling, punctuation, grammar?					
19. Sentence structure?					
20. Neat, professional appearance?					

first, then use the retrieve command to provide an on-screen version to play with. With your saved copy secure, you can, if necessary, reposition words, sentences, even paragraphs, easily tightening the organization. This is also the time to apply the spell-checking program, the thesaurus, and similar software packages to help you improve the earlier draft. If, however, you don't reread your papers before turning them in, you won't be able to evaluate their success. The check sheet has several other uses: You can exchange papers with a classmate to spot each other's strengths and weaknesses; your instructor may want to use the check sheet for similar purposes, having the entire class evaluate its own papers; or to point out your problems quickly (especially if your instructor doesn't have time to comment at length).

To review what a professional reader would look for, consider the following student papers, which we will analyze, one paragraph at a time, as a composition instructor might. The first paper closely follows the requirements for a five-hundred-word theme.

```
           THE STUDENT AND CLIFFS NOTES

     Not usually avid readers, students sometimes resort to
substituting Cliffs Notes for required reading books. Basically
honest, many of these students, under pressure of heavy
assignments and extracurricular activities, think of Cliffs
Notes as merely a harmless short cut to an assignment. Though
this short-cut approach may give them enough information to
write a plot summary, these students cheat themselves when they
take this easy way out.
```

This example fulfills most of the requirements for a short introductory paragraph. It starts with a general statement about substituting *Cliffs Notes* for required reading and ends with a specific *controlling attitude* (the *pointer*): students *cheat themselves* when they do this. The paragraph also tries to get reader acceptance by making a number of *positive* statements about students: They are "basically honest" and they're "under pressure of heavy assignments and extracurricular activities." But there is no real attempt to create interest or to project ethical appeal. And there's no *blueprint* to order the ideas of the paper.

Here's the first developmental paragraph.

```
     The student who depends on the Cliffs Notes summaries of
great literature deprives herself of an accurate presentation
of the original story. For example, if she reads only the
summary version of Twain's A Connecticut Yankee, which doesn't
```

try to present the satire, she may get the impression that Twain was making an early effort at some type of science fiction. She is robbed of experiencing the satire at first hand. The student who relies on the summary version of <u>Huckleberry</u> <u>Finn</u> misses most of the defining details of Huck's adventures, as in the Grangerford episode. She finds the story retold and compressed in a manner that would infuriate the author. The unfortunate student who bases her book report on the summary version of <u>The</u> <u>House</u> <u>of</u> <u>Seven</u> <u>Gables</u> will probably exaggerate the Pyncheon ancestors and the family curse, saying little about Hepzibah, Clifford, and the other characters. In summary form, mysterious deaths and family curses make better mystery stories than the effect of these circumstances on the characters.

This paragraph has a proper topic sentence (the first one in the paragraph), providing the first reason for the validity of the thesis: Students *deprive* themselves of an accurate representation of the original story. To support the *controlling attitude* of this topic sentence, the writer uses three short illustrations from three famous works of fiction to show how the summary versions change the originals. Because the *pointer* in the topic sentence is *deprives* and each illustration indicates how this deprivation comes about, the paragraph is properly focused: it has unity. Each sentence uses *student,* or the pronoun substitute *she* as its subject, resulting in coherence maintained through a consistent point of view. There are no mechanical errors.

Now look at the second developmental paragraph.

(1) In addition to being deprived of accurate presentations of literature, each time the student resorts to the <u>Cliffs</u> <u>Notes</u> version of a novel she misses practice in critical reading and evaluation. (2) From the summary alone the student gets no concept of the underlying theme of a story or of persistent themes that recur in one author's works. (3) Since the <u>Cliffs</u> version presents only basic plot movement, the reader has no way of interpreting the author's purpose in creating certain dialogue. (4) Rather than deciding for herself, she reads the <u>Cliffs</u> interpretations provided between the chapter summaries. (5) Further, since symbols, figures, dialogue, and point of view can't be adapted to summary presentation, the reader does not experience these artistic devices. (6) Finally, the student fails to see the detailed structure of the novel because the summary always emphasizes plot and action, often condensing many pages into a single paragraph. (7) Regardless of the importance of setting or characters in the original, the student will see plot as the dominant factor.

Again the first sentence is the topic sentence (highlighted). Because the *pointer* is *misses,* the rest of the paragraph must show why this practice is missed. The writer has developed the paragraph through reasons, providing three to support the validity of the *controlling attitude* represented by the pointer. The first reason is in the second sentence: the student misses the underlying theme or themes that recur in an author's work. The second reason is in the fifth sentence: the student misses the experience of basic artistic devices—symbols, figures, dialogue, point of view. The third reason appears in the sixth sentence: the student misses the detailed structure of the novel because a summary emphasizes plot and action only.

The paragraph maintains unity. The three reasons directly support the topic sentence, and these in turn are supported by other sentences. The third sentence, for instance, explains the first reason (given in the second sentence), and the seventh sentence explains the third reason (given in the sixth sentence). The paragraph holds together well. The subject of each sentence is *student* or a pronoun or noun standing for the student. To increase coherence, the student has used transition words. *Further,* in the fifth sentence, introduces the second reason, and *finally,* in the sixth sentence, introduces the third reason. In the first part of the topic sentence, notice the important transition linking this paragraph to the preceding one, improving the coherence of the whole paper.

Now let's consider the final paragraph.

---

(1) Of equal importance to the student who substitutes the Cliffs version for the original, she does not enjoy the power and majesty of the English language as it has been used by great authors. (2) She finds no new and interesting words to challenge her. (3) Because these summaries are intended primarily for a nonliterary audience, she encounters chiefly colorless words she already knows. (4) Comparing the Cliffs version with the author's, she finds the vocabulary confined to words with little connotative meaning. (5) The student will also find that most descriptive passages have been eliminated from the summary or drastically condensed. (6) The author has described the actions and scenes in image-evoking, carefully chosen words, but the Cliffs reader will find only dull, oversimplified language. (7) She discovers that she needn't use her imagination to recreate a character because she has a simplistic list of qualities provided in summary fashion. (8) Thus, she doesn't need the author's figurative language that enriches and encourages imagination. (9) The student misses not only the artistry of word choice and description, but the original combinations of words within sentences and sentences within paragraphs—the various ways in which writers create distinctive styles. (10) Since she is reading a condensed and altered version of the novel, she can't enjoy the author's original use of dialect or his ability to make the most ordinary things seem unique. (11) She misses the artistry of authors like Poe and Thomas Wolfe, who chose sound-evoking words, then arranged them in rhythmic, almost poetic sentences. (12) By reading these inaccurate, condensed

> presentations of great literature, the student denies herself
> the opportunity of reading the literature of the past, the
> value of developing a critical attitude toward literature, and
> the pleasure of enjoying the power and beauty of her own
> language.

Like the other developmental paragraphs, this final one begins with the topic sentence. The point it develops is that the student who reads summaries as substitutes for the real thing misses the full effect of the artistry used by great authors. The paragraph develops through the use of illustrative examples—the piling up of reasons for what the student misses. The last sentence is the concluding sentence. It restates the three reasons for the validity of the thesis statement as they appeared in the topic sentences of the developmental paragraphs. Some writers prefer to place the conclusion in a separate paragraph of its own—even if it consists of only one sentence. This technique can be very effective, especially if the conclusion adds new insight or summary effect.

Again, this paragraph is coherent and unified. All the sentences directly support the topic sentence. All the sentences use *student,* the pronoun *she,* or an equivalent subject. Transition words reinforce the coherence: *these summaries* (sentence three), *also* (sentence five), *thus* (sentence eight). Further, the beginning of sentence nine provides a major transition to the next group of ideas: *The student misses not only the artistry of word choice and description . . .* And the first part of the topic sentence, *Of equal importance . . . ,* connects this paragraph with the preceding one.

An outline will demonstrate the overall organization of the whole paper.

Thesis statement:	*Students cheat themselves when they choose the "easy way" of reading* Cliffs Notes *instead of required books.*
Reason 1: (*Topic Sentence*)	*They deny themselves an accurate presentation of the original story.*
Reason 2: (*Topic Sentence*)	*They miss the opportunity to practice critical reading and evaluation of literature.*
Reason 3: (*Topic Sentence*)	*They lose enjoyment of the power and majesty of the English language.*

This paper is good in organization, content, and mechanics. But it could be improved. The writer could add interest to the paper by slightly extending the comment "image-evoking, carefully chosen words," making it even more specific, perhaps by quoting a phrase or two. She could also quote some of the "dull, oversimplified language" for comment, perhaps adding a touch of humor. While these changes aren't necessary and could lengthen the paper, they could very well add the spark to make the result *excellent.*

For every paper you write, devise an interesting title to *anticipate* the thesis—at least in part. Here are some basic guidelines to follow:

1. Keep your titles short—five or six words.
2. Place no period at the end of your title.
3. Make no *direct* reference to your title in the first lines of your paper. (Don't say, for example, "This is seen in . . . ," where *this* refers to the title.)
4. Capitalize the first and last words of your title and all other important words, but do not capitalize articles *(a, an, the)*, conjunctions *(and, but, or,)*, or prepositions.
5. Make your title honest, but try to be creative.
6. Anticipate your paper's thesis if possible (in capsule, summary form).
7. Do not use a sentence for a title.
8. Use a colon to balance short title parts: *Getting Started: Discovery, Specific Focus, Thesis.*
9. You may use ALL CAPS for your title if you wish.
10. Do not put quotation marks around your own title.

Consider, for example, the title of the paper just analyzed, "The Student and *Cliffs Notes.*" In a general way it anticipates the whole paper, takes up only five words, has no final punctuation mark, and has all the words capitalized except the conjunction *and*. It's not a sentence, and it's an honest title because it provides a "capsule" summary of the paper. Although it fulfills the requirements for a good title, it probably could be improved. Try to suggest a more creative, interesting version.

Now let's look at another student paper.

BREAD OF LIFE

Buddha, Mohammed, Jesus, and their fellow-prophets have a tough modern competitor. Today's American bread-winner spends at least forty hours a week working for it and most of the rest of the time spending it. Money feeds us, clothes us, shelters us. It has become much more than the convenient bartering system devised by our ancestors to simplify the exchange of goods and services. Money has become the bread of life, with a following the traditional religious groups would rejoice to include in the Sunday collection. Money gained this great discipleship because people believe in it. Their faith in money makes it appallingly powerful. The worldwide symbol of secular salvation, money affects nearly every aspect of daily life in the global community. It is a potent symbol, it has become omnipotent, and it permeates the social fabric of people's lives. Money has become a worldwide religion.

Although this successful introductory paragraph uses the funnel effect well, the student probably made it longer than it needs to be. The writer tries to capture attention with an unusual title, echoed twice in the first half of the paragraph. Whether the result justifies this effort to create the religious analogy is an open question. If the first four sentences were cut, some important bridge words would be lost: "fellow-prophets," "tough modern competitor," "bread-winner," "system devised by our ancestors." Though this deletion would shorten the paper, some interesting, relevant details would be lost. Beginning with the fifth sentence, the paragraph quickly focuses on money as a "worldwide symbol of secular salvation," and then provides a *blueprint* to govern the order of ideas—shown underlined. The paragraph ends with a bold thesis statement (shown highlighted).

Here's the first developmental paragraph.

(1) The cornerstone of all religions is unshakable belief, often in unprovable ideas represented by one or more potent symbols. (2) Zeus existed for the Greeks who believed that he existed. (3) Similarly, money works in our supermarkets or department stores because the customers, the cashier, and the community believe it is more than just a piece of paper. (4) And although our money is guaranteed by the United States Treasury as "legal tender for all debts, public and private," that really doesn't mean anything to most people. (5) The treasury is simply the ark, money is the power inside. (6) No matter that money is backed by useless metals or empty promises. (7) The dollar or the mark or the yen or the peso remains the cornerstone of each society as long as people believe it is the symbol of success, the key to a better life. (8) The resulting wealth brought by this symbol has a great advantage over spiritual religion. (9) The riches gained through this symbol have become a promise of happiness in this life: you don't even have to die first.

Shown highlighted, the topic sentence opens the paragraph, provides through the words *potent symbols* an important tie to the introduction, and gives the first reason for the validity of the thesis statement. The topic sentence echoes the blueprint ("potent symbol") and provides a controlling attitude ("unshakable belief") to support the thesis and to direct the ideas of this developmental paragraph. As with religion, says the writer, people's *unshakable belief in a potent symbol,* money, gives it worldwide life and *power.* Money works because people everywhere *believe* in it (customers, cashiers, supermarkets, the dollar, the yen, the mark, the peso). It works everywhere because people assume it has *power* and believe it's a *symbol* of success. It works because the symbol is not spiritual and has become a promise of happiness "in this life" (an echo of "secular salvation" in the introductory paragraph). The paragraph ends with an effective punch-line: "You don't even have to die first." By repeating such words as *symbol* and *belief,* the young man who wrote this theme has created unity and coherence. By linking his reasons to the controlling idea of *unshakable belief,* he has provided strong support for the analogy on which the thesis is based. There are no mechanical errors. It is a successful developmental paragraph.

The student provides an important transition to lead into the second developmental paragraph:

---

(1) <u>Though the symbolic nature of money contributes to its worldwide worship</u>, its use to provide instant gratification explains money's worldwide omnipotence. (2) The appeal of money is powerful and widespread because it seems so worldly, tangible, useful. (3) Think about a child taught to put a coin in a gumball machine. (4) That child quickly learns an important simple equation: the coin equals a piece of gum. (5) Adults then generalize that simple equation: having money means immediate gratification of our needs and desires. (6) Universal application of this equation transforms money into a fearful power. (7) Moving out of its proper role as a universal medium of exchange for acquiring goods to fulfill basic needs, money becomes the need itself. (8) This belief that the medium of exchange is the source of life sustenance is worldwide: people are joined internationally in their common materialism with greater unity than any one cause or prophet ever achieved. (9) And because all humans have similar basic needs and use cash or credit to fulfill them, acceptance of money has become their powerful common ground.

Again the topic sentence opens the paragraph. To provide added coherence to the whole paper, this first sentence begins with an important transition (underscored) that echoes the topic of the previous paragraph—the "symbolic nature of money." The topic sentence also states the controlling idea of the paragraph, "worldwide omnipotence," as well as a *reason* for this power—"instant gratification." The paragraph then explains that money provides this instant gratification because it is worldly and tangible (2). The writer next uses a simple illustration to explain how we learn to equate money with instant gratification (3, 4, 5, 6). As a result, money is transformed from a medium of exchange used to fulfill basic needs into the *need itself* (7). The "common materialism" of people joins them worldwide in the belief that money itself is the source of "life sustenance" (8). "Worldwide omnipotence" comes about because all humans have similar basic needs that they equate with money (9). The writer provides a number of reasons as well as an illustration to show why belief in instant gratification gives money worldwide omnipotence.

In addition to the transition provided in the topic sentence itself (underscored), the writer uses a number of other "echo" words to improve coherence: *that* child, *then*, *that* equation, *this* equation, *this* belief. He also repeats certain key words to provide both unity and coherence: *money . . . it, people . . . their, gratification, power, needs*. The result is a tight, coherent, successful paragraph.

Another important transition (underscored) leads the reader into the third developmental paragraph:

---

(1) As a result of unquestioned faith in money and its power to provide instant gratification, money has so permeated the social fabric of people's lives that it has become indispensable to all the workings of society. (2) Industry creates jobs and produces goods. (3) People work for money to afford to buy these goods, creating a never-ending circle of producer-consumer. (4) Government, the overseer, fights the demons of monetary inflation and recession, trying to regulate and balance production and consumption. (5) Even in churches, people who seek a spiritual environment are confronted by the worldliness of the collection basket. (6) Like some self-evident truth, money is everywhere. (7) In their daily lives, people are either earning or spending money in some way. (8) All their possessions are money in its traded-in form, and their time is money-bought, either hourly or on salary. (9) If it has been filtered through an air conditioner or heater, the very air they breathe costs money.

The strong echo provided by the transition statement in the first half of its topic sentence ties this paragraph clearly to the previous two. This statement keeps the overall coherent framework of the paper clearly before the reader (seen also in the *blueprint* in the introduction). In addition, the topic sentence supplies the *third reason* in support of the thesis idea: money has become a worldwide religion because it has "permeated the fabric of people's lives" and has become *indispensable* (the controlling idea). The writer then uses a series of illustrative examples to support this third reason. These illustrations point to *industry* (2, 3), *government* (4), and *churches* (5), summed up in sentence six with the statement that "money is everywhere" (6). Daily life is controlled by earning or spending money (7), and all possessions represent "money in its traded-in form," while even time is "money-bought" (8). Even the air people breathe costs money (9). These illustrations strongly support the topic sentence assertion that money so permeates people's lives that it has become indispensable. It is this tight list of reasons that gives the paragraph its strong unity and coherence. And again there are no mechanical errors.

Instead of placing the conclusion within the final developmental paragraph, this writer chose to separate it and use it to echo all the significant ideas:

---

(1) Money touches our lives so completely that we stand the risk of being controlled by our own creation. (2) Our belief in money amounts to unshakable faith; because it works,

we use it everywhere. (3) Through the power of money we pay to
breathe, to eat, to sleep. (4) The same money that delivers us
buries us. (5) It permeates our daily lives: it motivates, it
governs, it grows with interest. (6) Money buys happiness: put
a coin in the vending machine for instant gratification. (7) We
believe in the symbol and the power. (8) We have transformed
our belief in money into a worldwide religion.

Because this paragraph is a concluding summary, it doesn't have a topic
sentence. It does, however, incorporate the thesis statement into its last sentence,
as if to say, "See? I told you so." The many highlighted words in this paragraph
show how carefully the writer chose the echo words. They remind the reader of the
initial blueprint *(potent symbol, omnipotent, permeates)* and the overall coherence and
unity of the paper. The writer's short sentences *quickly* place all the paper's
important ideas before the reader, a strong reminder of the paper's structure.
Whether or not we are convinced by this writer's analogy and its supporting
reasons, we can easily see the paper's thesis, organization, thought, and carefully
constructed sentences. Although the tone of the paper is consistently "serious," the
writer creates interest through the careful use of evocative words. Most readers
would judge this to be a successful paper, even though it is somewhat longer than
the basic five-hundred-word theme.

The next two student papers illustrate some common problems you may
encounter. Check them carefully and be sure you understand how to improve
them. Here's the first.

THE LIBRARY, THE TEACHER, AND THE STUDENT

(1) Students in the school I attended have certainly lost
the inquiring mind, if they ever had it, and they no longer
even want to think for themselves. (2) It seems, in fact, that
our whole society has lost the zest for inquiring because of
the loss of ideals and qualities. (3) I cannot account for
society's loss, but among students in my school I can see at
least two reasons: inadequate libraries and prejudiced
teachers.

This introductory paragraph isn't bad. Though all the parts are there, the student
hasn't organized them or created a good *funnel effect*. Apparently the first sentence
is the thesis statement, but it's composed of two independent clauses: *Students in
the school I attended have certainly lost the inquiring mind* and *they no longer even want
to think for themselves*. Because the two clauses carry equal weight (both are
independent), the construction results in a confusing thesis statement. A reader

can't tell which subject is the *focus* of the paper because the sentence provides two *controlling attitudes*. Look at the sentence closely, however, and you'll see that the student says the same thing in both clauses. Here's what the writer probably intended as the thesis statement: *students no longer want to think for themselves*. This idea should be given the important position in the sentence and, to create a better funnel effect, it should be placed at the end of the paragraph with the two reasons (the **blueprint**) given in the third sentence. Rephrased and placed in the funnel position at the end of the paragraph, this sentence might look like this:

> *(4) Because of inadequate libraries and prejudiced teachers, students no longer want to think for themselves.*

The blueprint, shown underscored, precedes the actual thesis and anticipates the reasons to be discussed in the paper. Because it's a more general statement, the second sentence could serve as the paragraph's opening, though it needs to be revised to eliminate two vague words, *ideals* and *qualities*. In recasting, make these words more specific. One possible version might begin like this:

> *(1) It seems that our whole society has* **lost** *the zest for learning as well as the desire to read. (2) Nowhere is this* **loss** *seen more, perhaps, than among our students. (3) But the* **loss** *isn't entirely their fault.*

This three-sentence beginning uses the original paragraph's strongest quality—the repetition of the key word *loss* to provide continuity and coherence. The repetition ties the three sentences together.

The first developmental paragraph discusses the first reason students do not want to think for themselves.

In my school, the library was pathetically inadequate. If we wanted to know about the latest scientific developments, we had no reference books to examine except a fifteen-year-old encyclopedia. We could read no recent scientific magazines, because there were none, not even any fifteen years old. The most weighty current magazine in the library was The Reader's Digest, hardly the one in which to research a topic in, say, biology. If we were interested in literature, about the best we could do for modern fiction was Seventeen by Booth Tarkington or perhaps The Virginian. No teacher of any subject ever assigned us library work or outside reading. On the few occasions we did venture into the library on our own initiative, old Miss Spence, who had been librarian for twenty years, made it clear that she was not interested. If we came into the library, it only meant trouble for her. Under these conditions it's not surprising that the students did little inquiry into important human problems. They did not even know what these problems were; they had no way of knowing.

This paragraph appears to be a good one. It starts with a topic sentence with a pointer, *pathetically inadequate*. Basically, it gives three reasons in support of the validity of this topic sentence: (1) resources for scientific research were nonexistent; (2) literary research, particularly modern, was equally difficult; and (3) the teachers and the librarian were uninterested in encouraging library work. Each reason is supported by illustration, and the paragraph ends with a summary sentence. The paragraph reads well as a unit. Note, for instance, the repetition of *fifteen* in the first part of the paragraph and of *library* and *librarian* in the last part to help coherence. Unity is maintained because all the evidence offered supports the topic sentence.

Here is the last paragraph.

---

(1) We have modified our society a great deal in the past few decades. (2) With the new advances in knowledge and in working and living conditions, we have come to expect more from other people than from ourselves. (3) Students revel in the new prosperity, buying things, having fun, and joining clubs. (4) The sole aim of their lives has become to have pleasure, so much so that they simply do not have time for school or studies or satisfying their natural curiosity. (5) In fact, they do not even notice these things, because they do not contribute to what they consider their pleasure. (6) Teachers foster this pursuit of pleasure in their students by trying to make their students all conform to what they think students ought to be and to think. (7) Students are expected to parrot on quizzes the ideas the teacher has given out in class. (8) They do not want us to think for ourselves but to go to established authorities for even simple ideas and explanations. (9) These teachers, and other forces in society, who rebel against nonconformity (something may or may not be right, but they won't try to find out if it is or not) make certain that a teacher with other ideas is not allowed to exist in their little world. (10) This is well illustrated by the case of Mrs. Jane Doe, a former teacher of mine. (11) In her English classes, she discussed everything, always taking the view opposite that of the majority of her students. (12) She would rant in class in her attacks on the established order of society or politics or tradition, and actually spoke in favor of Communism just to get her students to argue with her. (13) Her attacks forced her students to think to support their views. (14) Forcing her students to think was the best thing she did for her students. (15) But Mrs. Doe was accused of being a Communist and fired because the other teachers, the school administrators, and the community did not appreciate her value. (16) With the lack of research facilities in the school library and with this sort of narrow-mindedness from our teachers, students at the school I attended cannot think for themselves.

This paragraph is a jumble of ideas without unity, and what seemed to be a promising paper falls to pieces. The introductory paragraph announces that the paper will develop two reasons for the validity of the thesis statement: Students do not want to think for themselves because (1) the library is inadequate and (2) the teachers are prejudiced. This paragraph should be the one that develops the controlling attitude represented by the pointer *prejudiced,* but the word does not even appear in the paragraph.

What has happened? The student may have started writing the paper without thinking it through. Then when she reached this last paragraph, she wasn't sure what to use to support the idea about the teachers being prejudiced. Rather than going back and reorganizing—not much change needed—she plunged ahead and ruined the paper. Or, she may have failed to see that the last paragraph discusses two subjects, not one. She changes direction in the middle of the paragraph. Through the fifth sentence, the paragraph has to do with the hectic life students lead and how it stops them from thinking. The remainder of the paragraph, however, is concerned with teachers' narrow-minded conformity and the way it restricts student thinking. Each of the two main ideas should have been developed in a separate paragraph. This paragraph is a good example of the use of hazy, undefined terms *(advances in knowledge and in working and living conditions, forces in society)* that allow the writer to wander off with no particular point being supported. It lacks a controlling attitude.

The third paragraph might be questioned at several points. The trouble is largely a matter of diction—the use of hazy, general words instead of specific ones that convey exact meaning. For instance, look at the beginning of the second sentence: *With the new advances in knowledge and in working and living conditions.* . . . What precisely does the general term *advances* mean to the writer? How can the reader know what she means? We can guess, but we can't be certain. In addition, how have these *advances* led us *to expect more from other people than from ourselves?* Because the writer doesn't answer this question and doesn't define *advances,* the sentence seems meaningless. The instructor might mark this sentence simply with a question mark in the margin, or say it is "general" or "vague." These comments indicate that the reader can't determine what you mean and that you need to be more specific.

The ninth sentence should also be questioned. It begins *These teachers, and other forces in society, who rebel against nonconformity (something may or may not be right, but they won't try to find out if it is or not)* . . . , and stops readers cold. They can't possibly continue into the sentence after this point without rereading this beginning carefully to determine precisely what is being said. The parenthetical material is confusing; something is being defined, but what? Further, the sentence introduces a new subject, *other forces in society,* that appears irrelevant to the discussion. The dependent clause following this phrase, *who rebel against nonconformity,* is twisted in such a way that the reader must stop to figure it out. Ordinarily, we speak of rebelling against conformity rather than against nonconformity. We rebel against what is established. Nonconformity could hardly be said to be the established way of life in our society. So the reader is confused by this clause. *Who support conformity* is a much better way of saying it here.

The illustration of the teacher who refused to conform isn't good enough. It makes the reader think the school may have been justified in firing the teacher. She was apparently hired to teach English, but the illustration suggests that she taught everything but English. If she *ranted* in her classroom, it would make the school's case more secure. But this may be another instance of the writer's difficulty in choosing precise words.

Read the next paper all the way through.

EXERCISE IN OUR DAILY LIVES

Exercise should play a very large role in daily life. Everyone, no matter what age, needs exercise every day. However, with modern life being what it is, few older people get the daily exercise they need. Probably television as well as other modern inventions plays a part in producing the physically unfit American.

There are many exercises that will help people keep physically fit, if they are done every day. First, there are sit-up exercises that anyone can perform for a few minutes every day. If more people would do sit-up exercises on a regular schedule, fewer people in America would be sick. Younger people need to play games to keep themselves physically fit. Football is one of the best games a young person can play for this purpose. But any game that requires running and bending and stretching will do the same thing. Of course, young people should take advantage of the athletic programs in their school and of the school gymnasium on every occasion. Body-building centers are springing up all over the United States. In these centers, anyone from the youngest person to the oldest can set up an exercise program under the supervision of an expert in body building. Or, of course, a family can always buy exercise equipment such as stationary bicycles, barbells, and slant boards on which to exercise daily. If more people would exercise daily, they would find they feel better all the time.

Television and other modern inventions could possibly be a factor that produces the physically unfit American. Television can be very educational. There are many educational programs for adults as well as for the young generation. "Face the Nation," for example, and news programs such as "Sixty Minutes" can help the people of the United States learn more about the advancing world. But mostly, television is just a waste of time, being concerned altogether with entertainment programs. Another modern invention that contributes to the physically unfit American is the automobile. People no longer walk anyplace. If they have to go only two blocks to the grocery store, they get in the car and ride there instead of walking. Even the young people don't walk, but expect their parents to give them a car at an early age. If people are going to sit for hours in front of their television sets and ride in their cars everywhere, they need to get exercise by doing sit-ups or working out on gym equipment.

In our progressing world, everyone seems to be looking for more and more entertainment and for easier ways of doing things. It is easier for a mother to have her children watch entertainment programs on television while she does her work

> around the house than it is to put her housework off while she
> takes her children outside for some healthy exercise or outdoor
> play. By doing this is the mother making things easier for
> herself or is she thinking about her children's welfare? A good
> mother will let her children play outdoors while she does her
> housework. Under the same conditions, adults will watch
> television rather than exercise as they should.

You should recognize that the paper is ineffective and should be able to point out its chief weaknesses. If an instructor tried to mark everything unacceptable in this paper, the margins wouldn't accommodate the marks and comments. Perhaps personal conferences with the instructor would guide this student writer.

One of the chief weaknesses of this paper is its content. The very title, "Exercise in Our Daily Lives," suggests emptiness and dullness. Almost any reader who sees the thesis statement, *Exercise should play a very large role in daily life,* knows the paper will not be vital. First, *very large* is not specific. How much exactly is a *very large role*? Second, who wants to read about so commonplace a subject, one that everyone knows about already? A more limited subject would improve the focus: "Running for Life."

Despite the confusion apparent in the introductory paragraph, the reader may find three points the paper uses to support the thesis: (1) Everyone needs exercise every day; (2) few older people get the daily exercise they need; and (3) television and other modern inventions produce the unfit American. None of these supports the thesis statement *as given.* We need go no further into the paper than the brief introductory paragraph to predict the results—an unacceptable paper.

The rest of the paper bears out such a prediction. The paragraphs aren't unified. Each jumps from subject to subject, changing direction every sentence or so. Some second-paragraph material is discussed in the third, and some in the third is discussed again in the fourth. Therefore, the paragraphs cannot be coherent; no use of coherence devices will help these paragraphs unless they are first rewritten for unity. Diction and sentence structure will have to be revised. Some sentences, possibly the result of too little thought or too hasty revision, come out unintentionally humorous. Look, for instance, at the last sentence. The writer has just explained that many mothers allow their children to waste time watching television because it speeds up housework. The last sentence says: *Under the same conditions, many adults will watch television in their spare time rather than exercise as they should.* The reader is tempted to counter, "Under what conditions? While their mother is taking care of them?"

Before you begin the writing assignments, here's a final student theme for analysis. Its six paragraphs are numbered for easy reference. Note that it has four developmental paragraphs rather than the three suggested in the basic diagram for Theme Pattern B. And the conclusion has been expanded into a full paragraph. Decide whether this expanded theme still meets the suggested guidelines for a short paper. Check it for thesis statement, topic sentences, and supporting information, using the check sheet for the whole paper to guide your evaluation of the paper's effectiveness. List your responses to the check sheet's twenty questions on a sheet of note paper and be prepared to discuss your conclusions.

THE UMBRELLA MAN

1   At least two defensible truisms apply to Americans. Both are exemplified by the multiplicity of "conspiracy" and "coverup" charges following the assassination of President John Kennedy. Fortune-seeking authors who refused to believe the simple answer––that one man could kill a president––found a ready audience in millions of Americans who were eager for a mystery. The House Select Committee on Assassination convened for a second attempt (the first was the Warren Commission in 1964) to end these theories. The "umbrella man" conspiracy theory, one of those considered by the committee, illustrates two truisms: that Americans love a murder mystery and that they love to make things complex.

2   The Umbrella Man was caught in photographs just at the time of Kennedy's assassination. He was a member of the crowd in Dealey Plaza that November day, and as he opened his black umbrella the shooting began. People who studied the film and the assassination immediately understood the plot. The umbrella was a signal for the gunman (or gunmen) to fire. These "experts" concluded that split-second timing was critical. Perhaps it covered up the fact that more than one gun had been fired. The scheme would have been complicated and difficult to carry out, but nothing less could be expected of men who wanted to kill a president.

3   Because the Umbrella Man's story was widely circulated in the mass media, Americans across the country quickly adopted the conspiracy idea. After all, the murder was not yet solved and a mystery remained. In his book Shadows of Doubt (Hicksville, N.Y.: Exposition Press, 1976), Robert Meunier summarized the support for this theory. He writes that the umbrella opened just as the shooting began and then the Umbrella Man simply walked away. It was as if he knew what was going to happen and had his escape planned. The mystery deepened because, since it was warm in Dallas that day, there was no need for an umbrella, and despite the massive press coverage the Umbrella Man had not been identified. For many people this was very mysterious and adequate proof of his involvement in a conspiracy. Perhaps even now, they feared, he lived in Havana, basking in his success.

4   To the dismay of theorists their ideas were exploded. On September 21, 1978, Louis Witt, a thirty-year-old Dallas warehouse foreman, better known as the Umbrella Man, appeared before the House Committee to tell the true story. The Waco Tribune Herald (September 22, 1978) quoted Witt as he explained why he was carrying an umbrella: "I was going to do a little heckling." The umbrella was supposed to be a sore spot to the Kennedy family because it symbolized appeasement, which Joseph Senior supported before World War II.

5   Witt went on to explain his feelings after the shooting saying, "I can assure you I was not at all cool. Knowing I was there with this stupid umbrella and heckling the president. . . . It was kind of a practical joke gone sour." He hadn't come forth sooner because he didn't believe the matter important. And so, the umbrella was a symbol of appeasement, not a signal for murder; Witt was there for a "practical joke," not as part of a plot. And he refused to come forth more out of embarrassment than guilt. Witt's explanation, while not describing perfectly logical actions, was certainly believable. It was believable because there were more Americans interested in heckling the president than there were Americans interested in shooting him. But, most of all, it was believable because it was simple. There were no conspirators, no planning, and no split-second timing; so much for complexity. All Witt wanted to do was wave his umbrella; so much for mystery.

6   The Umbrella Man will soon be forgotten because the mystery is solved and the complex plot dispelled, but it is only one of many theories and conjectures surrounding the Kennedy assassination. The House Select Committee on Assassination soon released its verdict, and it echoed the Warren Commission——that one man, acting alone, killed President Kennedy. If you are one who loves a murder mystery and won't accept simple explanations, I hope you remember the Umbrella Man before you believe another conspiracy story.

EXERCISES

A. 1. Select one of the following general subjects to develop into a short paper.

Advertisements	Televangelists
TV Commercials	Minorities
Overpopulation	Pollution
TV Programs	Sexism
Movies	Transportation

If you are going to do Writing Assignment *B* or *C,* read them before choosing the subject for paper *A.*

2. Using one or more of the *discovery* methods studied in Chapter 3, logically divide your general subject into as many restricted ones as you can. Then choose one of these restricted subjects for development in a short paper of approximately five hundred words.

3. Using the *directed discovery questions* studied in Chapter 3 (or any other method that works for you), decide on a sharply focused *controlling attitude* for your subject. Keeping your restricted subject and controlling attitude in mind, phrase a good thesis statement for your paper.

4. Decide on three or four reasons to support the controlling attitude of your thesis statement. If you have problems, return to the *question approaches* explored in Chapter 3 for help. Once you've decided on the reasons in support of your controlling attitude, phrase them into a *blueprint* that can either (1) precede the thesis statement, or (2) become part of the thesis sentence. (Before you continue, your instructor may want to check what you have done. In any case, you should have good notes to represent these first four stages of the thinking and writing process.)

5. Write an introductory paragraph (about one hundred words) that (1) begins with one or two statements about the *general* subject you began with, (2) creates a *bridge* to the restricted subject you decided to use, (3) includes a blueprint to represent your supporting reasons, and (4) ends with a sharply focused thesis statement.

6. Now write a short paper (four or five good paragraphs) developing the reasons you discovered during the *prewriting* part of this exercise. In one paragraph, use reasons as the basic method of development; in another, use either comparison or contrast; and in another use some form of illustration or definition. Or, if you wish, you may combine methods within a developmental paragraph.

7. Underline your thesis statement and all topic sentences.

8. Beside each developmental paragraph, write in the margin the chief method (or methods) of development you used in that paragraph.

9. Before you turn in your paper, use the check sheet on page 195 to evaluate and, if necessary, to revise what you have written.

B. After your instructor has evaluated the paper you wrote for Exercise *A,* read it again and consider the following questions:

1. Does the paper sound convincing to you?

2. What reader did you have in mind when you wrote it?

3. Did you try to get your reader's interest? How?

4. Check the exercises on page 191, then list the "feeling" words in your paper. Now rewrite the first two paragraphs of Paper *A,* trying to improve reader interest and reader acceptance, but this time assume you are writing to a specific person, perhaps one of the following:

a. Your best friend (same sex).

b. A small group of very conservative women (or men).

c. An important authority figure (congressman, mayor, father, minister).

d. Any special person of your own choice.

Keep your ideas, thesis, organization, and illustrations basically the *same* as they were in Paper *A.* Concentrate on changing the interest level and tone to fit the chosen reader(s). In parentheses immediately below your paper's title name your reader, like this: (Reader: My best friend, Zeba.)

C. Here's another way to learn about creating an interesting tone in a paper. First, reread the examples given in Chapter 1 (page 7) and then look carefully at these three paragraphs (all written by the same student). Try to determine what three "voices" the student used.

1. I took the ball on the handoff from the quarterback. I hid the ball behind my outside thigh as one does on a bootleg. The ball was hidden so well it fooled the end and the linebacker. Then I simply outran the rest of the clods to the goal.

2. Charlie's fake on that play was great—he was the fullback who took the first fake and dived into the line. The end and linebacker tackled him, thinking he had the ball. This enabled Fred to turn the end and cut up the field for the score.

3. The Slip Yeomen slid by the Elm Lions by a score of 7–0. The only score came late in the last half, when the right halfback took the ball from the quarterback and cut up field for 70 yards. But the play was a team effort: all the blocks and fakes were perfectly executed because the team had worked the play for the past two weeks.

What other things have changed in these paragraphs with the change in "voice"? (Consider such things as choice of words, pronouns, and general "feeling.")

Now try to do something similar with the first two paragraphs of Paper *A* or *B*. This time, assume a *role;* pretend you are someone other than yourself with characteristics you know well. Again, keep your ideas, thesis, organization, and illustrations basically the same as they were in Paper *A* (or *B*); make changes to fit the new "voice" you have assumed in the paper. Here are some role suggestions (you may use others):

    a. Your father (or mother)
    b. An excited young girl (or boy)
    c. Your grandmother (or some other relative)
    d. A housewife with no high school education
    e. A salesman who never stops selling
    f. A conservative politician

In parentheses immediately below your title, identify the "voice" you are trying to project, like this: (Writer: Sarah, age 12).

D. If you study the techniques you used in *B* and *C,* you should be able to write a theme on one of the following:

    1. Changing Tone in a Paper
    2. Creating Reader Interest in a Paper
    3. Some Effects of "I" and "He" in a Paper

You should discuss this paper in class before trying to write it; your instructor may want to give you some additional suggestions.

8

Researched Writing and the Long Paper

Chapter 7 brought together the basic parts of a five-hundred-word theme, provided a picture-outline showing the interrelationship of the parts, supplied you with a check sheet for the whole paper, and asked you to evaluate a number of complete papers. It also further explored additional problems in tone, reader interest, and point of view—all important elements in any successful paper. Add to this information what you learned in the first six chapters, and you should be able to tackle the long paper, the subject of the present chapter. This point is worth emphasizing: *All the skills and principles you learned to use in writing a short paper apply to the longer one.*

This chapter asks you to review and apply those skills as you research and write a longer paper using reliable information sources. As you move through the chapter, you will be asked to think and write your way through the following assignments:

1. Choose two or three general subject areas you would like to research. Choose only subjects that you find interesting or useful.
2. By using logical division (analysis), for each of these general subjects devise a limited subject you can discuss in five to ten typed pages. Do some preliminary searching and reading.
3. For each of these limited subjects phrase several questions to suggest what you will investigate *about* the subject. Choose one of these limited subjects for investigation. Continue your preliminary searching and reading.
4. Devise a preliminary working bibliography to show that you have begun to investigate your chosen subject.
5. After doing some additional reading and thinking, devise a first-try purpose statement in the form of a simple assertion, or a question, or a thesis.

6. Use this purpose statement to write a first-try introductory paragraph to lead a reader into your paper and its limited subject.
7. Summarize reliable, relevant information on four-by-six-inch note cards to show the extent of your research.
8. Classify (sort) your information into major subject categories and devise a brief working topic outline.
9. Write a first draft of your research paper.
10. Complete and submit the final draft of your paper (including complete note cards, final bibliography, and first draft) together with a detailed, final topic (or sentence) outline.

Reprinted by permission: Tribune Media Services.

WHAT IS A RESEARCHED PAPER?

Even though you may begin the search for a long-paper subject by using the *discovery* techniques of *free association,* you continue this search by using the techniques of the *directed discovery process* you studied in Chapter 3. The information used in the paper is "directed," first, by the sources you use (books, people, magazines); then you further expand, control, or limit that information by applying the skills you developed in "Getting Started: Discovery, Specific Focus, Thesis" (Chapter 3). Depending on its specific purpose, who will write it, and who will read it, the long paper has been given many names: *researched paper, research paper, investigative paper, library paper, term report, technical report, problem-solving paper, thesis, dissertation, reference paper.* Although all of these require the skills and principles presented in the first seven chapters of this book if they are to be effective and successful, they differ from the basic short paper in a number of important ways.

1. Length.   To begin with, they are longer. Excluding theses and dissertations, which can vary in length from about fifty to several hundred pages, the long papers this chapter prepares you for will range in length from five to ten pages. *Length will depend on your instructor's requirements and the time available for the project.*

2. Documentation.   Researched papers are *documented* because they are reports based on information sources. They contain internal documentation (citations) to identify for the reader all quoted, paraphrased, or summarized material. They may also contain footnotes or explanatory [end]notes to clarify, extend, or comment on the meaning of internal documentation (citations). They may use information from books, magazine articles, newspapers, encyclopedias, official government documents, and other standard, *reliable* information sources. They may refer to interviews, whether conducted in person or by phone. They may use information from unpublished reports, papers, or theses. They may even report, objectively and accurately, original experiments conducted by the writer of the research paper. But whatever the information sources, they all must be clearly identified in acceptable documentation form.

3. Research and Its Purpose.   The word *research* implies a systematic investigation of *available information* in some specific field of knowledge. It may be a survey (review or analysis) of the available information on one specific topic. This kind of researched paper surveys the information available in *many* sources and then reports it in a *single* long paper. The basic purpose of this kind of paper is to collect, summarize, and report that information. It brings together in *one* paper the current information previously scattered throughout many sources.

   In fact, all meaningful research is motivated by some *purpose*. A researched paper may have as its purpose:

> to report current views on a specific topic
> to determine the answer to a focused question by reporting current information
> to explore the validity of one idea or principle by examining *many* views
> to recommend a specific course of action by analyzing and reporting various available options
> to advocate *one* specific point of view (or thesis) by reporting supporting authoritative views
> to correct misunderstanding of a specific topic by reporting reliable information

But beyond these fundamental purposes your research paper will give you the experience of independent study—discovering, organizing, developing, and reporting information on a specific topic of your choice. A secondary though important purpose of the research paper assignment is to extend your *searching skills* by extending your knowledge of a good library's incredible information sources.

4. Form.   Your researched paper takes a special form. Whether you follow the style of MLA or APA, the paper will include *internal documentation* (citations) to identify information sources. It will also provide a bibliography, entitled "Works Cited," "References," or "Works Consulted." The longer the paper, the more likely it is to use headings to indicate major units (MLA sometimes follows this practice). A long research paper also usually has a concluding unit (or summary) consisting of one or more complete paragraphs. These too may be set off by a heading. The paper is typed (double-spaced) with adequate margins (at least one inch), usually has a title page (paper's title, writer's name, recipient's name, date), and repeats the writer's name on each page (just before the page number in the upper right corner). For these and other conventions of form, check the sample paper, "Monkey Talk."

5. Evaluation.   Some research papers do more than simply discover facts and report them in a detailed, orderly, objective manner. They may *evaluate* the facts, provided that the researcher has enough reliable information, insight, and education to make a concluding judgment or recommendation. Carefully pursued, research can teach you how to discriminate between useful and worthless opinions.

6. Audience.   Most research papers (including technical reports) are aimed at a specific audience (reader). They must, therefore, meet the needs and requirements of that audience. In a classroom situation, the research paper is aimed primarily at the *instructor.* In a business situation, a research report would consider the requirements of a supervisor and, perhaps, others who will be reading it. Your instructor will help you decide on what audience to consider.

7. Research Situations.   At work, in school, and at play, you already know that many situations require reliable researched information. This means that you should be clear on the *purpose* of any research you do. Phrased as questions, here are some examples to suggest research situations and the purposes they imply:

> Because she wants to buy two new computers for the office, your supervisor calls you in and asks, *"What would you recommend to fit our expanding needs as well as our limited budget?"*
> In late August, for six days only, you will fly to Moscow for a vacation visit and are faced with this question: *How do I plan the trip and the visit?*
> While introducing *Macbeth,* your English instructor comments that actors are superstitious about performing in the play and gives this assignment: *"Is there any factual basis for this fear and superstition?"*
> A friend, who is buying a used car, asks: *"What make and model has the best repair and replacement record?"*

Our lives are filled with questions:

> *What is the legal status of abortion in the United States?*
> *What employment prospects are there in the area of environment protection?*
> *What kinds of jobs hold up best during good (or bad) times?*
> *In what ways do humans exhibit territorial behavior?*
> *How do psychologists define "deviant behavior"?*
> *How widespread are deviant lifestyles?*
> *How does language influence and control its users?*
> *Do television ads encourage harmful behavior?*

Is world population out of control?
How does the increasing number of people in the United States affect everyday lives?
What effects has the legalization of drugs had in the Netherlands?
How easily can a person become addicted to the use of hard drugs?
What do American personnel managers look for in a prospective employee?
What college is best suited to my interests and budget?
What has caused teenage birthrates to increase after years of decline?
Can AIDS be transmitted through simple physical contact?
Does alcohol damage our brain cells?

The best kind of purpose is to find a question you really want to answer or a problem you really need to solve.

Whether informative or evaluative, research should lead you to a *way of learning* you'll find useful for the rest of your life. Writing a research paper requires you to learn and apply many basic strategies and skills. It is a method of investigating, summarizing, and reporting information you have gathered—from magazine articles, books, pamphlets, questionnaires, libraries, professional people, government documents, even letters. And, because the researched paper does more than merely explain something the writer is interested in, it designs purpose, form, and style to fit the requirements of a specific reader. It can *report* facts and summarize them without making an inference. Or it can, in addition, make an inference from the facts. Or its purpose may be to *solve a problem* or *answer a question,* providing a solution that the facts convincingly support.

The check sheet in the next section of this chapter provides an overview to guide you through the process of conceiving and writing a short research paper. Note the skills you use during each stage of the process.

CHECK SHEET FOR WRITING A RESEARCH PAPER

The check sheet on page 219 outlines the information you will be studying in the rest of this chapter. It identifies all the stages you will go through in creating an effective research paper.

The five major parts of this check sheet (A–E) should be familiar to you. They represent what you have already learned in writing a five-hundred-word theme. Before studying how each of these parts relates to the long paper, you should review the suggested relevant chapter, since much of the discussion of the research paper assumes that you understand the earlier material. Also, note that the three chapters on revision (9, 10, and 11) following this one provide useful suggestions on writing and revising your paper to make it more effective. Work through the ten stages of the process as explained in this chapter and you should be able to make the transition from the short papers you've been writing to the research paper you now will be asked to write.

CHECK SHEET FOR WRITING A RESEARCH PAPER	
A. Seeing the whole paper (Review Chapter 2)	
Know what the finished product looks like, study a sample.	
B. Choosing a subject (Review Chapter 3)	
1. Discover a suitable subject.	
2. Limit the subject with a specific controlling attitude or question.	
3. Write a purpose statement.	
C. Getting the facts (Review Chapters 3 and 6)	
4. Discover suitable information sources.	
5. Survey the information sources, prepare a working bibliography.	
6. Take exact, relevant notes, design a rough plan.	
D. Organizing the facts (Review Chapter 2)	
7. Classify the facts into major subject categories.	
8. Devise a preliminary topic outline.	
E. Writing the paper (Study Chapters 9, 10, 11)	
9. Write the first draft.	
10. Revise the paper, make the final copy, provide a final outline.	

EXERCISES: WARM-UP ASSIGNMENT

This assignment will help you get ready for work on the researched paper. It has these important aims:

To get you to think about possible report subjects
To get the research process started
To practice taking accurate notes on bibliographic information
To practice reporting and documenting information sources
To practice evaluating information you've researched.

Do the assignment carefully, step by step; take notes and list questions you would like to discuss in class after you've handed in the assignment. Before beginning this assignment, discuss it in class with your instructor.

A. Choose *any* subject that interests you. (It doesn't have to be the subject you finally choose for your research paper.) The questions listed on page 217 ("Research Situations") may provide some subject ideas; the list on page 236 can suggest others. First, write down the subject; then write a separate, one-sentence comment to explain what you'd like to learn about that subject. Following the examples given in "Research Situations," try to restate your comment as a question.

B. Find three short journal (magazine) articles that provide useful information about your subject. The articles must come from three different magazines. Different issues of the same magazine may be used. Write down the complete *bibliographic information* for each article:

1 The author's full name.

2. The complete title of each article (within quotation marks).

3. The name of the magazine(s), underlined.

4. The date of the magazine (month, date, and year).

5. The numbers of the pages on which the article appears.

C. For each article write a one- or two-sentence comment to explain what the article says about your subject. (You could combine parts *B* and *C* of this assignment.)

D. Write three paragraphs of approximately 150 words each about your subject. Here are the requirements for these paragraphs:

1. In each paragraph you must refer to or use information from *two* of the articles you've read.

2. By the end of your third paragraph you must have used information from all three articles.

3. You may quote *short* passages, if you wish, but these cannot be more than one sentence long. Put "quotation marks around these passages, followed by the author's last name and the page from which the quote comes" (Jefferson 739). [Note how I've used the quotation marks and the page reference example in the previous sentence.] Do not use more than three *short* quotations in each paragraph.

4. Don't summarize the articles. In your own words explain what information they give about your subject.

5. At the end of the third paragraph, write two or three sentences explaining which of the three articles was most helpful and why.

E. Write a concluding statement:

1. After you've finished the three paragraphs, write a carefully worded, one-sentence statement explaining what you have learned about your chosen subject.

2. Using this sentence as your basis, write a short, *pointed* title for your three-paragraph assignment.

SEEING THE WHOLE PAPER

Know what the finished product should look like; study examples. You can write a more effective research paper if you have a good idea of what the product looks like. Length aside, how does it differ from the five-hundred-word papers you've been writing? This section will help you visualize the whole researched paper by asking you, first, to study carefully the picture-outline of "Monkey Talk" on page 221.

First, notice that the paper has five major units (**I–V**). Except for the last ("Conclusions"), each unit has two or more paragraphs. These are arranged to lead the reader through an introduction, the body of the paper, and the conclusion. Like a five-hundred-word theme, then, "Monkey Talk" has a beginning (**I**), middle (**II, III, IV**), and ending (**V**), each serving a specific purpose: (1) to introduce, (2) to investigate, to develop, and report, and (3) to conclude.

Introduction.   Usually a researched paper's introduction (**I**) has more than one paragraph; "Monkey Talk" has two. The first paragraph introduces the general

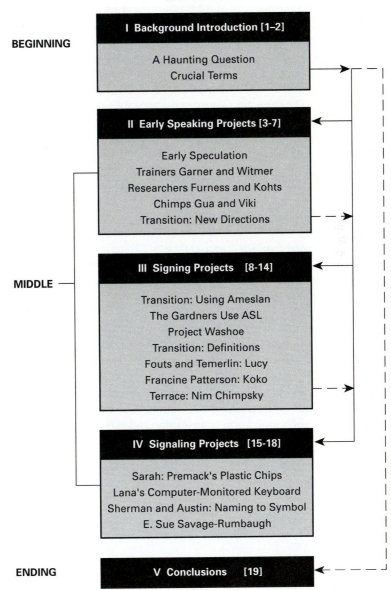

MONKEY TALK

BEGINNING

I Background Introduction [1–2]

A Haunting Question
Crucial Terms

II Early Speaking Projects [3-7]

Early Speculation
Trainers Garner and Witmer
Researchers Furness and Kohts
Chimps Gua and Viki
Transition: New Directions

MIDDLE

III Signing Projects   [8-14]

Transition: Using Ameslan
The Gardners Use ASL
Project Washoe
Transition: Definitions
Fouts and Temerlin: Lucy
Francine Patterson: Koko
Terrace: Nim Chimpsky

IV Signaling Projects   [15-18]

Sarah: Premack's Plastic Chips
Lana's Computer-Monitored Keyboard
Sherman and Austin: Naming to Symbol
E. Sue Savage-Rumbaugh

ENDING

V Conclusions   [19]

subject—communicating with apes. The second paragraph focuses attention on certain key terms, including "communicating partners," and, in its last sentence, clearly anticipates the main body of the paper (**II** to **IV**) with a leading thesis question: *What conclusions can be drawn from the **speaking, signing, and signaling** skills researchers have taught to our primate neighbors?* This thesis question serves as a blueprint to anticipate the three main units of the main body of the paper.

Body.   The three developmental paragraphs of the five-hundred-word theme (see diagram, page 22) have been replaced by three major units (**II** to **IV**), each with many paragraphs (numbered 3 to 18). This middle part of the paper provides the information needed to answer the question asked in the introduction. The body of an acceptable freshman research paper should have three or four main units, each comprised of several paragraphs. Here the three units in the body can be compared to the three developmental paragraphs of a five-hundred-word paper. The organization of "Monkey Talk" will become clearer if you review the diagram given in Chapter 2 to help you picture deductive organization (see *Theme Pattern B,* page 23). Notice that the last paragraph (7) of "Early Speaking Projects" (unit **II**) concludes the unit and provides a *transition* to anticipate the subjects of the next two major units ("Signing Projects" and "Signaling Projects"). Similar transitions appear throughout the paper.

Conclusion.   In the five-hundred-word paper following the deductive pattern, the ending was a concluding restatement of the thesis, presented as the last sentence in the final developmental paragraph. In "Monkey Talk" the ending is a separate unit (**V**), summarizing the important conclusions from all the other units. It answers the question, "What conclusions can be drawn?"

Now, using this picture-outline as a guide, read "Monkey Talk" carefully, looking for anticipation, transitions, and echoes.

```
                           MONKEY  TALK

                               by

                         J.  P.  Decker
```

```
                    Professor Harry Kroitor
                        Composition 101
                        10 December 1993
```

Decker — 1 —

MONKEY TALK

1   Is it possible to establish two—way communication with apes? Could they be taught a <u>human</u> <u>language</u>? For over four hundred years the anthropoid apes have been the subject of speculation (Schaller 3–5). Because of their superficial similarity to humans, chimpanzees and gorillas have been studied extensively to see if they could be taught to communicate using some form of language. And though this interest in ape language studies declined in the 1980s (Linden, <u>Silent</u> <u>Partners</u> 8), Penny Patterson's declaration that "'language is no longer the exclusive domain of man'" continues to haunt researchers who had been involved in earlier studies (Terrace, "Nim Chimpsky" 65).

2   The history of this research shows that certain key terms have become crucial in the studies: <u>communication</u>, <u>language</u>, <u>grammar</u>, and <u>sentence</u>. In <u>Animal</u> <u>Language</u> Bright points out that among animals of all kinds "By far the most common use for sound . . . is to communicate" (11). But what is "communication"? Bright says that " . . . an animal has communicated with another when it has transmitted information that influences the listener's behavior" (11). This definition works all right until the communicating partners are humans and apes. Researchers have repeatedly tried to establish such "communicating partners," concentrating on three basic

Decker — 2 —

approaches—-speaking, signing, and signaling. They report both

failure and spectacular success. Because some recent studies

have raised doubts about the meaning of earlier research

results, a useful way to approach the subject is with a

question: What conclusions can be drawn from the speaking,

signing, and signaling skills researchers have taught to our

primate neighbors?

3   From the early 1700s to the time of Charles Darwin,

speculation about the human place in the animal world was

widespread (Glass et al. 33–40, 145–172). Even the philosopher

Schopenhauer wondered about humans, chimpanzees, and orangutans

(Glass et al. 428). Though this early speculation was mostly

about anatomical similarities, some observers were also

interested in behavioral correlations. Darwin had suggested

that "there was a biology to man's behavior," perhaps related

to the behavior of other animals (Linden, <u>Apes</u> 228). In the

early 1900s Eugene Marais had studied baboons in the wild,

". . . suggest[ing] that, along with other primates, man

possessed two memories," an instinctive one related to

"collective primate history," and a "causal" memory that made

it possible for humans to learn from their experiences. Marais

also insisted that "non-primate mammals were dominated by

hereditary memory while primates were dominated by causal

memory" (Linden, <u>Apes</u> 227). This distinction was to become

important in reevaluations of the ape language projects.

4   The earliest of these language projects focused on

teaching apes to speak. In 1896 R. L. Garner speculated that

"chimpanzees . . . possessed a limited natural language," and

Decker — 3 —

claimed that he had taught a young chimpanzee to say _feu_, the
French word for fire (Rumbaugh et al., _Primate_ _Behavior_ 363).
About ten years later, L. Witmer maintained that he had taught
Peter, "a performing chimpanzee," to say the word _mama_ and to
imitate the sound "p" (Rumbaugh et al., _Primate_ _Behavior_ 364).

5   During this same period (1913 to 1916), two other
researchers worked on speaking projects. William Furness worked
for several years with two orangutans and a chimpanzee. He
manipulated the mouths of the apes to get them to imitate
sounds. He claimed that "one of the orang—utans learned to
pronounce _papa_, _cup_, and _th_," and that the animals "could
follow simple commands, but he felt that this" apparent
understanding of language resulted because the animals used
"his gestures and facial expressions as cues to the correct
response to a particular command" (Rumbaugh et al., _Primate_
Behavior 364). This view would come to dominate future
ape—language criticism. The second researcher, a Russian named
Kohts, didn't try to teach speaking directly. Instead, for
nearly three years she kept the chimp Joni within a normal
family environment to see if the animal would naturally learn
language skills. Joni "never tried to imitate vocal sounds made
by human beings" (Rumbaugh et al., _Primate_ _Behavior_, 364).

6   After 1925, there were two other attempts to teach apes to
speak. For nine months Winthrop and Kellogg kept a
seven—year—old chimpanzee, Gua, with their infant son, Donald.
Both Gua and Donald received the same treatment and training,
including lip manipulation. Neither Donald nor Gua learned to
pronounce spoken words during the 9 months of training. More

Decker — 4 —

ambitious, the second attempt is the story of the chimpanzee

Viki. In the late 1940s, Keith and Cathy Hayes

> . . . conducted the most extensive home-raised ape speech
> study. . . . They raised Viki, a chimpanzee, in their home
> from shortly after birth until she died at the age of 6
> years. They claimed correct pronunciation and usage of
> four, heavily accented English words: <u>mama</u>, <u>papa</u>, <u>cup</u>, and
> <u>up</u>. They, too, used manipulation of the ape's mouth and
> lips, which was phased out as Viki gradually came to
> approximate the actual words. Again, the claim was made
> that their subject could comprehend spoken language.
> (Rumbaugh et al., <u>Primate</u> <u>Behavior</u> 364)

Though a kind of two-way communication was established with

Viki, it had little to do with human language.

7   Although they produced no speaking apes, perhaps the real

significance of these early speaking projects is that they

established an unmistakable new kinship between humans and

once-feared apes. This learned kinship became the almost

unrecognized assumption upon which all subsequent projects

proceeded. Also significant, these experiments challenged the

all-important assumption concerning the uniqueness of human

speech (Rumbaugh et al., <u>Primate</u> <u>Behavior</u> 364). This challenge

took the form of signing and signaling projects.

8   The most significant signing projects came mostly in the

1970s with the first systematically researched apes: Washoe,

Lucy, Ally, Koko, and Nim. Because the "spontaneous and

imitative gestures" of apes were well known among researchers

(Froman 125; Rumbaugh et al., <u>Primate</u> <u>Behavior</u> 365), they

decided to use Ameslan (American Sign Language; ASL).

9   R. Allen and Beatrice T. Gardner began ASL experiments

with Washoe, an eleven-month old, wild-born female chimp.

Washoe lived in a trailer in a stimulating, homelike

environment. The only language Washoe was ever exposed to was
ASL. According to the Gardners, at the end of 51 months Washoe
had a vocabulary of 132 signs and a much larger "receptive
vocabulary" (Gardner and Gardner, <u>Evidence</u> 244–46).

10   The Gardners' experiments provided evidence that two-way
communication was possible between chimp and man. To support
this view the Gardners described Washoe's ability to use the
sign for the word <u>more</u> in such contexts as "more tickling,"
"more brushing," and "more food" (Gardner and Gardner, <u>Evidence</u>
247). A second important result, they said, was Washoe's use of
<u>Wh</u> questions in the form of <u>what</u>, <u>who</u>, <u>where</u>, and <u>when</u>. Her use
of and response to these questions, they maintained, showed a
grasp of a basic concept of human communication, the gathering
of information (Gardner and Gardner, <u>Evidence</u> 248–50). Washoe's
ability to use and understand language was further illustrated,
they said, when she began combining and recombining signs and
responses into meaningful sequences in different situations
(Gardner and Gardner, <u>Evidence</u> 256).

11   But researchers argued about the definitions of <u>language</u>,
<u>grammar</u>, and <u>sentence</u> as applied to the imitative signing of
apes (Rumbaugh et al., <u>Primate</u> <u>Behavior</u> 372–74). To meet some
of the criticism of Project Washoe, the Gardners later refined
their signing methods when they worked with Moja and Pili, two
chimps who received around-the-clock attention and training
from birth (Gardner and Gardner, <u>Early</u> <u>Signs</u> 752–53).

12   Like the Gardners, Roger Fouts and Maurice Temerlin used
ASL in signing experiments. Fouts worked with Lucy, a
five-year-old chimp raised by Temerlin, who maintained that

Decker – 6 –

Lucy already understood and obeyed spoken words (Temerlin, _Lucy_

117). After five years of training, Fouts had taught Lucy

nearly two hundred signs, established her vocabulary at over

one hundred words, and observed her "creative integration" of

signs she had mastered. Temerlin describes this combination of

signs:

> . . . on three different occasions she learned a sign for
> cry, food, and hurt. Then, sometime later, she was shown a
> radish. When she bit into it she signed, "Cry hurt food."
> After that moment of creative integration, when shown a
> radish she always signed either "Cry food" or "Hurt food"
> or "Cry hurt food." This is not an isolated or a unique
> example. (Temerlin, _Lucy_ 120)

Temerlin was convinced that his "daughter Lucy" understood and

obeyed his spoken words and that she used ASL to communicate

her feelings. He provides this episode to illustrate:

> When she tired of the pictures she put the magazine down,
> crossed the room, stood before me on two legs wearing her
> play-face. This conversation ensued, Lucy speaking ASL
> while I replied in English.
>> Lucy: "Maury, tickle Lucy."
>> Maury: "No! I'm busy."
>> Lucy: "Chase Lucy."
>> Maury: "Not now."
>> Lucy: "Hug Lucy, hurry, hurry."
>> Maury: "In just a minute."
>> Lucy (Laughing): "Hurry, hurry, hug Lucy, tickle,
>> chase Lucy."
> How could I resist? (Temerlin, Lucy 125)

Though critics insist that Temerlin and Lucy were not engaged

in _language_ communication, almost no one says that

communication was not taking place.

13   Two additional signing experiments gained widespread

attention, one involving Koko, a gorilla, another with a

chimpanzee named Nim. In _Brain and Language_ (1978), Francine

Patterson documents her work with Koko, which is summarized by

Joel Greenberg in _Science News_. According to Greenberg, Koko had mastered "a working vocabulary of 375 hand signals," "20 percent more signs than . . . Washoe" (Greenberg, <u>Koko</u> 265). Unlike the Gardners and Fouts, Patterson and her trainers spoke English as they taught Koko how to sign, providing her with a computer terminal that could "produce a spoken word for each key, thereby affording the gorilla the opportunity to 'speak'" (Rumbaugh et al., <u>Primate Behavior</u> 366).

14   Herbert S. Terrace's signing experiments with Nim were even more painstaking than those conducted with Koko. Terrace used manual molding of signs, videotaped all typical signing interactions, and kept an audio cassette recording of the work (Rumbaugh et al., <u>Primate Behavior</u> 366–67). He presented the results in <u>Nim</u>, which reports all the learned signs as well as the emotional reunion with Nim after a one-year absence ("Epilogue: One Year Later" 228–34). Nim was overjoyed to see Terrace and had not forgotten his signing (Terrace, <u>Nim</u> 232–33). In this book and later in an article, however, Terrace recognizes that the signing may not be considered "language" because the "more than 20,000" sign combinations were not really "primitive sentences" but "were simply subtle imitations of the teacher's [signing]" (Terrace, "Nim Chimpsky" 68, 71). Although there seems to be no doubt that two-way communication occurred, whether it was true <u>language communication</u> remains arguable. Whether the signing is simply unthinking imitation or primitive language acquisition became an open question.

15   The questions raised by these signing experiments convinced researchers to use such signaling devices as plastic

Decker − 8 −

chips and computer−monitored keyboards. They "developed
artificial languages in which physical attributes of visual
symbols served as functional equivalents of words" (Rumbaugh et
al., _Primate_ _Behavior_ 367−68). Using plastic chips of different
colors, sizes, and shapes, David Premack trained a six−year−old
chimp, Sarah, to select and arrange "four or five chips in
given sequences." He considered her chip selection "to be
analogous to spoken words" (Savage−Rumbaugh 8). Instead of the
social interaction approach used in other ape−language
projects, Premack used a "problem−solving format" (Rumbaugh et
al., _Primate_ _Behavior_ 368). His aim was to eliminate minimal
cues from the teacher and simply test whether Sarah's response
choices were correct or incorrect (Savage−Rumbaugh 20).

16   Another important testing advance was introduced by Duane
Rumbaugh at the Yerkes Regional Primate Research Center. He
used computer−monitored keyboards and geometric symbols
(lexigrams) on colored backgrounds to train Lana. The computer
setup separated trainers from Lana and allowed for around−the−
clock monitoring and use of the system. Lana was trained to
combine "word lexigrams from various conceptually related
categories into appropriate stock−sentence patterns." This
approach let Lana use the system at any time and

> cause the computer to operate various food and liquid
> vending devices, to open a window for a view of the
> outdoors, or to provide music, projected slides, or
> movies. The computer was programmed to respond only to
> correct strings according to the rules of Yerkish grammar.
> (Rumbaugh et al., _Primate_ _Behavior_ 368)

Lana's manipulation of "Yerkish lexigrams" hasn't received the
same criticism previous experiments suffered. Experimenters

Decker – 9 –

maintained that Lana "had become sensitive to the rules of
Yerkish grammar" and that she "had learned to use lexigrams and
combine them in a rule-ordered fashion" (Rumbaugh et al.,
Primate Behavior 370).

17   The Yerkes project was later extended to include two young
male chimpanzees, Sherman and Austin. A major goal of the new
project was to determine whether apes could use their new
signaling abilities to "enhance" communication with each other
in ways not available through their "natural non-verbal
signals" (Savage-Rumbaugh 125). In Ape Language: From
Conditioned Response to Symbol, E. Sue Savage-Rumbaugh outlines
in great detail the procedures, precautions, and conclusions.
In addition to the training that Sarah had received, Sherman
and Austin were trained "in a social, preschool-like setting
with emphasis . . . on communication. [They] received human
companionship for almost all of their waking hours" (Rumbaugh
et al., Primate Behavior 370).

18   She concluded (among other things) that Sherman and Austin
could use their "learned symbol skills" to "communicate
information to one another" that couldn't be sent by "typical
chimpanzee non-verbal signals" (Savage-Rumbaugh 147). The
chimpanzees, she said, "were aware of the nature and purpose of
their communications in a way that other animals engaging in
similar tasks seem not to have been" (Savage-Rumbaugh 147). In
the Foreword to her book, Terrace praises the "patient and
exacting approach that was followed to instill symbol use in
minds which . . . cannot process language normally" (Savage-
Rumbaugh xviii). He says that " . . . the study of the use of

Decker – 10 –

individual symbols by an ape is a highly profitable enterprise"
that "avoids the all–or–none problems of interpretation
encountered by studies . . . focused on grammatical competence"
(Savage–Rumbaugh xix).

19   These extensive research projects in speaking, signing,
and signaling show that the terms <u>language</u>, <u>grammar</u>, <u>word</u>, and
<u>sentence</u> must be redefined for human and ape contexts. At first
the apes' imitative behavior in signing and signaling projects
went unrecognized and led to unwarranted assumptions about "ape
language," "words," and "communication." The signaling work
with Lana, Austin, and Sherman largely overcame the problem of
unintended cueing from trainers, leading finally to basic
communication through the use of symbols. The ape projects
moved from simple, imitative naming to symbolic and social
communication. Sherman and Austin represent an important
breakthrough to a higher level of symbolic functioning, showing
that "chimpanzees can master referential use of learned
symbols" (Rumbaugh et al., <u>Primate</u> <u>Behavior</u> 379). E. Sue
Savage–Rumbaugh says that we cannot understand "word
acquisition" if we focus "on the mere occurrence of words.
Instead, we must focus . . . on the exchange of meaning between
parent and child, or teacher and chimpanzee . . . "
(Savage–Rumbaugh 17). The research with Austin and Sherman
included this component, leading her to conclude that the
"chimpanzees had developed a capacity of fundamental importance
to language––the ability to use arbitrary symbols
representationally" (Savage–Rumbaugh 376).

Decker — 11 —

WORKS CONSULTED

Altman, Stuart A., ed. Social Communication among
    Primates. Chicago: U of Chicago Press, 1967.
Bright, Michael. Animal Language. London: British
    Broadcasting Corp., 1984.
Fleming, Joyce Dudney. "The State of the Apes."
    Psychology Today Jan. 1974: 31–44.
Froman, Robert. The Great Reaching Out: How Living Beings
    Communicate. Cleveland: The World Publishing Co.,
    1968.
Gardner, Beatrice T., and R. Allen Gardner. "Evidence for
    Sentence Constituents in the Early Utterances of
    Child and Chimpanzee." Journal of Experimental
    Psychology: General 104 (1975): 244–67.
Gardner, R. A., and B. T. Gardner. "Early Signs of
    Language in Child and Chimpanzee." Science 187
    (1975): 752–53.
Glass, Bentley, Owsei Temkin, and William L. Straus, Jr.,
    eds. Forerunners of Darwin: 1745–1859. Baltimore:
    The Johns Hopkins Press, 1959.
Greenberg, Joel. "Ape Talk: More than 'Pigeon' English?"
    Science News 10 May 1980: 298–300.
———. "Koko." Science News 14 Oct. 1978: 265, 270.
Kupferberg, Herbert. "Primate Time on Television."
    Parade 20 Jan. 1974: 3.
Laidler, Keith. The Talking Ape. New York: Stein and
    Day, 1980.
Linden, Eugene. Apes, Men, and Language. New York:
    Penguin Books, 1976.
———. Silent Partners: The Legacy of the Ape Language
    Experiments. New York: Time Books, 1986.
Patterson, Francine. "The Gestures of a Gorilla: Sign
    Language Acquisition in another Pongid Species."
    Brain and Language 5 (1978): 72–97.
———. Koko's Kitten. New York: Scholastic, Inc., 1985.
———. Koko's Story. New York: Scholastic, Inc., 1987.
Premack, D. "On the Assessment of Language Competence in
    the Chimpanzee." Behavior of Non-human Primates.
    Eds. A. Schrier and F. Stollnitz. Vol. 4. New York:
    Academic Press, 1971.
Reynolds, P. C. "Social Communication in the Chimpanzee."
    The Chimpanzee: Anatomy, Behavior, and Diseases of
    Chimpanzees. Ed. Geoffrey H. Bourne. Vol.
    1. Basel, Switzerland: S. Karger, 1969.
Rumbaugh, Duane M., ed. Language Learning by a Chimp: The
    Lana Project. New York: Academic Press, 1977.
Rumbaugh, Duane M., E. Sue Savage-Rumbaugh, and John L.
    Scanlon. "The Relationship between Language in Apes
    and Human Beings." Primate Behavior. Ed. James L.
    Fobes and James E. King. New York: Academic Press, 1982.
    361–85.

Decker — 12 —

Savage—Rumbaugh, E. Sue. <u>Ape</u> <u>Language</u>: <u>From</u> <u>Conditioned</u>
    <u>Response</u> <u>to</u> <u>Symbol</u>. New York: Columbia UP, 1986.
Schaller, George B. <u>The</u> <u>Year</u> <u>of</u> <u>the</u> <u>Gorilla</u>. Chicago: U
    of Chicago Press, 1964.
Sebeok, Thomas A., and Jean Umiker—Sebeok, eds. <u>Speaking</u>
    <u>of</u> <u>Apes</u>: <u>A</u> <u>Critical</u> <u>Anthology</u> <u>of</u> <u>Two—way</u>
    <u>Communication</u> <u>with</u> <u>Man</u>. New York: Plenum Press,
    1980.
Temerlin, Maurice Kahn. <u>Lucy</u>: <u>Growing</u> <u>Up</u> <u>Human</u>: <u>A</u>
    <u>Chimpanzee</u> <u>Daughter</u> <u>in</u> <u>a</u> <u>Psychotherapist's</u> <u>Family</u>.
    Palo Alto, California: Science and Behavior Books,
    1975.
———. "My Daughter Lucy." <u>Psychology</u> <u>Today</u> Nov. 1975:
    59—62, 103.
Terrace, Herbert S. <u>Nim</u>. New York: Alfred A. Knopf,
    1979.
———. "How Nim Chimpsky Changed My Mind." <u>Psychology</u>
    <u>Today</u> Nov. 1979: 63—76.

CHOOSING A SUBJECT

If you have reviewed the material in Chapter 3, you should find choosing a subject for your research paper an interesting challenge rather than a major stumbling block. To begin with, note that the five steps given in Chapter 3 on page 56 have been condensed into three on the research check sheet:

1. Discover a suitable subject.
2. Limit the subject with a specific controlling attitude or question.
3. Write a purpose statement.

Let's consider each step closely.

Discover a Suitable Subject

If your instructor doesn't provide a list of general subjects or questions suitable for research, you will have to find your own. Although you were cautioned to use only specific *facts* to support the thesis of your five-hundred-word paper (see pages 146–52), you were encouraged to use facts from your personal experience or knowledge. In choosing a general subject for your research paper, again you may select one you are already familiar with; your supporting facts, however, must come from authoritative information sources. Use the discovery process discussed in Chapter 3 and the question approach of Chapter 6. Let your mind actively play with possibilities, and you'll find that many of the general subjects listed on page 58 will provide general subject areas suitable for formal research. (For additional research subjects, see page 217 and also Exercise C on page 241.) Here are some with obvious possibilities:

Accidents	Laws	Pollution
Advertising	Computers	Population
Animals	Novels	Slums
Censorship	Planes	Space
Congress	Plays	Television

If you chose *planes,* for example, you could focus on *major causes of airplane accidents in the United States;* your research problem would then be to find authoritative books, articles, or government documents that provide factual information to use in your paper. *Advertising* might suggest a research problem in *federal government regulation of deceptive advertising practices in the sale of nonprescription drugs* (or other products). *Pollution* might lead you to investigate *the legal action taken by the federal government to free the air of automobile pollutants* (or pollutants from steel or chemical plants). A little thought about the general subject of *population* could suggest research into *the success of birth control practices* or *family planning* in a specific country (India or China, for example). And *television* could suggest an investigation of *the effect on preschool-age children of the portrayal of violence on television*. The possibilities are almost unlimited, depending on how actively involved you let your mind become and how much personal interest you can generate. You must make the discovery process work for you.

The student who wrote "Monkey Talk" began with the general subject *communication,* became interested in communication between man and other animals, and then zeroed in on apes as a suitable subject for research. To be suitable, the limited subject chosen must be one for which factual, authoritative information sources are available, usually in the library. Until the student checked the library, therefore, he couldn't be certain that the ape-communication subject was suitable. To be safe, you should try to think of several subject possibilities before heading for the library; then, depending on what a quick, first search reveals, you can settle on the subject for your paper.

Limited Subject Area	Limited Predicate Area (Controlling Attitudes)
Accidents: plane accidents in the United States	major causes of
Advertising: deceptive advertising practices in the sale of nonprescription drugs	federal government regulation of
Pollution: to free the air of automobile pollutants	legal action taken by the federal government
Population: birth control practices in India	success of
Television: portrayal of violence on television	effect on preschool-age children

Before making a final decision, however, note that a subject is *not* suitable for a research paper if:

1. It is based on your personal experience alone.
2. All the information about the subject comes from a single reference source (for example, an encyclopedia, or one book, or one article).
3. It is too general to lead to specific research information.
4. It is too technical for you or your reader.
5. Opinion about the subject is wholly subjective (personal) or hopelessly conflicting.

In contrast, a general subject is probably suitable for a research paper if:

1. It is personally interesting to you and your reader.
2. It is discussed in a number of articles and books.

3. It readily suggests a number of meaningful, limited subjects.
4. It can be limited and focused with a specific controlling attitude.
5. It has been investigated objectively (scientifically) and described in factual, nonemotional language.

If you apply these criteria to the general subject of "Monkey Talk," *communicating with apes*, you'll see that it meets all the requirements.

Limit the Subject with a Specific Controlling Attitude or Question

From your work on the five-hundred-word paper, you already know why a general subject is unsuitable (see pages 57–64 in Chapter 3). The discussion you have just read about choosing a suitable research subject shows this limiting process in action. If you examine each illustration closely, you'll see at once that both the subject area and the predicate area of the problem statements have been limited.

To discover one, limited subject area is to choose for your paper a subject that can't be significantly divided further; it is the key to unity of thought. (See pages 61–64 in Chapter 3.) To discover a single, limited predicate area is to decide on a controlling attitude (the "pointer") for your paper that tells the reader what you are going to investigate *about* the limited subject area. (See pages 65–70 in Chapter 3.)

In "Monkey Talk," the last sentence of the second paragraph presents the limited subject area and limited predicate area of the paper:

> *What conclusions can be drawn from the speaking, signing, and signaling skills researchers have taught to our primate neighbors?*

If you look for it, you'll see that the first two paragraphs have a funneling effect leading up to this question/problem. The writer's thinking process might have occurred in this sequence: communicating— communicating with animals—apes, gorillas—baboons, orangutans—two-way communication—language—speaking, signing, signaling skills—conclusions to be drawn.

The last two parts of this sequence represent the subject and predicate areas conveyed by the thesis question:

Limited Subject	Controlling Attitude
speaking, signing, signaling skills taught to apes	conclusions to be drawn

Depending on how long a paper you wanted to write and what you wanted to emphasize, the subject area could be limited further.

Write a Purpose Statement

Writing a purpose statement requires you to *review* the prewriting thinking process that led you to the focus of your research subject—the long paper's limited subject and controlling attitude. Because it is really a thesis, the purpose statement should help you find out if you are ready to research, organize, and write the paper. You write it *before* writing the paper and only *after* you have done some preliminary reading and information gathering. Reading some magazine articles about your general subject—for example, communicating with animals—will help you find a specific subject to explore. The sooner you begin reading, the fewer false starts you will have. Some of the stages in this thinking process can be represented like this:

> I wonder what's been written about animal-to-human communication?
> I know that a lot of work has been done with dolphins and whales.
> I'm more interested in the way humans relate to chimps and gorillas.
> I wonder, do we really "talk" to these apes?
> I've read some articles on teaching apes sign language.
> I'd like to find out more about so-called "ape languages."
> I wonder what problems the researchers have run into?

> *In my long paper I'd like to report what the researchers have found out about teaching apes to communicate with humans.* [preliminary purpose statement, thesis idea]

With more reading and thinking, you could make this purpose statement more specific and more like a carefully controlled thesis (as you have just seen in the section above on limiting the subject by using a controlling attitude).

However, since you already have the completed paper on "Monkey Talk" to look at, you can easily see the subject and control of its purpose statement. Also, you'll see that the purpose statement for "Monkey Talk" can be represented in three basic ways:

1. Assertion:

> *In this paper I will* **discuss what conclusions can be drawn** *from experiments devised to teach apes to communicate using speech, signing, and signaling skills. (Theme Pattern A—Inductive Organization)*

This straightforward statement, similar in approach to Theme Pattern A, commits the writer to a *discussion* of the conclusions that can be drawn from three types of experiments. In the form of an assertion, it is simply a rewording of the thesis question, "What conclusions can be drawn?"

2. Question/Problem:

> **What conclusions can be drawn** *from the speaking, signing, and signaling skills researchers have taught our primate neighbors [apes]? (Theme Pattern A—Inductive Organization)*

This question/problem approach also implies an inductive organization. The writer adopts a "let's wait and see" attitude, promising to present the available information and *then* conclude (or perhaps evaluate). The writer promises to answer the question at the end of the paper.

3. Thesis Statement:

> *Although researchers have successfully communicated with apes in a number of ways, they* **have failed to teach them to speak,** *they* **have misunderstood the results of signing experiments,** *and they* **have only recently understood the tie between signaling skills and symbolic communication.** *(Theme Pattern B—Deductive Organization)*

The implied question of approach one and the stated question of approach two are *answered* here in the form of a thesis controlled by: *failed, misunderstood,* and *recently understood.* As you learned in Chapter 2, this *deductive* approach really requires a complete thinking through of the information. After all, you couldn't know what conclusions to draw unless you had sifted through the evidence. However, you present the *conclusion* (the answer to the question) *as if* it were a fact. In effect you are saying, "I know *X* is true because . . . " You will present *reasons* (evidence) to support the thesis, as you learned in "Paragraph Development by Reasons, Causes, or Consequences" in Chapter 6. This is also the pattern of "People Problems" in Chapter 2.

Each of these three purpose statements implies a slightly different handling of the information gathered in the research process. If you are writing a *problem-solving paper,* you will write a purpose statement similar to the first two. If you are writing a more "argumentative" paper in which you are trying to "prove" a point with reasons or evidence, your purpose statement will be similar to the third one.

Examine "Monkey Talk" carefully, and you'll see that with only very slight changes in wording, especially at the end of the third paragraph, the paper can be made to fit all three approaches.

EXERCISES

  A. List the most important changes you would have to make in "Monkey Talk" to make it fit the *thesis approach.* In your list, pay special attention to transitions between major parts (or paragraphs) and to statements that would "echo" the thesis as the paper progresses.

  B. 1. Evaluate and comment on the suitability of each of the following as an approach to writing a research paper.

   a. *Purpose statement:* In this paper I will investigate contemporary readers' responses to Keats's poems when they were first published.

   b. *Question approach:* How did contemporary readers respond to Keats's poetry when it was first published?

    c. *Thesis approach:* Although some contemporary readers recognized Keats's poetic ability, most did not react favorably to his poems when they were first published.

  2. Which approach gives the writer the greatest freedom in presenting information? Why?

  3. Suggest some other words to replace *investigate* in the purpose statement. Be prepared to discuss the differences in *controlling attitude* implied by your suggested substitutions.

C. Using the question approach studied in Chapters 3 and 6, devise questions that might be suitable for a research paper on at least four of the following general subjects.

   1. Character contrasts (or comparisons) in one of Shakespeare's plays
   2. Offshore oil drilling (problems, advantages, methods)
   3. Character contrasts (or comparisons) in a novel you've studied.
   4. Censorship of high school textbooks (how, by whom, effects, consequences)
   5. Cigarette smoking (causes, effects, ads, laws)
   6. Urban renewal (plans for, slum clearance, obstacles to)
   7. Science fiction (role of computer, alien types, recurrent themes)
   8. Computer education (courses in schools, pros, cons)
   9. Computer (languages, kinds, software, hardware)
  10. Communication skills (in specific jobs, in everyday life)
  11. Women/men characters in short stories
  12. Love poems
  13. Energy sources.

To get you started, here are some questions based on some of these general subjects.

What is special about the way Emily Dickinson handles the theme of love in her poems?

What image do Hemingway's women (men) characters project in some of his most famous short stories?

To what extent are school textbooks censored in (*name a state*)?

Who is responsible for the censorship of high school textbooks in (*name a state*)?

What is the popular role of the computer in science fiction?

What are the most recent advances in solar energy applications?

GETTING THE FACTS

You will remember from Chapter 4 that every statement in your research paper should in some way explain or support the controlling attitude toward the limited subject **(unity).** Your paper must have one subject, one controlling attitude, and one tone. Equally important, you will remember that your paper must also have logical direction, created through interlocking connection within and between paragraphs **(coherence).** All facts must be relevant, and you must give them the kind of direction that guides the reader to see and accept their relevance. Your knowledge of unity and coherence will help you understand some of the choices you must make in the next three stages of the research process:

4. Discover suitable information sources (articles, books, interviews, etc.).
5. Survey the information sources; prepare a working bibliography.
6. Take exact, relevant notes; design a rough plan.

Again we shall consider each stage of the process in detail.

Discover Suitable Information Sources

You can gather information in many ways and from many sources. Consider, for example, a *problem-solving paper,* such as "How Safe Are Children's Toys?" (Chapter 2). The inductive organization implied by a question/problem approach allows you to present a series of investigations before reaching a final conclusion. And these investigations can tap many sources.

1. Observation.   Direct personal observation of many toys would lead you to discover for yourself some of the most obvious safety hazards. (Fire hazards and chemical dangers would require professional analysis.) You would check systematically and take careful notes. Your paper would describe what you found and reach a conclusion based on the toys examined.

2. Interviews.   In almost all subject areas you can find professionals, experts who might be willing to tell you what they knew about the problem you were investigating. You could talk to a toy manufacturer — perhaps by phone — and get information you could use in the paper on toys. Or, you might know of a professor at your college who was a safety expert and who had done some research on safety hazards in children's toys. Each interview — in person or by phone — can be cited as an information source, similar to the way in which you would use a magazine article.

3. Questionnaires.   You could devise a questionnaire with probing questions designed to identify hazard problems in toys. These questionnaires would be sent to people who might have the information you need — toy manufacturers, retail stores, toy stores, parents, government agencies. Although this method can provide useful information, devising the questionnaire, analyzing the information, and summarizing the results requires special skill and care.

4. Experiments.   Though the problem of safety hazards in children's toys doesn't easily lend itself to scientific experimentation, with other subjects you might very well set up an experiment to discover information — growing strawberries, incubating chicken eggs, growing a variety of plants under varying light.

5. Reading.   The most reliable information on most subjects is probably in professional magazine articles, reports, or books. Professional writers create good research reports from information gained in all these ways. Consider all important information sources unless your instructor tells you otherwise. You will probably get most of your information through *reading,* that is, through "re-searching" what has been written about a specific subject.

A check of its bibliography shows that the writer of "Monkey Talk" got information from books and articles describing *experiments* conducted by researchers. This kind of reading can be the most important key to writing a research paper. If you need statistics, facts, professional opinions, the testimony of experts, or documents to investigate your subject, you must check articles in reliable magazines, books by experts, or various reports or records, including *government documents*. And to find these you must know how to use the library and its resources, especially the following: the computer catalog and the card catalog, indexes to magazines and newspapers, abstracts (summaries of articles in magazines), and reference books.

The Library Computer Catalog and Card Catalog

Although the card catalogs of most libraries are still important research tools, they are rapidly being supplemented or replaced by *computer catalogs*. And the information printed in a great many of the indexes, abstracts, bibliographies, and reference works mentioned later in this section (pages 247–48) have been stored in *computer databases*. The computer has become an indispensable storage and research tool.

The computer catalog.   To transfer millions of bits of information from cards in the standard catalog into a *computer catalog* takes years. Libraries involved in this process usually maintain the old catalog, though they may not keep it up to date. During the transition, new acquisitions usually are added only to the computer version. Meanwhile, your researching will be more complete and successful if you learn how to use both catalogs. On your first visit to the library, therefore, ask the reference librarian about the computer resources available.

If the library has a computer catalog, you can access it from various computer terminals set up in the building, or you can access it by telephone from home with your personal computer (if your computer has been set up for this purpose). Depending on the kind of computer catalog your library has created, you should be able to ask for information by *author, title,* or *subject*. If the asked-for information appears on the computer screen, it should provide a call number and essentially the same details you would find on a card in the card catalog (check the illustration on page 245). Searching by subject, whether by computer or in the card catalog, will be more efficient if you note the subject *cognates* (synonyms); these appear as item number *7* on the sample catalog *card*. You can find additional subject cognates by checking *The Library of Congress Subject Headings*.

Computer databases.   Suppose you've checked the *Readers' Guide to Periodical Literature* for articles about animal communication and found nothing. Suppose, further, that you'd like to have in a single, huge computer source a list of articles from 500 popular magazines—all classified by author and subject—including all those appearing in *Readers' Guide.* Such a list, updated monthly, exists and is called the *Magazine Index;* it contains nearly two million records. This list is a *database,* a computerized list combining several printed bibliographic indexes.

Like such printed *indexes* as *Books in Print* or *Engineering Index,* most databases are bibliographies, lists of citations to articles found in hundreds of magazines, professional journals, conference proceedings, and similar sources. The difference is that the items are stored in a computer database to provide virtually instant access through author, title, and subject. *Compendex,* for instance, is the database corresponding to the *Engineering Index.* Similarly, companies have created databases for the printed versions of *abstracts* (see page 248). For example, the database titled *Biosis* is the computer version of *Biological Abstracts; PsycINFO* is the computer version of *Psychological Abstracts,* and *INSPEC* combines into one computer database the references listed in three separate publications—*Physics Abstracts, Computer and Control Abstracts,* and *Electrical and Electronic Abstracts.* Some databases—for example, *Harvard Business Review Online*—are "full text," providing a computer version of all the articles appearing in the corresponding printed publication, *Harvard Business Review.*

Over 3,000 huge computer databases contain information on nearly any subject you can think of—book reviews, career placement, chemistry, medicine, biosciences, science, technology, engineering, social sciences, humanities, education, dissertations, books in print, government documents, agriculture, and many others. A database titled *Electronic Yellow Pages* contains over two *million* entries from nearly 500 telephone books. Another, *Academic American Encyclopedia,* available through various suppliers, contains over 30,000 articles, each some 300 words long. One called *Newsearch* classifies over 2,000 items from 1,700 newspapers and magazines—for the current month only.

Nearly all computer databases are available to libraries and individuals through subscription to three database suppliers: DIALOG, BRS (Bibliographic Retrieval Service), and ORBIT. Of the three, DIALOG is the largest, able to supply to its subscribers over 200 databases containing over 100 *million* units of information. Though there is some overlapping, the other two suppliers have nearly 100 available databases each. Large modern libraries subscribe to these supplier services and offer the databases to library users either free or for a small fee. *BRS/After Dark* and *Knowledge Index* are two database sources widely used by libraries.

Although only some of these computer databases are available in school libraries, all can be searched through your personal computer at home—if you have the right equipment and can pay for the cost of the services. You can have the world at your fingertips if you're willing to learn how. The best guide to the use of computer databases is probably Alfred Glossbrenner's *Complete Handbook of Personal Communications* (New York: St. Martin's Press, 1989).

The card catalog.   Your library's card catalog will help you find the information sources you need, *including* the indexes, abstracts, books, magazines, and reference books that will guide you to *additional* information sources. The card catalog is a file of cards identifying everything on the shelves of the library, including books, magazines (usually called *periodicals*), sets of books or reference works, pamphlets, microfilms, microcards, and often other library holdings as well (maps and government documents, for example).

For each holding, you will find at least two cards in the catalog, an *author card* and a *title card,* filed in different places. In addition, most catalogs have a *subject card*. As you will see in a moment, this means that you have two or three different ways of finding the item you need. Some libraries file author and title cards in one catalog and subject cards in another, keeping the two groups clearly separated.

To see how the system works, study this illustration of an author card, noting the eleven numbers used to identify the card's different parts:

```
   QL           2
 1 775      Altmann, Stuart A        3
   A4.8         Social communication among primates, edited by Stuart
                A. Altmann. Chicago, University of Chicago Press [1967] 4

              5 xiv, 392 p. illus., plates. 24 cm.

                Based on an international symposium on communication and social
   ALSO IN      interactions in primates held in Montreal, Canada, Dec. 27-31, 1964, 6
                during the annual meeting of the American Association for the
   Veterinary L. Advancement of Science.
      11        Includes bibliographies.

                              ✓
              7 1. Primates–Behavior. 2. Animal communication.    I. American
                Association for the Advancement of Science. II. Title.

                QL775.A48            599.8              65–25120
              8                               9                    10
                Library of Congress         [12]
```

1 Call number in the library being used. You must have this number to find the work.
2 Author's name, with last name given first.
3 Title of the book.
4 Publication data: Place of publication (Chicago), publisher (University of Chicago Press), date (1967).
5 Description of book: 14-page introduction, 392 pages of text, illustrations, special illustrations (plates), 24 centimeters in height.
6 Additional information about the book; the book has extensive bibliographies.
7 Other listings in the card catalog, indicating places to look for this card and related works: Check under *Primates—Behavior* and *Animal communication* in the subject catalog; there is a title card also filed, under *Social communication*. . . . For computer research, these subject *cognates* (synonyms) must be used *exactly* as they are listed here.
8 Library of Congress call number for libraries using this system. Smaller libraries usually use the Dewey system.

9   Dewey Decimal call number for libraries using this system.

10   Order number of the card from the Library of Congress, from which additional cards may be bought.

11   Another copy of this book is found in the Veterinary Library at this institution.

↙   Indicates that this author card was filed in the *subject* catalog under *Animal communication.* An identical card is filed under *Altmann* in the author catalog.

Knowing your alphabet and how the library uses it to arrange the cards in the catalog will keep you from missing cards by going to the wrong part of the alphabet (often far enough away so that merely flipping through the cards won't help). Here are some basic rules to remember:

1. In titles beginning with *A, An,* or *The,* these words are ignored and the card is filed under the next word.
2. The basic arrangement is word by word, alphabetized letter by letter to the end of the word. *Book* World comes before *Book*binding; *New* York and *New* Zealand both come before *New*ald and *New*ark.
3. Initials come before words beginning with the same letter: *ASST Handbook* is filed before *Aakhus,* Theodore.
4. Personal names come before titles beginning with the same word: Adam, James, and Adam, William, are both filed before the novel *Adam and Eve.*

When in doubt, ask a reference librarian for help, for filing can become a very complicated problem. Don't be intimidated by the card catalog; it is the most powerful research tool you have at your command. Learn to make it serve you well. Remember, however, that the most up-to-date information is usually in magazine articles, which you can find by using *indexes, abstracts,* and *bibliographies.* For a list of subject headings to check in these publications (and in the card catalog), be sure to check *The Library of Congress Subject Headings List,* which provides the *cognates* (synonyms) for your subject that you may not be able to think of. (See item number 7 on the sample library card.) These cognates are especially important in accessing *computer databases* in any library computer catalog.

Indexes.   Don't let the word *index* bother you; it comes from a Latin word, *indicare,* meaning "to indicate," usually where to find something. The indexes you must learn to use are simply bibliographies, *alphabetical lists of titles*—usually of the individual items in magazines (articles), anthologies (poems, stories, articles, essays), newspapers (articles), and other collections *whose contents cannot be located by checking only the card catalog.* In some ways, these indexes are even more important than the card catalog, for they indicate where you can find information that you are unlikely to discover in *any other way.* Also, an index will locate articles for you on subjects about which, perhaps, no *book* has been written. Searching *only* the catalog for a book about "teaching apes or chimpanzees how to talk" could lead you to assume erroneously that little or nothing had been written on the subject; almost always, searching the indexes will lead you to usable information. Using computer databases is another way of accessing these indexes and eliminating card catalog limitations.

The most important indexes for your search will provide lists of articles that have appeared in magazines (periodicals, journals). Only one index lists "general magazines" (periodicals in which you would find *general* articles about various subjects). All other indexes are specialized, each one listing only articles concerning a fairly specific subject area. The only general periodical index is *Readers' Guide to Periodical Literature* (1900–   ). Because some popular magazines often publish important technical articles, the *Readers' Guide* is probably a good *starting* place. But because it lists only popular magazines, your search *must* go beyond it, to the specialized indexes and bibliographies. Every subject you can think of (and many you can't) has a specialized index, and many, especially in the sciences, appear as *abstracts* (brief summaries). We'll take a brief look at abstracts in a moment. The following list includes only a few of the most important specialized indexes. Find out which of these indexes your library has and list call numbers for all of them.

> *Agricultural Engineering Index*
> *Applied Science and Technology Index* (formerly *Industrial Arts Index*)
> *Art Index*
> *Biological and Agricultural Index*
> *Business Periodical Index*
> *Computer Literature Index*
> *Congressional Information Service Index to Publications of the United States Congress*
> *Current Index to Journals in Education*
> *Education Index*
> *Engineering Index*
> *Film Literature Index*
> *Humanities Index*
> *Index to Government Periodicals*
> *Library of Congress Subject Headings List*
> *Monthly Catalog of United States Government Publications*
> *Monthly Checklist of State Publications*
> *New York Times Film Reviews*
> *New York Times Index*
> *The Newspaper Index*
> *Science Citation Index*
> *Social Sciences Citation Index*
> *Social Sciences Index*
> *Television News Index and Abstracts*
> *Ulrich's International Periodicals Directory*

Because these books indicate where to find articles from many hundreds of magazines, they are indispensable in any serious research. For example, the *Applied*

Science and Technology Index analyzes hundreds of magazines in the fields of aeronautics, automation, chemistry, construction, electricity, engineering, geology and metallurgy, machinery, and physics—and this is a partial list. And the *Engineering Index* covers every aspect of the field, analyzing some 2,000 magazines! Ask your reference librarian for a list of *indexes* available in your library, and be sure to ask your instructor about the *MLA International Bibliography of Books and Articles on the Modern Languages and Literatures.*

Abstracts.   An index simply locates materials; an abstract also locates materials, but in addition it briefly describes the essential points of the article, pamphlet, book, report, or other publication listed. These descriptions are short, often just a single sentence, but sometimes as long as several hundred words. Like the indexes, abstracts are also indispensable to serious research, especially since they cover almost every conceivable subject area. Here are a few of the hundreds of abstracts published:

> *Abstracts of English Studies*
> *Biological Abstracts*
> *Chemical Abstracts*
> *Field Crop Abstracts*
> *Forestry Abstracts*
> *Geoscience Abstracts*
> *International Abstracts of Biological Sciences*
> *Metallurgical Abstracts*
> *Nuclear Science Abstracts*
> *Petroleum Abstracts*
> *Physics Abstracts*
> *Psychological Abstracts*
> *Sociological Abstracts*
> *Soils and Fertilizers*
> *Vitamin Abstracts*

How many *abstracts* does your library have? Locate at least four of these publications in the library, take descriptive notes about how they are set up, and bring several short sample entries to class for discussion. What problems did you run into? Why might you find them useful? If your library has computer databases you can use, check to see which abstracts are available. A computer search can save hours of time.

Other library sources.   Develop the habit of beginning your search by checking encyclopedias and other basic reference sources. This kind of quick check will provide introductory information on your subject and, often, useful bibliographies (as at the end of encyclopedia articles). The variety of these important information sources can be seen from this very brief list. Find out which of the following encyclopedias your library has and list the call numbers of all of them.

Encyclopaedia Britannica, 15th ed., 32 vols.
Encyclopedia Americana
Encyclopedia of Anthropology
Encyclopedia of Banking and Finance
The Encyclopedia of the Biological Sciences
Encyclopedia Canadiana
Encyclopedia of Computer Science and Technology
Encyclopedia of Crime and Justice
Encyclopedia of Psychology
International Encyclopedia of the Social Sciences
McGraw-Hill Encyclopedia of Science and Technology
The Negro in American History
The Oxford Companion to American History
The Oxford Companion to American (or English) Literature
Princeton Encyclopedia of Poetry and Poetics
Princeton Handbook of Poetic Terms

Also, check your library to see what publications it has to help in biographical studies (authors, historical figures, kings, presidents, famous personalities). List the call numbers for those you can find in the library and add to this list any other titles you think could be useful.

Biography Index
Chambers's Biographical Dictionary
Current Biography
Dictionary of American Biography (DAB)
Dictionary of National Biography (DNB)
Notable Women in America

If you are researching a literary subject, what reference works does your library have to help you locate articles about English and American literature? In addition to the *Cambridge Bibliography of English Literature,* what special bibliographies are available to you? Does your library have the *MLA International Bibliography* (which lists articles and books in English and American literature)? Find the call numbers for *Literary History of the United States, Literary History of England,* and *The Reader's Encyclopedia.* What different kinds of information do these reference works have? Take notes and come prepared to describe these reference sources and discuss your findings.

For more information about the library and its resources, try to find a book that tells you more about libraries—their catalogs, reference works, indexes, abstracts, and bibliographies. These will tell you much more than this brief summary can suggest. Here are examples of several such books you might look for:

Barton, Mary Neill, and M. V. Bell, *Reference Books*
Galin, Saul, and Peter Spielberg, *Reference Books*
Gates, Jean Key, *Guide to the Use of Books and Libraries*
Sheehy, Eugene P., *Guide to Reference Books*, 10th ed., 1986
Shove, Raymond, and others, *The Use of Books and Libraries*
Walford's Guide to Reference Material, 4th ed., 1980–1987. 3 vols.
White, Carl M., and others, *Sources of Information in the Social Sciences*

These brief pages on the library have shown you where to look to discover suitable information sources for a research paper. In summary, your first search steps should include the following:

1. Find and read a book about libraries and their resources.
2. Read an encyclopedia article on your subject for basic information and references.
3. Check the subject card catalog for leads in your subject area (check cognates for key words).
4. Check the *Reader's Guide to Periodical Literature* for general articles on your subject.
5. Check relevant specialized indexes to find articles on your subject.
6. Check abstracts for additional articles.
7. Use the leads you have to check author cards in the catalog for cross-referenced subject listings and bibliographies.
8. Check your library's computer resources.
9. Ask your reference librarian for help.

You should now be ready for the next step in getting your facts together.

Survey the Information Sources; Prepare a Working Bibliography

At this point, your instructor may ask you to submit a *working bibliography*, a tentative list of books, articles, and other sources you think will be useful in providing the facts needed for the subject of your research paper. Depending on your instructor's requirements, this list may take the form of a *set of three-by-five-inch index cards* (which you should make for yourself in any case), or it may take the form of an alphabetized list on one or more sheets of regular theme paper (see the bibliography following "Monkey Talk" on page 234).

To compile this list, you will have to make a separate card for each bibliography item you discover that seems relevant to your subject. Be selective; list only those works that seem specifically relevant, otherwise your list will seem padded and will certainly be too long. On each card, carefully write all the information you need, following exactly the *order* and the *form* that the reference will have in the bibliography at the end of your paper (this will make the final compilation much easier, for you can then simply transfer the information directly into the bibliography for your paper). The two sample bibliography cards on page 251 follow the form used in the bibliography of "Monkey Talk."

Linden, Eugene.
    Apes, Men, and Language.
    New York: Penguin
    Books, 1976.

Terrace, Herbert S.
    "How Nim Chimpsky
    Changed My Mind."
    Psychology Today Nov.
    1979: 63 – 76.

Later, when your instructor has approved your bibliography cards (or your list), add to them the call numbers you find in the card catalog. Then, as you check each source to see if it is relevant and suitable, you may add a brief comment to remind yourself of the first impression you got when you scanned the information. If any source seems clearly useful, you should read it and begin to take notes, summarizing, quoting, and paraphrasing information you hope to use in the paper. Set up to follow MLA style, these two sample bibliography note cards illustrate only two of the many kinds of references that can appear in the working bibliography.

The Modern Language Association (MLA) and the American Psychological Association (APA) require their authors to follow their documentation styles—two basic and widely used styles. The illustration given in the following section are based on the two manuals these organizations have published to guide authors:

MLA: Walter S. Achtert and Joseph Gibaldi, *The MLA Style Manual* (New York: The Modern Language Association of America, 1985).
APA: *Publication Manual of the American Psychological Association,* 3rd ed. (Washington: American Psychological Association, 1983).

The illustrations are shown as they would appear *typed,* with italics indicated by underlining and with the correct spacing shown between the three (or four) basic units that make up all bibliographic references:

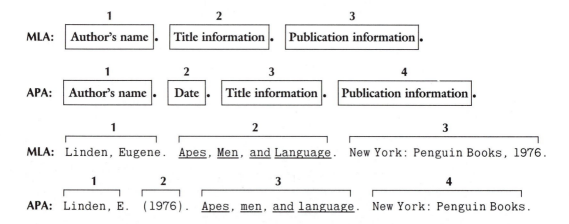

The greatest variation will usually appear in the last unit, where "publication" can include the titles of books, magazines, and other works *within which* the work represented by the "basic title" is printed. As you check the illustrations given in the following section, note how the three-unit or four-unit pattern works.

DOCUMENTATION METHODS: BIBLIOGRAPHIES, CITATIONS, NOTES

All researched papers *must* be documented: directly quoted, paraphrased, or borrowed information must be acknowledged. On this everyone agrees. But what is the *best* form for bibliographies, citations within paragraphs, or notes at the end of a paper? On this nearly everyone disagrees. The truth is, there is no "right way" to document a paper. The method of documentation any writer uses is dictated by the reader or publisher of the paper. In a classroom situation, you follow the method required by your instructor, and the method will vary—from English to biology to engineering to agriculture to chemistry. And if you were working at a job in which reports had to be written, you'd follow the method and style of your supervisor or the company. If you become a published writer and submit an article or a paper to a publisher (or a magazine), you would have to follow the method required by that publisher (magazine). The "right" way to document a paper, therefore, is to follow the requirements of the writing/publishing situation.

MLA and APA Bibliography Styles.   Because your instructor will likely ask you to follow the style of either MLA or APA, each of the following *bibliography* examples appears in both forms. In *PMLA (Publications of the Modern Language Association)* such items would appear in a section at the end of the paper titled "Works Cited"—works actually referred to or quoted from. If the paper uses APA format, this section would be titled "References." Another title option for this section sometimes allowed in classroom situations is "Works Consulted" (to tell the reader that some of the works in the bibliography were consulted but weren't actually used in the paper).

A BOOK BY ONE AUTHOR

MLA   Bright, Michael. <u>Animal</u> <u>Language</u>. London:
          British Broadcasting Corp., 1984.

APA   Bright, M. (1984). <u>Animal</u> <u>language</u>.
          London: British Broadcasting Corp.

A BOOK BY TWO OR THREE AUTHORS

MLA   Mathes, J. C., and Dwight W. Stevenson.
          <u>Designing</u> <u>Technical</u> <u>Reports</u>.
          Indianapolis: Bobbs, 1976.

APA   Mathes, J. C., & Stevenson, D. W. (1976).
          <u>Designing</u> <u>technical</u> <u>reports</u>.
          Indianapolis: Bobbs.

A BOOK BY MORE THAN THREE AUTHORS

MLA   Nilsen, Alleen Pace, et al. <u>Sexism</u> <u>and</u>
          <u>Language</u>. Urbana: National Council of
          Teachers of English, 1977.

APA   Nilsen, A. P., Bosmajian, H., Gershuny, H.
          L., & Stanley, J. P. (1977). <u>Sexism</u> <u>and</u>
          <u>language</u>. Urbana, IL: National Council
          of Teachers of English.

WORKS OF SEVERAL VOLUMES WITH ONE TITLE BY A SINGLE
AUTHOR

MLA   Johnson, Edgar. <u>Charles</u> <u>Dickens</u>: <u>His</u> <u>Tragedy</u>
          <u>and</u> <u>Triumph</u>. 2 vols. New York: Simon,
          1952.

APA   Johnson, E. (1952). <u>Charles</u> <u>Dickens</u>: <u>his</u>
          <u>tragedy</u> <u>and</u> <u>triumph</u>. (Vols. 1-2). New
          York: Simon & Schuster.

LATER EDITIONS OF AN EARLIER BOOK

MLA   Kroitor, Harry P. The Five-Hundred-Word
           Theme. 5th ed. Englewood Cliffs, N.J.:
           Prentice Hall, 1994.

APA   Kroitor, H. P. (1994). The
           five-hundred-word theme (5th ed.).
           Englewood Cliffs, N.J.: Prentice Hall.

AN EDITED BOOK (COLLECTION, ANTHOLOGY)
WITH SELECTIONS BY SEVERAL AUTHORS

MLA   Fobes, James L., and James E. King, eds.
           Primate Behavior. New York: Academic
           Press, 1982.

APA   Fobes, J. L., & King, J. E. (Eds.).
           (1982). Primate behavior. New York:
           Academic Press.

A CHAPTER OR ESSAY IN AN EDITED BOOK

MLA   Rumbaugh, Duane M., E. Sue Savage-Rumbaugh,
           and John L. Scanlon. "The Relationship
           between Language in Apes and Human
           Beings." Primate Behavior. Eds. J. L.
           Fobes and J. E. King. New York:
           Academic Press, 1982. 361-85.

APA   Rumbaugh, D. M., Savage-Rumbaugh, E. S., &
           Scanlon, J. L. (1982). The relationship
           between language in apes and human
           beings. In J. L. Fobes & J. E. King
           (Eds.), Primate behavior (pp. 361-385).
           New York: Academic Press.

ARTICLES IN (MONTHLY) MAGAZINES

MLA   Fleming, Joyce Dudney. "The State of the
           Apes." Psychology Today Jan. 1974:
           31-44.

APA   Fleming, J. D. (1974, January). The state
           of the apes. Psychology Today, pp.
           31-44.

AN ARTICLE IN A JOURNAL WITH CONTINUOUS PAGINATION
THROUGHOUT ANNUAL VOLUMES

MLA Gardner, R. A., and B. T. Gardner. "Early
Signs of Language in Child and
Chimpanzee." <u>Science</u> 187 (1975):
752–53.

APA Gardner, R. A., & B. T. Gardner. (1975).
Early signs of language in child and
chimpanzee. <u>Science</u>, <u>187</u>, 752–753.

AN ARTICLE IN A JOURNAL THAT PAGES EACH ISSUE
SEPARATELY

MLA Lyon, George Ella. "Contemporary Appalachian
Poetry: Sources and Directions."
<u>Kentucky Review</u> 2.2 (1981): 3–22.

APA Lyon, G. E. (1981). Contemporary
Appalachian poetry: sources and
directions. <u>Kentucky Review</u>, <u>2</u>(2),
3–22.

AN ARTICLE FROM A WEEKLY OR BIWEEKLY PERIODICAL

MLA Greenberg, Joel. "Koko." <u>Science News</u> 14
Oct. 1978: 265–70.

APA Greenberg, J. (1978, October 14).
Koko. <u>Science News</u>, pp. 265–70.

AN ARTICLE FROM AN ENCYCLOPEDIA OR REFERENCE WORK

MLA Green, Benny. "Jazz." <u>Encyclopaedia
Britannica</u>: <u>Macropaedia</u>. 1974 ed.
[This article is signed "B.Gr." and the author can be
identified from the special list of authors given at the back
of the index volume.]

APA Green, B. Jazz. (1974). In <u>Encyclopaedia
Britannica</u>: <u>Macropaedia</u>. 12th ed.

A SIGNED NEWSPAPER ARTICLE

MLA Witzel, David. "The Satire of <u>Doonesbury</u>."
<u>The Houston Post</u>, 2 March 1989: C5.

APA Witzel, D. (1989, March 2). The satire of
<u>Doonesbury</u>. <u>The Houston Post</u>, sec. C,
p. 5.

AN INTERVIEW YOU CONDUCT (IN PERSON OR BY PHONE)

MLA   Andropolis, Charles G. Professor, Dept. of
            Biochemistry, Texas A&M University,
            College Station, Texas. Personal
            interview. 12 February 1990.
            [You could also have a "Telephone interview," a "Response
            to a letter," or similar variations.]

APA   Andropolis, C. G. (1990, February 12).
            [Professor of Biochemistry, Texas A&M
            University.] Personal interview.

AN UNSIGNED ARTICLE FROM A POPULAR WEEKLY MAGAZINE

MLA   "Fire When Ready, Ma'am." _Time_ 15 January
            1990: 29.

APA   Fire when ready, ma'am. (1990, January
            15). _Time_, p. 29.

A SIGNED ARTICLE FROM A POPULAR WEEKLY MAGAZINE

MLA   Dunne, Philip. "Dissent, Dogma and Darwin's
            Dog." _Time_ 15 January 1990: 84.

APA   Dunne, P. (1990, January 15). Dissent,
            dogma and Darwin's dog. _Time_, p. 84.

A TELEVISION OR RADIO PROGRAM

MLA   _The First Americans_. Narr. Hugh
            Downs. Writ. and prod. Craig
            Fisher. NBC News Special. KNBC, Los
            Angeles. 21 Mar. 1968.

APA   Downs, H. (Narrator). (1968, March 21). _The
            first Americans_. NBC News Special. Los
            Angeles: KNBC.

Take Exact, Relevant Notes; Design a Rough Plan

The key to taking notes is your *controlling attitude*. If this attitude is clear and limited properly, you should be able to tell what information to take from your source. If you have written a careful purpose statement, it will provide two useful guides to taking notes:

1. An exact, limited controlling attitude
2. The basic approach to developing this attitude

If you check the purpose statements given for "Monkey Talk" (p. 239), you'll see that all three have a clear controlling attitude:

"discuss what **conclusions** *can be drawn"* [assertion]

"What **conclusions** *can be drawn?"* [question]

"have failed to teach them to speak, . . . have misunderstood the results of signing experiments, . . . have only recently understood the tie between signaling skills and symbolic communication" [these are the **conclusions,** restated as a thesis]

The key to note-taking is the word *conclusions,* which identifies the controlling attitude (as shown on page 238). The student would look for information that could be used to show the results of the *teaching experiments* in speaking, signing, and signaling (the subject area). Also, the way in which each purpose statement is worded influences the way in which the information will be used in the paper. The *assertion* statement says the paper will discuss the conclusions; the *question* version implies that the results will be examined and then a *conclusion* will be reached (perhaps with an *evaluation* added); the *thesis* version clearly presents a specific *thesis* to be *supported by evidence* in the paper. Early in your investigation, decide exactly what you hope to show and how you plan to go about it; these two factors will influence the information you choose from the sources, how much you will need, how detailed you must be, and how you use the information in the paper.

Write your notes on a four-by-six-inch card, with the information source clearly indicated. For example, look at paragraph 9 of "Monkey Talk." As the internal documentation at the end of the paragraph suggests, all the information in this paragraph, including the two quoted words, comes from one source. The note card with the necessary information might look like this:

```
B. J. & R. A. Gardner - Evidence
 - reviewed the Hayes failure
 - Chimps have the intelligence
 - find the right "Channel"
 - Washoe experiment -
     Chimp 11 mo. old - wild-born
     was taught only ameslan
     she used & interpreted signs
     learned - training & observation
     after 51 mo., a vocab. of 132
     signs & a much larger
       "receptive vocab."
                              pp. 244-46
```

The complete source reference would appear on the *bibliography card* describing the Gardner work referred to here as *Evidence.* All these facts and the phrase "receptive vocabulary" will be found on pages 244–46 in the article by the two Gardners in the *Journal of Experimental Psychology* (indicated by the short title *Evidence*). The notes simply list the facts considered relevant. Almost no quotation marks are needed because nothing substantial is quoted *as phrased* in the original source. Note, however, that even though no quotation marks appear, *all* borrowed facts must be documented if you are to avoid the charge of plagiarism. You must indicate where all the *ideas* come from, whether you quote directly or not. If you make your notes brief enough and then phrase your sentences from these notes without looking at the source, you aren't likely to duplicate the exact phrasing of the source. The result should be a summary or paraphrase similar to paragraph 9. Your instructor may require more than the one citation the student used to tag his paragraph, though here that's probably unnecessary.

Here's one more example of completed note cards. Here the note cards again provide a short-title identification. These two cards provide the information that appears in the quotation in paragraph 12, identified by the internal documentation at the end of the quotation (Temerlin, *Lucy* 125).

Temerlin, Maurice K. - *Lucy*
"When she tired of the pictures she put the magazine down, crossed the room, stood before me on two legs wearing her play-face. This conversation ensued, Lucy speaking ASL while I replied in English.
Lucy: "Maury, tickle Lucy."
Maury: "No, I'm busy."
Lucy: "Chase Lucy." (p. 125)

Temerlin, - *Lucy* - 2
Maury: "Not now."
Lucy: "Hug Lucy, hurry, hurry."
Maury: "In just a minute."
Lucy (laughing): "Hurry, hurry, hug Lucy, tickle, chase Lucy."
How could I resist?" p. 125

Once you have gathered all the information you think you'll need, move on to the last two phases of the research project—organizing the facts and writing the paper.

ORGANIZING THE FACTS

In any long researched paper a major problem is to organize the gathered facts into major units (parts) and subunits (usually paragraphs), and then to devise an outline to guide you in the actual writing process. This process is represented by steps seven and eight on our check sheet:

7. Classify the facts into major subject categories.
8. Devise a preliminary topic outline.

Classify the Facts into Major Subject Categories

The greater the number of facts, the greater the need for careful, efficient classification. (Review Chapter 2, especially the section on outlining, and Chapter 3, pages 80 and 83). Most information can be classified (i.e., arranged and organized) in many ways, depending on the writer's purpose and controlling attitude. Information about *shirts,* for example, can be classified according to *material, color, use, cost.* In "Monkey Talk" the information is classified by experiment, the easiest and most obvious grouping. Could it be reorganized and presented in some other way? Would the paper work if all the information were classified under each of the following: *language used, participants, problems?* What problems would this arrangement create? What information would be included in a major unit (of three or more paragraphs) describing Washoe, Lucy, Nim, Sherman, and Austin *only as participants?*

The aim of classification should be to decide from your note cards what major parts the paper is to have and what paragraphs will comprise each part. For each part and each paragraph a "pointer" or controlling attitude should determine what information you will include. Your aim is to make certain that each part and each supporting paragraph has unity. Probably the most difficult kind of information to control comes under the heading of "background" or "history." In long papers, some background information or history is usually needed to place the research within a broader context. Such an introductory unit can also serve to create reader interest and establish the general tone of the paper; but the unit shouldn't take more than two or three paragraphs. The first unit of "Monkey Talk" seems to be designed to create interest. Does it succeed? Could it be deleted? What function does the second unit serve? Could the information in these units be reclassified more efficiently? The result of classification should be a preliminary outline of the paper. For "Monkey Talk," this preliminary outline should be general and brief; it might look like this:

Background—animal communication—question
Speculation about apes—results
Attempts to teach apes to speak—conclusions
Work with Ameslan (signing)—results, conclusions
Other projects
Summary, conclusions

If your classification is effective, you should later be able to translate these preliminary notes and your note cards into a more detailed outline.

Devise a Preliminary Topic Outline

Whether your instructor requires it or not, devise a good topic outline for your paper, including enough detail so that major parts and paragraphs can be seen at a glance. A good outline will keep you on track as you write the paper, though you should be prepared to change it if, during the writing process, you discover something relevant and important you have omitted. When you have completed the paper, rewrite the outline to make it represent exactly what you have written. Turn in the outline with the paper so that it can help guide the reader through your paper. Study the form and the details of the following final topic outline for "Monkey Talk," using it as a basis for the outline of your own paper. For additional information about outlining, study pages 80, 83, and 188, and review the section on outlining, Chapter 2, page 34.

```
              TOPIC OUTLINE FOR RESEARCH PAPER

    Title: MONKEY TALK
    Question: What conclusions can be drawn from the speaking,
              signing, and signaling skills researchers have taught
              to our primate neighbors? [end of paragraph 2]
      I. Background Introduction [1-2]
         A. A haunting question [1]
         B. Crucial terms [2]
     II. Early Speaking Projects [3-7]
         A. Early speculation: Darwin and Marais [3]
         B. Trainers Garner and Witmer [4]
         C. Researchers Furness and Kohts [5]
         D. Chimps Gua and Viki [6]
         E. Transition: new directions [7]
    III. Signing Projects: Ameslan and Beyond [8-14]
         A. Transition: Using Ameslan [8]
         B. The Gardners' choice of ASL [9]
            1. Washoe's environment [9]
            2. Washoe's signing vocabulary [9]
         C. Project Washoe [10]
            1. Two-way communication [10]
            2. Washoe's combining forms [10]
         D. Transition: Troublesome definitions [11]
```

WRITING THE PAPER

Of the ten steps listed on the check sheet for writing a research paper, only two necessary and important procedures remain:

9. Write the first draft.
10. Revise the paper, make the final copy, provide a final outline.

If you've been attentive and interested, the actual composing process has been going on in your head ever since you began gathering facts. And, when you began classifying the information on your note cards, you may very well have begun jotting down sentences or writing leads to follow. At this point, however, you must concentrate on the actual writing itself.

Write the First Draft

Some instructors require a first draft of the paper to be turned in with the final copy. Comparing the two versions can show a reader how you used the available information, how carefully you revised the first version. If the two are exactly alike in wording, you probably didn't put the revision process to work, but merely recopied the original.

As you write and revise, be wary of sexist language, since many readers are offended by male-dominated allusions. Such expressions as "the reader . . . *he*" and "everyone must do *his* job" and "the doctor . . . *he*" should be used only when the context demands the male reference. One way to avoid the use of sexist language is to alternate references, using "doctor . . . *she*" as often as "doctor . . . *he*" (for example). Not all readers like that solution, however. Another common way around the problem is to use the expressions "he/she" or "he or she," but most careful writers consider these awkward and find other solutions. Perhaps the most widely used method of avoiding sexist language is to substitute *people* for *everyone* and to use plurals where possible:

> If we are to succeed, people must do *their* jobs.
> Doctors find that *they* can treat patients better if . . .
> If readers practice, *they* can increase *their* reading speed.
> Writers must avoid sexist language if *they* want to succeed.

Set up internal documentation as you write. One useful purpose of the first draft is to set up the citations within the text of the paper. If you have written your note cards carefully, noting sources and page references accurately, you should have no trouble simply adding the citations *as you write*. Using the simplified internal documentation methods required by MLA and APA makes this job easy.

The hard part at this stage is to get moving and keep moving. (You might check some free association and clustering suggestions in Chapter 3.) One way to get the first draft moving onto the blank page or computer screen is to rely on your memory and the brief, *preliminary* outline. Get your fingers moving. Try writing a few sentences about each of the general "subject headings" you listed. If you're working with a computer, start typing. Think what you would like to include under each heading, and begin:

```
Background--animal communication: In this section I'd like to include
some information about animal communication. We don't have to talk to
animals to communicate. Dogs and cats obey our commands. People train
animals to do things all the time. But does this have anything to do with
animal language?
```

There you are. Writing. Immediately go to each of the other headings and do the same. This process will: (1) force you to write something, (2) tell you if you have a focus in mind, (3) begin organizing your ideas, and (4) activate the free association process you learned about in Chapter 3. This preliminary warm-up completed, you can begin writing the first draft in earnest.

Writing the first draft provides the opportunity to *reconsider* the subject limits and the goals you've set. As you write, you should be critical enough to think of all sorts of questions:

> Do I need this information in the paper? Does it fit my limited subject?
> Does this information belong in this paragraph?
> Have I classified the information effectively?
> What's my purpose? Do I still have a clear controlling attitude?
> Am I keeping my thesis question in mind?
> Can I focus my thesis question more precisely?
> What audience (reader) am I writing for? Only my instructor?
> Do I really understand what my instructor wants?

These questions are so basic that they should automatically influence the writing process. When you come to revise this first draft, you'll approach this critical questioning process more systematically, using the check sheet on page 195 and the guidelines on page 219.

Simplified Documentation Methods

In the past, traditional form required that citations be placed as independent "endnotes" at the end of the paper or, in the occasional journal, as footnotes at the bottom of the page. The present practice in *PMLA* (the journal widely used as a style model in the humanities) is to place all citations within the text in the form of *internal* (parenthetical) *documentation*. The American Psychological Association (APA) uses a similar method. The following examples illustrate the use of internal documentation: complete short citations appear within parentheses within the text.

INTERNAL DOCUMENTATION

The first example comes from the beginning of paragraph 2 of "Monkey Talk":

```
grammar, and sentence. In Animal Language Bright points out
that among animals of all kinds "By far the most common use for
sound . . . is to communicate" (11). But what is
"communication"? Bright says that " . . . an animal has
communicated with another when it has transmitted information
that influences the listener's behavior" (11).
```

Because both the title of the work and the name of the author appear in the first sentence, the only citation required for the quote is the page number, given in parentheses (11) and followed by a period. Because the author's name appears in the third sentence also, the only citation required is the page number. Note that including title and/or author within the text proper often improves readability and simplifies the parenthetical citation.

This next example comes from paragraph 3 of "Monkey Talk":

```
In the early 1900s Eugene Marais had studied baboons in the
wild, " . . . suggest[ing] that, along with other primates, man
possessed two memories," an instinctive one related to
"collective primate history," and a "causal" memory that made
it possible for humans to learn from their experiences. Marais
also insisted that "non-primate mammals were dominated by
hereditary memory while primates were dominated by causal
memory" (Linden, Apes 227).
```

The quotation begins with an *ellipsis* (. . .) to indicate that part of the quoted sentence is left out. (Note that the periods of the ellipsis are spaced and separated from the first word of the quotation.) Also, because the first quoted word is *suggested* in the original, the [ing] is put within brackets to indicate the change. The information about Marais comes from Eugene Linden's book, *Apes, Men, and Language*. Since neither his name nor the work's title appears in the text, the normal citation would be (Linden 227). But if you check the bibliography of the paper, you'll find two works by Linden; therefore, some kind of short-title identification is required here. In this example only the first word of the full title has been used (Linden, *Apes* 227).

The following example (from paragraph 12 of the paper) illustrates how to *single space* and *indent* a longer quotation (more than five lines) within the typed text:

```
[5 spaces]
───→. . . on three different occasions she learned a sign for
      cry, food, and hurt. Then, sometime later, she was shown a
      radish. When she bit into it she signed, "Cry hurt food."
      After that moment of creative integration, when shown a
      radish she always signed either "Cry food" or "Hurt food"
      or "Cry hurt food." This is not an isolated or a unique
      example. (Temerlin, Lucy 120)
```

The quoted passage is indented five spaces from the left margin of the paper's regular text. Again, ellipses (. . .) begin the quote to indicate omitted material.

Note that *no quotation marks* begin or end this passage because it's indented and set off from the rest of the text. Within the passage, however, regular (rather than single) quotation marks appear around words quoted in the original. As required by MLA form, note, too, that the citation appears *after the period at the end of the quote* (rather than before it as in the examples given above). Finally, again the citation must include a short title because the bibliography contains two works by Temerlin (Temerlin, *Lucy* 120).

This final example comes from paragraph 3 of "Monkey Talk":

> From the early 1700s to the time of Charles Darwin, speculation about the human place in the animal world was widespread (Glass et al. 33–40, 145–172).

The general statement made here is backed by information on many pages (33–40, 145–172) from *Forerunners of Darwin: 1745–1859,* a book *edited* by three people and containing a collection of essays by many writers. The citation includes only the last name of the first editor plus *et al.,* which means "and others" (from the Latin, *et alii,* with the second word abbreviated). This method prevents the internal documentation from becoming too cluttered with names. Similarly, in paragraph 4 the citation (Rumbaugh et al., *Primate Behavior* 363) refers to an essay by Rumbaugh and two other authors within a book titled *Primate Behavior.* The title is given within the citation to distinguish it from another work by Rumbaugh listed in the bibliography.

Unlike "Monkey Talk," these examples from the paper are not in MLA style. To illustrate how they would appear in APA style, here they are again. The first quotes from *Animal Language:*

> In Animal Language Bright points out that among animals of all kinds "By far the most common use for sound . . . is to communicate" (1984, p. 11). But what is "communication"? Bright says that ". . . an animal has communicated with another when it has transmitted information that influences the listener's behavior" (p. 11).

Note the differences. APA style requires the use of *p.* or *pp.* for all specific page references. In addition, authors are always identified with a publication date, placed in parentheses immediately following the author's name or, as in this example, within the parentheses giving the page reference. This example could also begin with "Bright (1984) . . . ," omitting the title. The page references would remain the same, except "1984" would be deleted in the first citation.

Here's the Linden example from paragraph 3 of "Monkey Talk":

> In the early 1900s Eugene Marais had studied baboons in the wild, ". . . suggest[ing] that, along with other primates, man possessed two memories," an instinctive one related to "collective primate history," and a "causal" memory that made it possible for humans to learn from their experiences. Marais also insisted that "non-primate mammals were dominated by hereditary memory while primates were dominated by causal memory" (Linden, 1976, p. 227).

The only difference here is that within the parentheses APA replaces *"Apes"* with the date and adds a *p.* before the page number. The date identifies which of the Linden works is being quoted.

This same identification method is used in the indented quote from paragraph 12 of the paper:

> [5 spaces]
> → . . . on three different occasions she learned a sign for cry, food, and hurt. Then, sometime later, she was shown a radish. When she bit into it she signed, "Cry hurt food." After that moment of creative integration, when shown a radish she always signed either "Cry food" or "Hurt food" or "Cry hurt food." This is not an isolated or a unique example. (Temerlin, 1975, p. 120)

As in MLA style, the citation is placed *after* the final period in the quotation. As with the Linden example, the date replaces *Lucy* to identify which Temerlin work is being quoted.

A major difference between the two styles involves citations referring to multiple authors. APA allows the use of *et al.* only if *six* or more authors are involved; otherwise, *all* the authors' names must be listed, as in the example from paragraph 3 of "Monkey Talk":

> From the early 1700s to the time of Charles Darwin, speculation about the human place in the animal world was widespread (Glass, Temkin, and Straus, 1959, pp. 33–40, 145–172).

Note that all three authors' names are listed, the date is included, and the required *pp.* is placed before the page numbers.

There are advantages and disadvantages to both methods. Your instructor will tell you which to use. If you end up using APA style, a useful exercise would be to revise all the citations in "Monkey Talk" to fit APA style. You can get additional information from the two style manuals referred to on page 252 and from the MLA–APA bibliographic listings on pages 253–56.

ENDNOTES

In printed form (for example, in magazines and journals), endnotes normally appear immediately following the last paragraph of the paper. In a typed paper, however, your instructor may ask you to begin endnotes on a new page (or not to use them at all). Endnotes are given various headings: "Notes," "Endnotes," "Reference Notes," "References," and in APA format, "Footnotes." Since the purpose of internal documentation is to eliminate all endnotes and footnotes if possible, when they do appear they usually are "content notes," designed to expand or comment on something within the text. They are identified within the text with *superscripts*[1] as shown here and numbered consecutively. In *PMLA* such content notes are often very long explanations and the heading used is "Notes." In APA format the content notes are called "Footnotes" even though they appear as endnotes following the last paragraph of the paper. Here's what you might find if you checked the end of the paper to see what the superscript "1" refers to:

```
                            NOTES

     1 A superscript is a raised numeral placed within the text
to tell the reader that information appears at the end of the
paper. Both MLA and APA use these superscripts for explanatory
purposes, to provide additional supporting references, perhaps,
or to refer to contradicting opinions. They are not used to
provide the information given through internal documentation.
For additional information about endnotes, check Achtert and
Gibaldi's MLA Style Manual (1984) or any issue of PMLA. Though
some publications still place footnotes at page bottoms, this
method has largely been replaced by internal documentation.
```

OTHER DOCUMENTATION METHODS

Check the magazines on your library shelves and you will find *dozens* of documentation methods. All, however, are variations of the ones discussed in this chapter. Here you will be introduced to a compact method of citation that requires an alphabetized, *numbered* bibliography plus the internal documentation method.

Look again at the example quoting from Bright's *Animal Language*. If you check the bibliography of "Monkey Talk," and number the items, the Bright reference would be *2* and the two Linden references would be *12* and *13*. If the works in the bibliography are numbered, these numbers can then be used for citation purposes. The Bright example would look like this:

```
In Animal Language Bright points out that among animals of all
kinds "By far the most common use for sound . . . is to
communicate" (2:11). But what is "communication"? Bright says
that " . . . an animal has communicated with another when it
has transmitted information that influences the listener's
behavior" (2:11).
```

"Tagging" the citation by referring to author, title (and sometimes date) within the text is a standard method in many fields, whether internal documentation is used or not. Here the (2:11) is especially appropriate because author and title already appear in the text. MLA suggests the form (2, 11).

And since the Linden book referred to in paragraph 3 of the paper is item number *12* in the bibliography, that example would look like this:

```
In the early 1900s Eugene Marais had studied baboons in the
wild, " . . . suggest[ing] that, along with other primates, man
possessed two memories," an instinctive one related to
"collective primate history," and a "causal" memory that made
it possible for humans to learn from their experiences. Marais
also insisted that "non-primate mammals were dominated by
hereditary memory while primates were dominated by causal
memory" (12:227).
```

Many variations of this "number style" exist; all depend on an alphabetized, numbered list of *works cited,* and all use internal documentation and some kind of "tagging" to help clarify the source. Don't use the number style without your instructor's approval. If this method is used, you should also be prepared to hand in for approval a first draft with all the "tagging" and internal documentation already complete.

CHECK SPACING AND FORM FOR ACCURACY

The first draft is also the best time to get the spacing and form of all internal documentation and bibliography items accurate. If your instructor decides to require MLA form, you can use "Monkey Talk" as a guide. For items in your bibliography that don't match those given in "Monkey Talk," you have the additional examples of bibliography style on pages 253–56.

Although this summary of bibliography and internal documentation form does not cover all the problems you are likely to encounter, it provides the basic approach used in deciding the form of all entries. A useful way to solve additional problems is to ask your instructor for a scholarly journal to use as a model, which you can then consult for your specific difficulties by checking its bibliography, citations, or endnotes. In the humanities, the journal most widely used as a model is probably *PMLA*. In any case, bibliography and internal documentation form must fulfill the requirements of the reader (your instructor, or the editor of the journal in which the paper appears). In the sciences and in engineering, documentation form varies considerably from field to field, so that choice of a specific journal to follow as a model is extremely important and should be attempted only with permission of your instructor. Your instructor will also tell you whether you may use footnotes, explanatory "Endnotes," or "Notes" (as explained on page 267). And you will need to know if the paper's bibliography section is to be titled "Works Cited," "References," or "Works Consulted." If you decide to provide a list of "Works Consulted" (as in "Monkey Talk"), be sure to include all works actually cited and only a few *carefully* selected works you consulted but didn't actually use.

Write with Your Controlling Attitude in Mind

As you write the first draft, keep the controlling attitude clearly in mind. Somewhere in each major unit, this attitude should be "echoed" (restated) or in some way implied. The result will be a series of reminders to your reader that you have indeed delivered what your introduction promised. In addition, the echoes will improve the coherence of your paper, since they serve as interlocking connections to guide the reader through the paper. If you write your first draft with care, with special attention to the controlling attitude, unity, coherence, and documentation, writing the final version will be much easier.

REVISE THE PAPER; MAKE THE FINAL COPY; PROVIDE A FINAL OUTLINE

As with the short paper, revision of the first draft should be used as an opportunity to correct errors in mechanics, documentation, form, and wording. Delete or condense as you think necessary, add explanations where clarity is questionable, or additional evidence where support of a thesis seems inadequate. Check for unity and coherence, wordiness, jargon, trite expressions, and the "Who-which-that disease," as well as for faulty punctuation and spelling. Look for passive-voice constructions that add unnecessary words, and for problems in grammar. These and other problems you will find discussed in Part Two of this book, "Revision—Mechanics and Style." (See page 272 for more information about the revision process.)

In appearance, your final paper should look like "Monkey Talk." Here are some final guidelines to follow. Check each in the sample paper:

1. Type, using double spacing for all parts of the paper, including bibliography and indented quotations. Though this is the standard practice for submitting papers for publication, in a classroom situation a paper's indented quotations are often single spaced, as are the bibliography, notes, and any footnotes. Use only good white paper, never erasable bond.

2. Prepare a title page with the following information: on the upper half of the page type the paper's title (all caps), your name several lines below the title (upper and lower case); on the lower third of the page type the name of the course, the instructor's name, and the date.

3. Include a topic outline (usually immediately following the title page) which presents the paper's title, a thesis/question (or a purpose statement), and a paragraph-by-paragraph list of topics. (For long paragraphs you may also include subtopics.)

4. Repeat the paper's title at the top of the first page of the text, usually in all caps. (Some readers prefer a title in upper and lower case here.) Count it (as page one), but do not type a number on this page.

5. Beginning with page 2, type your name and the number of each page at the top (usually lined up with the right margin).

6. Place the bibliography, with entries alphabetized according to authors' last names, at the end of the paper on a separate page, and number it also.

7. Indent five spaces to set off all extended quotations (usually five or more lines in typed form). Type them single spaced unless your instructor tells you to double space them.

8. If your paper requires explanatory "Notes" to clarify something within the text or to extend citation information, create a separate section for these notes and place them immediately following the last paragraph of the text, preceding the bibliography.

9. Unless your instructor requires it, do *not* place your research paper in a slippery plastic folder or any other cumbersome folder. (A plain manila filing folder usually works well.)

10. If you use a laser printer to create the final draft of your paper, *underline* major titles to indicate that they will appear in italics. Don't use the printer to create the actual italics. (If your instructor asks you to use *Headings* for the major sections of the paper, by all means use the laser printer to **boldface** them; use the same **Boldface Headings** in your topic outline.)

In subject, form, and appearance, "Monkey Talk" is an effective researched paper. Its subject is limited, its controlling attitude is focused by a question thesis, its information comes from a number of reliable sources (both articles and books) and can't be gathered from one reference source alone. Though some of the information in the sources is technical, the researchers' conclusions can be understood by any intelligent reader.

The paper's detailed topic outline shows that it is thoughtfully organized with a specific purpose in mind, guided by four key words: *speaking, signing, signaling,* and *conclusions.* Presented in the thesis question at the end of paragraph 2, these key words come at the end of the funnel effect provided by the first two paragraphs. Check the opening sentences of all the paragraphs and you'll see that most of them contain obvious echoes of previous information and serve as transitions to provide overall coherence and unity. The paper's last paragraph briefly restates the important conclusions provided by the researched information. It's clear that the paper *reports* the views of scientific researchers; it is not an expression of personal opinion.

Except in the use of the title "Works Consulted" for the bibliography (instead of "Works Cited"), the paper follows MLA form exactly. Parenthetical documentation follows required MLA form without interrupting the flow of the text. Because the overall appearance projects care and thought, the first impression a reader will get (a kind of *ethical appeal*) is very positive. And *that*, clearly, is the first impression you will want to create with any paper you write.

9

Mechanics: Grammar, Punctuation, Spelling

REVISION

Before tackling some of the most common problems in mechanics, let's briefly consider the revision process as it applies to your five-hundred-word theme or research paper.

The Importance of Revision

Like the prewriting process (thinking, discovering, planning, organizing), revision is important and requires both time and concentration. Student writers who neglect these two phases of the overall writing process usually turn out less effective work. Professional writers, however, welcome revision time because it provides additional opportunities to reconsider or add new supporting ideas and to make their style distinctive. As a result, their writing carries a *personal mark* (style), not accidentally, but because they consciously revised it to make it say exactly what they wanted it to say. These last chapters ask you to revise *seriously* and continually through all phases of the writing process to achieve the two broad purposes you are striving for:

1. Strength, clarity, and directness of well-supported thought—getting the reader to say, "I understand."
2. A *tone* of self-confidence and conviction —getting the reader to say, "I agree."

Although you can achieve the first of these purposes partly through the effective use of grammar, punctuation, and spelling, success depends far more on the larger problems of rhetoric—controlling focus, unity of thought, organization of ideas, and coherence. But both purposes also depend on diction (appropriate word choice, concreteness, directness) and effective sentence structure, as you will see in the chapters you are about to study. Equally important, the revision process lets you become more aware of your own style and ways to improve it. Careful revision gives you a chance to reconsider your ideas and listen to how the writing sounds.

Revising Rough Draft into Final Copy

The first complete copy of your theme or paper is the rough draft. Although this is often the copy some students turn in, it is only the first stage of the actual writing process described in the early chapters of this book. With a completed rough draft, you will have managed to get your ideas fairly well organized and most of your supporting evidence down on paper or into your computer. At this point you'll need some systematic revision, perhaps consulting the check sheets on pages 195 and 219.

If you've been working on a computer all along, revising is a constant process. You can easily change a word or sentence with a few keystrokes. Because deleting and reworking are much easier on the computer, you should take full advantage of the process to evaluate what you are composing. Type a sentence, then reread it. Change individual words or restructure the whole sentence. But make sure it fits the paragraph and the paper. In addition to this ongoing process, however, you should have another revision session when the first draft has been completed. Having saved a copy of your first draft (to hard disk or floppy), you can retrieve the document to work with on the monitor screen—without fear of "messing up a clean page." If you have spell-check software or a program that checks grammar and sentence structure, now is the time to apply it. Once you've completed the revision, again save the draft to disk, this time as "Draft 2" (or the equivalent). Print out both copies, compare them, and decide whether you need to make additional changes.

Whether you work on a computer or from a typed or written page, at this point take the time to revise systematically. Here's a summary of things to do and look for:

1. Reread your first and final drafts slowly, systematically, and thoroughly, moving from the title to the last word in the conclusion and bibliography. Read aloud, *listening* to the words and their effect; read silently, concentrating on ideas and their continuity.
2. Check the introduction to see if the thesis (problem statement or question) is clear and focused with a specific controlling attitude.
3. Check each paragraph to see that the topic sentence and the support clearly reflect the thesis.
4. Compare your paper with its outline to see that only relevant ideas and paragraphs are included.

5. Check each developmental paragraph for unity, making sure it concentrates on only the main idea of the topic sentence.

6. Check for coherence *within* paragraphs and transitions *between* them, providing transitions where you've neglected them.

7. Study the introduction to see if reader interest and acceptance can be improved, changing words that don't seem to fit the tone you are trying to project. (See check sheets, pp. 355, 385.)

8. Look for vague, general words, substituting concrete, specific ones where necessary. (More information on diction is presented in Chapter 10.)

9. Check closely for problems in grammar, punctuation, and spelling, with special attention to subject–verb agreement, pronoun reference, illogical sentence fragments, run-on sentences, and dangling modifiers (reviewed for you later in this chapter).

10. For a research paper, recheck documentation and bibliography form, accuracy of page references, and basic typing requirements. (See pp. 253, 263, 270.)

The Revising Process

Whether you're working on a computer or from a typed or written page, revising should be a continuous, ongoing process through all writing stages. This summary list should tell you at once that revising is more than simple recopying. It's also more than just correcting most of the spelling errors and making certain that commas and periods are acceptably used—though these are important because they are so basic. Most student revising falls short in the larger problems of rhetoric:

Revising for **focus**—controlling attitude, topic sentences (Chapter 3)
Revising for **unity**—all ideas are right on target (Chapter 4)
Revising for **coherence**—transitions, interlocking connection (Chapter 4)
Revising for **emphasis**—making major ideas stand out (Chapter 3)
Revising for **tone**—ethical appeal, audience appeal (Chapter 5)
Revising for **vagueness**—making words specific, concrete (Chapter 10)
Revising for **directness**—cutting, deleting wordiness (Chapter 10)

Can you read through your rough draft once and improve all these (as well as look for problems in mechanics)? Not likely. This, then, is the most important rule in the revising process:

Reread your paper several times (preferably aloud), each time revising systematically as you read.

The aim of this unit will be to get you to think about revising as an ongoing process and to decide how best to tackle your personal writing problems.

Here's the introductory paragraph from a student theme titled "Is It Fear?" As you read this paragraph, list words, phrases, punctuation, or other things you think need improvement. You will check your effectiveness in a moment.

IS IT FEAR?

Throughout mans life there are many feelings he posesses which cannot be clearly expressed. When explained in words the true feelings and meanings of these sensations are lost, people are often put into situations which make them react strangely. How does man show his feelings toward these situations and what are the involuntary reactions which overcome man caused by? Some illustrations of mans reactions can be seen in the following illustrations.

You probably noticed most of the mechanical problems on first reading:

Throughout	⟶	throughout (spelling)
mans	⟶	man's (apostrophe needed)
posesses	⟶	possesses (spelling)
in words	⟶	in words, (comma with opener)
are lost, people	⟶	are lost. People (comma splice)
these situations	⟶	these situations, and (comma, main clauses)
mans	⟶	man's (apostrophe needed)

If you caught all these, you did fine. However, don't stop after you have corrected basic problems in mechanics. What remains is a poor introductory paragraph because it is careless about the larger elements of rhetoric. Look at the paragraph again and see if you can cut down on the number of words, clarify the meaning, and focus the controlling attitude more effectively. After you've thought about your changes, examine these suggested revisions to the paragraph.

---

wordy, *omit* { Throughout man's life there are many

sensations? feelings he possesses which cannot be clearly

expressed. When explained in words, the true } *vague,*

feelings and meanings of these sensations are } *general*

lost. People are often put into situations which

shift in person

people   their

make them react strangely. How does man show his

in?   *causes*

feelings toward these situations, and what are

shift { the involuntary reactions which overcome man *people*

caused by? Some illustrations of man's reactions } *wordy*

can be seen in the following illustrations.

Keeping these revisions in mind, let's rewrite the paragraph:

> Many sensations cannot be clearly expressed. When explained in words, the feelings and meanings tied to these sensations are lost. People are often put into situations which make them react strangely. How do people show their feelings toward these situations, and what causes the involuntary reactions which overcome people? People's reactions can be seen in the following illustrations.

Although this version is much improved, does it *point* clearly and specifically to something that will be explained and developed in the essay? How specific are such words as *sensations, feelings, situations,* and *illustrations?* A reading of the whole essay shows that it's really about *stress reactions* and how hard it is to describe them or explain the fear behind them. Here with a new title is an improved version of the paragraph, pointing more specifically to the controlling attitude of the whole essay and to some of the stress reactions that will be discussed.

EXPLAINING STRESS REACTIONS

People have trouble explaining their feelings. On a page, fear, anger, love, hostility, and terror are merely words. To describe these emotions seems to rob them of the meaning and sensation they have in experience. Personal threat, involvement in an accident, breaking the rules of accepted social behavior can make most

]— Mentions specific emotions

]— Suggests more specific situations

> people react strangely. They can be
> overcome by sensations that seem to
> take over, causing involuntary
> reactions. Everyone reacts to   Thesis statement +
> threat and fear in <u>unique</u> <u>ways</u> <u>that</u>   controlling attitude
> <u>often</u> <u>defy</u> explanation.

Now the thesis of this paragraph tells the reader that the essay will be about the *unique ways that often defy explanation* when people react to stress and fear. Clearly, a good paper goes through many revision stages, each requiring concentration on specific problems. Perhaps the most efficient approach would be to begin by revising for wordiness, clarity, focus, coherence, logical support, and broader rhetorical elements. Usually a separate run-through is needed to check for mechanical things like punctuation, spelling, and grammar. Working on a computer *requires* this separate run-through. Finally, reading the paper aloud may help you spot additional problems in focus and logical support. You must decide on the approach that works best for you.

After you are satisfied that you have made all necessary revisions, recopy (or retype) the paper. Give this second copy the same close scrutiny you gave the first and don't hesitate to make additional changes where necessary. You may need to make still another copy before you are satisfied that you have written a paper as exact in idea and as polished in expression as you can make it. Never turn in a paper that has not gone through this revision process, and do not get someone else to do all the revising for you.

When you are satisfied that the revision is as good as you can make it, recopy the paper as neatly as possible (or type it). Although manuscript neatness is not in itself a virtue, you shouldn't make your paper difficult to read; there is no need to prejudice your reader against your ideas with a messy-looking paper. Remember, if your reader is an employer, he or she won't tolerate messy work. Whether you write or type, get into the habit of making the final copy a finished product you can be proud of, one that projects a positive ethical appeal.

TEST YOUR REVISION SKILLS: GENERAL PROBLEMS IN EXPRESSION

Revise and rewrite these sentences to improve clarity, directness, and general effectiveness. Be prepared to hand in the exercise and explain the changes you have made. Use this assignment as a test of your basic revision skills.

1. I would like you to provide the accountant with information about the bank's financial condition.
2. Because of rising costs, we would like to suggest that you purchase the computer hard disks without further delay.

3. I am writing this letter to you in order to ascertain the true facts concerning the refund delays.

4. There are four subjects discussed in the project report. These are as follows: feasibility, development, cost, planning for the future.

5. In effective systems usage of computers to attain maximum operating efficiency time is absolutely essential.

6. In my experiments, I have endeavored to ascertain the truth and to utilize it in the full and complete report I have attached for your consideration.

7. With reference to safety requirements, the entire staff must employ utmost precaution at all times. In the event of fire, the first thing you must do is to sound the alarm.

8. We would like you to obtain for us a duplicate copy of the report for our files.

9. The reason the plants are stunted in growth is due to the fact that they have been damaged by the high salt and chlorine content of city water.

10. It's usual to select regional managers to whom salesmen send reports and depend on for sales guidelines.

11. The bottom line is that you can't pass without studying.

12. On the other side of the ledger is the fact that he was speeding like crazy when he skidded off the road and the accident occurred.

13. Juan's employment was terminated due to the fact that his supervisor felt that an excessive number of hours per day were being spent in other than gainful pursuits.

14. In order to purchase a plane ticket to Chicago Pat sold the watch which had been given to her for her birthday.

15. Plans to attend the community college were made by Teresa and her husband; their applications had been mailed months ago.

16. The noisy, inattentive students sprawled grotesquely in the abused and battered seats of the incredibly crowded classroom, ignoring the absolutely riveting history lecture of the old but eager professor.

17. The consumption of alcoholic beverages among the younger generation is apparently escalating.

18. The historic library, which was scheduled to be torn down, had suffered broken windows and lost bricks, which worried the planning committee, which was fighting hard to preserve the old structure.

19. Before accountants write their financial reports, many writing problems have to be solved by them. These include planning, developing, organizing, writing and revising, all of which precede the production of the report itself.

20. Suddenly the puppy saw the cat. He jumped in front of the cat. The cat was hissing. He dodged back and forth. He was barking furiously.

21. I like a mystery story with exciting action and which keeps me guessing.

22. Knowing they might lose the game created short tempers among the players.

23. I think that driving in heavy freeway traffic is nerve wracking. Michael enjoys the challenge and excitement of driving in freeway traffic. I hate driving in heavy freeway traffic.

24. It's easier to spot grammar mistakes than correcting them, which can create problems if time is short, or if you are tired.

25. Some are born great, some achieve greatness, and some have greatness thrust upon them.

GRAMMAR

Most of the chapters in Part One conclude with a brief section of Review Terms, usually divided into a unit of rhetorical terms followed by a list of grammatical terms. In fact, you couldn't really understand the early chapters without some knowledge of grammar. So don't worry; you already know a great deal of grammar. The main purpose of the following unit on grammar is to review the major problems that repeatedly occur in most student writing. But before beginning this review, complete the pretests on grammar and punctuation to see if you can describe and correct the basic problems they cover. You can then test yourself again after you've completed the chapter. Your instructor may also want you to complete the spelling pretest at this point.

GRAMMAR PRETEST

Most (not all) of the sentences given below contain *only one* of the following grammatical problems:

0. Sentence contains no grammatical problems.
1. Subject and verb don't agree.
2. Pronoun does not agree with its antecedent.
3. Dangling modifier—verbal phrase doesn't clearly refer to any word in the sentence.
4. Misplaced modifier—word or word-group needlessly separated from the term it modifies.
5. Sentence fragment—incomplete grammatical construction not clearly connected to other meaning in context.
6. Run-on (fused) sentence—sentences run together with no conjunction or punctuation between them.
7. Faulty verb form—illogical shift in tense.
8. Faulty parallel structure—unequal grammatical elements placed in a series.

Use the numbers (including "0") given above to identify the one grammatical problem in each sentence below. First decide what problem the sentence has, and then place in the blank provided to the left of each sentence the *one* number from the above list that best identifies the grammatical problem. If the sentence has no problem, place a "0" in the blank. *Note:* Your instructor may ask you to provide a correction below each sentence, especially if you don't know the grammatical terms used in the list.

Example: 3   *After eating the meal, the newspaper was read.*

Correction: *After eating the meal,* **we** *read the newspaper. Since the verbal phrase* **after eating the meal** *does not clearly refer to any word in the sentence, you would place the number 3 in the blank. In the correction, the verbal phrase modifies the word* **we;** *almost any pronoun* (**I, he, she, they**) *or proper noun* (**Grace, Andy**) *could be substituted for* **we.**

_____ 1. The professor told them to watch the movie, take notes on it, and that they would have a test next week.

_____ 2. When faced with the evidence, not one objection was raised.

_____ 3. The doctor said that she was leaving town during the last consultation.

_____ 4. Each of the ten corporations distributed their profits this year.

_____ 5. To grow good plants, feed them regularly.

_____ 6. Unemployment, along with taxes, influence how people vote.

_____ 7. Good notes as well as a good textbook makes test taking easier.

_____ 8. I already have many interesting ideas for my research paper. Although, I haven't yet done any serious research in the library.

_____ 9. I already have many interesting ideas for my research paper, although I haven't yet done any serious research in the library.

_____ 10. Some people have trouble relaxing others can't get motivated.

_____ 11. The secretaries and the boss usually answers the phone.

_____ 12. Neither the secretaries nor the boss answers the phone.

_____ 13. Don't panic. Choose. Reject any notions that you have nothing to write about.

_____ 14. The first thing you'll want to do is to rent a car for personal use upon arriving at the airport.

_____ 15. No single group of voters represent the whole country.

_____ 16. After eating the meal, the table should be cleared and wiped clean.

_____ 17. His political career, unlike most people who run for political office, continued after he was convicted of tax fraud.

_____ 18. To write good papers, well-conceived, detailed outlines are needed by a student.

_____ 19. Excessive errors in the game was the chief reason for her failure.

_____ 20. If you don't learn to turn out the lights when you leave a room, it will probably raise your light bill. This can be very discouraging.

_____ 21. After removing the dishes from the sink, they are placed on the rack to dry.

_____ 22. If the board of directors controls the school system, they may change the textbooks.

_____ 23. Zeba said she would give me a raise this year. But without definitely committing herself.

_____ 24. Grace kept pictures of all the people she had known in a large shoe box.

_____ 25. While answering the telephone, my cat ran out the front door.

Acceptable and Unacceptable Grammar

What we call grammar is simply a description of the way a language works. Grammar describes how the structured parts of a language—especially its words and sentences—use the vocabulary of that language to communicate meaning accurately and acceptably. What is "acceptable"? Even though you may have become accustomed to speak of "good" grammar and "bad," the communication situation determines what is acceptable usage in written and spoken communication. The spoken language, for example, takes great liberties with grammar and varies considerably from community to community and from group to group within a community. The written language, where you might expect greater conformity to what is generally "acceptable," also varies from writer to writer, again depending on the demands of the communication situation.

However, consider these statements:

It don't matter to me.

He ain't bad for a beginner.

Anyone with a high school education should recognize the first statement as grammatically unacceptable because the verb *do* takes the form *does* with *he, she,* and *it.* A verb must *agree* with its subject. To some readers, the second statement will seem "acceptable" in certain informal situations; to most, however, *ain't* is a grammatically questionable form in most communication situations. Although speakers and writers do take liberties with language, they avoid constructions that are clearly ungrammatical or nonstandard usage.

Now consider the following statement:

Assuming this hypothesis to be true, the conclusions can be justified.

At first glance, many readers would say that the statement is "acceptable." But is the statement clear? Who is doing the *assuming? Justified* to whom? Here are several possible interpretations of the statement:

If I assume this hypothesis to be true, I can justify my conclusions.

If the researcher assumes this hypothesis to be true, she can justify her conclusions.

Confusion arises because *assuming* does not clearly *modify* any word in the original sentence; it isn't grammatically tied to any word. Careful speakers and writers avoid these dangling modifiers and strive for unmistakable clarity because they don't want to be misunderstood.

After a brief review of grammar, this unit concentrates on writing that is clearly ungrammatical or nonstandard, on the kind of grammar that muddies or wipes out meaning and can lead to misunderstanding between the sender and the receiver of a message. Let's begin with a brief look at how the English language works, since that is what grammar is all about.

Learn How Language Works

You will eliminate many of your grammatical and punctuation problems and greatly improve your ability to communicate complex ideas if you:

Understand the components of basic sentence **patterns** and how their **signaling systems** work.

Know the basic **functions** that single words and longer components can perform within a sentence.

Practice rearranging, changing, and **combining** the components and basic sentence patterns to communicate complex ideas.

These processes represent three basic ways of describing how language works. The first concentrates on the ways in which we organize the components into a few basic *structures,* the second describes what *functions* the components perform, and the third shows how a few basic patterns can be *recombined* to create very complex structures. Though you may not know it, you are already quite familiar with all three methods. The aim here is to help you become more conscious of your skills so that you can avoid common word-blocks to clear, effective communication.

Understand the Basic Terms and Basic Sentence Patterns

Grammatically speaking, we can communicate with one another because we have learned through personal experience to use words as "labels" for persons, actions, things, ideas, places, events, and all the other elements of the world around and within us. We learn the labels and the patterns first by imitating what we hear as children and then, later, by imitating what we see in written form. Once we've learned to speak and to read, we already know the grammar of the language, though we may not know the terms used by grammarians to describe the communication process. You may have experienced this difference working the grammar pretest, probably recognizing some of the problems without really knowing what to call them. Your first goal, then, should be to understand these terms; your second will be to understand the basic sentence pattern and its components.

Knowing the terms will pay off in the revision process if you systematically search the first draft of your paper for the grammatical problems described by these terms. Also, you need them throughout this book, as a check of the review terms at the ends of Chapters 1 through 4 will show. Similarly, understanding how the components of an English sentence work together will help as you write the first draft of your paper and then again as you revise it. *Practice* in expanding, combining, and repeating these components and the basic sentence pattern will improve both the clarity and the maturity of your writing style.

UNDERSTAND THE BASIC TERMS

Recheck the review terms at the end of the first four chapters, and you'll see that most of the grammatical terms you need to know have already been used in this book. *Any good dictionary will define these terms for you.* Like all words, those used to describe how language works are simply "labels" for things we want to communicate. In grammar, these labels are for *words,* their positions, and their *functions* in the sentences used in communication. Consider this simple *sentence:*

6 2   3   3   1   3   1   5   4 6 4   1
In their first English class, college students quickly learn to write themes

7 6   4   2
and to revise them.

We can "label" each word in this sentence according to the function it performs *in this sentence;* i.e., how it relates to other words. If the function of the word changes, then the grammatical label may change, as in the following illustrations:

1   4
love is blind; I **love** freedom

3   1
college students, students in **college**

6   5
in class, come **in**.

The numbers above the words point out those with similar grammatical functions and represent nearly all the basic terms you must know:

1: nouns   5: adverbs
2: pronouns   6: prepositions
3: adjectives   7: conjunctions
4: verbs

Here are some simple definitions for these "basic parts of speech" (as traditional grammarians refer to them).

1

Nouns.   Any word that names something is labeled a noun. Nouns that name a general class of things are labeled *common nouns:* boy, girl, city, house, nation, class, student, theme, noun, verb (the last two words name groups of words). Nouns that name particular persons, places, or things are labeled *proper nouns:* Larry, Hazel, Houston, Texas, City National Bank, Abraham Lincoln, Africa, Mars (a planet), *David Copperfield* (a book). Nouns that name a group of persons, places, or things as if they were a single unit are labeled *collective nouns:* crowd, bunch, flock, family, herd, audience, committee, jury. When phrases (any word-group) and clauses (any **SVC** word-group) function as nouns, they are labeled *noun phrases* or *noun clauses:*

Larry liked riding his   (Noun **phrase,** *naming what*
motorcycle.   *Larry liked to do)*
What you did before class *is not*   (Noun **clause,** *identifying*
relevant.   *something done)*

An **SVC** is a word-group consisting of a *subject*, a *verb*, and a *complement* (as described on page 286).

2

Pronouns. Words that substitute for nouns ("take their place") are labeled pronouns. The noun a pronoun substitutes for ("stands for") is called the **antecedent,** and the relationship between pronoun and antecedent must be unmistakably clear from the context. Depending on whether they function as subjects or objects (see the SVC pattern), or indicate possession, pronouns change their form, as shown by these *personal pronouns*:

Subject	Object	Possession
I ⟶	me ⟶	my, mine
we	us	our, ours
you	you	your, yours
he	him	his
she	her	her, hers
it	it	its
they	them	their, theirs
who	whom	whose

Depending on their functions, pronouns may be grouped as follows:

Personal (substituting for the names of persons): see table above
Relative (linking subordinate clauses): who, whom, whose, which, that, whoever, whomever
Demonstrative (pointing to an antecedent): this, that, these, those, such
Indefinite: any, each, few, anyone, everyone, no one, some, someone

3

Adjectives. Any word or word-group that modifies a noun is labeled an adjective. To *modify* is to describe or in some way change the meaning of a word. *The, a,* and *an* are usually called adjectives, though they are often referred to as *articles.*

The **deep-green** *sea roared against* **the black, jagged** *rocks.*

The *end* of the movie *provides* the *key* that solves the mystery.

The first illustration contains a compound adjective and a series of adjectives; the second contains an *adjective phrase* and an *adjective clause*.

4

Verbs.   Verbs are words that express action or motion *(walk, run, kill, jump)*, being *(am, become)*, or state of being *(suffer, rejoice, please, delight)*. Verbs requiring an object to complete their meaning are called *transitive verbs* (he *lifted* the weight; she *hit* the ceiling); those that require no object to complete their meaning are called *intransitive verbs* (she *talks* constantly; he *works* well; she *talks*, he *works*, they *play*). Verbs are said to be in the *active voice* when their *objects receive* the action, and in the *passive voice* when their subjects receive the action:

He hit *the ball; the ball* was hit *by the batter.*

Note that the noun *ball* functions first as the object of *hit,* and then as subject of *was hit.* Subjects and verbs must *agree:* I *begin,* he *begins,* they *begin;* I *am,* she *is,* we *are;* he who *fights* and *runs* away may live to fight another day; these men *have sacrificed* for us. Subject–verb agreement is one of the most frequent grammatical problems in student writing. Related verb forms include *present participles* (verb + *ing*), *past participles* (verb + *ed* in regular verbs), *infinitives* (to + verb), and *gerunds* (present participles that function as nouns).

5

Adverbs.   Adverbs are words that modify verbs, adjectives, or other adverbs. Most adverbs function to describe or qualify time (when?), place (where?), direction (in what direction?), degree (how much? how little?), or manner (how?). A phrase or clause may function as an adverb.

> *When?*—now, immediately, today, ago, yesterday, soon, tomorrow, always, ever, never
> *Where?*— above, below, near, here, there, where, upstairs
> *In what direction?*—forward, onward, away, left, north
> *How much? how little?*—far, little, very, completely, barely, nearly, scarcely
> *How?*—gladly, carefully, nicely, sadly, learnedly
> *Adverb phrase*—Hazel arrived *after Larry.*
> *Adverb clause*—We know the value of rain *when the fields are dry.*
> *Adverbs*—I *slowly* moved forward, *carefully* turned *left,* and *soon* discovered the raccoon *nearly* hidden *in the bushes.* (Note the adverb phrase.)

6

Prepositions.   Words that link nouns or pronouns to the rest of the sentence are called prepositions. A preposition and its *object* are called a *prepositional phrase,* which functions usually as an adjective or an adverb. The oldest English prepositions include: after, at, but, by, down, for, in, of, over, since, through, to, under, with.

Because **of** *the storm, half* **of** *the students came* **to** *school late.*

By *late morning, she finally arrived, walked* **to** *her seat, and removed her books* **from** *the bottom* **of** *her bag.*

The second illustration has three prepositional phrases that function as adverbs and one that functions as an adjective.

Conjunctions.   Conjunctions are words that join single words, phrases, or clauses, and sometimes paragraphs. Coordinating conjunctions join elements of equal grammatical rank; subordinating conjunctions join unequal grammatical elements.

> Coordinating: *and, or, but, nor, yet, for*
>
> Subordinating: *if, unless, because, since, for, as, that, though, although*

Some conjunctions appear in pairs (correlative) that join equal elements: *both . . . and, neither . . . nor, either . . . or.*

> *Investigation revealed that* **neither** *the students* **nor** *the teacher was to blame.*

Faulty parallel structure occurs when the words, phrases, or clauses joined by coordinating and paired conjunctions are of unequal rank. For more information on coordination and subordination, study pages 373–77.

UNDERSTAND THE BASIC SENTENCE PATTERNS

An English sentence is not just a string of words stuck together at random. It follows basic patterns, in which certain components fit together in an orderly sequence.

SUBJECT AREA	PREDICATE AREA	
1	2	3
SUBJECT	VERB	COMPLEMENT
S ——————————	— V ——————	——➤ C
Students	write	themes.
(doer/actor)	(action)	(receiver/object)
(noun function)	(verb function)	(completing function)

Although this illustration simplifies the process, it represents the basic **SVC** (subject–verb–complement) pattern from which all sentences can be built. This is true because the 1-2-3 order can be varied, each component can be expanded into a complex word-group, and the basic pattern can be expanded and repeated in various ways. A simple grammatical sentence is an independent unit of expression consisting of a *subject area* and a *predicate area*.

1. Using word-groups to expand components.   The following sentences have word-groups functioning as subject, as verb, and as complement.

What you did before class *is not relevant*.

The game will be starting *soon*.

Larry liked riding his motorcycle.

Lisa learned how to influence her friends.

2. Using combination (coordination) to expand components.   A sentence can be expanded by combining (coordinating) several components or complete SVC patterns. To combine or coordinate components requires the repetition of grammatically equal units, whether words, phrases, or clauses. The result will be *parallel* (balanced) structure.

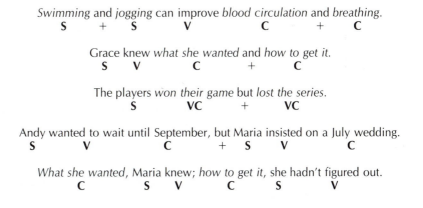

Notice that in the last illustration the usual SVC order is changed for special effect and the two basic sentence patterns are exactly parallel in structure, part for part as well as in the order of parts.

3. Using subordination.   Any component of the SVC pattern can be expanded or modified by a word or word-group subordinated to it. In the following sentence, the basic SVC pattern (independent clause) is *players lost series,* with the beginning word-group as a subordinate modifier.

Although they won their last game, the fired-up **players lost** *the* **series**
which they tried so hard to win.

What does the subordinate clause at the end of the sentence modify? The sentence
combines three SVC groups. What are they? What two words serve as "signals" to
the reader?

In most sentences you will almost automatically "hear" the SVC pattern at
work. More important, listen for it and make it work for you. Use the pattern to
expand simple sentences into complex ones; experiment with the SVC *order* to gain
special effect in appropriate situations; coordinate, subordinate, modify, combine.
Building sentences can become a fascinating game, for the combinations are
virtually limitless. If you can really hear the components repeated in a sentence,
you'll become aware, also, of a fundamental basis for parallel structure: several
components or SVC patterns coordinated in a series.

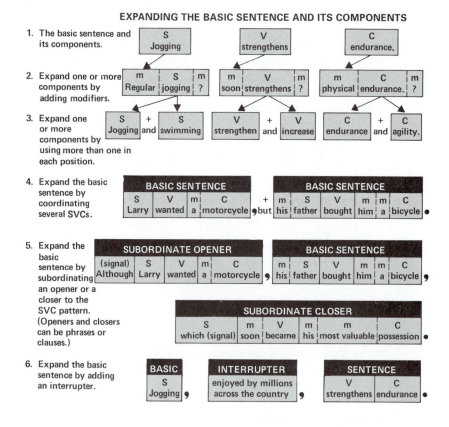

Although this diagram on Expanding the Basic Sentence summarizes the
most important ways to expand components and combine SVC patterns, in
Chapter 11 you'll find additional comments on the SVC pattern and how to make

it work for you, especially when you add modifiers before or after any of the components (pp. 367–69).

EXERCISE

> Your instructor may ask you to do the exercises on pages 369 and 380, which provide basic sentence patterns for expansion and subordination.

Now, with the basic terms and the basic sentence patterns clearly understood, you should be able to master the following problems in grammar with very little difficulty.

GRAMMATICAL WORD-BLOCKS TO ACCURATE COMMUNICATION

Only a handful of grammatical problems account for most of the questionable constructions in student papers. About half of them require an understanding of basic grammatical terms, and the rest require knowledge of the SVC pattern and how it works. All these problems appear in the list at the beginning of the grammar pretest (p. 279).

AGR

Agreement: Subjects, Verbs, Nouns, Pronouns

Agreement is the grammatical relationship between words that change form, usually to indicate number (singular or plural) and person (first person: *I, we;* third person: *he, she, it, they*). In addition, a few nouns and pronouns change form to indicate *case*—whether they are functioning as subjects, objects, or possessives (see the examples under pronouns). When using these words with changing forms, you must match singular with singular, first person with first person, plural with plural. Here are the major problem areas in agreement.

☐ **AGR 1**

Make the verb and its subject agree in number.   In revising your work, check the subject–verb relationship in the SVC pattern to be sure they agree. If you have trouble finding the subject of a sentence, first find the verb, since it describes action and is usually easy to spot. Then you should be able to discover what is doing the acting—your subject. *Most* of the time, you automatically use a singular verb with a singular subject (or a plural with a plural) because the construction is firmly established in your speech patterns:

Singular: *The bird sings, the girl talks, I am, it flies.*

Plural: *The birds sing, the girls talk, we are, they fly.*

But your sentences are almost never this simple, so that you can easily become careless in making subjects and verbs agree. The following illustrations identify the chief causes of faulty subject–verb agreement.

☐   **A.**

Watch the *-s ending*. With subjects (nouns) the *-s ending* is a plural form; with verbs it is a singular form. Check yourself by *quickly* scanning the following pairs of subjects and verbs to spot those with faulty agreement: *I don't, we don't, they don't, he don't, the student writes, the woman writes, it don't, Hazel don't, women writes, changes comes, changes come, he come late, they came late, he says, I says, the jury votes, scientist ask.*

☐   **B.**

Don't be misled by plural words placed between the subject and the verb.

Faulty: *Every **magazine** in those racks **are** coming apart.*
Revised: *Every **magazine** in those racks **is** coming apart.*

Faulty: *Repeated **use** of too many long words **irritate** me.*
Revised: *Repeated **use** of too many long words **irritates** me.*

Faulty: *The **student** as well as the teachers **were** pleased.*
Revised: *The **student** as well as the teachers **was** pleased.*

☐   **C.**

Two subjects joined by *and*, regardless of their number, require a plural verb.

Faulty: *A **hammer** and **saw is** in the tool chest.*
Revised: *A **hammer** and **saw are** in the tool chest.*

Faulty: *A limping **dog** and a ruffled **cat was** all that remained after the fight.*
Revised: *A limping **dog** and a ruffled **cat were** all that remained after the fight.*

☐   **D.**

All indefinite pronouns take singular verbs: *each, neither, either, anybody, anything, someone, somebody, another, everything, nobody, nothing.* Each of these is (not *are*) singular in meaning, even when connected to a plural word (*each* of the girls *is*, *neither* of the men *is* a pro).

> *Each* **has** *a preference; nobody* **shirks** *jury duty.*
>
> *Either* **is** *acceptable; nothing* **is** *absolute.*
>
> *None of these students* **is** *a failure.*

Although you will often hear the expression *none of them are*, you'll find that careful speakers and writers use the singular, *none of them is*. In fact, *none* is frequently plural, depending on the meaning of the rest of the sentence:

> *None* **are** *so cruel as those who don't feel.*
>
> *None* **is** *so cruel as he who does not feel.*

Other indefinite pronouns that can be either singular or plural are *any, all, more, most,* and *some:* Some of the pie *is* better than none; when hope is lost, all *is* lost; some of the students *are* bound to pass; when nations make war, all *are* involved.

☐ **E.**

Double check correlative pronouns. *Either . . . or* and *neither . . . nor* take a singular verb if both subjects are singular. When one subject is plural, the verb usually agrees with the subject nearer to the verb.

> *Neither the student nor the teacher* **is** *to blame.*
>
> *Neither the teacher nor the students* **are** *to blame.*
>
> *Neither the students nor the teacher* **is** *to blame.*
>
> *Either you or I* **am** *mistaken. (Correct)*
>
> *Either you* are *mistaken or I* **am.** *(Better)*

The best solution to these troublesome contrasts is to keep the plural subject next to the plural verb. With some constructions, rewriting the sentence to avoid the problem may be the best solution.

☐ **F.**

Collective nouns take singular verbs. Because they are singular units with legitimate plural forms, collective nouns *(jury, committee, herd, family, kind, group, audience, majority)* require singular verbs unless the meaning of the sentence clearly demands the plural.

> *A* **jury decides** *a man's guilt; the* **jury are** *individuals who decide a man's guilt.*

*This **kind** of potato **is** best for baking. (Permissible)*

*These **kinds** of potatoes **are** best for baking. (Permissible)*

*These potatoes **are** best for baking. (Preferable)*

The British use a plural verb with most collective nouns, but American writers tend to make the distinctions suggested above.

Like collective nouns, numbers denoting a fixed quantity usually take singular verbs because the quantity is usually considered to be a unit.

*A hundred dollars **is** worth working for. (A unit)*

*A hundred dollars **are** counted carefully. (Individual dollars)*

*Forty students **is** too many for one class. (A unit)*

*Forty students **make** a lot of noise. (As individuals)*

□ **G.**

Double check agreement when the verb precedes the subject. When the verb comes before the subject, check the subject component carefully before deciding on number.

Faulty: *In the room there **is** a desk for the teacher and seats for all the students. (Desk and seats **are** in the room.)*

Faulty: *His chief support **are** his sister and brother. (The subject of the sentence is **support**.)*

Faulty: *There **is** his sister and brother to support him. (Sister and brother **are** the subject.)*

Revised: *His brother and sister **are** his chief support.*

□ **H.**

Nouns with plural forms but singular meanings usually take a singular verb. The following nouns are regularly singular: *acoustics, aesthetics, civics, economics, linguistics, mathematics, measles, mumps, news, physics.* Unless the sentence meaning demands a plural form, these nouns are followed by singular verbs.

*Acoustics **is** an interesting study.*

*The acoustics of the auditorium **are** excellent.*

*Mathematics **is** a science; physics **is** a science.*

*Athletics **provide** good exercise. (Various games)*

*Athletics **builds** firm muscles. (Activity in games)*

Measles **is** *a disease; mumps* **is** *a disease.*

The statistics **were** *assembled; statistics* **is** *a science.*

When subject—verb agreement becomes a problem, think and use your common sense. Be clear on the SVC pattern first, determine the exact meaning, and make the subjects and verbs agree. If you revise hastily (or not at all), you won't discover the problems, and readers will evaluate you and your work accordingly.

Copyright © 1977 by Field Newspaper Syndicate, Chicago, Illinois.

☐   **AGR 2**

Make pronouns agree with their antecedents.   Pronouns stand for the nouns or ideas they represent and, therefore, must agree with *them* in number. Relative pronouns *(who, which, that)* functioning as subjects must *clearly refer to* and *agree with* their antecedents. Also, since pronouns change their form with their case (subject or object), you must be clear on their function in the SVC sentence pattern; they can function as either subject or complement (object). Some problems in pronoun agreement occur because the noun to which the pronoun refers appears earlier in a sentence and too far away from its pronoun for the reference to be unmistakably clear. Or the pronoun may refer to either of two antecedents ambiguously. Occasionally the same pronoun (often *it*) may appear several times in a sentence but will refer to different antecedents. Part of the difficulty is that pronoun agreement and reference may be so clear in the writer's mind that the ambiguity doesn't register. Here are some illustrations of faulty pronoun agreement for you to study and correct by matching the pronouns with their antecedents.

A discouraging **student** *trait is* **their** *emphasis on grades.*

Each *of the students tried to follow* **their** *teacher's instructions.*

When a **boy** *or* **girl** *enters college,* **they** *find it different from high school.*

The school is old. The rooms are small and poorly lighted, with worn-out desks and faded chalkboards. The library is like a small closet. However, it *is still in good condition and should not be torn down.*

Larry is the student **whom** *I think* **will succeed.**

If the **administration** *wants the support of the* **students, they** *should listen to* **their** *problems.*

Grace missed her exam, **which** *caused much comment.*

If **you** *break the law,* **you** *may be arrested.*

He gave the information to John and I.

In the book **it** *says that pronouns must agree with antecedents.*

MOD

Check Modifiers for Clarity of Connection

Whether it consists of one word or a word-group, a modifier must be clearly tied to the word it describes or explains. Since the meaning of an English sentence depends largely on the position of its parts, careless placing of a modifier can change or obscure the meaning. And, as with pronouns, too wide a separation of the modifier from the word it describes can create confusion or unintended humor.

☐ **MOD 1**

Clarify dangling verbal phrases.   Study the following illustrations, noting two basic processes at work in the clarified versions: (1) adding words to clarify the relation of the verbal phrase to the rest of the sentence, and (2) rearranging words so that modifiers are next to the components they describe.

Confused: *Pregnant cows are required to teach courses in animal science.*
Clear: *To teach courses in animal science,* **we** *need pregnant cows.*
Clear: *To teach courses in animal science,* **professors** *need pregnant cows.*

Confused: *Sentences gain clarity* by eliminating wordiness.
Clear: **Your** *sentence will gain clarity if* **you** *eliminate wordiness.*
Clear: *To give sentences clarity, eliminate wordiness. (***You** *is understood before* **eliminate.***)*

Confused: When picking a location to camp, *there are several factors to consider.*
Clear: *When* **you** *pick a camp site, consider several factors.*

Confused: To write well, *good books must be read.*
Clear: *To write well,* **you** *must read good books.*

Confused: After sitting there awhile, *it began to rain.*
Clear: After I *had been sitting there awhile, it began to rain.*

☐   MOD 2

Place modifiers next to the words they describe.   Because position is a key to meaning in the English sentence, you can change meaning unintentionally by carelessly placing a modifier. The modifier *only* is a good example:

She said that she made only one mistake.

She said that only she made one mistake.

She said only that she made one mistake.

Only she said that she made one mistake.

Sometimes the careless positioning of a modifier will make it seem to refer to two things at the same time. Here are some "squinting modifiers":

She agreed **on the next day** *to help me.*

The motorcycle which was whining **noisily** *roared up the road.*

Larry promised **when he was on his way home** *to stop at the store.*

They decided **when both teams lost** *to begin recruiting.*

Several students **I know** *missed two major quizzes.*

In all these sentences the **boldface** modifiers should be positioned to project one meaning only. You should be able to write at least two unmistakably clear sentences for each illustration.

FRAG

Sentence Fragments

☐   FRAG 1

COMPLETE THE MEANING OF ALL
GRAMMATICAL FRAGMENTS

Complete grammatical fragments by making them *independent* units of expression with a subject area and a predicate area. They must communicate a *complete* thought even if part of the SVC pattern is missing. Often a fragment results when you use a *verbal phrase* as if it were a complete SVC pattern:

> *They had a great time at the lake.* **Swimming near the shore and fishing off the pier.**

> *Student athletes want to do well.* **To succeed not only as athletes but also as scholars.**

> *She made little progress.* Finally **giving up all her efforts.**

The **boldface** fragments can be corrected in several ways. Each verbal phrase can be *expanded* into a complete SVC pattern with the addition of a subject and verb: *they swam and fished, they want to succeed, she finally gave up.* Often the fragment can be *tied* simply to the rest of the sentence:

> Swimming near the shore and fishing off the pier, they . . .

> *Student athletes want to succeed not only as* . . .

> *She made little progress, finally giving up* . . .

Occasionally you may want to *subordinate* one of the ideas involved:

> Because she made little progress, *she finally gave up* . . .

If you do subordinate, be careful not to use a subordinate clause as if it were a complete (independent) sentence:

> *Larry had some definite ideas about college.* Although he had never been on a college campus.

In this example, replace the first period with a comma and tie the subordinate clause to the independent clause. And, since it modifies the subject *Larry,* it is probably better positioned at the beginning of the sentence next to the word it modifies. Some subordinate clause fragments sound deceptively complete:

> *When several students asked for make-up quizzes.*

> *Which isn't true of the last examination I took.*

Placed within the context of a paragraph, these subordinate clause fragments could easily be mistaken for complete, independent sentences. The *signal word* at the beginning of the **SVC** pattern should alert you to the subordination.

☐ **FRAG 2**

USE RHETORICAL FRAGMENTS SPARINGLY

Fragments are nonsentences because they lack crucial parts of the **SVC** pattern. You should be able to recognize two kinds: *grammatical fragments* and *rhetorical fragments*. Today many writers and most writing handbooks recognize the difference between the two. Grammatical fragments are not acceptable; with care, rhetorical fragments may be used sparingly for emphasis or attention-getting. The context provided for the fragment defines the difference between the two kinds. Complete all grammatical fragments by expanding them into *independent* units of expression with a subject and a predicate area, or tie them to independent **SVC**s. Check the context of all rhetorical fragments; make sure they are so closely tied to the thought around them that their meaning is clear enough to let them stay as fragments.

Grammatical Fragments	**Rhetorical Fragments**
I can remember father barbecueing hamburgers. He liked them cooked rare. *Mother jogging in blue sweat pants.* **Option:** *But what I remember most is* mother jogging in blue sweat pants. [expanded]	I can remember father barbecueing hamburgers. He liked them cooked rare. *What do I remember most? Mother jogging in blue sweat pants.* [expanded context]
We often ate on the back patio. *Because it allowed us to relax.* **Option:** We often ate *on the back patio because* it allowed us to relax. [tie-in subordinate clause]	We often ate on the back patio. *Why? Because it allowed us to relax.* [expanded context]
Drivers also take unnecessary chances when they try to pass cars in heavy, fast, oncoming traffic. *Sometimes a fatal collision, sometimes the fatal scramble for nonexistent space on the shoulder of the road.* **Option:** Drivers also . . . oncoming traffic. *This sometimes leads to a fatal collision, sometimes to the fatal scramble for nonexistent space . . .*	Drivers also take unnecessary chances when they try to pass cars in heavy, fast, oncoming traffic. *What are the results? Sometimes a fatal collision. Sometimes the fatal scramble for nonexistent space on the shoulder of the road.* [See page 29.]
They had a great time at the lake. *Swimming near the shore and fishing off the pier.* **Option:** *Swimming near the shore and fishing off the pier, they had . . .* [direct tie-in]	"They had a great time at the lake." "Doing what?" "*Swimming near the shore. Fishing off the pier.*" [a dialogue]
She made little progress. *Finally giving up all her efforts.* **Option:** *Because she made little progress, she finally gave up all her efforts.* [subordination]	No one can write well without practice. *No one.* *Now for the final point.* What did George do? *Nothing, as usual.*

The italicized grammatical fragments can be corrected in many ways. Each verbal phrase can be *expanded* into a complete SVC pattern with the addition of a subject and verb: *they swam and fished, this sometimes leads to, she finally gave up*. Or, as the options show, the grammatical fragment often can be tied to the rest of the sentence or subordinated.

RUN-ON

Learn to Spot and Correct Run-on Sentences

If you carelessly run together two independent **SVC** patterns without joining them with conjunctions, you will create run-on (fused) sentences:

$$\boxed{\text{SVC}} \qquad \boxed{\text{SVC}} \; . \quad \text{(Run-on, fused)}$$

$$\boxed{\text{SVC}} \; , \text{ and } \boxed{\text{SVC}} \; . \quad \text{(Joined)}$$

$$\boxed{\text{SVC}} \; . \; \boxed{\text{SVC}} \; . \quad \text{(Separated)}$$

Here are some examples:

Zeba has her mind made up nothing you can say will change it.

Clearly, this is the $\boxed{\text{SVC}}$ $\boxed{\text{SVC}}$. pattern, with no punctuation and no conjunction. Suppose you added a comma:

Zeba has her mind made up, nothing you can say will change it.

Although this version recognizes the two **SVC** patterns, it has not corrected the problem. Instead, the version has become a *comma splice* (a splice is a connection or joining):

$$\boxed{\text{SVC}} \; , \boxed{\text{SVC}} \; . \quad (\textit{Wrong;} \text{ comma splice})$$

The original run-on sentence and this comma splice can be corrected in four ways:

1. $\boxed{\text{SVC}}$, and $\boxed{\text{SVC}}$. (Coordination)

2. $\boxed{\text{Because } \textbf{SVC}}$, $\boxed{\text{SVC}}$. (Subordination)

3. $\boxed{\textbf{SVC}}$; $\boxed{\textbf{SVC}}$. (Coordination)

4. $\boxed{\textbf{SVC}}$. $\boxed{\textbf{SVC}}$. (Coordination)

Following these four patterns, correct the Zeba run-on in four ways.

> Wrong: Water skiing is great fun, *however try it only if you can swim.*
>
> Correct: Water skiing is great fun; *however, try it only if you can swim.*

Correct pattern: $\boxed{\textbf{SVC}}$; $\boxed{\text{however, } \textbf{SVC}}$.

> Correct: I seldom eat avocados; ***in fact,** I don't like them.*

$\boxed{\textbf{VERB}}$

Correct Illogical Shifts in Verb Tense

If you understood the unit in Chapter 4 on "Coherence through Consistent Point of View" (see p. 98), you should have little trouble with shifting verb tenses. There you learned that sentences in a paragraph won't *interlock* properly if the verb's *tense* changes from sentence to sentence. Here you are reminded to be *logical* and *consistent* in all time references. You are already familiar with *present, past,* and *future* forms of hundreds of common verbs (I *walk,* he *walks;* I *walked,* he *walked;* I *will walk,* he *will walk*). Wherever possible, use these as models to guide you with verbs you have trouble with, keeping a list of *principal parts* for review purposes *(write, wrote, written; choose, chose, chosen; drink, drank, drunk)*. Then consider the following guidelines.

☐   **VERB 1**

Make verb tenses logically fit time references.   Verb tenses change to indicate time references extending from the *present* (here and now) back into the *past* (yesterday, last year) and forward into the *future* (tomorrow, next year).

1. *Present.* Use present tense to indicate action going on *now,* in the present: She *works (is working)* at a dress shop; She *works* every day (customary, habitual action). Also, use the present tense to describe events in stories or plays, or other literary works: When Juliet *wakes* in the tomb, she *finds* Romeo dead;

the friar *begs* her to leave. Additional uses of the present include the following:

Aristotle knew *the world* is *round.*	*(Timeless truth or fact is in present tense, even though the main verb is past)*
I start *my vacation next Tuesday.*	*(Present used instead of future,* will start.*)*

2. *Past.* Use the past tense for all action taking place *before* the present and not extending into the present.

I saw *her at the dress shop last year.*

She worked *at the dress shop. (Does she work there now?)*

I watched *television last night and* saw *a fine movie. (Both verbs are past tense.)*

3. *Future.* Use future tense for all action expected *after* the present. Future time can be expressed in several ways.

She will work *at the dress shop next week. (Straight future.)*

She is going to work *at the dress shop next week. (Future expressed by* is going.*)*

> *When she* works *at the dress shop next year, she will earn more. (Future expressed by present tense.)*

We need to consider two more verb tenses, represented by the following: *she has worked* and *she had worked.* Here's where these fit on the time scale.

she had worked	she worked	she has worked	she ⟨ works / is working	she will work
ACTION TAKES PLACE IN THE PAST			PRESENT	FUTURE
(Past Perfect Tense)	(Past Tense)	Takes place in the past but extends into the present → (Present Perfect)		

Here are sentences that show all five tenses in action:

By the end of last year, she had worked *at the shop for three years. She* worked *nearly every night last month, she* has worked *every night this week, she* is working *tonight, and she probably* will work *every night next week.*

Although these are unusual sentences, they illustrate the time references governing the sequence of tenses. The two added tenses in the illustration are called the *present perfect* and the *past perfect*.

4. *Present Perfect.* Use the present perfect tense for past action extending into the present. In the illustration, *she has worked* refers to past action taking place before "tonight" (i.e., "every night this week"). But the action also extends into the present, since "she is [still] working." Here's another example: She *has phoned* me many times.
5. *Past Perfect.* Use the past perfect tense for past action *completed before some specified time* in the past. In the illustration, *she had worked* is correct because it refers to past action completed "by the end of last year" (all in the past). Here's another example: I *had talked* to her several times before I *left* the house.
6. *Future Perfect.* Use the future perfect tense for action *to be completed before* some *specified time* in the *future*. Example: She *will have worked* four years at the dress shop by December. The future perfect tense has not been shown on the time chart because it is rarely needed.

☐ **VERB 2**

Keep a list of troublesome principal parts. A good dictionary gives you the principal parts of verbs immediately following the main entry: *see* (main entry, present stem, infinitive form as in *to see*), *saw* (past tense), *seen* (past participle, when different from the past tense, as in *had seen* and *have seen*), *seeing* (present participle). Most verbs are *regular,* forming the past by simply adding *-d* or *-ed* to the infinitive form (*work, worked; tame, tamed; hire, hired; talk, talked*). The verbs you are likely to have trouble with are *irregular,* changing their infinitive form for past tense and participle (as the verb *see* does in the illustration above).

Use a dictionary to look up the principal parts of the following troublesome irregular verbs.

begin	do	run
blow	drink	shrink
choose	get	sing
come	lead	swim
dive	ring	swing

Once you have looked up these principal parts, practice writing for each verb the five tenses shown on the time scale above.

PARALLEL STRUCTURE

Correct Faulty Parallel Structure

Faulty parallel structure can occur when a series of words or word-groups (phrases or clauses) are joined by conjunctions. Though not a serious grammatical problem, faulty parallelism can easily obscure meaning and mess up the natural flow of words in a sentence. You will find additional illustrations of this problem in Chapter 11 on sentence revision under *coordination* (pp. 373–77). The signal words for coordination are coordinating conjunctions: *and, or, but, nor, for, yet.* You have already seen these at work in combining sentence components to achieve *balanced,* complex sentences (pp. 105 and 287). Here you are reminded only that any three or more equal grammatical elements can appear in a series—nouns, verbs, participles, clauses, prepositional phrases, or any sentence component. Here are some illustrations. Problems in parallelism appear in **boldface.**

Faulty: *The instructor told the students* **to study** *the chapter,* **to take notes** *on it, and* **that they would be tested** *on the material.*

Correct: *The instructor told the students* **to study** *the chapter,* **to take notes** *on it, and* **to prepare** *for a test on the material. (Three parallel infinitive phrases)*

Awkward: *I shall consider the* **origin** *of the ecology movement and* **how it has progressed.**

Better: *I shall consider the* **origin** *and the* **progress** *of the ecology movement. (The subordinate clause has been replaced by a noun.)*

Awkward: *Grace is* **attractive, assertive,** *and* **thinks a lot.**

Better: *Grace is* **attractive, assertive,** *and* **thoughtful.**

Awkward: *I like a mystery story* **with exciting action** *and* **which keeps me guessing.**

Better: *I like a mystery story* **that** *has exciting action and* **keeps me guessing.** (that *is understood before* keeps.)

PUNCTUATION PRETEST

Most (not all) of the examples given below contain one (occasionally more) of the following punctuation problems:

0. Sentence has no punctuation problems.

1. Period or semicolon needed: run-on sentences.

2. Comma(s) needed as coordinator—items in a series.

3. Comma needed as coordinator of independent clauses (**SVCs**).

4. Comma needed to set off dependent opener.

5. Comma needed to set off dependent closer.

6. Comma(s) *not* needed with restrictive interrupter.

7. Comma(s) needed with nonrestrictive interrupter.

8. Comma splice: full stop *or* conjunction needed with independent clauses (**SVCs**).

9. Semicolon needed to separate independent clauses (**SVCs**) *or* for clarity.

10. Semicolon fault: semicolon used between components of unequal grammatical rank.

11. Colon needed as anticipator.

12. Apostrophe needed for possession.

13. Apostrophe needed for omissions *or* other special uses.

14. Apostrophe is misplaced *or* not needed at all.

15. Quotation marks needed around direct speech or quoted words.

16. Quotation marks needed with titles or names.

17. Additional punctuation needed with quotation marks.

18. Underline title to indicate italics.

Use the numbers (including "0") given above to identify all punctuation *errors* in the sentences below. First decide what punctuation error(s) the sentence has; then place in the blank provided to the left the numbers from the above list that best identify all the punctuation *errors*. If you think the sentence has no punctuation problem, place a "0" in the blank. *Note:* Your instructor may ask you to provide a correction within or below each sentence, especially if you don't understand the descriptions of punctuation uses given in the list.

> Example: *4, 5, 5   As he fell Larry grabbed the branch which broke off in his hand sending him plunging into the cold water.*
>
> Correction: *As he fell, Larry grabbed the branch, which broke off in his hand, sending him . . .*

Three commas are needed: one to set off the dependent opener (4), one to set off the first dependent closer (a *which*-clause) (5), and one for the final dependent closer (a verbal phrase) (5). The numbers in the blank name the problems; the correction shows how the punctuation would be placed.

_____ **1.** In Annie Hall Woody Allen plays a comedian.

_____ **2.** Irelands countryside is similar to Englands countryside.

_____ **3.** Andy went to the pet store, he came home with a cat.

_____ **4.** Maria and Manuel traveled to Washington to visit the Smithsonian but neither of them enjoyed the museum exhibits.

_____ **5.** The ship's computer clearly said my name is HAL.

_____ 6. We had to buy our tickets get some popcorn and find our seats.

_____ 7. Computers are everywhere; although not everyone wants to use them.

_____ 8. Dont smoke cigarettes and dont experiment with drugs.

_____ 9. One of our great problems is population control, however no one seems interested in doing anything about it.

_____ 10. Big-city slums cause crime; crime costs money.

_____ 11. Big-city slums cause crime, crime costs money.

_____ 12. The Greenhouse Effect is more than a theory its one of many environmental problems facing the planet today.

_____ 13. Yesterdays parade was dull one fire truck one marching band and three horses.

_____ 14. A Clockwork Orange and Dr. Strangelove made Stanley Kubrick famous, he's one of films' brightest directors.

_____ 15. By the year 2000 the average cost of a new home will be $200,000.

_____ 16. His voice was shaky will you leave please he asked.

_____ 17. The title of the Post article was Acid Rain Burns Politician.

_____ 18. You wrecked Lisas car nothing you say can change that.

_____ 19. All mechanics who boycott Tuesdays flights without permission will be fired.

_____ 20. Though no longer able to pass the course the students attended class anyway.

_____ 21. On August 26 1920 American women gained the right to vote; but only after a long hard fight.

_____ 22. An interrupter, which immediately follows and restricts the meaning of the subject, should not be set off with commas.

_____ 23. The opener can be any word, phrase or dependent clause its followed by a slight pause and lowering of the voice.

_____ 24. Football requires the best in strength and endurance; track, the best in speed and agility.

_____ 25. The ringing bells played in and out of the dark rainfall causing the man to pause breathe out little clouds and look up through the naked trees.

PUNCTUATION

Listen carefully to the way you talk, and you'll soon discover that you punctuate by using *pauses* and the *sound* of your voice. Although the pauses are sometimes hardly noticeable, at other times they are very definite. Have you noticed that at times the sound of your voice seems to go higher? The key to punctuation is to translate these sounds and pauses into a written form that accurately conveys your intended meaning. That's what punctuation marks are all about. They take the place of voice signals that clarify meaning and prevent misunderstanding.

For example, when you ask a question, the sound of your voice usually goes *up* and you *pause*. When you translate this into written form, how do you signal your reader that you are asking a question? When you begin a sentence with an opener, you normally pause slightly. Or, if you interrupt the flow of a sentence, again you usually pause slightly. But when you complete a sentence, the pause is more definite and the sound of your voice goes down. If you check the sentences in this paragraph, you'll see that most of them illustrate the use of the punctuation mark they are describing. Begin to study punctuation, therefore, first by *listening;* then use your knowledge of grammar and sentence components to discover why some sentence structures require special punctuation signals while others don't. This unit will review the following punctuation signals: period [.], comma [,], semicolon [;], colon [:], apostrophe ['], and quotation marks [" "].

The Period: Stop Signal for the Sentence

Use the period to signal a full stop for the end of a sentence. In speaking, you signal this stop by a definite pause and a lowering of the sound of your voice. Keep in mind the SVC sentence pattern, and you should be able to place the period stop signals in the following series of sentences.

> *She came to school early preparing for her quiz before class was important she discovered while studying how much she already knew learning this gave her more confidence therefore she did well*

Counting the period at the very end, you should have five. Which SVC components have been expanded into word-groups? Would you place a comma before the word *therefore?* (See pp. 298–99 on run-on sentences and comma splices.)

Like the period, the question mark (?) and the exclamation mark (!) also signal full stops. If your sentence is to be understood as a question, use the question mark, which signals a rising sound in the voice as well as a definite pause. *Do you understand?* As its name suggests, the exclamation point "exclaims": it signals an increase in loudness of voice and a full stop signal. *What a mess!* Use the exclamation mark only for truly important emphasis.

The Comma: Pause Within the Sentence

The comma is probably the most used and most abused punctuation signal. Like all punctuation signals, it is important because it clarifies meaning by indicating relationships between sentence components within the SVC pattern. In speaking, you signal the comma with a slight pause and a slight lowering of the sound of your voice. If you doubt this, read this sentence aloud, listening for each pause, noticing the sound of your voice. To understand the way in which the comma signal functions, you need to remember the SVC pattern and know how its components can be expanded (see pp. 287–88). Most comma signals function in one of four ways—as coordinators, openers, closers, or inserters.

1. The comma as coordinator.   As used here, the word *coordinator* means to join single words or word-groups (phrases or clauses) of the same grammatical rank.

(a) *Items in a series.* The comma signal *plus* a coordinating conjunction *(and, but, or, nor, for, yet)* tells the reader that the grammatical elements belong together as a series or group. Here are some examples.

For breakfast he ate **bacon, eggs,** *and* **toast.** *(Three nouns)*

Before every exam, she **read, studied,** *and* **summarized** *each chapter in the book. (Three verbs)*

It was still raining, and Larry was **wet, irritable,** *and* **exhausted.** *(Three completers; two SVC patterns)*

Notice that the comma signals two kinds of coordination in the last illustration:

$$\boxed{\textbf{SVC}} \text{ , and } \boxed{\textbf{SVC, C, and C}} \text{ .}$$

(b) *Independent clauses.* Use a *comma plus a coordinating conjunction* to join two independent SVC patterns:

$$\boxed{\textbf{SVC}} \text{ , and } \boxed{\textbf{SVC}} \text{ .}$$

If you use only the comma to join two independent SVC patterns—omitting the conjunction—you will create a *comma splice,* an error you should avoid:

$$\boxed{\textbf{SVC}} \text{ , } \boxed{\textbf{SVC}} \text{ . (Wrong)}$$

In the unit on the run-on sentence (p. 298), you've already seen this illustration of the comma splice:

and

Zeba has her mind made up, ↑ *nothing you can say will change it.*

To correct this error, insert the coordinating conjunction as shown. Remember, too, that you can't use a conjunctive adverb *(however, also, furthermore, moreover, still, then)* as a coordinating conjunction. The result will still be a comma splice:

Zeba has her mind made up, **furthermore** *nothing you can say will change it. (Wrong; comma splice)*

In summary, use of the comma as coordinator can be illustrated by two simple diagrams:

a, b, and **c**   Use commas to coordinate three or more words with the *same* grammatical function, and three or more phrases or clauses with the *same* grammatical function. (See also pp. 373–77)

| SVC, | for
and
but
or | SVC. | Use a comma *plus* a coordinating conjunction to join two *independent* **SVC** patterns (i.e., two sentences). |

2. The comma as opener.   Use the comma to signal an *opener* preceding the basic SVC pattern, especially if the meaning is ambiguous or can be misunderstood. Here's the diagram:

$$\boxed{\text{opener}} \text{ , SVC.}$$

The opener can be any word, phrase, or *dependent* (subordinate) clause. *In speaking,* you would normally pause slightly and lower your voice slightly after the opener (as in this sentence, after *in speaking*). Here are some additional illustrations of openers:

At the beginning of the semester, *the students were eager to learn.* *(Introductory prepositional phrase)*

However, *by the end of the term they had lost their enthusiasm.* *(Conjunctive adverb begins and pauses. Would you put a comma after the word* term?*)*

Although they were no longer interested, *the students did well.* *(Introductory subordinate SVC pattern; i.e., a dependent clause)*

For example, *everyone received at least a* B *grade in the course. (Short, interruptive phrase followed by a pause)*

During the night *she heard strange noises.*

At noon *everyone went to the cafeteria. (Short prepositional phrases that aren't interruptive are seldom followed by a comma)*

3. The comma as closer.   Use the comma to signal a *closer* following the basic SVC pattern, especially if the closer is interruptive. Here's the diagram:

$$\text{SVC, } \boxed{\text{closer}} \text{ .}$$

The closer can be any word, phrase, or *dependent* (subordinate) clause. Look at the openers in the above illustrations, *for example.* You could put all of them at the ends of the sentences following the SVC patterns, *though not all would be preceded by a comma.* In which would you use the comma signal to indicate an interruptive pause? Closers can also be appositives or afterthoughts, *ideas that expand the sentence, definitions that clarify a word in the basic SVC pattern.* In the preceding sentence, did you notice the way in which two closers were used to clarify the meaning of *afterthoughts?* Here are some additional illustrations:

> *Monday was a hot day,* hotter than predicted. (**SVC** + *closer*)
>
> *As he fell, Larry grabbed the branch,* which broke off in his hand, sending him plunging into the cold water. *(Opener* + **SVC** + two closers—one a dependent clause, the last a participial phrase)
>
> *You'd better study your math for tomorrow,* just in case we have a quiz. *(****SVC*** + dependent clause as a closer)*
>
> *It was an easy quiz,* much easier than I thought it would be. *(****SVC*** + dependent clause as a closing contrasted element)*

The closer in the last illustration is so parenthetical that it could be enclosed in parentheses (   ). Some writers would put a dash before *just in case* (in the third sentence) to indicate a more abrupt pause than the comma signals.

4. The comma as inserter.   Commas should be used to indicate interruptions or breaks in the natural flow of a sentence. Use commas

> to set off ("insert") parenthetical expressions and interrupters
> to set off appositives and contrasted elements
> to set off geographical names, items in dates and addresses

Put commas on *both* sides of a NONrestrictive word, phrase, or clause *inserted into* the SVC pattern, especially if it interrupts the natural flow of the sentence. Most examples will follow this form:

S, | interrupter | , VC.

SV, | interrupter | , C.

An interrupter can be a word, a phrase, or a dependent SVC pattern (clause). An interrupter, **which often appears immediately after the subject,** may also be inserted between the verb and the completer. However, an interrupter **that immediately follows and restricts the meaning of the subject** should NOT be set off with commas (as in this sentence). An interrupter **that immediately follows the subject, therefore,** may or may not be set off by commas, depending on its relation to the subject. For example, look at the sentence immediately preceding this one. In that sentence, "that follows the subject" is a restrictive interrupter with no commas before or after it. But the word *therefore,* as a nonrestrictive interrupter, is set off by two commas. Here are some additional illustrations.

All students ⟨ *who cut classes unnecessarily* ⟩ *will be penalized.*

> (Ask: Will ALL students be penalized? Since the answer is "no," the interrupter functions as a restrictive element limiting the meaning of the subject. Do NOT use commas with such restrictive interrupters.)

College students, ⟨ *who represent a highly skilled group* ⟩ *,*

must accept the responsibility of leadership.

> (Ask: Does the dependent clause define or limit which college students have the responsibility? Here, "college students" means, simply, ALL college students. The dependent clause just supplies additional information. Put commas before and after such NONrestrictive interrupters.)

College students ⟨ *who graduate with distinction* ⟩ *represent a highly skilled*

group of future leaders.

> (Ask: Do all college students belong to the "highly skilled group of leaders"? No, only those who graduate with distinction belong to this group. The dependent clause, "who graduate with distinction," defines and limits the subject. Do NOT put commas around such restrictive, limiting interrupters.)

In general, you can tell if an interrupter is restrictive or nonrestrictive by reading the sentence without the interrupter present. If the basic meaning remains unchanged without the interrupter, it is NONrestrictive (put in commas). If the basic meaning seems distorted without the interrupter, it is restrictive (no commas). Use this test on these examples:

> *Students who can't communicate effectively usually don't make good leaders.*
>
> *High school graduates who contribute significantly to the productive working group often aren't appreciated by many employers.*
>
> *My old car which was in need of a paint job was easy to sell.*
>
> *An old car which is badly in need of a paint job may be hard to sell.*

Here are some additional examples of comma uses.

> *The students knew,* **however,** *that they would be penalized.*
> *(NONrestrictive interrupter:* **SV, interrupter, C.***)*
>
> *Hazel,* **the banker's wife,** *works as a secretary.*
> *(NONrestrictive appositive; use commas)*

Larry, **not his brother,** *will pay for the damaged car.*
(NONrestrictive contrasted phrase; use commas)

His son **Larry** *will pay for the damaged car.*
(Restrictive appositive; i.e., not "his son John" or "his son Peter")

Dallas, **Texas,** *is the setting for the television show* Dallas. *(Use commas to set off geographical names. Notice that* Texas *may be thought of as equal to the nonrestrictive clause, "which is in Texas.")*

After Pat arrived in **Spokane, Washington,** *she applied for a job on* **January 3, 1984,** *but she began working on* **Tuesday, February 14, 1984.**
(Use commas with geographical names, and with items in dates and addresses.)

Pat applied for her job in **January 1984** *but didn't accept it until Tuesday,* **14 February 1984.**
(Commas may be omitted when the day of the month is not given or when the day precedes the month.)

"I believe," **she said,** *"that you have no choice left."*
(Dialogue needs special punctuation. Here, "she said" is really a nonrestrictive interrupter inserted into the quoted sentence.)

"That's it," **she said.** *"You have no choice left."*
(Here "she said" functions as a closer for the first sentence unit. The word You *begins a new sentence.)*

She will see, **if she uses common sense,** *that she has made a mistake.*

(**SV,** ⏐ subordinate clause interrupter ⏐ , **C.**)

You should be able to see from these illustrations that a *restrictive* interrupter (no commas) is essential to the *meaning* of the basic SVC pattern, limiting or defining the meaning in some way. The *nonrestrictive* interrupter (use a pair of commas) provides related, additional information but does not *limit* or define the meaning of the basic SVC pattern.

The Semicolon: Stop Signal that Ties

The semicolon signals a *full stop* between independent SVC patterns closely tied in meaning. Use the semicolon where you could also substitute a period; other uses are uncommon. Here's your pattern:

The students were confused ; no one knew the answer.
    Independent SVC   **Independent SVC**

As you can see, the semicolon "ties" the two statements together, as a coordinating conjunction would; it links only *independent* SVC patterns (i.e., two independent clauses). To use the semicolon between SVC patterns of unequal grammatical rank results in a lopsided construction, sometimes called a **semicolon fault.** It is lopsided because the semicolon, like the period, signals a full stop and a lowering of the voice, after which we normally expect an independent SVC pattern. Read the following illustrations aloud, comparing the punctuation signals:

> *None of the boys dated Marilyn; although she was intelligent, alert, and properly reserved. (Semicolon fault)*

> *None of the boys dated Marilyn; she was intelligent, alert, but too properly reserved. (Correct)*

> *None of the boys dated Marilyn; although she was intelligent and alert, she was too properly reserved. (Correct)*

In the first illustration, the semicolon ties a *dependent* SVC pattern to an independent one; in the second, it ties together two independent SVC patterns. In the third, however, you have three SVC patterns, one of them dependent. Which is it? How can you tell? Justify the punctuation in the third illustration. What comma "rule" governs the comma after the word *alert?* Could a period replace the semicolon in the first illustration? Apply this test to the following illustrations to discover which uses of the semicolon are acceptable.

> *A fierce rain filled the gutters with water; causing them to overflow onto yards and walkways.*

> *Although Agnes did her best to explain her failure in math; her parents still scolded her severely.*

> *The astronaut was not merely following instructions; he had to use his own judgment repeatedly.*

> *Steve didn't work very much; in fact, he hardly ever worked.*

> *He has his mind made up; therefore, nothing you say will change it.*

> *Football requires the best in strength and endurance; track, the best in speed and agility.*

> *Football requires the best in strength and endurance; but track requires the best in speed and agility.*

> *The committee consisted of Ralph Brigand, the president of the Snook Bank, I. M. Stealing, the manager of the phone company; and the mayor.*

The last illustration is a special case: occasionally you need semicolons to clarify a series of words or word-groups confused by too many commas. Where else would you place a semicolon in this sentence?

The Colon: A Pause that Points

The colon signals a pause that anticipates; it points forward, usually to a list of items to follow. This is what the colon does: it directs attention forward. You also know the colon in the *Dear Sir:* that begins business letters, where it seems to say, "Read on." The following examples show the colon's several functions:

> *This chapter discusses three subjects: grammar, punctuation, and spelling. (Correct)*
>
> *This chapter discusses grammar, punctuation, and spelling. (Better)*
>
> *She could only think of one thing: marriage. (Correct)*
>
> *She could think only of marriage. (Better)*
>
> *Remember this: Don't panic. (Correct)*
>
> *The following cities have smog problems: Los Angeles, New York, Pittsburgh, and New Orleans. (Correct)*

You could also use either a comma or a dash in the third example, making it less formal.

The Apostrophe: The Mark of Possession or Omission

Use the apostrophe to indicate possession, omission in contracted words or dates, and certain plurals. The apostrophe's use will be simpler if you remember that its most common uses are to signal possession *(one student's exam, many students' exams)* or omission *(it's for it is, '79 for 1979)*.

1. Possession.   To indicate possession, always begin with this pattern:

$$\boxed{\text{[word]'s}}$$

Whether your word is singular or plural, one word or a compound, first name or last name, write it down first, and then add *'s*, as shown in the diagram. As the following examples show, this method doesn't always work; however, it does help prevent some common errors with plurals and compounds, and it makes it easy to see whether your ending is *'s* or *s'*. Study the examples below carefully, noting where the *s* has been dropped. Can you see the pattern for dropping this *s*?

SINGULAR	PLURAL
one [girl]'s mother	many [girls]'s̶ mothers
one [man]'s tie	many [men]'s ties
a [lady]'s hat(s)	many [ladies]'s̶ hats
a [woman]'s face	many [women]'s faces

a [boy]'s book   many [boys]'s̶ books

a [box]'s lid   many [boxes]'s̶ lids

[James]'s book   [Dick and Jane]'s book

[Mr. Jones]'s house   the [Joneses]'s̶ house

[brother-in-law]'s wife   two [brothers-in-law]'s wives

As you can see, the system works reasonably well. Very few singular forms containing an *s* or *s*-sound deviate from the rule. Two examples are *Moses* and *Jesus*, which drop the *s*, with possessives of *Moses'* and *Jesus'*. Say the word aloud, and if the combination of *s's* makes the word unpronounceable, drop the final *s*. The same holds true for plurals with *s* endings: *ladies, boxes, Joneses.* If you know the plurals of compound words *(mothers-in-law, courts-martial, sisters-in-law)*, adding the *'s* should be easy. Last names are also easy if you form the plural first and then add *'s*, deciding whether to keep the *s* by pronouncing the name:

Mr. Smith's car.	The Smiths' house. (The Smiths live there.)
Mrs. Brown's car.	The Browns' children.
Mr. and Mrs. Pettit.	The Pettits are at home, but the Pettits' children are away.
One Jones, two Joneses.	There are six Joneses—if you don't count the Joneses' dog and cat.

Notice, too, that *Dick and Jane's book* means one book shared (owned) by two people, but *Dick's and Jane's clothes* means individual ownership.

Personal pronouns are already possessive and need no apostrophe: *its, his, hers, theirs, ours, whose.* Remember that *it's* always means *it is* and who's always means *who is*. And don't try to make a noun plural by adding *'s*: one *try* and many *tries* (not *try's*), one *cry* and many *cries* (not *cry's*).

2. Omissions.   Use the apostrophe to indicate omissions in contracted words or dates:

can't, didn't, he's (for he is), it's (for it is), you're (for you are)

'79 for 1979, '84 for 1984, class of '85 (meaning 1985)

3. To indicate certain plurals and abbreviations.   Use the apostrophe plus an *s* to indicate the plurals of lower case letters and abbreviations followed by periods:

We have too many Ph.D.'s in physics and English. (Do not **italicize** *the 's.)*

Lisa never crosses her **t***'s, and her* **till***'s seem to be* **tell***'s.*

Here's how the second illustration would look typed:

```
Lisa never crosses her t's and her till's seem to be tell's.
```

Use the apostrophe plus an *s* to indicate certain plurals, abbreviations that have no periods, words referred to as words, and plurals of capital letters:

> *In the 1960's stories about UFO's were common.*

> *In the 1960s stories about UFOs were common.*
> (Typed: 1960s UFOs)
> *(Apostrophes may be omitted.)*

> *Lisa's 6's and her A's aren't legible.*

> *Lisa's 6s and her As aren't legible. (Apostrophes may be omitted.)*
> (Typed: 6s <u>As</u>)

> *The sentence contained three **and's** and four **on's**.*

> *The sentence contained three **ands** and four **ons**. (Apostrophes may be omitted.)*
> (Typed: three <u>ands</u> and four <u>ons</u>)

Quotation Marks

Quotation marks, either double (" ") or single (' '), are popularly referred to as *quotes*.

1. Put double quotation marks around the actual words of a speaker.
2. Put double quotation marks around words within your sentence when you quote them exactly as written in the original source.
3. Omit quotation marks around longer, indented quotations.
4. Put double quotation marks around certain titles and names.
5. Put single quotation marks around quoted material that appears *within* material that already has quotations marks around it.

1. Quoting the actual words of a speaker.   Look at any short story or novel and you'll find this use of quotation marks:

> *"Anyone can make a mistake," she said, smiling pleasantly.*

> *Then she added, "It's no big deal. Let's forget about it."*

Use commas to set off expressions such as *she said* and *she asked*, and observe the punctuation rules for complete sentence units.

2. Quoting the words of others within your own sentences.   This kind of quoting is probably the kind you will use most, especially in a research paper. Here's an example:

> *Both chimps received care similar to that given human infants, including "around-the-clock feedings, diapering, inoculations, . . . and body contact whenever they were awake" (Early Signs 752). Equally important, teachers in the project included . . .*

Variations of this can be seen in passages that quote famous words or phrases: How many people really understand the meaning of "give me liberty, or give me death"? Or: When people say, "all men are created equal," do they really understand the statement's full implications?

3. Quoting longer passages.   In papers prepared for the classroom, longer quoted passages—usually more than five typed lines—are set off from your own words, indented five spaces, and single spaced. *No quotation marks are placed around these indented passages.* In professional papers submitted for publication, MLA style requires double spacing for these indented quotations, as well as for notes and bibliographies. For theses and dissertations, however, MLA suggests single spacing for indented quotations, notes, and bibliographies. (See also Chapter 8, pp. 264, 270.)

4. Quoting titles and names.   Do not put quotation marks around major titles—names of books, movies, magazines, newspapers, pamphlets, plays, long poems, musical works. These are *italicized* in printed form and appear underlined in your writing. Here are some examples as you would type them:

```
Time and Newsweek are popular magazines. Both magazines
reviewed Home Alone 2 and Aladdin, as well as Terminator 2. The
New York Times also reviewed these films, and so did the
Houston Post. Magazines and newspapers also review books of all
kinds, including The Hitchhiker's Guide to the Galaxy and
Huckleberry Finn.
```

However, articles or chapters or sections *within* these major publications appear within double quotation marks—including titles of essays, chapters, short stories, paintings, poems, television programs. Here are some examples:

Poe's "The Raven"
Michelangelo's "David"
Thoreau's "Civil Disobedience"
Twain's "A Humane Word from Satan"
Hawthorne's "Young Goodman Brown," in *Twice-Told Tales*
The chapter "The Asexual Amoeba," in the book *Primitive Organisms*

5. Quotation marks within quotation marks.   Use single quotation marks to indicate quotations within quotations.

Lisa said, "Pat keeps calling my goal 'an impossible dream.'"

Pat says, "Nobody who has read Thoreau's 'Civil Disobedience' can argue with my position."

In Primitive Organisms *Brown points out that the "amoeba reproduces asexually, and not by the process described by Smith as 'a combination of budding and simple cell division.'" (In this example, the writer is quoting Brown from* Primitive Organisms, *and that quotation includes one from Smith.)*

SPELLING PRETEST

A. Most *(not all)* of the word-groups below contain one *or more* spelling errors. To the left of each word-group, identify each misspelled word by placing an *X* under the number corresponding to the word. If you think the word-group has no misspelled words, place an *X* in the "0" column.

0	1	2	3	4	5

1. ceiling 2. arguement 3. unecessary 4. seize 5. evened

1. neice 2. conceive 3. weild 4. grief 5. irresistible

1. adviseable 2. desireable 3. detestable 4. blame-able 5. analyse

1. disappear 2. mileage 3. noticeable 4. serviceing 5. reprieve

1. mother-in-laws 2. conferred 3. occurred 4. regretting 5. conscientious

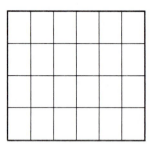

1. mistatement 2. acheive 3. temperment 4. benefited 5. leveling

1. blaming 2. height 3. foreign 4. eighth 5. propelling

1. accommodate   2. accidentally   3. supersede 4. precede 5. exceed

1. defenite 2. occasionally 3. incidentally 4. alloted 5. discription

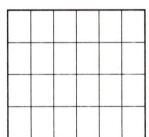

1. the Kellys (plural) 2. trys 3. attorneys 4. heroes 5. echos

1. judgement 2. duly 3. disservice 4. changeable 5. hoeing

1. valleys 2. mispronunciation 3. niece 4. taxis 5. crammed

1. advise (noun) 2. advise (verb) 3. chose (past tense) 4. chose (present tense) 5. irritible.

0	1	2	3	4	5

1. repitition 2. surprize 3. permissable 4. familiar 5. similiar

1. perscription 2. seperate 3. benificial 4. forty 5. dissipate

1. irresistable 2. hypocrisy 3. goverment 4. hinderance 5. desirable

1. sacrilegious   2. playwright   3. embarrassed 4. procedure 5. psychological

1. preference 2. prefered 3. supress 4. mischievious 5. devide

1. useage 2. doseage 3. sacrafice 4. occassion 5. dependant

1. allottment 2. hypocrit 3. desease 4. laborously 5. gaiety

1. payed 2. villian 3. exercise 4. professor 5. tommorrow

B. To the left of each word-group, identify the CORRECT spelling by placing an *X* under the number corresponding to the word that fits the given definition. If you think there is no correct answer, mark the "0" column.

the RESULT (noun):
1. affect 2. effect

to ACT UPON, to INFLUENCE:
1. affect 2. effect

to MAKE HAPPEN, BRING ABOUT:
1. affect 2. effect

RULE OF ACTION, GENERAL TRUTH:
1. principal 2. principle

HEAD PERSON:
1. principal 2. principle

FOREMOST, MOST IMPORTANT (adjective):
1. principal 2. principle

0	1	2	3	4	5

REFERENCE TO, MENTION OF (something):
   1. illusion 2. allusion 3. delusion

FALSE IDEA, MISCONCEPTION:
   1. illusion 2. allusion 3. delusion

A FIXED MISCONCEPTION:
   1. illusion 2. allusion 3. delusion

HE HAS A GUILTY:
   1. conscious 2. concious
   3. conscience 4. concience

HE IS AWAKE, OR:
   1. conscious 2. concious
   3. conscience 4. concience

to GIVE AN EXAMPLE:
   1. site 2. cite 3. sight

a LOCATION OR PLACE:
   1. site 2. cite 3. sight

ACT OF SEEING, SOMETHING SEEN:
   1. site 2. cite 3. sight

WRITING MATERIALS:
   1. stationary 2. stationry 3. stationery

NOT MOVING:
   1. stationary 2. stationry 3. stationery

ROUGH, UNEVEN:
1. course 2. coarse 3. corce

a WAY, PATH, or DIRECTION:
1. course 2. coarse 3. corce

to GO BEFORE:
1. procede 2. proceed 3. precede 4. preceed

to MOVE FORWARD, ADVANCE:
1. procede 2. proceed 3. precede 4. preceed

0	1	2	3	4	5

to SUFFER THE LOSS OF:
1. loose 2. lose

NOT TIGHT, FREE:
1. loose 2. lose

AN ASSEMBLY:
1. counsel 2. council 3. consul

ADVICE (noun):
1. counsel 2. council 3. consul

to ADVISE (verb):
1. counsel 2. council 3. consul

SPELLING

Why improve your spelling? And does it matter outside the classroom? To begin with, hundreds of personnel managers across the country list careless spelling as the single most irritating problem in job applicants' letters. They routinely reject job applicants with obvious spelling problems. Also, careless spelling may very well reflect careless work habits or lack of self-pride—qualities few employers will tolerate. Clearly, accurate spelling is important.

As with punctuation, to improve your spelling, you will have to get your eye to cooperate with your ear; what you see on the page should represent the sounds you hear. This cooperation will succeed, however, only if you give it a chance to work for you. To succeed, you will have to develop a positive, ongoing attitude toward spelling accuracy. Become aware of accurate pronunciation and match it with the written word. Hear the word, say the word, write the word. Learn some basic guides to spelling improvement and put these to work for you. Also, you will want to keep a list of your special spelling problems. More important, however, classify your special words into groups, each group representing a basic problem shared by all the words in that group. This process should let you concentrate on only a few basic principles rather than individual words, greatly simplifying the amount of remembering you have to do. Use the problem areas discussed in this unit as the bases for classification, beginning your list with the words you missed in the spelling pretest. Later, add words collected from your daily reading and writing. After you have studied the material in this unit and the words on your list, check your progress by working the spelling test at the end of this chapter. And, most important of all, be sure you own a good dictionary. Look up all words you are uncertain of and check the special section on "Spelling" (it gives you all the "rules").

Sound and Sense in Spelling

Words come *before* spelling rules. The rules are only guides, *inferred* (see p. 131) from groups of words sharing spelling similarities. Classifying your personal spelling problems should lead you to *infer* "guides" to improve your spelling habits.

Sound.   The inability to translate the spoken word into its current, accepted written form causes *all* spelling errors. With certain words, however, pro*nun*ciation itself is the key to the misspelling. As you study the words in this unit, therefore, pro*nounce* every syllable in a word; don't add any that aren't there. *EnvIRONment* and *FebRUary* are good examples of words in which careless spoken and written omissions occur. *Athlete* (not *athelete*) and *mischievous* (not *mischieVIOUS*) are good examples of words that tend to be given syllables that aren't there. As your first step toward improved spelling, classify the following words into two groups—those to which you might *add* syllables, and those from which you might *omit* syllables; circle the part of each word that represents its problem area.

accidentally	generally	probably
athlete	government	quantity
candidate	grammatically	recognize
disastrous	hindrance	remembrance
drowned	lightning	representative
entrance	literature	sophomore
environment	occasionally	umbrella

Some important pronunciation/spelling problems are also suggested by these words: *irrelevant, perspiration, prescription, cavalry.* What happens when you spell these words? Can you find others like them? Using sound as your basis, devise a way of remembering the spelling of *definite* and *repetition.*

Words that sound alike.   Some words sound alike but don't look alike; more important, they mean different things. Students most frequently misspell words found in these two word-groups:

their teacher	*two* books (not three)
I went *there*	*too* many books
they're (they are)	go *to* the game

Keep a list of sound-alike words that give you trouble. Begin by reviewing the meaning of each word in every group of these **homonyms** (sound-alikes):

accept, except	cite, sight, site
advice, advise	coarse, course
affect, effect	conscience, conscious
choose, chose	council, counsel

decent, descent, dissent   quiet, quite
formally, formerly   right, rite, write
irrelevant, irreverent   sense, since
its, it's   there, their, they're
lead, led   threw, through
lose, loose   to, too, two
passed, past   weather, whether
precede, proceed   whose, who's
principal, principle   your, you're

Keep your ear and eye alert for other homonyms (there are a great many others); add them to this list as you find them.

Prefixes.   A prefix is a syllable added to the beginning of a word to modify or change its meaning. Almost always the prefix is simply *added* to the beginning of the word; both the prefix and the word are retained completely in the resulting word, thus:

$$[\text{prefix}] + [\text{word}] = \textbf{new word}$$
$$[\text{un}] + necessary = unnecessary$$
$$[\text{il}] + logical = illogical$$

It's less important to remember where these prefixes came from than to know how to spell them and how they change the meaning of the word they're added to. Most of those in the present grouping have a negative effect: They usually mean *not* + the *word*. Here are the ones you will run into most often: *dis-, il-, im-, in-, ir-, mis-, un-*. If you simply write down the prefix first, then add the word, you shouldn't have trouble deciding where the "double" letters appear (and don't appear) in the following words: *disappear, dissimilar, disservice, dissatisfy, disappoint, illegal, illegible, illogical, immaterial, immoderate, immoral, immortal, immovable, inappropriate, innumerable, irrational, irreconcilable, irregular, irrelevant, irreligious, irresistible, misspell, misfire, misspeak, mistype, misbehave, misstatement, missent, misunderstand, unnamed, unnatural, unnecessary, unnerved, unnumbered, unpinned.*

Suffixes.   A suffix is a syllable added to the *end* of a word to modify or change its meaning. Here you will be concerned with a very limited but most important group of suffixes—those that begin with a vowel, including the *-ing* used to form present participles of verbs and the *-ed* used to form past participles. These are the important ones: *-able, -ible, -ing, -ed, -ance, -ence, -ers*. Is it *occured* or *occurred*? What's the difference between *striped* and *stripped*? Is it *shipper* or *shiper*? You will bring thousands of words under control if you remember the following three and what happens to them when you add one of the suffixes beginning with a vowel:

1. Ship   + -ed = Ship*p* ed   (*ALWAYS* double the consonant.)
2. Occur + -ed = Occur*r* ed   (*ALWAYS* double the consonant.)
3. Color + -ed = Color ed   (Do *not* double the consonant.)

Let's examine each of these to be sure we have the word-class spotted.

1. *Ship.* One syllable, ends in a single consonant. The doubling rule applies to *all* monosyllabic words ending in a single *consonant,* if the suffix beginning with a vowel is added. Note the number of words involved: *shipped, shipping, shippable, shipper; cram, crammed, cramming, crammable, crammer; drop, dropped, dropping, droppable, dropper.* And there are thousands of monosyllabic words: *spin, span, sin, sun, stop, crop, mop, tan, ban, mar, bar,* etc.

2. *Occur.* More than one syllable, the accent (stress) on the *last* syllable (the one next to the suffix we'll be adding). The doubling rule applies to all words of *more* than one syllable also <u>IF</u> they end in a single consonant and the accent is on the last syllable. Read the following words aloud and listen to where you place the *stress* (accent): *occur, allot, repel, infer, refer, excel, dispel.* As long as the stress remains on the last syllable, the consonant doubles; but note what happens here: *infer, inferred, inferring, inferrable, inference.* In the last of the series, the stress has shifted: from *in*<u>FER</u> to <u>IN</u>*ference,* which has only one *r.*

3. *Color.* More than one syllable, ends in a single consonant, stress is *not* on the last syllable: <u>COL</u>or, <u>COL</u>ored, <u>COL</u>oring, <u>COL</u>orable. All words like *color,* then, do *not* double that last consonant. This word-group is unusual, however, since the doubled consonant is also accepted for many of the words: <u>BEN</u>efit, <u>BEN</u>efited or <u>BEN</u>efitted; <u>COUN</u>sel, <u>RI</u>val, <u>MOD</u>el, <u>MAR</u>vel, <u>TRA</u>vel, and <u>YO</u>del all have the alternate spellings. Still, the rule applies, and you can never go wrong when you do run into words (like *color*) for which there is no alternate spelling: <u>E</u>ven, <u>E</u>vened, <u>E</u>vening, <u>E</u>vener.

Other suffix "rules" can be as useful as these three. Some of them involve single letters: *c* and *g* become soft when followed by an *i* or *e,* as in *slice, city,* and *age;* for this reason, the *k* is added to *mimicKing* and *picnicKing,* to maintain the hard sound. But *change* and *notice* already have the *e* to keep the sound soft and, therefore, must retain it, even when a suffix beginning with a vowel is added, as in *chanGEable* and *notiCEable.*

Final *e* and common sense. Many suffixes take care of themselves if you use common sense when adding them. For example, you'll have less trouble with the *-ally* suffix if you first check to see if the word has an *-al form:*

accident + *-al* = accident*al* + *-ly* = accident*ally*
occasion + *-al* = occasion*al* + *-ly* = occasion*ally*
incident + *-al* = incident*al* + *-ly* = incident*ally*

What should you do when the word ends with an *e*? Here are two simple guides:

1. *Retain* the *e* when adding a suffix beginning with a consonant: *care* + *FUL* = *careFUL; care* + *LESS* = *careLESS; rude* + *NESS* = *rudeNESS.*
2. *Drop* the *e* when adding a suffix beginning with a vowel: *come* + *ING* = *comING; desire* + *ABLE* = *desirABLE; ride* + *ING* = *ridING.*

Common sense should take care of such exceptions as *hoeING* and *awFUL.*

-cede, -ceed, -sede. These troublesome endings will be easier to handle if you remember just a few words. Look at *superSEDE*. It is the only word in English with the "seed" ending spelled *sede*. Like *hypocrISY*, it's in a class by itself. Only three words end in *ceed*: *exCEED*, *proCEED*, and *sucCEED*. All others ending with the "seed" sound are spelled *cede*, as in *preCEDE*, *reCEDE*, and *interCEDE*. The word *proCEDure* doesn't even qualify as an exception, since it doesn't *end* with the "seed" sound.

-able, -ible. There are also "rules" describing the spelling patterns of *-able/-ible* words, but the best of these depend on a knowledge of Latin. However, some major *-able/-ible* groupings can still readily be suggested with a handful of words:

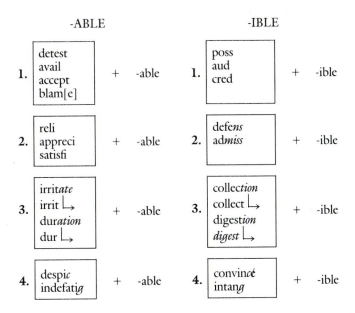

You should be able to infer the "rules" from these examples.

USE THE *-ABLE* SUFFIX WHEN:
1. The base is a complete word.
2. The base ends in *i*.
3. The base also forms a word with the *ay* sound in it.
4. The base ends in a hard *c* or *g*.

USE THE *-IBLE* SUFFIX WHEN:
1. The base is an *in*complete word.
2. The base ends in *ns* or in *miss*.
3. The base word also forms an *ion* word *directly*.
4. The base ends in a soft *c* or *g*.

But note the following exceptions: *equitable, formidable, memorable, probable; irresistible, contemptible, discernible, flexible.*

-yze, -ise, -ize. You are likely to run into only two words ending in *yze*: *analYZE* and *paralYZE*. Those ending in *ise* include *surPRISE*, *exerCISE*, and *comproMISE*, representing the three groups of the most common *-ise* words, *-prise, -cise,* and *-mise.* Most other words ending with this sound have the *ize* ending: *criticIZE, emphasIZE, realIZE, recognIZE, stabilIZE.* Only a few words don't fit the pattern: *advertise, merchandise, despise, chastise, franchise.*

The ie/ei rule.   For these words, remember the old rhyme:

I before *e*
Except after *c,*
Or, when sounded like *ay*
As in *neighbor* and *weigh.*

What the rhyme says is that when the sound is *ee,* write *ie* (except after *c,* when you write *ei,* as in *receive*).

Here are a few examples. In all the following words, the sound is *ee,* hence the spelling is *ie* (because no *c* is involved): *yield, wield, relief, pierce, niece, grief, field, chief.* In the following words, however, even though the sound is *ee,* we must shift to *ei* because a *c* is involved: *receive, perceive, deceive, conceit, ceiling, conceive.* And here are words in which the sound is NOT *ee* and, therefore, *ie* can*not* be used: *weigh, sleigh, vein, heir, neighbor, reign, height, eight, foreign.*

Exceptions: either, weird, seize, forfeit, protein, counterfeit. Memorize these; the rule doesn't apply to them.

Clearly, so brief a look at spelling as this can't discuss more than a few "rules"—those generalizations inferred from an examination of words with similar problems. From the discussion, however, you should be able to devise a classification scheme of perhaps a half-dozen categories to represent your personal problems in spelling. With a little ingenuity, you can probably come up with "rules" or remembering devices of your own. If the device works, use it.

SPELLING REVIEW TEST

A. Most *(not all)* of the word-groups below contain one *or more* spelling errors. To the left of each word-group, identify each misspelled word by placing an *X* under the number corresponding to the word. If you think the word-group has no misspelled words, place an *X* in the "0" column.

0	1	2	3	4	5

1. cieling 2. arguement 3. unecessary 4. seize 5. evened

1. peirce 2. cheif 3. weird 4. inumerable 5. dissappoint

0	1	2	3	4	5

1. court-martials (plural) 2. occuring 3. regretta-ble 4. concientious 5. counseled

1. digestable 2. inference 3. stopping 4. benefit-ting 5. servicing

1. disappear 2. disatisfy 3. mispell 4. ilegal 5. reign

1. defendible 2. defensible 3. correctable 4. pre-dictible 5. desireable

1. temperment 2. acheive 3. misstatement 4. height 5. foriegn

1. accomodate 2. accidently 3. supercede 4. pre-ceed 5. excede

1. irritible 2. defenite 3. paralyze 4. emphasize 5. surprize

1. allotted 2. discription 3. incidently 4. evidently 5. repitition

1. conceivable 2. convenience 3. privilege 4. sepa-rate 5. predominant

1. atheletic 2. disasterous 3. optomistic 4. hinder-ance 5. occurrence

1. advise (noun) 2. advise (verb) 3. chose (past tense) 4. chose (present tense) 5. it's (posses-sive)

1. the Kellys (plural) 2. the Kelly's house (plural, possessive) 3. trys 4. attornies 5. heroes

1. familiar 2. similiar 3. hypocrasy 4. brother-in-laws (plural) 5. valleys

1. criticisim 2. conscientious 3. mischievious 4. embarassed 5. sacrilegious

1. exagerate 2. surpress 3. catagory 4. fourth 5. fourty

B. To the left of each sentence, place an *X* under the number corresponding to the word on the right that fits into the blank.

1	2	3

The _____ called a meeting of all teachers.

Honesty is the _____ guiding us.

→ 1. principle
2. principal

The _____ guide we followed was honesty.

Bad study habits _____ grades adversely.

→ 1. effect
2. affect

The _____ of bad study habits is poor grades.

He projected an _____ of honesty.

She made an _____ to the coming party.

→ 1. allusion
2. illusion
3. delusion

Hitler had a _____ of racial supremacy.

I'm barely _____ in the morning.

→ 1. conscience
2. conscious

His _____ kept him honest.

The _____ for the building was cleared.

→ 1. cite
2. site
3. sight

The building was a beautiful _____.

Be sure to _____ an illustration.

The _____ was filled with trees and traps.

→ 1. coarse
2. course

The material had a _____ texture.

The animal was finally _____.

Her dress was long and _____.

→ 1. lose
2. loose

Because he studied, he could not _____.

Last night I _____ not to study.

→ 1. choose
2. chose

Today I _____ to rest.

Tomorrow I will _____ a new plan of action.

1	2	3

The teacher provided good _____ to the students.

The students had a _____ to represent them.

The teacher promised to _____ the students.

The _____ consisted of students and teachers.

Sarah served as United States _____ in Brazil.

1. council
2. counsel
3. consul

GRAMMAR REVIEW TEST

Most *(not all)* of the sentences given below contain *only one* of the following grammatical problems:

0. Sentence contains no grammatical problems.
1. Subject and verb don't agree.
2. Pronoun does not agree with its antecedent.
3. Dangling modifier—verbal phrase doesn't clearly refer to any word in the sentence.
4. Misplaced modifier—word or word-group needlessly separated from the term it modifies.
5. Sentence fragment—incomplete grammatical construction not clearly connected to other meaning in context.
6. Run-on (fused) sentence—sentences run together with no conjunction or punctuation between them.
7. Faulty verb form—illogical shift in tense.
8. Faulty parallel structure—unequal grammatical elements placed in a series.

Use the numbers (including "0") given above to identify the grammatical problem(s) in each sentence below. First decide what problem(s) the sentence has; then place in the blank provided to the left of each sentence the numbers from the above list that best identify the grammatical problem(s). If the sentence has no problem, place a "0" in the blank. *Note:* Your instructor may ask you to provide a correction below each sentence, especially if you don't know the grammatical terms used in the list.

Example: 1   *The problem of drug use and its effects are examined.*

Correction: *The problem of drug use and its effects* **is** *examined. Because the subject* **problem** *is singular and the verb* **are** *is plural, you would write the number 1 in the blank to show that the subject and verb do* not *agree. Here's the basic SVC pattern: The* problem *. . . is examined.*

_____ **1.** My sister Teresa wants to be an actress but dancing is my future profession.

_____ **2.** The complaining sales manager attacked neither the marketing program of her sales force nor offered a plan of her own.

_____ **3.** Each of the students tried to read their assigned chapters.

_____ **4.** The effects of emotional stress on efficient performance is discussed.

_____ **5.** The newspaper revealed that neither the city council nor the mayor were guilty of wrongdoing.

_____ **6.** After eating dinner, the table should be cleared and cleaned by each person.

_____ **7.** When first tasted, you will find the sensation of hot peppers unusual.

_____ **8.** Some say party politics is a dirty business others insist that party politics help develop strong character.

_____ **9.** A lineup of the suspects help a victim to pick out her assailant.

_____ **10.** Sometimes he won small sums of money, but they were quickly lost the next time he went to the gambling casino.

_____ **11.** Zeba let him believe that she'd take the job. But without definitely committing herself.

_____ **12.** A person should examine the candidates before they vote.

_____ **13.** While taking a bath, the phone began to ring.

_____ **14.** The teacher's responsibility is to the students they can't concentrate on pleasing their principal.

_____ **15.** The new babysitter is experienced, skilled, and you can depend on him.

_____ **16.** Michael told Matthew that he was obsessed with his job.

_____ **17.** To create an exotic meal, a well-stocked kitchen is needed by the cook.

_____ **18.** If you want to do well in this course, come to class and pay attention. Never putting off the papers until the last minute.

_____ **19.** Right where I want to park the car is a motorcycle and a bicycle.

_____ **20.** I already had many fears about computers, although I haven't yet sat behind the keyboard of one.

_____ **21.** He cooked the whole meal for us, and the dessert was also made by him.

_____ **22.** Unscrew the valve; then steel wool should be used to clean the rubber ring. When finished, the whole unit should be rinsed before assembly.

_____ **23.** When only a kitten, my father brought Morris home. Before Kevin was born.

_____ **24.** There is an estimated five billion people on this planet.

_____ **25.** Anyone can make their garden successful. Although it does take some planning and hard work.

PUNCTUATION REVIEW TEST

Most (not all) of the examples given below contain one (occasionally more) of the following punctuation problems:

0. Sentence has no punctuation problems.

1. Period or semicolon needed: run-on sentences.

2. Comma(s) needed as coordinator—items in a series.

3. Comma needed as coordinator of independent clauses (**SVCs**).

4. Comma needed to set off dependent opener.
5. Comma needed to set off dependent closer.
6. Comma(s) *not* needed with restrictive interrupter.
7. Comma(s) needed with nonrestrictive interrupter.
8. Comma splice: full stop *or* conjunction needed with independent clauses **(SVCs).**
9. Semicolon needed to separate independent clauses **(SVCs)** *or* for clarity.
10. Semicolon fault: semicolon used between components of unequal grammatical rank.
11. Colon needed as anticipator.
12. Apostrophe needed for possession.
13. Apostrophe needed for omissions *or* other special uses.
14. Apostrophe is misplaced *or* not needed at all.
15. Quotation marks needed around direct speech or quoted words.
16. Quotation marks needed with titles or names.
17. Additional punctuation needed with quotation marks.
18. Underline title to indicate italics.

Use the numbers (including "0") given above to identify all punctuation *errors* in the sentences below. First decide what punctuation error(s) the sentence has; then place in the blank provided to the left the numbers from the above list that best identify *all* the punctuation *errors*. If you think the sentence has no punctuation problem, place a "0" in the blank. *Note:* Your instructor may ask you to provide a correction within or below each sentence, especially if you don't understand the descriptions of punctuation uses given in the list.

> *Example:* **13, 12, 1, 12** *It's a student's right to ask questions the teacher's job is to answer them.*
>
> Correction: *It's a student's right to ask questions; the teacher's job is to answer them.*

One apostrophe is needed in *it's* to indicate omission (13); two apostrophes are needed to indicate possession: *student's* (12) and *teacher's* (12). The example consists of two run-on sentences (1), which require a period to separate them; or, as the correction shows, a semicolon can be used to separate the two independent SVCs (9). Errors in order: 13, 12, 1/9, 12.

_____ 1. Bessies car didnt get fixed, its still in her garage.
_____ 2. Mike left only one thing on his plate broccoli.
_____ 3. Im only human said Andy, I don't have all the answers.
_____ 4. Spiders considered by some people to be insects belong to a different class the arachnids.
_____ 5. Two things, which most students always need, are money and time.
_____ 6. Lori's decision was final she wouldn't take the out-of-town job.
_____ 7. Thomas my only son was born on March 2, 1989, in Houston, Texas.
_____ 8. Its all in a weeks work.

_____ **9.** Theyre going to the mall its stores are having a clearance sale.

_____ **10.** Five dollars worth of gasoline wont get you home from here.

_____ **11.** The class was fun; although the students had five papers to write.

_____ **12.** People, who use drugs, are often considered antisocial.

_____ **13.** This chapter the longest in the book discusses three subjects grammar punctuation and spelling.

_____ **14.** He paused, he aimed, he fired.

_____ **15.** Maria won the mile Grace won the hundred-yard dash and Andy easily won the broad jump.

_____ **16.** The opener can be any word, phrase, or dependent clause its followed by a slight pause a lowering of the voice.

_____ **17.** The student was delayed because of a flat tire but he made it to professor Maxs ten oclock class the most important one of the day.

_____ **18.** Nobody wanted to date Manuel, although good-looking and intelligent he talked too much and was too impulsive.

_____ **19.** Nobody wanted to date Manuel; although he was good-looking and intelligent.

_____ **20.** You are he said angrily impossible to get along with.

_____ **21.** If you spend more time writing your papers you can improve your grade.

_____ **22.** One of the worlds great problems according to Time magazine is population control and yet no one seems to be doing much about it.

_____ **23.** Although population control is a worldwide problem the income tax system rewards people for having children.

_____ **24.** Our air water and soil have been contaminated.

_____ **25.** Population is a worldwide problem, however the income tax system still rewards people for having babies.

10

Revising Your Paper: Diction

Have you really thought about the way words work? If someone says, "Living in the city is great," are you certain you understand what is meant? At first, the words *living, city,* and *great* seem to be reasonably clear. But *are* they? If you take another look at the problem suggested by the cartoon on page 350, you should be able to come up with questions about each word and discover problems in meaning. Choosing specific rather than general words and pointing them unmistakably is a skill you can learn and develop, provided you aren't satisfied with the first word that comes to mind. You can say, "I like my steak medium rare"; or, you can revise this and announce, "I prefer sirloin to T-bone steak, and I like it grilled—charred on the outside, hot, juicy, and pink within."

Revising your diction in this way after you've completed the first draft of your paper will pay off. You'll learn to get rid of lazy verbs and tired expressions, to eliminate the *who–which–that* disease and the involutions of passive constructions, and to delete irritating ten-dollar words in simple, fifty-cent situations. You'll discover how to make words comfortable in each communication situation by projecting a suitable tone. You'll choose cautiously from such alternatives as *concede, admit, confess, acknowledge* and *clever, sly, cunning, shrewd, calculating, smooth*. Revise your diction, and your writing will gain directness, clarity, and strength. Choose each word for maximum reader impact; then watch for and enjoy the results. Make revision a creative game.

Assuming you've been working on a computer all along, the creative game of revising words for maximum impact enters a completely new dimension. Changing words and phrases, replacing or moving them, comes with a flick of the finger and a simple move of the cursor. Before making any changes, however, *always* be certain you've saved your original draft (to floppy or hard disk). Once you've made the changes, print a hard copy and compare the versions for effectiveness—reading them aloud if necessary. With the computer, other revision tasks also move into new dimensions. Is that the right word? The best word? Check the thesaurus. Is the sentence structure "standard"? Use the software program designed to check grammar and basic sentence sense. Making changes on a monitor screen provides a new freedom that pen or typewriter don't approach. If you're willing to play, and know your word processing program, you can create parallel columns, place the original draft in column one, use column two for the ongoing revision, and compare the new version with the original as you move along. The opportunities are there; you need only to take them.

AIDS TO STRENGTH, CLARITY, DIRECTNESS

By all means enjoy the game. Here are some creative plays you may have forgotten.

Change the Passive Voice to Active Voice

English verbs have two voices—active and passive. For example, consider these sentences:

Andy | _hit the ball._

The ball | _was hit by Andy._

The first sentence is in the active voice. The subject of the sentence, _Andy,_ is doing the hitting, the action expressed in the sentence. The second is in the passive voice. The subject of this sentence, _ball,_ is _receiving_ the action. Or, to put it another way, the first sentence (active) follows the normal word order for English sentences— subject, verb, complement, or _actor, action, receiver of action._ The second sentence (passive) turns this normal word order around. What was the complement of the first sentence becomes the subject in the second sentence. Its order is _receiver of action, action, actor._ The problem is that the actor is often vague and sometimes simply omitted.

Look at this example.

```
     (1) To call a telephone on your own party line proceed as
follows: Lift the receiver and wait for dial tone. (2) The
regular seven-digit number of the desired station is dialed,
the busy signal will be heard, and the calling party then
places the receiver on the hook. (3) The desired station is
then signaled. (4) After a reasonable time, remove receiver and
start talking.
```

The writer of these directions has shifted from active to passive and back to active in four brief sentences. The resulting jumble is enough to cause telephone subscribers to hesitate making calls on their own party lines. The first sentence is in the active voice. The subject *you*, the actor, is understood. *You* are to lift the receiver and *you* are to wait for the dial tone. The second sentence, however, shifts to the passive. There is no one dialing, and no one is hearing the busy signal. The actor is missing in the passive sequence. The last part of the second sentence shifts again to active voice. The calling party acts. Again, in the third sentence, no one is signaling the desired station, and the sentence is passive. The final sentence returns to the active voice with an understood *you* as the actor. These directions do not communicate clearly. If the understood *you* had acted throughout (that is, if the author had remained in the active voice), there would be no confusion about following the directions. Here is a revision of the paragraph.

```
      (1) To call a telephone on your own party line proceed as
follows: Lift the receiver and wait for the dial tone. (2) Dial
the regular seven-digit number of the desired station, listen
for the busy signal, and then place the receiver on the hook.
(3) Signal the desired station. (4) After a reasonable time,
remove the receiver and start talking.
```

The passive voice isn't always inappropriate, of course, or there would be no need to have it in the language. But you must be careful to use it appropriately and unobtrusively. If, for instance, you don't know who performs the action, or if the actor is too unimportant to the thought of the sentence to be worth mentioning, you could appropriately use the passive verb. If you write, "Highway 6 was completed last May," no one is likely to insist that you change this passive construction to active by naming the engineering firm that built the road. But you probably don't need to leave this sentence in the passive voice. You can easily make it a phrase and put it into a longer, active sentence, for example: "Highway 6, completed last May, has increased trade in Boonville by fifty percent," or "Completion of Highway 6 last May boosted trade in Boonville."

This example acceptably uses the passive voice:

> *After the operation, Ernest was moved to his room and was given a sedative by the nurse who was to watch over him during his long convalescence.*

In this sentence, we can take it for granted that a doctor performed the operation and that an orderly moved Ernest to his room. There is no point in mentioning them, for they are unimportant in this context. Notice that the remainder of the sentence continues in the passive, *was given by the nurse*, instead of *the nurse gave*. This use of passive is appropriate because to change it to active would change the point of view in midsentence. To make it active you would have to change this part of the sentence to an independent clause preceded by a comma: . . . room, *and the nurse who was to watch over him during his long convalescence gave him a sedative*. A second objection to this active form of the verb is the distance between the subject of the clause, *nurse*, and its verb, *gave*. Ordinarily, they should be as close together as possible.

You can use the passive, then, when the actor is unknown or unimportant or when the active voice would interfere with style or cause a clumsy construction. Usually you should change any passive sentences to active ones. Sometimes students use passive constructions to avoid using the first person *I*. For example, sentences such as this one appear frequently: *C. Goehring's* Life in the Jungle *was selected for a book report because of the interest of its subject matter to this reader*. Note that no one has selected a book in this sentence. *This reader* may have, but who is he? Better by far to say in a forthright manner: *I selected C. Goehring's* Life in the Jungle *for a book report because its subject matter interested me*. Furthermore, do not refer to yourself in writing as "the author" or "this writer." Trying to eliminate the first person often leads to a poor use of the passive or to clumsy circumlocutions.

These examples of poor use of the passive come from student papers.

> *Coffee had to be drunk and cookies eaten before games were played. (No one in this sentence is doing anything. Change to something like: The visitors had coffee and cookies before playing checkers and Monopoly.)*

> *Games to be played were checkers and Monopoly. (Again, no one is playing the games. Make it active this way: They will play checkers and Monopoly.)*

> *8:15 was shown by the clock on the wall. (Very simple to change. The sentence shouldn't start with numbers, and the clock should be doing the action expressed here, so make it the subject of the sentence: The clock on the wall showed 8:15.)*

EXERCISES

    A. Change passive verbs to active in these sentences.
       1. Her skirts were always too short, Pat's parents insisted, and when she got a veto on her white leather suit, tears were shed.
       2. When the fourth child came, all plans to move to Chicago in the spring were given up by the McLain family.
       3. More than ten pounds of beef and forty sacks of peanuts were eaten by the two dieters per week on their low-carbohydrate diet.
       4. In 1980, her case was called incurable by every doctor in the Miami area of Florida.
       5. "All that I hope to be, I owe to my beloved oilwell," was the twist Miss Susie gave the Lincoln quote.

6. The centerpiece was arranged by the secretary, while doughnuts and coffee were set out on tables in the foyer by the clerk-typist.
7. Plans to attend the first session of summer school were made by the Harter girls.
8. The hay was thrown over the fence by Farmer Swenson, whose cows were then called by their owner to "Come and get it!"
9. Michael's closet held more than fifty sports shirts, but every time, he chose the blue-gray plaid.
10. The house on Glade Street was pink and brown with a most vulgar green on the roof, and the color combination was loudly bemoaned by the neighborhood, as it was by the new owner.
11. Facts could not be ascertained, and so no decision was reached by the Committee to Remove Uncooperative Members from the club rolls.
12. Lisa pranced home to stun her father with the news that she would be blasted off to California for the summer with the girls.
13. Complaints were heard by the young man when he announced to his parents that he had just quit his new job.
14. The mystery of the missing books was finally solved by the librarian at the Saturday meeting of the student shelvers.
15. Because of the development of seven new cavities, the afternoon was unpleasantly spent in the dentist's office.
16. Excellent recommendations were given on the application sent by the artist from Virginia.
17. Practice was continued until the target was hit by every marksman.
18. On November 15, agreement was reached among the Brechner Boulevard neighbors over rights to the water tank.
19. Amazing progress has been made by the Dade County Chamber of Commerce.
20. All the potato salad, as well as the Greek olives and the pickles, was eaten before mid-afternoon.

B. Write a set of instructions for one of the following:
1. Tying a shoelace
2. Brushing teeth
3. Folding a paper plane (or hat)

C. Exchange instructions for B with someone in your class. Then, following your classmate's instructions *exactly,* perform the steps. Make a list of problems you discover.

Avoid Listless Verbs

"Listless verbs" are sluggish, uninteresting, and inexact. They deaden your writing. As you revise, change as many of these as possible to lively verbs with exact meanings.

are	go
is	say
it is	see
had	there are
has	there is
have	

Look at the verbs shown highlighted in this paragraph:

```
        The Volkswagen is unexcelled for dependability. It is
well-behaved under driving conditions in which other cars are
kept off the road. Unlike conventional cars with their engine
over the front wheels, the VW engine is in the back, which
gives superior traction to the rear wheels. As a result, the VW
can climb steep, slippery hills with ease or it can go with
sureness through ice, snow, mud, and sand. Furthermore, other
cars are easily out-performed by the VW even under the most
extreme temperature conditions because there are no radiator
problems in the VW. The VW engine is air-cooled; thus there are
no leaks, rust, or antifreeze problems peculiar to conventional
cars. Any time, summer or winter, day or night, the VW is ready
to go anywhere.
```

Every verb in this paragraph, with the exception of *gives* and *climb,* appears on the list. Further, a poor use of the passive also appears in midparagraph. Can you spot it? It marks a change in point of view.

This paragraph as it stands is not the worst one ever written, but making it better is simple. Just change the verbs (automatically taking care of the passive construction).

```
        Unexcelled for dependability, the Volkswagen behaves well
under driving conditions that frighten other cars off the road.
Unlike conventional cars with their engines over the front
wheels, the VW, with its engine's weight in the back of the
car, allows the rear wheels superior traction. As a result, the
VW climbs steep, slippery hills with ease or cruises securely
through ice, snow, mud, and sand. Further, the VW outperforms
other cars even under the most extreme temperature conditions,
because it needs no radiator. The air-cooled engine thus
develops no leaks, rust, or antifreeze problems peculiar to
conventional cars. Any time, summer or winter, day or night,
the VW stands ready for anything.
```

In this revision, none of the listless verbs appear. No change in point of view mars the paragraph's coherence. No weak use of the passive confuses the reader.

Occasionally, you will find it necessary to use some of the listless verbs. Fine! As long as you don't overuse them to the point that your writing becomes boring. A good rule to follow is: *Change any verb that does not draw a picture.*

EXERCISE

Change all colorless verbs in these sentences to stronger, active ones.

1. The tour conductor said that we could not lean over the wooden railing.
2. There is a fat little green pig with roses on his back placed on the dresser.
3. The painter came down the shaky ladder and put his pan and brush down on the floor in disgust.
4. The driver drove his truck down the road, passing cars on the icy road very carelessly.
5. The girl was crying when she said that the police were after her.
6. The teacher could see the chalk dust all over the floor, and some of it was on her desk and some was even on the windows.
7. Sylvia gave a loud cry when she realized that the telephone call was long distance from her sister Laura in New Jersey.
8. Every time one of the carbonated drinks was opened, out came a gush of purple pop with a hissing noise, and I had to put it down and run to keep from getting wet from the spray.
9. Jackson had a stomachache, so he said, and he told us that there were six other leading athletes who had stomachaches, too.
10. We went first to Los Angeles and then went on to Seattle, not getting to the convention until Thursday afternoon.

Examine All Uses of "Who," "Which," and "That"

The overuse of *who, which,* and *that* weighs writing down with deadwood—unnecessary words. These words introduce dependent adjective clauses. Reducing the clauses to phrases almost always results in economy in wording and an increase in interest. Look at this example.

> *Smith's* Guide to Spain, *which was first written over fifty years ago, has gone through nine revisions, of which the latest was in 1978.*

If you drop the first *which* and the first *was,* along with the *of which* and the same listless *was,* you will have a stronger, more economically worded sentence that sounds more direct.

> *Smith's* Guide to Spain, *first written over fifty years ago, has gone through nine revisions, the latest in 1978.*

In the next sentence, the *who* is unnecessary.

> *Jack Jones is a man who calls every trick.*

(Let us assume from his name that Jack Jones is a man. Then strike is a man who, and you have cleared away four words of deadwood. Yet the meaning is intact.)

Jack Jones calls every trick.

In the next sentence, the *that* is unnecessary.

Peterson's poem, "The Way to Heaven," is a poem that needs no explanation.

(As in the previous sentence, delete is a poem that and you have eliminated a weak is and an unnecessary that.)

Peterson's poem, "The Way to Heaven," needs no explanation.

Note the number of *who*'s, *which*'s, *that*'s, listless verbs, and other deadwood in this paragraph.

```
 1        The university catalog can be used to good advantage by
 2     the freshman who is bewildered by university life. It is
 3     revised every year in order that it will be up-to-date.
 4     First of all, there is in this catalog a list of all the
 5     courses which are offered by the university. These courses
 6     are arranged alphabetically by department in order that the
 7     student may choose which courses he wants to take. It is
 8     also from this list of courses of each department that a
 9     degree plan for the student can be devised, which will be
10     within the limits of the regulations of the university.
```

Line 1:
Listless verb, *can be used.*

Lines 2–3:
A *who* followed by the listless verb *is*. Write *freshmen bewildered by university life* and avoid both. *It is* at the beginning of the next sentence and *in order that* need revision. Why not leave this whole sentence out and substitute the one word *current* before *university* in the first line?

Lines 3–4:
Listless verb *will be*. Problem avoided if you delete this whole sentence as suggested. *First of all*. Do not use this expression. If you must use a *first*, be certain you also use a *second*. In any case, delete *of all*. Do not use *firstly* or *secondly* at any time. Eliminate *there is*.

Lines 5–6:
Which followed by listless verb *are* needs examination. Listless verb *are* needs revision. *In order that*. Do not use this phrase; . . . *to allow students a choice of courses* is better here.

Line 7:
Which avoided by the revision suggested for line 5. *It is,* at the beginning of the next sentence, needs to be removed by revision.
Line 8:
Of courses of each department has too many *of*'s. Remove one *of* by writing *of departments' courses.*
Line 9:
Listless verb *can be* needs changing. *Which* followed by listless verb *will be* also needs revising.
Line 10:
Of the regulations of the University. Delete one *of* by writing *of university regulations.*
All lines:
The passive construction in every sentence underlies most of the problems in the paragraph. The active voice usually will eliminate *which, who, that,* and listless verbs.

Here is a revision of the paragraph. Notice the difference in length with the deadwood deleted.

```
    The current university catalog offers help for bewildered
freshmen. It lists all university courses alphabetically by
department, allowing the student, if he follows university
regulations, to choose his own courses and devise his own
degree plan.
```

Look now at a paragraph by Robert Louis Stevenson. Here no *which* or *who* clutters the thought. No overuse of listless verbs deadens it. Some passive constructions appear. Can you spot them? Verbs are italicized.

> These long beaches *are* enticing to the idle man. It *would be* hard to find a walk more solitary and at the same time more exciting to the mind. Crowds of ducks and sea gulls *hover* over the sea. Sandpipers *trot* in and out by troops after the retiring waves, *trilling* together in a chorus of infinitesimal song. Strange sea tangles, new to the European eye, the bones of whales, or sometimes a whole whale's carcass, white with carrion gulls and poisoning the wind, *lie* scattered here and there along the sands. The waves *come* in closely, vast and green, *curve* their translucent necks, and *burst* with a surprising uproar that *runs* waxing and waning, up and down the long keyboard of the beach. The foam of these great ruins *mounts* in an instant to the ridge of the sand glacis, swiftly *fleets* back again, and *is* met and buried by the next breaker.[1]

Three listless verbs appear in this paragraph—*are* in the first sentence, *be* in the second sentence, and *is* in the last sentence, and these are all passive. But these are

[1]Robert Louis Stevenson, in "The Old Pacific Capital," first published in *Frazier's Magazine,* November 1880.

the only listless verbs and the only passive constructions in the paragraph. Notice the preponderance of strong active verbs—*hover, trot, lie, curve, burst, runs, mounts, fleets.* Note also the absence of *which* and *who.*

EXERCISE

Revise the following sentences to eliminate *who, which,* listless verbs, and other deadwood.

1. Larry decided to take the commuter flight to New Orleans, which would get him to Baton Rouge twenty minutes earlier than planned.
2. Pat talked to Lisa, who wasn't interested, about her own plans to go to college, which she thought everyone would want to know about.
3. Michael's father, who had once been a cop, and who knew a lot about drugs, counseled Michael to use common sense and restraint.
4. Sarah and Carol decided to major in engineering, which was contrary to popular opinion, and which their parents had disapproved. They decided to follow their own interests rather than bow to friendly pressure.
5. Joe McCown is the man who contributed all his ranch income to the orphan whom the police found in the house, which was deserted and which no one ever visited.

(NOTE: If you have to use them, how do you decide between *who* and *whom?* It is simple. *Who* and *whom* will be found only in dependent clauses. Remove the clause from the sentence and substitute *he/she* or *him/her* in place of the *who* or *whom.* If *he* fits, then *who* is the correct form; if *him* fits, choose *whom.* (Use the same method with *she* and *her.*) For example, in the fifth sentence *who* is found in the clause "who contributed his ranch income." If you try both *he* and *him* in place of the *who* you will find that only *he* will fit properly: *He contributed his ranch income.* So *who* is correct here. *Whom* is found in the clause "whom the police found." You will find that only *him* can be substituted for *whom: The police found him.* So *whom* is correct in this clause. If the subject is plural, substitute *they* for *who* or *them* for *whom.*)

6. The choice which was made was between Michael and him, neither of whom had any experience in typing, which was required of the person who was to be employed. (Is this *whom* correct?)
7. There is no reason for the president, who is Patricia Harter, to take offense at the motion, which is aimed at electing a vice-president, who is to help her with her duties.
8. The story, which was exciting, was about a campus murder, which occurred at an Eastern school, and which involved a secret affair between a coed and her teacher.
9. *Oliver Twist,* which is a novel by Charles Dickens, was made into a musical, which was titled *Oliver,* which starred a cast of incredible children and character actors.
10. Geoffrey Chaslin, who played the lead in *A Man for All Seasons,* which is a play about Sir Thomas More, visited London last year in order to become better equipped to play the role.

**Get Rid of Deadwood—Trite Expressions, Exhausted Phrases,
Wordiness**

Through constant use, some words simply wear out. The experienced reader
dislikes them, the immature writer often thinks they're great. Trite expressions and
exhausted phrases often create wordiness—deadwood that usually can be cut out.
You probably recognize these tired phrases: *holding the bag*, and *work like a dog*. But
certain combinations of ordinary words also have become trite:

not only . . . but	and so forth
like mad	proved to be
such as	first and foremost
the following	each and every

Here's the kind of writing created by the uncritical use of these expressions:

```
     He not only started weeping like mad, but also gave me a
list of items to buy for the party, such as the following:
party hats, confetti, horns, and so forth. These things proved
to be so much fun that we had a ball.
```

Trite words and lazy expressions lead to deadwood. So do exhausted phrases of all
kinds. An exhausted phrase is just that—worn out from too much use. But often
it is also just a lazy expression, stuck in by the writer unthinkingly. Usually you can
either eliminate these lazy, worn-out phrases or replace them with a single, strong
word. Each sentence below contains at least one exhausted phrase, in boldface for
emphasis. Avoid them and others like them.

Due to the fact that *I had gained too much weight in the past month,
I turned down his invitation to dinner. (Always substitute* because *for
due to the fact that. It works every time.)*

This apathy has spread over the **entire world.** *(Why not just* world?*)*

Our **ever-growing population** *will be a problem in* just a few short
years.

To this rule I was no exception.

We crossed the street **in order** *to avoid meeting him. (We crossed the
street to avoid meeting him. Always delete* in order.*)*

In this fast-moving world, *the scientist must* keep abreast *of
technological advances.*

In this land of ours today, *no one can really be a* **rugged individualist.**

So for many years to come *we will feel the effect of Watergate.*

Yes, truly it can be said that *young people today are rebellious.*

Ours is becoming a **push-button society.**

Texas Avenue will soon reach the limit of its capacity, **as far as traffic is concerned.** *(A particularly poor one)*

These tired expressions take up valuable space without adding anything to the thought. Avoid them *like the plague* (another one).

The following lists give you examples of several kinds of deadwood. Learn to eliminate or replace these exhausted expressions.

TRITE EXPRESSIONS

tough as nails	hard as a rock
the bottom line	nerves of steel
all part of the game	holding the bag
work like a dog	never say die
sly as a fox	busy as a bee
slippery as an eel	dry as a bone
on the line	each and every
for the most part	stubborn as a mule

WORDINESS: EXHAUSTED PHRASES

EXHAUSTED	BETTER
due to the fact that	because
in order to	to
of great importance	important
in the event of/that	if
make contact with	phone/write/call
it is the belief of	believes
in spite of the fact that	because/since
despite the fact that	because/since
at all times	always
during the time that	while/when
will you be kind enough to	please
in the very near future	soon (or, specify a time and date)
in a hasty manner	hastily
with reference to	about/concerning
without further delay	at once (or, specify a time and date)

at the present time	now/presently
in most cases	usually
in all cases	always
on the grounds that	because
we would like you to	please
until such time as	until
for the purpose of	because

WORDINESS: REDUNDANCY, REPETITION

REDUNDANT/REPETITIOUS	DIRECT, STRONGER
stunted in growth	stunted
exactly identical	identical
consensus of opinion	consensus
if and when	if (or when)
my personal opinion	my opinion
in today's modern world	today
true facts	facts
absolutely complete	complete
absolutely essential	essential
each and every one of us	each person/everyone
basic fundamentals	basics (or fundamentals)
he is five years of age	he is five
in this day and age	today

Here are wordy sentences using some of these trite, exhausted expressions. Very quickly think of how to make each direct and stronger.

> *In today's modern world, finding out the true facts in foreign affairs becomes increasingly difficult.*

> *I am writing for the purpose of updating our information. Would you be kind enough to give this matter your full thought and consideration?*

> *It is the belief of everyone who was involved that during the time that we were away someone broke in for the purpose of robbery, despite the fact that we had taken full and complete precautions.*

You should now be ready to do Exercises *A* and *B*, which follow.

EXERCISES

A. Pick out all trite and exhausted words and phrases in this paragraph.

> Yes, truly the American way is the one which is best
> suited to serve the needs and desires of the people of this
> far-flung world of ours today. Even if one of the various and
> sundry philosophies which oppose our way of life were to win
> out and conquer our country as well as all others, there are
> various means through which we could make a comeback. We could
> pull the rug out from under our enemies by stirring up a
> hornet's nest of far-flung, ever-increasing destruction of
> enemy material, that is, as far as their supply lines are
> concerned--trains, airplanes, and so forth--so that they would
> not have a leg to stand on, as far as fighting us is concerned.
> It would, therefore, prove to be the case that in order to keep
> us under their thumb, our enemies would have discovered that
> they have bitten off more than they can chew and would be
> facing an impossible task.

B. Rewrite these sentences to remove exhausted words, phrases, and wordiness.

1. In view of the fact that our process is absolutely unique, a patent should be obtained as soon as possible.
2. I would like you to get in touch with me in the very near future.
3. In order to assist you in purchasing this absolutely essential repair kit, let us recommend the following time-saving procedures.
4. The bottom line in the classroom is efficient study techniques.
5. When the going got tough, Lisa decided to turn the job over to Pat, who has since avoided her like the plague.
6. I'm writing for the purpose of getting this show on the road.
7. In the event of fire, all persons in the building should vacate the premises without further delay.
8. Will you be kind enough to do the exercise carefully?
9. This special service costs the sum of $35.00 per month.
10. We sat under the sheltering arms of the gnarled old oak, at which point in time I noticed that she had clearly suffered the ravages of time.
11. Each and every one of us must do their duty.
12. In this modern day and age, we must all do our utmost to conserve energy and be responsible members of the community at large.
13. In view of the fact that you are already a week late, you must turn in your research paper without further delay.
14. At twenty-three, Lisa isn't getting any younger. Time waits for no one.
15. In my personal opinion, I believe that the reason for failure is due to the fact that students are not sincere and earnest. They fail to give thought and consideration to their assignments.

Avoid Forcing Your Reader to Love It

If you grow too enthusiastic about your subject, you may stretch the credibility of your readers. By making excessive statements intended to convince them of the worth of your subject, you are, in effect, attempting to force them to fall on your side. These sentences do just that:

Horseshoes is a delightful game that can always be enjoyed by everyone, young and old. (Maybe horseshoes is delightful, but there is no *game that everyone will always enjoy).*

There's nothing as exciting as a good football game. (To some people there may be activities that are considerably more exciting—reading a book, for instance.)

Irma's Last Love *is the most fascinating book ever written. (To the writer, but perhaps not to the reader.)*

No one will regret making this trip into the depths of Devil's Canyon. (Not even someone who slips and breaks a leg on the descent?)

The point: Don't tell your readers how wonderful something is; make them *feel* it through the quality of your writing. Then you won't need to tell them.

Avoid Using Nouns as Adjectives

In most sentences, nouns serve as *subjects* and/or *objects* (completers). In the subject position, the noun says what the sentence is about. In the object position, the noun completes the meaning of a verb or verbal. Using nouns as adjectives can create clumsy constructions:

the gasoline and diesel fuel tax increase bill (why not call it "the bill to increase the tax on gasoline and diesel fuel"?)

in an election year, avoid new revenue enhancement measures (no new taxes)

food service operation (is it a restaurant?)

individual need satisfaction (what does this really mean?)

government consumer protection act (an act to protect consumers?)

Consumer Product Safety Commission (this arm of the government assaults English with "consumer product safety regulations control")

Many nouns serve efficiently as modifiers: "*deer* crossing," "*game* plan," "*traffic* control." But other short-cuts are questionable: "*audience* effects," "*curriculum* unit" (course?), "*science* knowledge," "*expansion* and *utilization* plans." If the *noun modifier short-cut route* doesn't help clarify meaning, avoid it.

Do Not Preach

"Preaching" usually takes the form of moralizing in writing. Rarely do readers want a lecture on what their moral positions should be or on what they should believe.

If you present convincing evidence, you will not have to state the moral conclusions for the reader. Look at these examples of student moralizing.

> *Young people should try to understand their parents.*
>
> *If we all love our country, no foreign ideology can ever take us over!*
>
> *Everyone should strive to live a more moral life.*
>
> *Students, awaken! We must not let our sacred traditions be taken away from us.*

Examination of these "preachy" sentences discloses the use of certain words that make the sentences preachy. These words divide naturally into two classifications.

1. FALSE WORDS

always	everything
ever	never
every	nobody
everybody	no one

When you use these words without qualification you say something about everyone or everything in a class. Almost no conclusion about everyone or everything can be valid. You can write that everyone must die some day or that everyone has been born; but otherwise, someone, somewhere, proves the exception to most statements about *all* people. (Note that this last sentence did not say that someone proves the exception to *all* statements about all people.) The ridiculousness of using these words becomes apparent when you see a sentence such as this one:

> *Everybody always likes everything about every film that Hitchcock makes, and no one ever criticizes his techniques.*

2. COMMANDING WORDS

Such words as *must, ought to, should,* and *had better* demand obedience to the writer. Such admonishment is more likely to make the reader resentful of your ideas than receptive to them.

Avoid Stilted Wording and "False Tone"

When writers try to impress their readers by using big words and flowery phrases inappropriately, they create stilted writing. They go out of their way to make a simple statement complicated by using longer words and more words than the thought warrants. The result is lack of communication because ideas are obscured rather than clarified by the clutter of words. Look at these examples and their simplifications:

The consumption of alcoholic beverages among the younger generation is escalating. (Young people are drinking more.)

Felicitations on the auspicious occasion of your natal day. (Happy birthday.)

I desire to pen my memoirs. (I want to write an autobiography.)

He matriculated with the earnest desire to graduate in three years, but due to certain problems that presented themselves, he was forced to accept a grade of failing in two courses of study and finally found it necessary to withdraw from two others, which left as a remainder only one course, on which his instructor awarded him a grade of C−. (Although he wanted to graduate in three years, he failed six courses, dropped three, and barely salvaged three in his first semester.)

You can frequently improve the "false tone" created by certain words simply by substituting stronger, one-syllable equivalents. Supply stronger substitutes for the words in this list.

assist	utilize
demonstrate	discontinue
permit	transmit
inquire	endeavor
procure	purchase
indicate	sufficient
terminate	encountered
ascertain	employs

What, for example, would you do with the following sentences to eliminate the "false tone"?

Please permit me to assist you by demonstrating the proper procedure.

We endeavor to ascertain the truth and to utilize it in creating public confidence.

I purchased sufficient food for the picnic.

EXERCISE

Revise moralizing, stilted wording, and "false tone" in these sentences.

1. Our company would like to assist you by demonstrating the proper procedure for auditing the financial records which you have sent us.
2. If you want to utilize the computer to its fullest, you must discontinue the practice of using the typewriter to type your papers and endeavor to learn all the word-processing procedures.
3. Permit me to assist you and demonstrate the proper use of this machine.

4. If you can ascertain the true facts in the situation, your initial task will be to procure sufficient money and material to construct the structure.

5. She has the ability to discuss at length any topic of conversation that is introduced, despite the fact that she sometimes is less than expert in the field under discussion.

6. His employment was terminated due to the fact that his employer felt that an excessive number of hours per day were being spent in other than gainful pursuits.

7. We would like to suggest that you purchase the engine parts without further delay.

8. In my experiments, I endeavored to ascertain the truth and to utilize it in the full and complete report I have attached for your consideration.

9. The consumption of alcoholic beverages among the younger generation is apparently escalating upward.

10. If you will be kind enough to provide a topic outline with your research paper, I'll try to ascertain the effectiveness of the organization in the paper.

11. We are in disagreement with our clients, and we have encountered sufficient discrepancies in purchase procedures to warrant the actions taken.

12. And so in conclusion, let me say that each and everyone of us should strive in unison to extirpate from our society the evils of drug abuse.

13. The dearly loved one passed away on Tuesday last, survived by her grieving husband and children.

14. We are writing in reference to your company's desire to participate in our new developmental program.

15. Inasmuch as inflation has elevated our costs, we are not in a position to purchase additional material at this time. We shall employ every method possible to get moving again. You can be sure that you will hear from us in the near future.

Avoid "Fine Writing"

Some beginning writers believe that a fancy and elaborate style is elegant. Be warned that it is not. For instance, a freshman English student had difficulty understanding why her instructor marked her down when she wrote the following:

> *Lush, well-maintained grounds combine with the harmonic grace of the buildings to give a deep majestic glow to the grounds. Flying everywhere, beautiful birds lend their melodious tones, while squirrels flit from tree to tree, chattering ecstatically.*

In trying to be artistic, the student said nothing. English instructors usually call this "fine writing," and they are not giving it a compliment. A good rule to follow is this: Write briefly, plainly, and sensibly. Don't put on airs or use flowery words. Say what you mean. Be direct.

Avoid Unessential "ly" Words

Most "ly" words are adverbs and modify verbs or adjectives. When used to modify verbs, "ly" words often allow authors to deaden their writing by selecting listless verbs instead of searching for strong active verbs to make their writing more specific. For instance, you could write "He ate voraciously," but "He gobbled his food" draws a better picture. Sometimes the "ly" words are unnecessary, as in these sentences:

I have completely exhausted my supply. [Delete *completely.* If you have exhausted it, it is exhausted. There is nothing more to say.]

There was really no reason for his success. [Delete *really.* It is a filler word, as are most of the "ly" adverbs.]

His remarks were truly nonsense. [Delete *truly.* If they were nonsense, that is all there is to it. Another word used as a filler.]

Here are some "ly" words you probably should avoid. Check your papers to be certain you don't overuse these words.

absolutely	positively	truly
completely	purely	undoubtedly
extremely	really	unfortunately
fortunately	surely	unquestionably
hopefully		

Avoid Vague Words

Like some exhausted or lazy phrases, vague words are those the writer uses from habit, or without thought, as substitutes for specific words with exact meaning. Vague words carry little meaning because they are general. For instance, this sentence says nothing: "The many different factors involved created various problems for many people." This sentence communicates nothing specific to the reader and there is no point in writing it.

Here is a list of vague words to avoid. When you are tempted to use one of them, mark it out and select a more specific term.

a lot	factor	many	pretty
aspect	field (of)	much	provide
characteristic	innumerable	nice	several
consideration	interesting	people	thing(s)
contains	item	pertains	variety
deal	large	phase	various
different	lots of		very

Most beginning writers have to make a special effort to avoid the words on this list, but eventually the effort will pay off. Remove these words from your vocabulary. Otherwise, you may end up saying nothing, as did the students who wrote these sentences:

There are lots of ways to consider making a living.

There are many and various sweaters to be made in all sizes and colors.

The many different aspects of socialized medicine are interesting.

INTENTION AND AUDIENCE: TONE

As the heading to this section suggests, tone has to do with the intentions of the writer as found in the finished work and as perceived by readers (audience). Another way of looking at tone is to think of it as the writer's "voice"; in your papers it is your "voice" as your readers hear it, and it may not be the "voice" you intended at all. Once you freeze a word on paper, it loses much of the added power it would normally have if you spoke it. For example, try to *hear* how each of the following would *sound* if spoken according to the instructions given:

1. Good bye. (firmly, straightforwardly)
2. Good bye. (softly, almost with fear)
3. Good bye. (whispered, with love)
4. *Good bye!* (loudly, meaning "get lost")
5. Good *bye*. (loudly, to people at a distance)

Not everyone would say these in exactly the same way. Still, it's obvious that a writer loses some "voice power" when he puts his words down on paper. An added problem, too, is that readers may not hear what a writer intends. We read into

Source: By permission of John Hart and Field Enterprises, Inc.

things, we hear what we want to hear. Inexperienced writers often try to supply this missing intention by using adverbs excessively (as you learned earlier in this chapter).

You can see, then, that tone involves the three-part relationship represented in the diagram on page 351. The diagram suggests that you, as the writer (sender), need to decide on the tone or "voice" you will try to project in your paper (message); then you must make sure it is this tone that accompanies your message to the reader (audience). In the classroom, the reader (usually your instructor) will let you know that he "understands" and "agrees"; or he may disagree with you, and ask you to add more factual support. With published papers the information returning to the writer (through sales, criticisms, personal comment, perhaps) is less certain.

Tone is related to changes in the sound of the voice in speech, where it is

INTENTION AND AUDIENCE – TONE

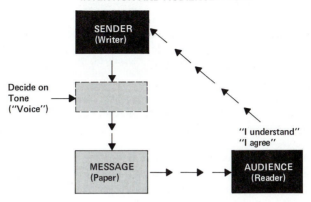

usually easy to spot the speaker's tone as approving (or disapproving), serious (or humorous), personal (or impersonal), direct (or sarcastic), formal (or informal), calm (or excited), and so on. It is the projection of this tone into the written work that helps a writer control the reader's attitude toward the ideas presented. If you recheck the section on introductory paragraphs, you'll find that you already know much about tone—how to get the interest of readers, how to get them to accept you and your ideas (see pages 120 to 127). Study and apply this definition of tone:

> *Determined by the writer's attitude toward subject and audience,*
> *tone consists of those qualities in a work through which a writer hopes*
> *to create a specific feeling in and get a specific response from the*
> *reader.*

"Qualities" implies logical thought as well as the psychological appeals used to create reader interest and to get reader acceptance. And since the "qualities" in question must be conveyed by words, they must be your starting point in controlling and projecting the tone you want your reader to hear. If, for example, you wanted your writing to project a tone of *seriousness,* you would use informal language and humor only with caution, or not at all. Similarly, a work can't be *personal* in tone if its language is too formal and technical.

This chapter has already shown you many ways inexperienced writers unknowingly create an undesirable "false" tone by using passive voice, listless verbs, too many adverbs, trite expressions, "fine writing," and *who* or *which* constructions that lead to "deadwood." In the following illustrations you'll see that in each the writer has tried to create a specific tone, carefully maintained throughout the work. To shift tone can damage or destroy unity, since a consistent tone helps hold the thoughts together. The comments on each selection point out some of the qualities of *thought* and *diction* that help create its specific tone. Also, all are introductory paragraphs, chosen because a writer must establish tone and interest at once if he is to keep his readers moving into the work.

A.

> Of all the *enemies* of mankind that have ever existed upon the face of the earth, there are some that simply *do not deserve* to be here. Ranked third in the all-time top ten *worst enemies*, just behind the *devil* himself and the *notorious snake*, is the cockroach. This *disgusting* little insect far exceeds his nearest competitor, the mosquito (who, for the sake of *those who may be curious*, could manage only an eighth-place finish behind such *powerful contenders* as *rats, buzzards, lions*, and *piranha*) because of his superior size and strength, and his *too-horrible-for-words* appearance. The cockroach should be *wiped out* at CCU because he is an eyesore, he *interferes* with one's learning, and he is a *hazard* to one's health.

Even a quick check of the italicized words in this paragraph reveals a negative tone: *enemies, worst, notorious, disgusting, horrible, eyesore*. This student clearly dislikes cockroaches; the controlling attitude of the thesis is that this insect "should be wiped out," and the paper develops the reasons pointed to in the rest of the thesis statement. But there is more to the success of this paragraph than a clear statement of disapproval. How, for example, has the student prevented the passage from becoming too serious? Do you think this passage would be as effective if both the subject and the tone were serious? The writer maintains the tone of playful seriousness throughout the paper with such comments as: "one of the little monstrosities galloping across the room," "he may be seen a few feet away just sitting and staring," "squatting in the corner surveying the situation," and "converge upon him armed with sticks, shoes, books, chairs." Professional humorists are well aware that exaggerating little things usually creates humor; do you think this student has carried exaggeration too far?

B.

> I am a gun nut, I suppose. My father made me a gun nut. He taught me how to shoot, and ever since what I would really rather be doing than anything else is shooting at small, innocent birds.[2]

You could never tell from introductory Paragraph *B* that Stewart Alsop is seriously attacking computerized bureaucracy. There is no thesis statement at the beginning, only a calculated tone of sarcastic playfulness created at once by the first sentence. The first sentence of the second paragraph echoes this tone: "To the non–gun nut, this may seem as mysterious as the nuttiness of the young does to the middle-aged." Maintaining his tone, he leads the reader surely toward the thesis (about halfway through) with the following statement: "What, indeed, you gonna do? So I took off most of an afternoon to be fingerprinted for J. Edgar Hoover's files, a messy and demeaning business." Only in the next-to-last paragraph does he give his reader a thesis:

> But surely there is a better way. Surely it is better to go to the root of the evil. Invention should have halted with the flush of the toilet a century ago—what sensible

[2]Stewart Alsop, "A Call to Revolt," from *Newsweek*, December 22, 1969. Copyright Newsweek, Inc., 1969. Reprinted by permission.

man has a good word to say for the ballistic missile or the bomb, or even for the automobile, and the airplane? But the worst invention of the lot was the computer.[3]

But the tone of sarcastic playfulness persists, partly because of exaggeration and partly because readers can't be expected to remain wholly serious as they read about the "flush of the toilet." Notice, too, that the first-person "I," used throughout, disappears in this paragraph. Why has the writer left it out?

C.

> When I hear about some *flagrant violation of human rights* in a far-flung place on the globe I react violently as any free, red-blooded American does. I get filled with righteous indignation. I get stirred. I get—*I get nervous is what I get.*[4]

Example *C* is the introductory paragraph to a short political article on the tense peace in the Middle East. Again the author chooses to withhold this thesis and concentrate on getting the reader interested and sympathetic. Aside from the personal "I," how does Goodman Ace keep you smiling as he heads toward a rather serious comment on peace? What is the effect of the contrast between the two comments in italics? The rest of Ace's article illustrates that *serious* commentary *can* be made while using a humorous or sarcastic tone—a difficult art, perhaps best illustrated in some of the writing of Jonathan Swift.

A main function of the "I" in Paragraphs *B* and *C* is to create a personal tone that can readily be turned into playfulness. Properly used, the "I" usually adds a feeling of first-hand observation; but it can be used to gain interest for very serious observations without the sugar-coating of humor seen in these first paragraphs. Here are some examples.

D.

> *A few mornings ago* I rescued a bat from the swimming pool. The man who owned the pool—*but did not own the bat*—asked me why. That question *I do not expect ever to be able to answer,* but it involves *a good deal.* If *even I* myself could understand it, *I* would know what it is that seems to distinguish *man* from the rest of *nature,* and why, despite all she has to *teach* him, there is also something he would like to *teach* her *if he could.*[5]

Paragraph *D* begins a fairly long paper on nature, the individual, and the species. The author concludes that nature has a "passion for mere numbers," disregarding individuals, and that some men have also become too "careful of the type" and too "careless of the single life." Only when the readers reach the last two paragraphs of the paper do they fully see the author's main point. In what ways does the author

---

[3]Alsop, "A Call to Revolt."

[4]From "Peace is Hell," by Goodman Ace. Copyright 1967 by Saturday Review Co. First appeared in *Saturday Review,* August 5, 1967. Used with permission.

[5]From *The Desert Year* by Joseph Wood Krutch. Copyright 1952 by Joseph Wood Krutch. Reprinted by permission of William Morrow & Company, Inc.

try to keep the paper from becoming too formal? What might you conclude about this writer's intention and tone from the italicized words? How does he create reader interest? How does the writer get you to think of him as serious, thoughtful, and questioning?

E.

> *A couple of years ago* I became involved on a panel for the Western Psychological Association which was about *something called* "The Psyche of a Scientist." It turned into a *kind of* psychodrama because *here were* all these psychologists, sociologists, and anthropologists, but I was the only *real live* scientist. The *tribe* I belong to is called biochemistry, which is sort of a subgroup in the *pecking order* of science somewhere below physical chemistry and above geology. And what *I* was listening to was a fantasy, or, *you might say,* the results of a *con job* by the *natives* on some *poor hapless explorers* who did not understand the *terrain* at all.[6]

The author of Paragraph *E* is beginning an outspoken attack on certain practices in the "science jungle," concluding (several pages later), "Until we become aware of these evils of big science we cannot hope to eradicate them." Judging from the words in italics, what would you conclude about the tone of this introductory paragraph? How many of the following descriptive terms would you use to identify the tone: *impersonal, objective, personal, formal, informal, casual, serious, direct, indirect, sarcastic.*

F.

> *I feel* that this award was not made to me *as a man*, but to *my work*—a *life's work* in the *agony and sweat* of the *human spirit*, not for glory and least of all for profit, but to create out of the materials of *the human spirit* something which did not exist before. So *this award is only mine in trust*. It will not be difficult to find a dedication for the money part of it *commensurate* with the purpose and significance of its origin. *But I would like* to do the same with the acclaim too, by using this moment as a pinnacle from which *I might* be listened to by the young men and women already dedicated to *the same anguish and travail*, among whom is already that one who will some day stand here *where I am standing*.[7]

In this famous address William Faulkner concludes that "man will prevail." He has chosen a moment of triumph to call for action. The tone he projects might be called "urgent"—a bid for attention in a time of need. How many personal "tags" can you discover in this paragraph? What is the effect of words like *travail,*

---

[6]From "The Science Jungle" by Paul Saltman in *Harper's Magazine*, February 1967. Copyright © 1967 Harper's Magazine.

[7]William Faulkner, "Nobel Prize Acceptance." Reprinted from *The Faulkner Reader*. Copyright 1954 by William Faulkner (Random House, Inc.).

commensurate, anguish, human spirit? Comment on the nature of the "ethical appeal" here. (See pages 120 and 123 for additional information.)

G.

> The School System has much to say these days of the virtue of reading widely, and not enough about the virtues of reading less but in depth. There are any number of reading lists for poetry but there is not enough talk about individual poems. Poetry, finally, is one poem at a time. To read any one poem carefully is the ideal preparation for reading another. Only a poem can illustrate how poetry works.[8]

The thesis statement at the end of introductory Paragraph *G* asserts firmly what this poet-critic will be discussing. Although the "voice" you hear is authoritative, it doesn't have quite the sense of personal argument that most of the previous paragraphs have. Of all the paragraphs, it is probably the most clearly *expository*, setting up a thesis and then supporting it in a fairly long paper. The writer decides to use the personal "I" very sparingly (there are only two or three, and they appear later in the discussion). Does he write in a way to create interest? What is the effect of the *parallelism* and *antithesis* in the first two sentences? (See page 105 for some hints.) Although there is no "I" in the paragraph, could you call it "impersonal"? Why not? (See page 69 for some comments about challenge and strength in thesis statements.)

To summarize. The questions to ask yourself when thinking about tone in a work include at least the following:

1. What specific response does the writer want from the reader? "I understand"? "I agree"? "I sympathize"?
2. How does the writer create interest?
3. What kind of person does the writer sound like? An authority? An objective commentator? An involved participant? A lively human being? Educated?
4. Are the words strong and expressive or weak and colorless? Is their effect "negative" or "positive"? Personal or impersonal?
5. Are the sentence patterns simple or complex? What effect do they have on the tone?
6. How serious is the thought presented? Is there any attempt to tone down the seriousness with humor or sarcasm?

If you look back at the diagram on page 351, you should see immediately how these questions apply to your writing and to the decision you make *before* you begin writing. The diagram shows that you, as writer, decide on the "voice" or tone *before* you begin to write the paper. If you are clear on "who you are," how serious, how informal, how personal, how assertive, you should be able to carry this attitude into the paper itself, giving it the *unity of tone* a good paper must have (see the two lightly shaded areas in the diagram).

---

[8]John Ciardi, "Robert Frost: The Way to the Poem," *Saturday Review,* April 12, 1958. Copyright 1958 by John Ciardi. Reprinted by permission of the author.

EXERCISES ON TONE

A. Here is a simple exercise that will make you aware of some of the limitations most of us have when we grab words from our vocabularies in a hurry.

Begin by looking at these words you probably learned before you first went to school. Check them quickly and decide their meanings:

arm   finger   worm   spoon   dish

You probably thought of them as nouns (names of things), just as you first learned them. But these "childhood words" can become strong *tone verbs* (words denoting action) if you think about them. For example: *Arm* yourself with strong verbs; don't *finger* your hair that way; he *wormed* his way into her affections; *spoon* out the ice cream generously; can you take it as well as *dish* it out?

Here is a list of "childhood words" classified into a number of obvious groups.

Animal Associations		Body Parts		Common Household Objects		Professions
ape	monkey	arm	palm	bed	pan	author
badger	paw	back	rib	book	paper	butcher
bug	pig	elbow	shoulder	box	pen	coach
claw	rat	eye	skin	chair	pencil	doctor
dog	snake	finger	toe	collar	pocket	engineer
feather	skunk	foot		cup	sheet	nurse
fox	weasel	hand		dish	spoon	pilot
hog	whale	head		fork	table	tailor
horse	wing	knee		ink	tap	tinker
hound	worm	neck		knife	wall	tutor

Notice the groups and their associations—with body parts, common animals, clothing, and other objects around the house, and professions. You'll need these words to complete this exercise. Begin by reading over the entire list to see if your mind is noun-centered as you check each word. All the nouns in the list can also function as verbs. Now, choose nouns from the list to function as VERBS in the following sentences as you rewrite them to make them stronger and more direct. (You may use colloquial or slang expressions if you wish.)

> *Example:*   Sarah *served as head* of the committee.
>   Sarah *headed* the committee.

   1. The man slowly pushed his way through the crowd.
   2. They supplied the men with guns.

3. The thief stuck the cashier with a knife and then put the money in his pocket.
4. Zeba nervously played with her pencil.
5. Carefully, Andy darkened the lines of the sketch with ink.
6. The bear tore a hole in the tent wall with its claws.
7. He tried to talk his way out of mowing the lawn.
8. Will you give me your support in the election campaign?
9. Mike looked at the girl smilingly before approaching.
10. "Stop repeatedly annoying me!" she cried furiously.
11. Agnes made a pig of herself at McDonald's.
12. Agnes selfishly took half the table to herself.
13. The sliding mud had built up a wall across the narrow gorge.
14. Agnes acted as chairperson for the meeting on weight control.
15. Maria gave Juan private instructions in algebra.
16. He tore part of the skin from the knuckles of his right hand.
17. The nurse slowly put the needle in his pocket when no one was looking.
18. Tom quickly hid his cheat notes in the palm of his hand.
19. After arranging the chocolates in the box, Agnes hungrily looked at them.
20. We won the basketball game against CCU by a huge score.

B. Come to class prepared to discuss *denotation* and *connotation*. In what ways are these important clues to tone? (Recheck Exercise C on page 191.)

C. Look again at Exercises C and D, pages 212 and 213. Using Exercise C as your model, write three different paragraphs on one of the subjects listed for you in Exercise A, page 152. Your instructor may want you to repeat the assignment with other topics to practice creating tone. (You'll find additional illustrations in Chapter 1, pages 6–7.)

REVIEW EXERCISE

Test your knowledge of this chapter by revising these sentences to improve clarity, directness, and tone.

1. Our expansion and modernization plans are proceeding on time, as scheduled.
2. You have two major problems to face. These are: (1) finding the necessary material, and (2) getting the money to purchase it.
3. I would like you to obtain for me a duplicate copy of the invoice which is dated 2 March 1924.
4. Our management has recognized the necessity of completely eliminating the undesirable vegetation surrounding the periphery of the facility.
5. The consumption of alcoholic beverages among the younger generation is apparently escalating upward.
6. Despite the fact that he laid his reputation on the line and worked like a dog, he found little support for his reelection.
7. Because all the true facts could not be ascertained and no decision had been reached by the Impeachment Committee, the President was allowed to keep continuing his defiance.
8. It is of very great importance to all that each and every one us observes consumer product safety regulations.
9. It is the belief of everyone who was present during the time the accident occurred that bad weather was the chief cause.

10. It is pretty difficult to provide completely accurate information and to make an analysis of the problem if various phases of the research are not unquestionable.

11. This city will soon reach the limit of its capacity as far as traffic is concerned unless a lot of consideration is given to implement solutions.

12. Tough as nails and hard as a rock, with nerves of steel, Superman came swiftly to the rescue of his fellow human beings.

13. Once you have purchased all the absolutely essential equipment, we would like you to get in touch with the head office.

14. It was decided by the principal that all students who were given make-up exams would be required to take the final exam, which was scheduled to be given immediately after classes that afternoon.

15. With reference to health safety regulations and requirements, all staff members must employ utmost precaution at all times during the day.

16. On the other side of the ledger is the fact that he was driving like crazy when the accident occurred.

17. Grace sold the book which had been given to her last Christmas in order to buy a ticket to Gainesville, which is where she had taken a new job.

18. The tall oak tree, which had replaced the scrubby hackberry tree, lost all its leaves and turned sick, which worried Lisa, who had done all she could to keep our old homestead attractive and pretty.

19. Before accountants write their financial reports, many writing problems have to be solved by them. These include planning, development, organizing, and writing, all of which precede the production of the report itself.

20. Suddenly Grace spotted Andy. She shouted furiously to attract his attention. She waved her hat. Andy kept right on going.

11

Revising Your Paper: Sentences

More than any other animal, humans seem to need to communicate with each other. They build complex communities requiring a subtle mixture of freedom and control. They invent machines, buildings, and ideas in response to their environment. They develop elaborate social systems and governments and territories that play on the harmonious interaction of natural hostilities. Cities, skyscrapers, computers, planes, love, democracy, country, war—without an efficient, effective communication system, these products of human labor wouldn't be possible. If you think about it, you'll discover three basic ways people communicate:

1. Through physical touch—a handshake, a pat on the back, a kick in the shins
2. Through body movement in space—pointing a finger, smiling, winking, nodding the head
3. Through visible and audible symbols—words and sentences, written and spoken

The subject of this book has been *written* communication—a complete paper, paragraphs, words, sentences.

But you've already seen from the discussion of tone in the previous chapter that one major problem is to make the written message represent the "voice" you have in mind and—equally important—to make sure that readers of your message understand what you want them to in thought and tone. The tone of voice, the wave of the hand, the pat on the back are absent in the sentences you write. One aim of sentence revision, therefore, should be to compensate for the loss of these in written communication; another is to create sentence patterns that give the most important ideas the strongest position.

SENTENCES IN GENERAL

Good sentences aren't born automatically. Not for anyone. They are created, with patience and skill, out of the accumulated knowledge of many years, out of the thoughts, feelings, words, and word patterns you *have available to you*. But unless you—and, in fact, anyone who wants to improve writing skill—consciously study how to improve, you may find that what is "available to you" are only the simple sentence patterns of your childhood. This chapter will help you recognize these basic patterns and improve them, and encourage you to experiment with them to gain new strength and emphasis.

You already know much about sentences. *Length,* for example. Short sentences move fast. Long ones, on the other hand, tend to move somewhat more slowly toward their final destination. You need both in your writing, and you need to know when to use them. You know also that there are many *kinds* of sentences, depending on how you classify them:

1. Grammatically—simple, compound, complex, compound-complex
2. Rhetorically—loose, periodic, balanced
3. Functionally—question, command, statement, exclamation

Why so many "kinds"? Each performs a specific job in communication. Because of their structures, some keep the reader involved by withholding the full meaning until the end of the sentence (as this one has done). Others make their point at once. Still others balance part against part, meaning against meaning. The five sentences immediately preceding this one, for example, illustrate five kinds. Which are they? Using different kinds of sentences gives your writing *variety* and prevents monotony. You can gain variety in sentence patterns in four basic ways: (1) *balance* (which you learned about on page 105 in the chapter on coherence); (2) *inversion* or unusual word order, a pattern different from the one a reader might expect; (3) *repetition* of phrases or clauses for effect, for emphasis; and (4) *omission* of certain words supplied by the sense of preceding passages. (Meaningful sentence fragments are an example: "How do you feel?" "*Sick.*") Most of the material on revision in this chapter can be studied under three broad headings just discussed: *length, kind,* and *variety.*

THE SIMPLE SENTENCE

One traditional definition of the sentence is that it's *a group of words containing a subject and a verb and expressing a complete thought.* Because this pat definition doesn't always fit, modern grammarians cautiously add qualifications. Perhaps the best definition says that *a simple grammatical sentence is an independent unit of expression consisting of a subject area and a predicate area.* To be "independent," the sentence must express a complete thought. But even single words like *help* and *incredible*—without proper "subject areas"—can be considered sentences when properly capitalized and punctuated.

Sentences come in all *lengths:* minute, medium, and mammoth. The sentence "unit of expression" can vary from a single word to more than a hundred. In English some of the most effective sentences are brief. For example, the shortest verse in the Bible, *Jesus wept,* expresses in its context more feeling and emotion than a longer sentence might. Similarly, Shakespeare controls the last words of the dying Hamlet: "The rest is silence." But sentences can also be indigestibly long. Very long sentences, however, are used infrequently and only for a special effect not easily conveyed by a series of shorter sentences. Here's how Hemingway tried to recreate the feeling of a bullfight in 151 words.

> Cagancho is a gypsy, subject to fits of cowardice, altogether without integrity, who violates all the rules, written and unwritten, for the conduct of a matador but who, when he receives a bull that he has confidence in, and he has confidence in them very rarely, can do things which all bullfighters do in a way they have never been done before and sometimes standing absolutely straight with his feet still, planted as though he were a tree, with the arrogance and grace that gypsies have and of which all other arrogance and grace seems an imitation, moves the cape spread full as the pulling jib of a yacht before the bull's muzzle so slowly that the art of bullfighting, which is only kept from being one of the major arts because it is impermanent, in the arrogant slowness of his veronicas becomes, for the seeming minutes that they endure, permanent.[1]

Because readers don't like to follow long involvements, professional writers tend to avoid these mammoth sentences. Most newspaper writers, for instance, prefer shorter units of thought, sentences cast for the most part in normal, expected English word order. Readers can recognize such sentences almost automatically.

Lewis Carroll, the author of *Alice in Wonderland*, recognized this fact long ago when he wrote the nonsense poem "Jabberwocky":

> *'Twas brillig and the slithy toves*
> *Did gyre and gimble in the wabe;*
> *All mimsy were the borogoves,*
> *And the mome raths outgrabe.*

Even though you don't know what *toves* or *borogoves* look like, or what *brillig* and *slithy* mean, you can still easily recognize that this verse is made up of English sentences. You can spot these unknowns as parts of speech: *brillig, slithy,* and *mome* are obviously modifiers (adjectives): *toves, wabe, borogoves,* and *raths* are nouns: *gyre, gimble,* and *outgrabe* are verbs.

Any group of nonsense words arranged in the patterns of English sentences can be recognized as sentences, as long as articles and prepositions are real. Look at these different sentence patterns using nonsense nouns, verbs, and verbals.

> *The junbig cranned a biglou.*
> *A biglou was cranned by a junbig.*

[1]Reprinted with the permission of Charles Scribner's Sons from *Death in the Afternoon* by Ernest Hemingway. Copyright 1932 Charles Scribner's Sons; renewal copyright © 1960 Ernest Hemingway.

Cranned by a junbig was a biglou.
After cranning a biglou, the junbig
  zlon up the donnen.

Each line represents a recognizable English sentence pattern. The first uses the basic word order of all English sentences, the normal SVC pattern (see also Chapter 9, page 286). Can you identify the patterns in the other lines?

SUBJECT AREA	PREDICATE AREA	
The boy	hit	the ball
ACTOR	ACTION	GOAL
Subject	Verb	Completer
S	**V**	**C**
1	2	3

A grammatical sentence normally has to have at least two of these parts—a subject area and a predicate area with a verb. Though the subject may be omitted if it's understood (as with *you*), the verb usually may not.

[You] *Get the book from the shelf.*

"What shall I get?" "The book, from the shelf."

Although the second group of words in the second example has no verb, it could very well project a complete thought if the context is conversational and clear. Normally a grammatical sentence expresses only *one* complete thought. If it has more than one, it's probably not *unified*. It won't point in one direction only, but in as many as there are topics in the sentence. For example:

My car broke down twice on the way to the campus, and I spent all day
Monday at registration.

Here two complete thoughts in two independent clauses have no clear logical relationship with each other. In effect, they point in different directions. Because this sentence has two independent, *unrelated* thoughts, it isn't a good one.

On the other hand, a group of words with a missing or incomplete thought is usually considered an unacceptable sentence fragment.

We arrived at 8:00 o'clock. Before the game started.

The first of these is independent, a complete thought; the second isn't. *Before* signals that this second group is a dependent unit (clause) and that somehow it must be made to stand alone or be tied to a complete and independent statement. Here the solution is easy: simply add the second unit to the first and replace the period with a comma:

We arrived at 8:00 o'clock, before the game started.

It could, of course, be tied to a new independent clause:

Before the game started, we bought peanuts.

Now look at these two groups:

He preached against three sins. Cards, whiskey, and tobacco.

The second group, made up of three nouns and one conjunction, has no predicate area and, therefore, no verb. Alone, it's an incomplete thought; tied with a colon to the preceding independent statement, it makes sense:

He preached against three sins: cards, whiskey, and tobacco.

You'll find a complete discussion of sentence fragments on page 295.

EXERCISE

Try your hand at spotting which of the nonsense word groups are complete sentences. Write *F* for fragments, *C* for complete sentences.

1. The junbig cranned a biglou.
2. The junbig cranning a biglou.
3. After the junbig had cranned a biglou.
4. There is the biglou the junbig cranned.
5. Since cranning a biglou, which was done by the junbig.
6. A biglou was cranned by the junbig.
7. The biglou being cranned by the junbig.
8. The biglou cranning junbig.

Emphasizing Words and Ideas in a Sentence

If placed in strong positions within the sentence, ideas and words gain emphasis. In English sentences using normal SVC word order, the opening and closing positions are usually most emphatic. Look again at this simple SVC sentence:

Actor	Action	Goal
The boy	hit	the ball.

The most important words in this sentence are in the most important positions. *Boy* (the actor) and *ball* (the goal) are the important key words. In this normal SVC pattern, the key words are in the emphatic positions. The end position can be considered stronger, however, because words and ideas in that position are usually those the reader sees last. Last seen, therefore last remembered.

This diagram illustrates the relative importance of these three (SVC) sentence positions.

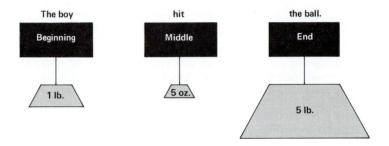

The three sentence positions have been arbitrarily assigned weights to suggest relative importance. The beginning position has been given a weight value of one pound; the middle position, five ounces; and the strong end position, five pounds. Now, by applying these weight values to the key words in a sentence, we can assign a weight to the whole sentence to indicate the strength of its emphasis. Look at this group of sentences.

1. However, *she* was an excellent *cook.*	5 lb., 5 oz.
2. *She* was an excellent *cook,* however.	1 lb., 5 oz.
3. An excellent *cook she* was, however.	1 lb., 5 oz.
4. *She* was, however, an excellent *cook.*	6 lb.
5. An excellent *cook,* however, was *she.*	6 lb.

In the first sentence, *she* in the middle position, gets a weight of only five ounces. *Cook,* in the end position, gets a weight of five pounds. Altogether, the whole sentence has a value, then, of five pounds, five ounces. In this sentence, one of the important positions, the beginning of the sentence, is taken by the unimportant word *however,* suggesting that this transition word might be better buried in the middle of the sentence. The second has even less emphasis. *She* is in the beginning position for one pound; *cook,* the other key word, is lost in the middle position and can be assigned an importance of only five ounces. The whole sentence, then, has a weight of only one pound, five ounces. In the third sentence, the position of the key words is reversed, and the value of the sentence remains the same as for the second sentence.

The fourth sentence, however, has a different arrangement. *She* is in the beginning position and weighs one pound, whereas *cook* is in the end position and weighs five pounds. The whole sentence weighs six pounds, more than any other so far considered. The reason for this is that the two key words come in the two important sentence positions. Note that the transition word, *however,* is in the middle position where it does not detract from the impact of the sentence on the reader. The fifth sentence also puts the key words in the important positions, but the difference is that the positions have been switched. The sentence emphasis remains the same on the surface because it is assigned the same weight as the fourth sentence. But the two sentences differ considerably.

The fourth sentence is in normal English word order, the basic SVC arrangement of sentence parts we ordinarily use in writing. The fifth sentence reverses the arrangement, and the very oddness of this switch makes it more emphatic if it appears in a context of sentences arranged in the expected SVC order. Only occasionally would you rely on a sentence like the fifth one—only when you want an unusual emphasis on the sentence. Although sentence variety is important, most of your sentences will probably follow the basic SVC pattern of the fourth sentence.

The Periodic Sentence

In any writing, the most powerful position for an idea—the one that gives it most emphasis—is usually at the end. In this respect, a sentence is no different from any other piece of writing. *The power spot in the sentence is at the end.* The main idea in a sentence, then, should come logically in this power spot. A sentence withholding its main idea until the end is called *periodic.* Look at this sentence:

Just as he bent over to tie his shoelace, a car hit him.

Here, the main idea, *a car hit him,* is at the end. Certainly the other idea in the sentence is less significant. In periodic sentences, important modifiers precede the independent SVC pattern; in loose sentences the modifiers come after the independent SVC pattern.

The Loose Sentence

More common in English, the *loose* sentence ends with a dependent sentence element—a subordinate element or a modifier. Rearranging the sentence just used as an example produces a loose sentence:

> *A car hit him,* just as he bent over to tie his shoelace.

The main clause (the independent SVC pattern) containing the main idea comes first in the sentence, whereas the subordinate element (the dependent clause) is at the end. Take care to keep the main idea in the main clause. If you don't, sentence emphasis goes askew. In this sentence, for instance, the insignificant idea is the main clause, and the main idea is in a dependent clause:

> *He bent over to tie his shoelace, just as a car hit him.*

The first part of the sentence is the main clause; the second part, the dependent clause. Such a sentence has no logical emphasis.

Here are more examples of loose and periodic sentences; the main idea (the independent SVC pattern) is italicized in each.

> *(Periodic) Having passed his house every day and knowing that it had been unoccupied for years,* I was surprised to see smoke coming from the chimney.

> *(Loose)* I was surprised to see smoke coming from the chimney, *because I had passed his house every day and knew that it had been empty for years.*

Periodic sentences build suspense to gain emphasis for the main idea. If the main idea is held to the last in the sentence and modifying elements are built up in the first part of the sentence, real suspense can be achieved to make the main idea hit the reader with force. For instance, a simple sentence of this type makes little impact on the reader:

> *The old woman fainted.*

But we can add a dependent element before this sentence, make it periodic in tone, and increase its impact:

> As confetti showered her head, *the old woman fainted.*

We can increase its impact even more by adding another dependent clause:

> As the laughing crowd swirled around her *and as confetti showered her head, the old woman fainted.*

To heighten the impact yet further, add another dependent element:

> As the band blared louder, *as the laughing crowd swirled around her, and as confetti showered her head, the old woman fainted.*

This type of period sentence is not as natural to the English language as it is to the modern Germanic languages. Most English sentences are loose in structure. That is, they are likely to be "strung" along with dependent elements at their end. They don't build to their point as the illustrative sentence above does. In English, the best sentences, then, are *periodic in tone but loose in structure.* You can achieve a periodic tone in three ways:

1. Suspending the subject
2. Suspending the verb
3. Suspending the complement

To suspend an element, delay its appearance in the sentence.

1. Suspending the subject.   Here's a sentence, simple in structure and English in word order:

> *The man hurried down the street.*

Here the subject is *man.* To suspend this subject and give the sentence a periodic tone, delay the point where it appears in the sentence. Just add simple adjective modifiers before the subject:

> *The* gray-haired old *man hurried down the street.*

Or you can add adjective phrases modifying *man:*

> Limping on his wounded foot, *the gray-haired old man hurried down the street.*

You can suspend this subject even further by adding another phrase:

> *Limping on his wounded foot and* staggering from side to side, *the gray-haired old man hurried down the street.*

The sentence now has become periodic in structure as well as in tone. You can change the structure by adding modifying elements at the end:

> *Limping on his wounded foot and staggering from side to side, the gray-haired old man hurried down the street* **littered with tin cans and shattered glass.**

2. Suspending the verb.   Using the same sentence and the same modifiers, you can delay the appearance of the verb in the sentence and create a periodic tone:

> *The man* **hurried** *down the street. (verb boldface)*

> *The man,* **old and gray-haired,** *hurried down the street. (modifiers boldface)*

> *The man,* **limping on his wounded foot,** *hurried down the street. (modifiers boldface)*

> *The man,* **limping and staggering,** *hurried down the street. (modifiers boldface)*

3. Suspending the complement.   In this same sentence, you can also suspend the complement. The phrase *down the street* is not actually a complement in the strictest sense. It is not a noun construction but an adverbial prepositional phrase. The word *complement* is used to mean a completer of the verb. *Down the street* fits this definition. Here it is suspended:

> *The man hurried* **down the street.** *(complement boldface)*

> *The man hurried* **limping and staggering** *down the street. (modifiers suspending the complement boldface)*

Caution: You can overdo suspension. If you suspend every SVC element in the sentence, the subject, verb, and complement can become too separated for quick understanding. Similarly, try not to separate any two SVC elements enough to interfere with the easy flow of thought. In the following sentence, for example, the student put too much space between the verb and its completing thought:

> *Chris attempted, even though his foot hurt him so much that he staggered as he ran, to reach the rifle.*

In this sentence, the verb *attempted* and the completer *to reach the rifle* (a verbal phrase) are separated by a long dependent clause. The resulting clumsy sentence is so involved that readers can forget the verb before they reach the completer. (If you have trouble with the grammatical terms in this section, review pp. 287–88 on sentence components.)

The Periodic-Loose Sentence

Consider these two sentences:

> *The ball soared toward the goalposts, which were fifty yards away from the kicker's toe. It wobbled end-over-end, but arced high and true.*

Because both sentences describe the same action, they can be combined easily into one. The second can be reduced to two modifying phrases and worked into the first, and the first sentence would be improved by deleting the *which*. As the independent, basic SVC clause in the sentence, take this one:

> *The ball soared toward the goalposts.*

Now, suspend the subject *ball* and the verb *soared* by adding modifying elements to the basic SVC pattern.

> Arcing high and true, *the ball,* wobbling end-over-end, *soared toward the goalposts fifty yards away.*

Or, you can suspend the verb and the complement with these same modifiers:

> *The* ball, wobbling end-over-end, *soared* in a high and true arc *toward the goalposts fifty yards away.*

These last two sentences are periodic-loose sentences because they have a periodic tone through the suspension of two sentence elements in the basic independent clause. The structure is loose because of the modifier *fifty yards away* at the end of the sentence.

EXERCISE

Your teacher may ask you to review pages 287–88 before doing this exercise. From each group of sentences, make one sentence by suspending two elements in the independent, basic SVC clause (italicized in each group).

1. *Bertha labored to secure bait to hook.* She winced as the worm tried to escape her uncertain grasp, and she hoped none of the other fishermen noticed her squeamishness.
2. *Ralph transported his aching jaws straight to the dentist's chair.* He held himself aloof with his shoulders erect as he marched through the reception room.
3. *The car coasted to a stop.* Its motor was dead. It bumped on one flat tire. It was long, shiny, and black.
4. *The legislature finally revoked the law.* The law had been impossible to enforce because the people held it in contempt. The legislature met in special session.

5. *The puppy barked at the cat.* He pranced and dodged back and forth. He was an excited puppy. The cat spat and hissed at him.

6. I hesitated for two weeks before making my choice, but I finally decided to attend Florida State University. *I think I made the best choice.* I had to choose between Florida State and the University of Dallas.

7. *Fleance broke up the rehearsal.* He entered from stage right. His wig was askew and his mascara was running. Lady Macbeth had just urged the assembly to "Take seats."

8. *The children giggled and cavorted.* They chanted "The one-eyed flea keeps bugging me." They marched out of step and ill-aligned.

9. The English teacher looked the Salutatorian straight in the eye. She was angry. *She said, "When you chose that topic for your research paper, I told you it wasn't worthy of you."* The Salutatorian was embarrassed and crestfallen.

10. *Grandfather inched up the stairs.* He grasped the handrail with one hand. He leaned on his cane with the other. He firmly planted both feet on each step.

SECONDARY SENTENCE PATTERNS: COORDINATION AND SUBORDINATION

So far in this chapter we have dealt mostly with one type of sentence—the simple sentence with normal SVC order and phrase or single-word modifiers for one or more of the elements. We have been dealing with this pattern:

I see the puppy. (S . . . V . . . C)

The idea expressed is approximately on the first-grade level and appropriate for a primer. But educated writers need to communicate more complicated ideas than this sentence pattern can express. For this purpose, English provides secondary sentence patterns. The two most useful types of secondary sentence patterns are:

(1) coordination (the simplest) and (2) subordination.

Coordination

Coordination is joining together similar grammatical constructions with a connecting word called a *conjunction*. In its simplest form, two or more nouns or two verbs or two modifiers, for instance, can be joined by the conjunction *and*.

Chris and Jane	read and write	swiftly and silently
bacon and eggs	happy and carefree	apes and monkeys and chimpanzees

Signal words for coordination (conjunctions), Group 1:

and	for	or	yet
but	nor	so	

Conjunctions in this group can be used to join *equal* grammatical structures only. That is, they can join together two independent clauses, two noun clauses, two prepositional phrases, two participles, or two of anything, as long as they are the same grammatically. They cannot join together, however, an independent clause and a dependent clause.

Caution: Group 1 signal words, especially *and,* are sometimes inappropriately used to string sentences together. This relatively short sample uses *and* four times:

> *I asked Dad for the car* and *then I picked up the corsage* and *got my date,* and *we went to the dance* and *had a wonderful time.*

Although this sentence does have coordination, it defeats the purpose of coordination. Certainly there are no complicated ideas here that could not be expressed in the simplest sentence pattern.

Signal words for coordination, Group 2:

also	furthermore	meanwhile	otherwise
anyway	hence	moreover	still
besides	however	nevertheless	then
consequently	incidentally	next	therefore
finally	indeed	nonetheless	thus

These signal words are used as conjunctions *only* to join two independent clauses. Often called *conjunctive adverbs,* they can function as adverbs or conjunctions.

To illustrate the use of this group of conjunctions, here are two sentences (two independent SVC patterns):

> *Marriage and hanging go by destiny. Matches are made in heaven.*

Because these two are connected in idea, they can be joined grammatically into one sentence in at least three ways:

1. Treat them as independent clauses (SVC patterns) and connect them with a coordinating conjunction:

> *Marriage and hanging go by destiny,* but *matches are made in heaven.*

The Group 1 conjunction *but* is appropriate here because it signals a *contrast* in ideas and correctly coordinates two independent SVC patterns.

2. Use a Group 2 conjunction (a conjunctive adverb) simply to coordinate the two independent SVC patterns:

> *Marriage and hanging go by destiny;* however, *matches are made in heaven.*

3. Join the two SVC patterns without using a conjunction if you want to emphasize the coordination and the close relationship:

Marriage and hanging go by destiny; matches are made in heaven.

PUNCTUATION OF COORDINATE ELEMENTS

Perhaps as much as 60 percent of your punctuation problems can be solved by knowing the Group 1 and Group 2 conjunctions and by understanding how they work.

1. Group 1 conjunctions *(and, but, for, or, nor, so, yet)*, when they join two independent clauses (SVC patterns), take a comma before them. See the diagram below.

(Independent clause)		(Independent clause)
_____A_____ ,	but	_____B_____ .

2. Group 2 conjunctions (*however, then, thus,* for instance) join two independent clauses together with a semicolon, in this way:

(Independent clause)		(Independent clause)
_____A_____ ;	thus,	_____B_____ .

3. Two independent clauses may be joined without a conjunction if a semicolon separates them:

(Independent clause)	(Independent clause)
_____A_____ ;	_____B_____ .

For additional information on punctuation, study pages 305–15.

EXERCISE

Supply the best mark of punctuation in the blanks of these sentences.

1. Great-grandfather would not refrain from chewing his noontime wad of tobacco _____ nor would great-grandmother give up dipping snuff, no matter how often we complained.

2. Santa brought Robin three dolls, a swing set, a CompuChron watch, and a plug-in refrigerator _____ but Bobby seemed satisfied with his new socks and corduroy jeans.

3. The veteran scholar took her first degree in the history and literature of Persia _____ the next step was to master the Arabic language.

4. From 6:00 to 10:00 in the evening he supplemented his income by teaching local teens to bowl _____ so for eighteen hours a day he was on somebody's payroll.

5. Just before school opened, Old Hat found her way to Rita's doorstep _____ and before Thanksgiving, Jet wandered in _____ then, on Easter Sunday morning, the cat they call Peeps made it a threesome.

6. Sandra seemed to sense that her partner held the trump ace _____ yet she deliberately underbid the hand.

7. No one claims that the red rambling roses are more attractive than the New York Pinks _____ I simply state that they are a showier flower.

8. Yupon and poison sumac grew on the upper ten acres _____ elsewhere over the ranch grew mesquite and huisache.

9. She tried first tape, then glue, and finally staples _____ however, Frances's Man in the Moon shadow box fell apart before fifth period.

10. The young wife insisted that air conditioning in that two-room west-side apartment was essential _____ her husband called her an extravagant simpleton.

11. If students live in Duncan Hall, or Dorms 11, 12, or 13, their laundry problems are solved _____ if they live in Milton Square or close to the Quadrangle, they practice the do-it-yourself system.

12. Bill bought shares in two local banks and spent two weeks fishing in Mexico _____ therefore his parents assumed that he could scrape by without further loans from them.

13. Mrs. Anderson embroidered icon after saintly icon _____ but she would not part with one of her collection, although they lay yellowing in the trunk of heirlooms in the parlor.

14. Six, seven, and eight come first _____ eleven comes somewhat later.

COORDINATE ELEMENTS IN SERIES

When more than two coordinate elements appear together, they are a series. Any three or more *equal grammatical elements* can appear in a series—nouns, verbs, participles, noun clauses, prepositional phrases, or any part of a sentence. This sentence shows verbs in a series:

Cathy ran, skipped, *and* jumped.

This one has three noun clauses in a series:

Herb never stopped to consider that the weather was not favorable, that the boys did not want to go, *and* that the highways would be too crowded for comfortable travel.

1. When coordinate elements are used in a series, a comma separates each element from the others. The two sentences just used as examples illustrate this punctuation. It may be diagrammed this way:

(First element)	*(Second element)*		*(Third element)*
_____A_____ ,	_____B_____ ,	*and*	_____C_____ .

The comma before *and* between the second and third elements is commonly left out. This practice is acceptable as long as the reader has no chance of assuming that the last two elements are linked together to the exclusion of the first.

2. The coordinate elements in a series must be parallel (that is, the same grammatically). The elements here are boldface:

Jessie did the job **quickly, competently, *and* hardly working at all.**

In this sentence, three adverbs are supposedly in a series; but one element in the series is not an adverb. This can be seen in a diagram.

Jessie did the job —
—*(1) quickly*
—*(2) competently*
and
—*(3) hardly working.*

The third element will have to be changed to make it parallel with the other two; that is, it must be grammatically the same. This sentence makes that change:

Jessie did the job —
—*(1) quickly*
—*(2) competently*
and
—*(3) easily.*

Jessie did the job quickly, competently, and easily.

Or look at this sentence:

The instructor told them to study Chapter IV, to make notes on it, *and* that they would have a quiz next period.

A diagram will expose the elements in this sentence that are not parallel.

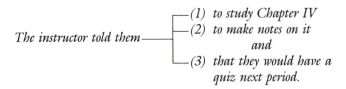

The instructor told them —
—*(1) to study Chapter IV*
—*(2) to make notes on it*
and
—*(3) that they would have a quiz next period.*

The first two elements of the series here are infinitive phrases (that is, *to* plus a verb plus a noun), but the third element is a noun clause (with *that* as the subordinating conjunction, *they* as the subject, and *would have* as the verb). Because these elements are not the same grammatically, the third element must be changed to make it an infinitive phrase starting with *to* plus a verb.

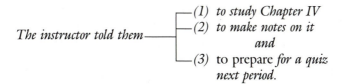

The instructor told them to study Chapter IV, to make notes on it, and to prepare for a quiz next period.

Here is a different one:

Although not many of the class went, those who did found the lecture heavy, dull, and the acoustics in the lecture hall adequate, although not everything could be heard.

Although this sentence appears to have a series of three, in truth it does not, because it has two subjects—*lecture* and *acoustics*. Look at this sentence in diagram form:

Although not many of the class went,

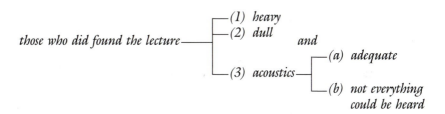

Acoustics (a noun) is not parallel with *heavy* and *dull* (adjectives), nor can these three be changed to make them parallel. But the sentence can be improved by making *lecture* parallel with *acoustics* (both nouns).

Although not many of the class went,

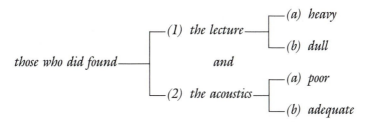

Although not many of the class went, those who did found the lecture heavy and dull, and the acoustics in the lecture hall poor but adequate.

All coordinate elements in a sentence must be clearly grammatically parallel, whether there are more than two elements or only two. Sometimes a fuzzy parallelism will confuse the reader temporarily, as in this sentence:

> *The lawyer begged that the accused be judged insane and committed to a mental hospital.*

Momentary confusion may result here because the reader may want to insert *be judged* before *committed*, because apparently *insane* and another adjective are being joined by *and*. A diagram illustrates the possible confusion.

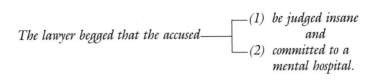

The solution is simple: The parallelism is made clear if *be* is put before *committed*, as well as before *judged*.

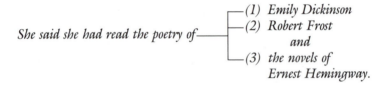

> *The lawyer begged that the accused be judged insane and be committed to a mental hospital.*

This sentence is similarly confusing:

> *She said she had read the poetry of Emily Dickinson, Robert Frost, and the novels of Ernest Hemingway.*

Here the writer has tried to create a series of three coordinate elements, but there are only two. Look at a diagram of this sentence as the author wrote it:

She said she had read the poetry of——
- (1) *Emily Dickinson*
- (2) *Robert Frost*
  and
- (3) *the novels of Ernest Hemingway.*

Obviously, *Emily Dickinson, Robert Frost,* and *the novels* are not parallel. *Poetry* and *novels* are, however. Here's a better construction for the sentence:

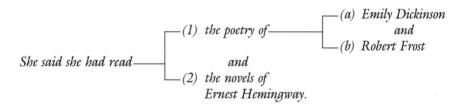

She said she had read the poetry of Emily Dickinson and Robert Frost, and the novels of Ernest Hemingway.

The comma is placed before the second *and* for clarity. Otherwise the reader might expect the material following *Robert Frost* to be a third element in a series. The comma specifies that it is not.

Here is another example of faulty parallelism:

His musical career, unlike most students who played in the band, continued after he left high school.

The fault here is one of logic. Careers and students are being compared, but they cannot be compared. It is like trying to make a comparison between apples and wood splinters; they have nothing in common. So they can't be made parallel in this way. A diagram of this attempted parallelism looks like this:

His musical career   *(1)* ⎯⎯⎯⎯⎯⎯
            unlike   ⎯⎯⎯⎯⎯⎯ *(continued)* . . .
    most students   *(2)* ⎯⎯⎯⎯⎯⎯

This sentence can be made logical and parallel:

His musical career   *(1)* ⎯⎯⎯⎯⎯⎯
            unlike   ⎯ *(continued)* . . .
the musical careers *of most students*   *(2)* ⎯⎯⎯⎯⎯⎯

Now careers are compared to careers, and the sentence is logically parallel. But a substitute, a pronoun for *career*, is more suitable than repeating the noun so soon after it first appears. The sentence then looks like this:

His musical career, unlike that of most students who played in the band, continued after he left high school.

EXERCISE

Correct any nonparallel elements you find in these sentences.

1. He studied the grouping of the stars in their constellations and how close Saturn is to Pluto.
2. The desk had a scratched top, a sticky drawer, and one leg wobbled.
3. Slicing away at the Winesap and whistling as he pared, Eric knew that the first cucumbers were already spoiled on the vine, how he would have to rebuild the chick roosts tomorrow, and his son had asked him twice to repair his toy truck.
4. She bought a pound each of nails, woodscrews, and a gallon of red paint.
5. Dr. Payne's tests, like all the other professors', were complex, detailed, and offered great difficulty.
6. Since he had already ruined his chances to recover the money and recouping his loss, Ronald shrugged, grinned, and, turning away, sauntered whistling down the hall.
7. Pete was quite slow in discovering that he had no singing voice, could not act, and his personality did not project well.
8. The gold plastic bracelet from the local dime store, added to Ruthie's talent on the dance floor and appreciating the excellent dance band, made the evening a mad memory.
9. Despite her aversion to seafood and liquor, she ate oysters, catfish, and drank beer.
10. Although the house was dark and because he knew the family was out of town, Manuel went ahead with his plan to repair the television set in the living room and resetting the loose tiles on the kitchen floor.

Subordination

In considering matters of sentence structure, *superior* constructions are independent clauses; they carry the main thought of the sentence and are complete in themselves. Words, phrases, and dependent clauses are *inferior,* or subordinate, because they do not consist of a complete thought; they are used most often as modifiers of some part of the independent clause. Sometimes they are used as the subject or verb or complement in an independent clause. Subordination, then, is changing what might be stated in an independent clause into an inferior or subordinate construction and attaching it to a part of another independent clause. Consider these two sentences:

> *John completed his final examination. Two hours still remained in the examination period.*

One of these independent clauses (independent clauses and basic SVC sentences are the same structurally) can be subordinated to the other and the two combined into one sentence. First, you must decide which idea in the two sentences is the more important, because it should come in the independent clause. Because it appears last, the writer apparently considers the idea of the second sentence the more important. You can subordinate the first independent clause to the second in one of these ways:

> When John completed his final examination, *two hours still remained in the period. (Independent clause reduced to a dependent clause.) Note that the only difference between an independent and a dependent clause is the presence of a subordinating conjunction,* when *in this sentence, at the beginning of the dependent clause. Other subordinating conjunctions are* after, although, as, as if, because, before, if, once, since, that, though, unless, until, when, where, while.

> Upon completing his final examination, *John discovered that two hours remained in the period. (Independent clause reduced to a prepositional phrase.)*

> Completing his final examination, *John discovered that two hours remained in the period. (Participial phrase)*

> His final examination completed, *John discovered that two hours remained in the period. (Absolute construction)*

> *John discovered* upon completing his final examination *that two hours remained in the period. (Prepositional phrase)*

> *John discovered that two hours remained in the period,* although he had already completed the final examination. *(A dependent clause with the subordinating conjunction* although. *The addition of the dependent clause makes the sentence loose in structure.)*

Here is a more complicated example:

> [1]*Our best quarterback was caught stealing CCC's mascot.* [2] *This happened at the beginning of the football season, and so* [3]*he was not allowed to play after the first game,* [4]*thus causing us to lose the championship.*

Written in primer style, this sentence is a string of independent clauses, except that the main point—we lost the championship—is in a participial phrase at the close of the sentence. Because it is the most important idea in these sentences, place this point in an independent clause to give it the most emphasis, and subordinate the inferior material. *This* (at 2) and *thus* (at 4) should be deleted. In this sentence, *this* is a pronoun with a vague reference; it doesn't refer the reader to a single noun, as it should, but to action expressed in the preceding sentence. *Thus* is used here as a conjunction. As one of the Group 2 coordinating conjunctions, it should join two independent clauses. Instead, here it joins an independent clause to a phrase. *Thus* can then be deleted without affecting the meaning of the sentence, creating no structural problem. Here's a revision with the main idea in the independent clause and the others subordinated to it. The ideas are numbered for comparison with the unrevised version.

> *⁴We lost the championship because our best quarterback, ¹caught ²at the beginning of the season stealing CCC's mascot, ³was not allowed to play after the first game of the year.*

In revising, remember to select the main point in your sentences and subordinate all others to it by casting them in dependent clauses, phrases, or single-word modifiers.

EXERCISES

One way to improve primer style—series of short, choppy sentences—is to practice combining groups of short sentences. These two exercises ask you to use your knowledge of coordination and subordination to combine short units into longer, more mature ones.

EXERCISE 1

Combine each of these groups of sentences into *single,* more effective sentences. Use any sentence patterns you want, but decide on a main idea (independent SVC pattern) for each and subordinate the other ideas to it. Here's one example to get you started:

PRIMER SENTENCES

Lisa had a sick dog.
The dog's name was Sampson.
She took her sick dog to the veterinarian.
She said she wasn't worried about Sampson.
The veterinarian said Sampson was suffering from food poisoning.

COMBINED

Although Lisa said she wasn't worried about him, she took her sick dog, Sampson, to the veterinarian, who said the dog was suffering from food poisoning.

A. 1. Nearly every summer night the cooling east wind crept through my bedroom windows.
   2. It made air conditioning unnecessary.
   3. It made a light blanket a warming comfort.
B. 1. The steep mountainsides were covered with snow.
   2. The snow fed several small streams.
   3. The streams raced down the slope and joined in the valley below.
C. 1. The grueling Boston Marathon was finally over.
   2. Lisa Harter crossed the finish line and collapsed onto the road.
   3. She was gasping for breath.

    4. She had pains in her chest.
    5. Her face was red with white splotches.
D. 1. The climber is nearing the mountaintop.
    2. His eyes are shining with triumph.
    3. He climbs faster and faster.
    4. He becomes careless.
    5. He suddenly trips and falls.
    6. He tumbles to the ground.
    7. He lies motionless there.
    8. He is a crumpled pile of legs, arms, and equipment.
E. 1. The IRS came up with a plan.
    2. The plan was designed to make income tax filing easier.
    3. At least for lower-income people it would be easier.
    4. The IRS sent out forms and instructions.
    5. The instructions are longer and more complex than the forms.

Combine the sentences in groups *F, G,* and *H* into a single unit of three or four sentences that might serve as the beginning of a paragraph:

F. 1. I was editor of CCC's *Star Trek Fanzine.*
    2. The fanzine is published by CCC's Science Fiction Club.
    3. The fanzine is published weekly.
    4. I was responsible for collecting Star Trek news.
    5. I was responsible only for information about Spock.
    6. I presented the information in a column.
G. 1. In each issue I concentrated on one Spock quality.
    2. I highlighted the quality in the title of each column.
    3. One column concentrated on Spock's physical appearance.
    4. Another column concentrated on Spock's mental abilities.
    5. One column concentrated on Spock's Vulcan background.
    6. I wrote a different Spock column each week.
H. 1. The longest Spock column I wrote was about his mental ability.
    2. One week I concentrated on a number of important mental qualities.
    3. It described Spock's ability to join other minds in a "mind meld."
    4. It also described Spock's computer-like ability to calculate.
    5. It described Spock's incredible memory.
    6. It described Spock's ability to block out pain.

EXERCISE 2

Make one sentence from each of the following groups of sentences. Cast the main idea in an independent clause and subordinate all other material.

1. It was dark and the night was cold and rainy. Zeba started cautiously down the path. It was slippery and clogged by roots and weeds.
2. The chair had one broken leg. It was old and its upholstery was tattered. It collapsed with Pete when he sat in it. A loud noise resulted.
3. The secretary ripped the paper from the typewriter roller. He gave a sharp exclamation and slammed his pencil on the desk.
4. The gringos crowded the Mexican streets. They all appeared overfed. They were all underdressed. They were making a noise.

5. The book lay by the window. The window was open. Wind flipped and tore the book's pages. The pages had been soaked with rain.

6. The university rates high scholastically. It has a library of four million volumes. Its teachers are internationally recognized. Its students are the best from quality high schools.

7. The American elk is a relative of the red deer of other continents. Its scientific name is *Cervus canadensis* of the family *Cervidae*. It is occasionally attacked by cougars. It is hunted by men everywhere.

8. They had loved their home. It had three bedrooms, a sun parlor, and impeccably kept gardens. But now the Church Street School had been built across the street. It housed the first graders who could not be accommodated in the old elementary school.

9. Jamie waltzed proudly around the floor. The hem of her stylish, black-sequined dress had come loose in two places. A lock hung limply from the back of her upswept hairdo. People were tittering. She did not know all this, of course.

10. Larry was only three-and-a-half when it happened. He can still remember Uncle Gene shooting the largest elk the state had recorded. The elk stood five feet, nine inches tall. It weighed 1,100 pounds.

STYLE

Style is the last of the major rhetorical subjects discussed in this book (the other two are organization and discovery). By now you are probably aware that nearly everything you have studied to this point is in some way related to style. The ideas you discover to write about, for example, may not be original; still, *how* you use them, what you decide to include or to omit, what illustrations you use as support—these may very well be original, and, because of this, have something to do with what we call style. Similarly, the organization you choose for these ideas is also probably your own, unlike the organization someone else might use for the same set of ideas. In revising diction and sentences, again the *choices* you make will probably distinguish your writing from that of others. *How* you decide to get your reader interested, *how* you create a tone or "voice" that will win your reader, are probably your own too. For no two writers solve the same communication problem in the same way. The resulting differences in the works may be explained as a matter of style.

To discuss style means trying to separate *what* is said from *how* it is said. Strictly speaking that's not possible. But for purposes of discussion it's useful to think about *the message* and *how it is sent* as if they were separate. Look at the following sentences:

1.

That such a life is likely to be ecstatically happy I will not claim. But that it can be lived in quiet content, accepting resignedly what cannot be helped, not expecting the impossible, and thankful for small mercies, this I would maintain. That it will be difficult for men in general to learn this lesson I do not deny. But that it will be impossible I will not admit since so many have learned it already.

Because this writer chose to use balance for his sentence patterns, he has given the passage a special effect (see page 105 for a discussion of parallelism, antithesis, and coherence in this passage). You notice it immediately because the word order is unusual; you know it's unusual because it departs from the "normal," expected pattern, *subject–verb–complement*. You notice, too, that he uses no simple, loose sentences; all are periodic and complex. Another writer might have done it differently:

2.

> I will not claim that such a life is likely to be ecstatically happy. But I would maintain that it can be lived in quiet content, accepting resignedly what cannot be helped, not expecting the impossible, and being thankful for small mercies. I do not deny that it will be difficult for people in general to learn this lesson. But I will not admit that it will be impossible since so many have learned it already.

Version 2 carries exactly the same meaning as the first; yet the *effect* is different. The "expected" word order moves the reader quickly to each main point: "I will not claim . . . ," "I would maintain . . . ," "I do not deny . . . ," "I will not admit. . . ." The effect is one of directness and strength. Version 1 *suspends* each main statement, making the reader wait for it until the end of each sentence. The effect on the reader is probably a "sense of expectation," but this would depend on the kind of ear that was listening. Still, though different readers might argue about the exact effects of the two versions, they could hardly fail to see that they were *intentionally different*. Expected (or unexpected) **word order, directness** of movement and meaning, **heightened reader expectation**—these are matters of style.

But style is also a matter of **sound.** Read Version 1 aloud and listen for the effects that parallel structure, antithesis, and inversion create. Some listeners would say the passage sounded "formal," "heightened," "elevated," perhaps too "contrived." Others might say, simply, that the passage was "hard to read." Their disagreement would be about the effects of writing styles. But if both readers had stored in their memories the same basic sentence patterns, the same vocabularies, the same sounds, they would disagree far less. For judging the effects of differing writing styles depends largely on what a reader has "inside" to use as a sounding board.

Suppose, further, that we altered Version 2 by changing some of the words, still keeping the meaning of the passages the same:

3.

> I won't say that such a life will lead to great happiness. However, I would say that it can lead to contentment and quiet, stoically accepting what can't be helped, not

expecting the impossible, and being thankful for small mercies. I don't deny that people will generally have a hard time learning this lesson. But I will not admit that it will be impossible since many men have already learned it.

The addition of contractions to Version 3 adds some **informality** to the **tone;** simpler balance adds to directness. Most of the word changes increase the informal tone *(say, great, happiness, contentment, hard time)*. The use of *however* plus a comma slows down the movement (compare the sound of "However, I would say . . ." with the sound of "But I would say . . ."). All these choices are also a matter of style. Considering the possibilities suggested by the three versions, trained writers would choose patterns and sounds and words that they felt their *readers would like.* Style, then, also includes **audience consideration.**

You can see that the writing style you decide to use in a particular situation involves many decisions, only a few of which have been suggested in this discussion. What matters most is that you see style as conscious **choice** and realize that there are many solutions to each problem in communication. If, for example, you chose to write all your sentences in the style of Version 1, you would probably lose most readers quickly. Similarly, extended passages in the style of the second or third versions, with all sentences marching forward in the "normal" *subject – verb – complement* pattern, would tend to sound monotonous. One solution to this problem would be to vary sentence patterns and lengths, though variety for its own sake shouldn't be your only aim. A study of style will increase the number of choices available to you and greatly expand the "sounding board" you have "inside." It should also add to your sense of "play" and discovery, for you should become increasingly aware of the power and richness of language. Although you can probably strive for some changes in style in your rough drafts, it is during the careful process of revision that you'll be able to discover the need for stylistic changes.

Style, then, is a matter of **personal choice**—of ideas, of words to carry the ideas, of sentences, of organization, of appropriate tone, of paragraphing. And because it is personal, your style is limited by who you are, by what knowledge and vocabulary you have, and even by the subjects you habitually write about (since they probably will appear repeatedly in your work). In this sense, style *is* the person; your style is *you*. In fact, you already have many writing styles of your own that reflect the limits just described. But just because style reflects your personality does not mean you're stuck with only one way of writing.

Because style is also the result of **conscious choice,** it is something you can therefore improve and change. If you let habit dictate your choice, as many beginning writers do, you'll find yourself tied to the diction and sentence patterns of your earliest training. (Remember the exercise on preschool words? See page 356.) To change your writing habits, however, you will first have to recognize what they are. That means putting to work everything you have learned in this book—as you discover and plan, as you organize and write, and, most important, as you revise. It also means studying the ways in which other writers (students and professionals) use words and sentences to solve their communication problems.

That is the basic approach: *Know your own style,* and *study the styles of other writers.* To summarize,

> *style can be defined as the individual, personal way in which you use your own knowledge and language to present your chosen subject to a specific audience in an appropriate "voice."*

The full implications of this definition are seen in the following check sheet on style; its questions will help you look for qualities in your own style and in the styles of other writers.

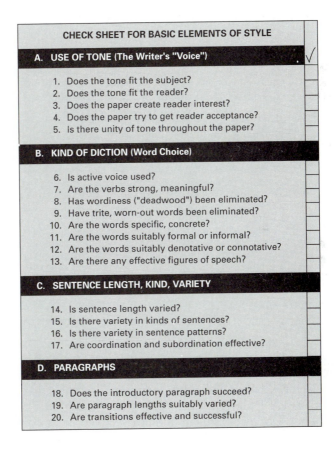

```
         CHECK SHEET FOR BASIC ELEMENTS OF STYLE

  A.  USE OF TONE (The Writer's "Voice")                  ✓

         1.  Does the tone fit the subject?
         2.  Does the tone fit the reader?
         3.  Does the paper create reader interest?
         4.  Does the paper try to get reader acceptance?
         5.  Is there unity of tone throughout the paper?

  B.  KIND OF DICTION (Word Choice)

         6.  Is active voice used?
         7.  Are the verbs strong, meaningful?
         8.  Has wordiness ("deadwood") been eliminated?
         9.  Have trite, worn-out words been eliminated?
        10.  Are the words specific, concrete?
        11.  Are the words suitably formal or informal?
        12.  Are the words suitably denotative or connotative?
        13.  Are there any effective figures of speech?

  C.  SENTENCE LENGTH, KIND, VARIETY

        14.  Is sentence length varied?
        15.  Is there variety in kinds of sentences?
        16.  Is there variety in sentence patterns?
        17.  Are coordination and subordination effective?

  D.  PARAGRAPHS

        18.  Does the introductory paragraph succeed?
        19.  Are paragraph lengths suitably varied?
        20.  Are transitions effective and successful?
```

You should now be able to put this check sheet to work. First, use it to analyze the two student selections below; take notes on each of the twenty questions on the check sheet and be prepared to support and illustrate your impression of the style. Both selections are by the same student writing on the same subject; the difference between them is that in the first the tone is supposed to be "confident," while in the second it's supposed to be "angry and disgusted."

```
                        A. THE FIRST DAY
                       (Tone: Confident)


        Tackling the closed door with her foot, she conquered the
hallway.   It was the noncommittal green used in military
installations.   But most of this color was obliterated by the
thundering herd of students.   The width of the hall was equal
to six students, shoulder-to-shoulder.   The length, about
thirty students.   And the hall held its capacity at this time.
But she made room.   Among the masses, she stood out. Marching
down the hall, heel first, she carried herself with confidence
and authority.
        Similar to Moses, she parted the sea of students, enabling
her to go from the left side of the hall to the right.   She
grabbed for the door. The doorknob was cold and uninviting. She
tried to force the locked doorknob to turn, then finally forced
the slightly ajar door all the way open.


                        B.  THE FIRST DAY
                         (Tone: Angry)


        Ramming the glass door with her foot, she stormed the
hallway.   It was the repulsive light-green used in military
installations. But this color was obliterated by the screeching
mob of students.   The width of the hall could only be measured
in terms of students--six students, shoulder-to-shoulder.   The
length, about thirty students.   And the hall was bursting at
the seams at this time.   Forced to make room, she was caught
up in the sweating, flowing current of bodies.
        Only through struggling and pushing and griping did she
manage to get across the hall.   She grabbed for the door, only
to find the doorknob shockingly cold and uninviting.   She
struggled with the doorknob, only to find the lock frozen and
the door already slightly ajar.   Infuriated by the wasted
effort, she swung the door completely open.
```

Do you think this student has succeeded in creating the two tones? Are there any differences in detail? Compare the verbs in the two versions; are they consistently different? Make a list of the words in each selection that seem to you most appropriate to the tone the student tried to create. Are the sentence patterns similar in both selections? Do you think they should be similar? If you didn't know that both versions were written by the same student, what evidence could be presented to show that they probably were, that they are stylistically similar, despite some difference in tone? Do you think the two passages are aimed at different audiences? Point to specific words or phrases that support your conclusion. How would you change the passages to make them appeal more clearly to two different audiences?

EXERCISES ON STYLE

A. One way to become conscious of sentence patterns unlike your own is to imitate sentences written by others. Here, for example, is a very famous sentence from Henry David Thoreau's *Walden:*

I went to the woods because I wished to live deliberately, to front only the essential facts of life, and see if I could not learn what it had to teach, and not, when I came to die, discover that I had not lived.

Although you should try to match the model in its major parts (phrases, clauses, balance, inversions), you may depart in minor ways, as a student has done in this imitation:

I questioned the system because I wanted to see how it worked, to determine its bad points, and see how effective it was, and then after thorough analysis, propose a system that would work better.

Here are some additional models with student imitations:

Model: *The cat shivered in the barnyard, wet from nosing her way through the dew-filled grass and covered with damp cockle-spurs.*

Imitation: *The woman ran in the race, wet from perspiring at every step and panting with laboring lungs.*

Model: *Disobedience, the rarest and most courageous of the virtues, is seldom distinguished from neglect, the laziest and commonest of the vices.*

Imitation: *Friendship, a rare and marvelous gift, is sometimes killed by hypocrisy, a shallow and worthless imitation.*

Model: *The human species, according to the best theory I can form of it, is composed of two distinct races, the people who borrow, and the people who lend.*

Imitation: *Friendship, as I see it, is based on two concepts, the idea of communication, and the idea of covenant.*

Model: *The apple tree never asks the beech how he shall grow; nor the lion, the horse, how he shall take his prey.*

Imitation: *The professor never asks the department head how he should teach; nor the gambler, the bookmaker, how he should place his bet.*

1. Write imitations of the five models given above (include Thoreau). First write down the model; read it carefully and listen to the sound and the rhythm; then write your imitation of it.

2. Write imitations of the first two sentences in Paragraphs *F* and *G* on pages 354 and 355 (Faulkner and Frost).

3. The following three sentences come from the paragraph by E. B. White on page 186. Write a coherent, three-sentence imitation.

> New York should have destroyed itself long ago, from panic or fire or rioting or failure of some vital supply line in its circulatory system or from some deep labyrinthine short circuit. Long ago the city should have experienced an insoluble traffic snarl at some impossible bottleneck. It should have perished of hunger when food lines failed for a few days.

B. 1. Use the style check sheet to analyze one of your own papers written earlier in the course. Take notes and be prepared to write a one-paragraph commentary on your style.

2. Using the style check sheet as your guide, analyze the style of the first two paragraphs in the section "Sentences in General" (page 360). Take notes. Be prepared to discuss and write about the four major subjects on the check sheet (tone, diction, sentences, paragraphs). If, for example, you think that the tone of these two paragraphs does *not* fit you (the reader), you should try to discover why. What can you discover about the length, kind, and variety of the sentences used?

C. Choose any five of the sentences you write for Exercise 2 on page 381. Rewrite each sentence twice, changing the *kind* of sentence (see page 360 for kinds of sentences) or the sentence pattern; keep the meaning and details of your originals. (You may get some additional ideas by rereading pages 366–69.)

12

The Essay at Work

This chapter provides review exercises that explore the ideas and strategies you have been learning throughout this book. Questions about thesis sentences, controlling attitudes, funnel effects, methods of paragraph development, pointers, writer's voice, tone, and many other important matters are designed to let you discover how far you've come. Following the review exercises, you will find a group of complete essays for analysis, class discussion, and as a source for controversial ideas you may want to explore further.

REVIEW EXERCISES

A.

The following six paragraphs make up the introductory unit of an essay titled "Telepower: The Emerging Global Brain." As you read these paragraphs, look for the "funnel effect"—the controlling focus—in the first paragraph and how it is refocused at the end of the unit.

1   The human use of communications contains the key to the future of our species. The linking of our optical and electronic technologies in new and different ways is not only the key to a new golden age, but a high-risk gamble as well. Our new telepower technologies can make us or break us.

2   The "global electronic machine" is where it all starts. This machine is far bigger than a nuclear aircraft carrier, a C5A cargo jetliner, or even a continuous-process automobile-manufacturing plant. It contains hundreds of millions of tons of coaxial cable buried underground and beneath the oceans. It includes electronic switches and exchange equipment with enough gold and silver to fully stock a large jewelry store.

Parts of the machine are invisible because they are flying in space—orbiting in circles a tenth of the way to the moon. Over a hundred of these space communications devices are relaying billions of messages around the world every year. The parts of the global electronic machine are now so numerous that no one can count them. Billions of telephones, television sets, facsimile devices, telexes, computers, and radios are linked to this massive network. Each year, the colossal machine grows by leaps and bounds as fiber-optic cables, new electronic switches, and new "ports" are added to accommodate more users around the world.

3   The machine is making the global village a reality. Soon, people in remote Tuvalu and Niue in the South Pacific will be able to call Chicago, Toulouse, or Chiang Mai, Thailand. In the 20 years since the moon landing, the number of people able to see global events on television has expanded sixfold from 500 million to 3 billion people. Our ability to share information and knowledge is today creating global trade and culture. Tomorrow, it will begin to form a global brain—a global consciousness.

4   The power of the global electronic machine is already awesome. Just one satellite, the INTELSAT VI, can send 200 simultaneous television channels— enough to send all episodes of *Dallas* and *Dynasty* ever made all at once. It could also transmit about a thousand 300-page books in the span of one second. In short, the global electronic machine, this multitrillion-dollar universal linkage, is very fast and very smart.

5   The many dimensions of our growing telepower will bring us both good and bad changes. On the debit side, it will bring us telewar, technology-based terrorism, technological unemployment, and information overload. Yet, this telepower will also bring hope for high-quality schooling, nutritional advice, and medical services through tele-education and telehealth techniques.

6   Well into the twenty-first century, there can even be hope for the building of a true global consciousness and ultimately for the emergence of a "global brain." Eventually, we may even see the evolution of a new human species.[1]

1. **a.** What earlier idea in the first paragraph is restated in its last sentence?
   b. What is the purpose of the last sentence of the first paragraph? Where can you find this idea restated toward the end of this selection?
2. What is the topic sentence of the second paragraph? What method of development is used in this paragraph? What personal pronoun is repeated to help give the paragraph coherence? To what noun does this pronoun refer? Which word is repeated most often in this paragraph?
3. What is the topic sentence of the third paragraph? What word in this sentence provides coherence through important transition from paragraph two? What is the controlling attitude—the pointer—in this topic sentence? How does the writer support and develop this controlling attitude?
4. What is the topic sentence in paragraph four? What important transition word appears again? What is the controlling attitude—the pointer—in the topic sentence? What method of development is used to make this pointer convincing?
5. What two ideas are echoed in the topic sentence of paragraph five? How do these two ideas control the information in this paragraph?

[1]Joseph N. Pelton, "Telepower: The Emerging Global Brain," *The Futurist,* September–October 1989: 9–10. Reprinted with permission by the World Future Society, 7910 Woodmount Ave., Suite 450, Bethesda, MD 20814.

6. What word in the last paragraph has been repeated a number of times in previous paragraphs? Would you guess that the last sentence of this paragraph is a conclusion to this introductory unit or an anticipation of what is to come in the rest of the essay? Why?

Here are the three concluding paragraphs of "Telepower." As you read them, try to decide whether they fit the introductory unit you've just read. For additional ideas you may want to read the entire essay, beginning on page 425.

> With telepower, one should maintain a long-term view, since we are ultimately creating not just a new technology, but in effect designing a new fate for our species. We humans are beginning to evolve in new ways. Each time we extend our global electronic machine so that everyone is more linked to everyone else, we become different. Each time we invent a higher level of artificial intelligence, our own intelligence is challenged in new and different ways. As we create new and more-intricate "smart" environments, we are altering our future.

> Biological evolution will no longer be in command as the forces of telepower reign supreme. As radical as it may seem, *Homo sapiens* may be replaced as the superior thinking being on Planet Earth during the course of the twenty-first century. What characteristics or skills the new species will possess is hard to say. The most likely key difference will be a brain of higher memory capacity, faster thinking skills, and improved communications skills. The new species will be more intelligent, more civilized, and perhaps even wiser—a species with a more-global consciousness and more-emphatic links to the rest of the species. The true mystery is whether this new "species" will be derived from humans, from bioengineering, from machines, or from another telepower source. Perhaps it will be dubbed *Homo electronicus*. Another century or so must pass before we know for sure.

> The evolution of this interlinked species that communicates directly with all other beings will indeed mark the beginning of an interlocked consciousness that can be called, quite simply, the Global Brain.[2]

1. Carefully consider the complete title of "Telepower." Now look again at the last sentence of the introductory unit you read above. How did the last sentence of the introductory unit prepare for the conclusion? What sentence in the *third* paragraph of the introductory unit also points to the middle part of the essay and the conclusion?

2. You've read only the beginning and ending of this long essay. Can you tell what it's about? Could the last sentence in the introductory unit be considered a thesis statement for the whole essay?

3. **Vocabulary:** *Tele* means "far," or "at a distance." The title of this essay, then, means "power at a distance." Explain how this idea applies to the essay. What is the meaning of *tele-education*? Can you think of any examples of "tele-education"?

   Here are some other words you may need to check in a dictionary: *species, coaxial, electronic, facsimile* ("fax"?), *satellite, simultaneous, evolution, evolve, Homo sapiens.*

4. Near the end of the selection the author invents the term *Homo electronicus*. What do you think he means by this term? Do you know anyone who might be called "Homo electronicus"? Write a paragraph to explain your view.

---

[2]Joseph N. Pelton, "Telepower: The Emerging Global Brain," *The Futurist,* September–October 1989: 13. Reprinted with permission by the World Future Society, 7910 Woodmount Ave., Suite 450, Bethesda, MD 20814.

5. If you're interested in the idea of a "global electronic brain," you may enjoy reading works by *cyberpunk* writers William Gibson *(Neuromancer, Burning Chrome, Count Zero)* and Bruce Sterling *(Mirrorshades, The Artificial Kid)*. The world of *Neuromancer* imagines a future with "console cowboys," and people with "cranial jacks" to plug into a global electronic network of "cyberspace."

B.

> Spacecraft that produce immediate, tangible benefits are a fact of life. Weather satellites continually track weather over the entire earth, and communications satellites relay messages and pictures between continents. Soon there will be a third type of practical spacecraft, another tool to help man understand and control his environment—the natural resources satellite. In its effect on the billions of persons who inhabit this planet, it may be the most important space program yet undertaken.[3]

1. This introductory paragraph skillfully introduces a broad topic and narrows it to a specific thesis statement. What is the broad topic?

2. What means does the author use to narrow the broad topic to one of its parts?

3. What is the specific thesis statement introduced in this paragraph?

4. What would you expect the author to discuss in the remainder of the paper?

C.

> If Man has benefited immeasurably by his association with the dog, what, you may ask, has the dog got out of it? His scroll has, of course, been heavily charged with punishments: he has known the muzzle, the leash, and the tether; he has suffered the indignities of the show bench, the tin can on the tail, the ribbon in the hair; his love life with the other sex of his species has been regulated by the frigid hand of authority, his digestion ruined by the macaroons and marshmallows of doting women. The list of his woes could be continued indefinitely. But he has also had his fun, for he has been privileged to live with and study at close range the only creature with reason, the most unreasonable of creatures.
>
> The dog has got more fun out of Man than Man has got out of the dog, for the clearly demonstrable reason that Man is the more laughable of the two animals. The dog has long been bemused by the singular activities and the curious practices of men, cocking his head inquiringly to one side, intently watching and listening to the strangest goings-on in the world. He has seen men sing together and fight one another in the same evening. He has watched them go to bed when it is time to get up, and get up when it is time to go to bed. He has observed them destroying the soil in vast areas, and nurturing it in small patches. He has stood by while men built strong and solid houses for rest and quiet, and then filled them with lights and bells and machinery. His sensitive nose, which can detect what's cooking in the next township, has caught at one and the same time the bewildering smells of the hospital and the munitions factory. He has seen men raise up great cities to heaven and then blow them to hell.[4]

---

[3]Louis F. Slee, "Coming: A Natural Resources Satellite," *Electronic Age,* Autumn 1966. Reprinted by permission of *Electronic Age,* Radio Corporation of America.

[4]Copyright 1955 by James Thurber. From "An Introduction" in *Thurber's Dogs* (New York: Simon & Schuster).

1. These two paragraphs fit tightly together. Explain why by commenting on the first and last sentence of the first paragraph and the opening sentence of the second paragraph.
2. What is the major method of development used in both paragraphs?
3. What is the function of the second sentence in the first paragraph? What is its relation to the word *but* that introduces the last sentence of this paragraph?
4. Comment on the major effects of balance in these two paragraphs (include parallelism and antithesis).
5. What is the main function of the first paragraph? Does it contain a thesis statement where you would expect to find it?
6. What has been added to the thesis statement in the second paragraph?
7. How would you characterize the tone of these paragraphs? Point to specific words and phrases that illustrate this tone.
8. Is the main subject of these paragraphs presented in the thesis statements or in the last sentence of paragraph two? Explain.
9. Comment on the length and kinds of sentences. Can you explain the writer's strategy of development?

D.

Here are the five opening paragraphs of an essay titled "Get Me a Ladder at the Library." As you read them, look for a "funnel effect" in the opening, for topic sentences throughout (with pointing controlling attitudes), and for methods of paragraph development.

1   When Chicago's new public library is completed in 1991, it will include a telecommunications hookup with all 86 branches, as well as a satellite downlink to draw programming from worldwide networks. Atlanta's public-library system operates its own channel on cable television, broadcasting literacy classes and interviews with authors. In Colorado more than 14,000 commuters a year find rides through a computerized information system run by the Pikes Peak Library District. And in Oregon the Salem Public Library lends audiovisual equipment and even personal computers. Welcome to the library of today.

2   Although books are still the chief business of libraries, these once quiet redoubts have vastly broadened their scope, branching out to serve their modern users' extended needs. One result is that despite tight municipal budgets and cutbacks in state and federal aid, American public libraries are experiencing a spirited renaissance. From 1988 to 1989, 111 new library buildings went up around the country, the greatest number in one year since 1979. Many of these were underwritten by new bond issues, voter-initiated taxes and private donations. Borrowers and browsers are streaming into the nation's 15,215 public libraries. In 1987, 57% of the American public used such facilities, up from 51% in 1978.

3   The revival knows no geographical boundaries. In 1985 Atlantans voted for a $38 million bond referendum that expanded the central library, constructed twelve new branches, started six modular libraries in public housing projects and bought $9 million in books. Washington State voters have gone to the polls at least nine times in the past five years to support bond issues aimed at renovating or building libraries. The budget for the New York Public Library soared from $60 million in 1981 to $127 million in 1989, thanks largely to government funds and the generosity of private donors. Even in oil-dependent Tulsa, citizens have voluntarily hiked property taxes to improve their libraries.

4   Perhaps the most impressive example is Detroit, a city ravaged by crime, poverty, a declining population and an eroding tax base. Practically the last thing local citizens might be expected to fight for is books, but they did just that when a money squeeze threatened to shut down twelve of the city's 25 branches in 1984. Detroit voters bailed out the libraries by approving a $1 million property tax by an impressive margin. In 1988 they renewed the levy. "People think their library will always be there," says Paul Scupholm, head of Detroit's independent Friends of the Library fund-raising group. "But when faced with its closing, they dig into their pockets."

5   Another reason for the energetic revival of libraries is that as city budgets have shrunk, library administrators and staffers have become more aggressive advocates. Once satisfied to stamp books and shush noisy patrons, librarians now write grant proposals, chat up community leaders and campaign for bond issues. Image is important. In 1988 the Public Library Association named its first ever marketing director in an effort to improve "customer" relations. "We're mobilizing our constituency," explains P.L.A. president Sarah Long. "We're targeting areas for special services."[5]

1. The first paragraph consists of five sentences. What is the purpose of the first four? What method of development does the paragraph use? What is the purpose of the last sentence (the fifth)? What is the overall effect of these five sentences?

2. What important transitional words appear early in the second paragraph? Do these words echo paragraph one or point to the ideas to come in the rest of paragraph two? Explain your view with examples.

3. What is the topic sentence of paragraph two? Does it appear in the position you expect? What two words in the topic sentence serve as the controlling attitude (pointer)? What method of development is used to support this pointer?

4. What is the topic sentence of paragraph three? What important transition word in the topic sentence echoes the previous paragraph? What is the predicate area of the topic sentence? What part of the predicate serves as the controlling attitude? What method of development is used to support this controlling attitude?

5. To what *previous* pointers does "most impressive example" refer? What is the topic sentence in this fourth paragraph? What one word controls the information in this paragraph? What method of paragraph development is used to support the assertion of the topic sentence?

6. What is the purpose of the phrase "another reason" at the beginning of paragraph five? What other words in the opening sentence serve the same purpose? What two words in this long first sentence serve as the pointer?

7. Discuss the unity and coherence of this five-paragraph unit by pointing to its dominant ideas and use of coherence devices.

E.

Though they are not produced in wide-screen Cinemascope, have never won an Oscar, and cannot be viewed on "Saturday Night at the Movies," electronic films are already smash hits in many important sectors of modern electronics technology. Increasingly, they are being "booked" into television equipment, computer logic and memory circuits, two-way communications systems, missile and spacecraft controls, and of course, pocket radios. In fact, if present trends continue, they may yet make the electronics industry the new "film capital" of the world.

As distinguished from photographic film, electronic films are delicate tattoos of electronically active material condensed, for the most part, from hot vapors onto cold, hard, insulating surfaces such as glass. Depending on the materials used and the manner in which they are deposited, such films—many of them 10 times thinner than the shimmering coat of an ordinary soap bubble—may act singly or in combination as whole electronic circuits or simply as components thereof from transistors, diodes, and oscillators to resistors, capacitors, and interconnection paths.[6]

These are beginning paragraphs from a long article. The first is an introductory paragraph, and the second is a paragraph of definition. Together they form the necessary introduction to the article.

1. What point is to be established in the article? What is the specific thesis statement for the article?
2. Is the introductory paragraph a good one? Why or why not?
3. In the second paragraph, is definition by classification used? If so, where is this definition found?
4. The author uses two other methods to make his definition clear. What are they?
5. In the first paragraph, why does the author use quotation marks around *Saturday Night at the Movies?* Why around *booked?* Why *film capital?* Would any of these be just as effective without the quotation marks?
6. In the first paragraph, why are commas placed after *Cinemascope, Oscar,* and *Movies?* Is the comma inside the quotation mark after *Movies* properly placed?
7. In the second paragraph, explain the comma after *film;* after *condensed* and *part;* after *cold* and *hard.*
8. Why are dashes used after *films* and *bubble?* Would commas serve just as well here?
9. What coherence devices are used in these paragraphs?
10. Analyze sentences for suspension of the subject, verb, or complement.

More than twice the length of a five-hundred-word paper, this next essay presents special problems in meaning and tone. A quick reading should tell you that the "writer's voice" in the essay does not *directly* present the author's meaning. Read it carefully to decide what its main points are; then reread for tone and other elements of style using the two check sheets as a guide (for the whole paper, page 195, and for basic elements of style, page 385).

F.

Unsolicited Opening Day Address by Prexy[7]

1   Ladies and gentlemen, welcome—and welcome back—to Diehard University. I shall start the academic year by describing the contract you have entered into by the act of enrolling in this university. That contract is clearly set forth in the university

[6]From Bruce Shore, "Electronic Films," *Electronic Age,* Summer 1966. Reprinted by permission of *Electronic Age,* Radio Corporation of America.

[7]John Ciardi, "Unsolicited Opening Day Address by Prexy." First appeared in *Saturday Review,* September 28, 1968. Copyright 1968 by Saturday Review, Inc. Reprinted with permission.

catalogue, but since literacy is no longer prerequisite to admission, let me lip-read the essential points of our agreement. As you emerge from this convocation you will be handed a digest of these remarks in attractively prepared comic-book form with all dialogue limited to basic English and with the drawings carefully designed to help you over any grammatical difficulties. Those of you, moreover, for whom the requirements of Sub-Literacy One have been waived, may dial AV for Audio Visual, followed by 0016, and a dramatized explication will appear on your TV sets.

2   Diehard, as you know, is no longer dedicated to excellence. The trustees, the administration, the faculty, and the federal government—not necessarily in that order—have concurred that excellence has been outnumbered. The restated policy of Diehard University is simply to salvage what it can from what little it gets from the too much being thrust upon it.

3   We recognize that the achievement of any given intellectual standard is no longer prerequisite to a bachelor's degree. The insistence of any educational institution is defined by its minimum standards, and Diehard no longer has any. As a contractual agreement, the faculty undertake to confer a bachelor's degree upon you in acknowledgment of four years of attendance.

4   If you are willing to settle for that degree, I suggest you do not waste money on textbooks. The presence of a textbook may tempt you to open it. The psychological consequences are obvious: if you must actually open a textbook in order to meet nonexistent minimum standards, how will you ever be sure you are not a moron? Your whole future career could be warped, in such a case, by guilt and uncertainty. Our educational activities, let me say, are so organized that any member of the in- or out-group of the affluent society can stroll through them in the intervals between political rallies, love-ins, water fights, sit-ins, sit-outs, sympathy marches, student elections, anti-raids and generalized adolescent glandular upheavals. These programs have been carefully constructed to assist your social development as students. I urge them upon you as the social duty of every minimalist. Diehard would serve no purpose were it to allow an intemperate emphasis on learning to deflect its minimalists from the fullness of their undergraduate social development and thus, indirectly, from future computerization.

5   To further that social development, Diehard imposes no rules of extracurricular behavior. We shall not act *in loco parentis*. With a mild shudder of revulsion, we return that function to your legal parents. We have problems enough with our own failures and cannot accept as ours the genetic failures of others.

6   This university has eliminated dormitories. Where you live, with whom you live, and what you do off campus are matters between you and your parents, or between you and the police, as the case may be.

7   You are free to demonstrate on all matters of conviction, or, simply, on all matters. For your convenience we have set aside a fireproof, waterproof, open-occupancy convention center called Hyde Park Hall. You are free to occupy it and to harangue in or from it at your pleasure. You have full license for all noncriminal acts that occur in Hyde Park Hall. Any criminal actions you may engage in there will be, of course, between you and the police.

8   Should you choose to act unlawfully in any of the otherwise assigned buildings of the university, you will be warned once that your actions are unlawful, and the police will then be summoned to take normal action against a breach of the peace.

9   The university will seek your advice on all matters of student organization, social development of the university, and community relations. We shall seek that advice temperately and with as much open-mindedness as we can achieve in our senility. In seeking it, however, we do not pledge ourselves to be bound by it. Where your views seem to be reasoned, they will be honored in reason; where they seem intemperate or shortsighted, they will be rejected in reason. A faculty–student board will be elected to study all grievances.

10   In no case, however, will that board, or any body of this university, consider a general amnesty as a condition for ending a demonstration that violates lawful procedure.

11   Diehard will not consider any request made by a minimalist for changes in the curriculum, faculty, or academic qualification. On these matters we ask nothing from you and we will hear nothing.

12   We do confess to a vestigial nostalgia for the long-honored and now outmoded idea of the university as a bookish community of learning. While most of you are pursuing your social development, therefore, the faculty will direct such students as are inclined to volunteer for it, in a course of study leading to the degree of Laureate in Arts or in Science. We shall continue to grant the Bachelor's degree in Arts or in Science without requirement, though to assist your social development we do invite you to attend various discussion groups to be held at carefully spaced intervals.

13   With those who elect the Laureate program, the university insists on a different contract. It insists that in the act of electing such a program, the student will have submitted himself to the faculty as candidate for a degree to be conferred at the discretion of the faculty. The faculty, having already thrown away minimums, must insist on reserving to itself the right to formulate maximums for those who are willing to reach for them. It is the student's business to qualify, or to revert (without prejudice), to the social development program leading to the degree of Bachelor.

14   I ask all those who are interested in a course of study to return tomorrow to start our further discussions. The rest of you may now return to your pads to drop out, turn on, and tune in. If you are arrested between now and your graduation, the university will credit the time up to your conviction toward your attendance and will do its best to readmit you upon completion of your sentence. By decision of the board of trustees, days of attendance completed while out on bail pending an appeal will be counted toward a degree.

15   If the police, that is, are willing to let you out of jail, and if you are willing to check in on the roster, we are willing to keep the attendance records and to grant appropriate degrees upon satisfaction of the requirement.

16   We are not willing to have our reading and discussion time interrupted by protest, no matter how passionate, that breaks the law. Nor are we willing to police the law. Criminality is the proper concern of the police; ours, we believe, is reasoned discussion. When the discussion goes beyond reason and to the point of interfering with the curriculum of those who have chosen one, we reserve the right to suspend or to expel you from the hazy premises of our failing venture into education for those few who are interested in the unlikely.

17   Hello. Goodbye. And may your standardization be your fulfillment.

1. What "role" has the poet-critic John Ciardi assumed as he writes this essay? If you didn't have the essay title, how could you tell?

2. List a number of reasons for Ciardi's use of the name "Diehard University." Is the "speaker" within the essay "for" or "against" Diehard U.? How can you tell? Is Ciardi "for" or "against" Diehard U.? How can you tell? (See Question 4.)

3. What is the effect of the *I–you* relationship established at the beginning and carried throughout? List other words and phrases that add to the conversational tone. (Consider the shift from *I* to *we*.)

4. Irony is a device used by writers who want to say one thing but mean another. How can you tell that Ciardi is using irony? (Consider such things as overstatement, understatement, and departure from the reader's expectations.) When writers are being ironical, how can you tell what they mean? Is it possible that the president of Diehard U. (the "speaker") is also being ironical? Explain your views.

5. List as many words and phrases as you can that seem to be overstatements (for example, *comic-book form, four years of attendance, moron, minimalist, diehard, full license, senility, without requirement*).

6. What is the function of the first three paragraphs? (Consider problems of introduction, tone, and thesis statement.)

7. What are the main points made in Paragraphs 4 through 13? Could you justify the use of so many short paragraphs? Could some of them be combined?

8. How do Paragraphs 14 through 17 tie the paper together? Are they a conclusion?

9. List a number of reasons why the last sentence in the essay may be considered its most important one.

10. Does Ciardi depend on stereotypes to make his exaggerations clear? List some examples.

11. When you are through reading this essay, do you "identify with" the speaker ("I"), the students addressed ("you"), or the writer (Ciardi)? Or none of these? Explain your views.

12. Using the check sheet for style as a guide, comment on the diction and sentences in this paper. List your observations and be prepared to support them.

13. Use the simplified check sheet for the whole paper (page 195) to evaluate the thought, organization, tone, and mechanics of this essay. Does this evaluation fit your first impression of this paper? Why or why not? List your observations and be prepared to support them.

14. This selection is neither expository nor purely argumentative. The irony makes it *satire*. Check the word *satire* in a good dictionary and be prepared to write an extended definition of this kind of writing.

G.

To entertain you and challenge your thinking, here's a carefully contrived essay by the novelist William Golding, author of *Lord of the Flies*. As you read it, notice how carefully Golding uses his storytelling ability *(personal narration)* to engage your attention. The all-important opener, "while I was still a boy," reminds readers—young or old—that the "voice" assumed by the writer is that of an older man thoughtfully remembering his young school days. The use of first person ("I") helps create a friendly tone, the *descriptions* capture attention and stimulate further interest, and the made-up dialogue (mostly in the first ten paragraphs) seems to say, "Hey, here's a story for you." The problem with all this enticement is that the short first paragraph unmistakably tells Golding's readers that this is really an expository essay with an argumentative edge. He's going to *explain* something.

Thinking as a Hobby[8]

1   While I was still a boy, I came to the conclusion that there were three grades of thinking; and since I was later to claim thinking as my hobby, I came to an even stranger conclusion—namely, that I myself could not think at all.

2   I must have been an unsatisfactory child for grownups to deal with. I remember how incomprehensible they appeared to me at first, but not, of course, how I appeared to them. It was the headmaster of my grammar school who first brought the subject of thinking before me—though neither in the way, nor with the result he intended. He had some statuettes in his study. They stood on a high cupboard behind his desk. One was a lady wearing nothing but a bath towel. She seemed frozen in an eternal panic lest the bath towel slip down any farther; and since she had no arms, she was in an unfortunate position to pull the towel up again. Next to her, crouched the statuette of a leopard, ready to spring down at the top drawer of a filing cabinet labeled A–AH. My innocence interpreted this as the victim's last, despairing cry. Beyond the leopard was a naked, muscular gentleman, who sat, looking down, with his chin on his fist and his elbow on his knee. He seemed utterly miserable.

3   Some time later, I learned about these statuettes. The headmaster had placed them where they would face delinquent children, because they symbolized to him the whole of life. The naked lady was the Venus of Milo. She was Love. She was not worried about the towel. She was just busy being beautiful. The leopard was Nature, and he was being natural. The naked, muscular gentleman was not miserable. He was Rodin's Thinker, an image of pure thought. It is easy to buy small plaster models of what you think life is like.

4   I had better explain that I was a frequent visitor to the headmaster's study, because of the latest thing I had done or left undone. As we now say, I was not integrated. I was, if anything, disintegrated; and I was puzzled. Grownups never made sense. Whenever I found myself in a penal position before the headmaster's desk, with the statuettes glimmering whitely above him, I would sink my head, clasp my hands behind my back and writhe one shoe over the other.

5   The headmaster would look opaquely at me through flashing spectacles.

"What are we going to do with you?"

Well, what *were* they going to do with me? I would writhe my shoe some more and stare down at the worn rug.

"Look up, boy! Can't you look up?"

6   Then I would look up at the cupboard, where the naked lady was frozen in her panic and the muscular gentleman contemplated the hindquarters of the leopard in endless gloom. I had nothing to say to the headmaster. His spectacles caught the light so that you could see nothing human behind them. There was no possibility of communication.

"Don't you ever think at all?"

No, I didn't think, wasn't thinking, couldn't think—I was simply waiting in anguish for the interview to stop.

"Then you'd better learn—hadn't you?"

[8]William Golding, "Thinking as a Hobby," *Holiday,* August 1961.

7   On one occasion the headmaster leaped to his feet, reached up and plonked Rodin's masterpiece on the desk before me.

"That's what a man looks like when he's really thinking."

I surveyed the gentleman without interest or comprehension.

"Go back to your class."

8   Clearly there was something missing in me. Nature had endowed the rest of the human race with a sixth sense and left me out. This must be so, I mused, on my way back to the class, since whether I had broken a window, or failed to remember Boyle's Law, or been late for school, my teachers produced me one, adult answer: "Why can't you think?"

9   As I saw the case, I had broken the window because I had tried to hit Jack Arney with a cricket ball and missed him; I could not remember Boyle's Law because I had never bothered to learn it; and I was late for school because I preferred looking over the bridge into the river. In fact, I was wicked. Were my teachers, perhaps, so good that they could not understand the depths of my depravity? Were they clear, untormented people who could direct their every action by this mysterious business of thinking? The whole thing was incomprehensible. In my earlier years, I found even the statuette of the Thinker confusing. I did not believe any of my teachers were naked, ever. Like someone born deaf, but bitterly determined to find out about sound, I watched my teachers to find out about thought.

10   There was Mr. Houghton. He was always telling me to think. With a modest satisfaction, he would tell me that he had thought a bit himself. Then why did he spend so much time drinking? Or was there more sense in drinking than there appeared to be? But if not, and if drinking were in fact ruinous to health—and Mr. Houghton was ruined, there was no doubt about that—why was he always talking about the clean life and the virtues of fresh air? He would spread his arms wide with the action of man who habitually spent his time striding along mountain ridges.

"Open air does me good, boys—I know it!"

11   Sometimes, exalted by his own oratory, he would leap from his desk and hustle us outside into a hideous wind.

"Now, boys! Deep breaths! Feel it right down inside you—huge draughts of God's good air!"

12   He would stand before us, rejoicing in his perfect health, an open-air man. He would put his hands on his waist and take a tremendous breath. You could hear the wind, trapped in the cavern of his chest and struggling with all the unnatural impediments. His body would reel with shock and his ruined face go white at the unaccustomed visitation. He would stagger back to his desk and collapse there, useless for the rest of the morning.

13   Mr. Houghton was given to high-minded monologues about the good life, sexless and full of duty. Yet in the middle of one of these monologues, if a girl passed the window, tapping along on her neat little feet, he would interrupt his discourse, his neck would turn of itself and he would watch her out of sight. In this instance, he seemed to me ruled not by thought but by an invisible and irresistible spring in his nape.

14   His neck was an object of great interest to me. Normally it bulged a bit over his collar. But Mr. Houghton had fought in the First World War alongside both Americans and French, and had come—by who knows what illogic?—to a settled

detestation of both countries. If either country happened to be prominent in current affairs, no argument could make Mr. Houghton think well of it. He would bang the desk, his neck would bulge still further and go red. "You can say what you like," he would cry, "but I've thought about this—and I know what I think!"

15   Mr. Houghton thought with his neck.

16   There was Miss Parsons. She assured us that her dearest wish was our welfare, but I knew even then, with the mysterious clairvoyance of childhood, that what she wanted most was the husband she never got. There was Mr. Hands—and so on.

17   I have dealt at length with my teachers because this was my introduction to the nature of what is commonly called thought. Through them I discovered that thought is often full of unconscious prejudice, ignorance and hypocrisy. It will lecture on disinterested purity while its neck is being remorselessly twisted toward a skirt. Technically, it is about as proficient as most businessmen's golf, as honest as most politicians' intentions, or—to come near my own preoccupation—as coherent as most books that get written. It is what I came to call grade-three thinking, though more properly, it is feeling, rather than thought.

18   True, often there is a kind of innocence in prejudices, but in those days I viewed grade-three thinking with an intolerant contempt and an incautious mockery. I delighted to confront a pious lady who hated the Germans with the proposition that we should love our enemies. She taught me a great truth in dealing with grade-three thinkers; because of her, I no longer dismiss lightly a mental process which for nine-tenths of the population is the nearest they will ever get to thought. They have immense solidarity. We had better respect them, for we are outnumbered and surrounded. A crowd of grade-three thinkers, all shouting the same thing, all warming their hands at the fire of their own prejudices, will not thank you for pointing out the contradictions in their beliefs. Man is a gregarious animal, and enjoys agreement as cows will graze all the same way on the side of a hill.

19   Grade-two thinking is the detection of contradictions. I reached grade two when I trapped the poor, pious lady. Grade-two thinkers do not stampede easily, though often they fall into the other fault and lag behind. Grade-two thinking is a withdrawal, with eyes and ears open. It became my hobby and brought satisfaction and loneliness in either hand. For grade-two thinking destroys without having the power to create. It set me watching the crowds cheering His Majesty the King and asking myself what all the fuss was about, without giving me anything positive to put in the place of that heady patriotism. But there were compensations. To hear people justify their habit of hunting foxes and tearing them to pieces by claiming that the foxes like it. To hear our Prime Minister talk about the great benefit we conferred on India by jailing people like Pandit Nehru and Gandhi. To hear American politicians talk about peace in one sentence and refuse to join the League of Nations in the next. Yes, there were moments of delight.

20   But I was growing toward adolescence and had to admit that Mr. Houghton was not the only one with an irresistible spring in his neck. I, too, felt the compulsive hand of nature and began to find that pointing out contradiction could be costly as well as fun. There was Ruth, for example, a serious and attractive girl. I was an atheist at the time. Grade-two thinking is a menace to religion and knocks down sects like skittles. I put myself in a position to be converted by her with an hypocrisy worthy of grade three. She was a Methodist—or at least, her parents were, and Ruth had to follow suit. But, alas, instead of relying on the Holy Spirit to convert me, Ruth was foolish enough to open her pretty mouth in argument. She claimed that the Bible (King James Version) was literally inspired. I countered by saying that the Catholics

believed in the literal inspiration of Saint Jerome's *Vulgate,* and the two books were different. Argument flagged.

21   At last she remarked that there were an awful lot of Methodists, and they couldn't be wrong, could they—not all those millions? That was too easy, said I restively (for the nearer you were to Ruth, the nicer she was to be near to) since there were more Roman Catholics than Methodists anyway; and they couldn't be wrong, could they—not all those hundreds of millions? An awful flicker of doubt appeared in her eyes. I slid my arm round her waist and murmured breathlessly that if we were counting heads, the Buddhists were the boys for my money. But Ruth had *really* wanted to do me good, because I was so nice. She fled. The combination of my arm and those countless Buddhists was too much for her.

22   That night her father visited my father and left, red-cheeked and indignant. I was given the third degree to find out what had happened. It was lucky we were both of us only fourteen. I lost Ruth and gained an undeserved reputation as a potential libertine.

23   So grade-two thinking could be dangerous. It was in this knowledge, at the age of fifteen, that I remember making a comment from the heights of grade two, on the limitations of grade three. One evening I found myself alone in the school hall, preparing it for a party. The door of the headmaster's study was open. I went in. The headmaster had ceased to thump Rodin's Thinker down on the desk as an example to the young. Perhaps he had not found any more candidates, but the statuettes were still there, glimmering and gathering dust on top of the cupboard. I stood on a chair and rearranged them. I stood Venus in her bath towel on the filing cabinet, so that now the top drawer caught its breath in a gasp of sexy excitement. "A–ah!" The portentous Thinker I placed on the edge of the cupboard so that he looked down at the bath towel and waited for it to slip.

24   Grade-two thinking, though it filled life with fun and excitement, did not make for content. To find out the deficiencies of our elders bolsters the young ego but does not make for personal security. I found that grade two was not only the power to point out contradictions. It took the swimmer some distance from the shore and left him there, out of his depth. I decided that Pontius Pilate was a typical grade-two thinker. "What is truth?" he said, a very common grade-two thought, but one that is used always as the end of an argument instead of the beginning. There is a still higher grade of thought which says, "What is truth?" and sets out to find it.

25   But these grade-one thinkers were few and far between. They did not visit my grammar school in the flesh though they were there in books. I aspired to them, partly because I was ambitious and partly because I now saw my hobby as an unsatisfactory thing if it went no further. If you set out to climb a mountain, however high you climb, you have failed if you cannot reach the top.

26   I *did* meet an undeniably grade-one thinker in my first year at Oxford. I was looking over a small bridge in Magdalen Deer Park, and a tiny mustached and hatted figure came and stood by my side. He was a German who had just fled from the Nazis to Oxford as a temporary refuge. His name was Einstein.

27   But Professor Einstein knew no English at that time and I knew only two words of German. I beamed at him, trying wordlessly to convey by my bearing all the affection and respect that the English felt for him. It is possible —and I have to make the admission—that I felt here were two grade-one thinkers standing side by side; yet I doubt if my face conveyed more than a formless awe. I would have given my Greek and Latin and French and a good slice of my English for enough German to

communicate. But we were divided; he was as inscrutable as my headmaster. For perhaps five minutes we stood together on the bridge, undeniable grade-one thinker and breathless aspirant. With true greatness, Professor Einstein realized that any contact was better than none. He pointed to a trout wavering in midstream.

28   He spoke: *"Fisch."*

29   My brain reeled. Here I was, mingling with the great, and yet helpless as the veriest grade-three thinker. Desperately I sought for some sign by which I might convey that I, too, revered pure reason. I nodded vehemently. In a brilliant flash I used up half of my German vocabulary. *"Fisch. Ja. Ja."*

30   For perhaps another five minutes we stood side by side. Then Professor Einstein, his whole figure still conveying good will and amiability, drifted away out of sight.

31   I, too, would be a grade-one thinker. I was irreverent at the best of times. Political and religious systems, social customs, loyalties and traditions, they all came tumbling down like so many rotten apples off a tree. This was a fine hobby and a sensible substitute for cricket, since you could play it all the year round. I came up in the end with what must always remain the justification for grade-one thinking, its sign, seal and charter. I devised a coherent system for living. It was a moral system, which was wholly logical. Of course, as I readily admitted, conversion of the world to my way of thinking might be difficult, since my system did away with a number of trifles, such as big business, centralized government, armies, marriage . . .

32   It was Ruth all over again. I had some very good friends who stood by me, and still do. But my acquaintances vanished, taking the girls with them. Young women seemed oddly contented with the world as it was. They valued the meaningless ceremony with a ring. Young men, while willing to concede the chaining sordidness of marriage, were hesitant about abandoning the organizations which they hoped would give them a career. A young man on the first rung of the Royal Navy, while perfectly agreeable to doing away with big business and marriage, got as red-necked as Mr. Houghton when I proposed a world without any battleships in it.

33   Had the game gone too far? Was it a game any longer? In those prewar days, I stood to lose a great deal, for the sake of a hobby.

34   Now you are expecting me to describe how I saw the folly of my ways and came back to the warm nest, where prejudices are so often called loyalties, where pointless actions are hallowed into custom by repetition, where we are content to say we think when all we do is feel.

35   But you would be wrong. I dropped my hobby and turned professional.

36   If I were to go back to the headmaster's study and find the dusty statuettes still there, I would arrange them differently. I would dust Venus and put her aside, for I have come to love her and know her for the fair thing she is. But I would put the Thinker, sunk in his desperate thought, where there were shadows before him—and at his back, I would put the leopard, crouched and ready to spring.

1. The one-sentence first paragraph announces the subject of the essay and adds two disclaimers. What is the subject and to what two other ideas does Golding tie it? Are you ready to accept all three ideas without question? Explain why or why not.

2. After reading it, find three reasons to explain why Golding's essay can be considered an exercise in logical analysis (division); be prepared to illustrate your reasons. Now write a five-hundred-word theme to support this thesis: *Golding develops "Thinking as a Hobby" through the use of logical division.*

3. If "Thinking As a Hobby" is an expository essay, would you normally expect the kind of writing you find in paragraph two? Explain your answer.

4. Paragraph three links pure thought, nature, and love to the statuettes appearing in paragraph two. Explain the connections.

5. How much of Golding's essay is taken up by *description?* Carefully list at least six things Golding describes. Do you find them interesting? Why do you think Golding included them? Choose two and explain how you think they fit into the essay.

6. What are the three types of thinking Golding presents? Using your own words, describe each type.

7. According to Golding, which is the best type of thinking? Do you agree with him? Find three good reasons to support your view. Write a five-hundred-word theme titled "The Best Type of Thinking." If you wish, begin your theme with: *According to William Golding in "Thinking as a Hobby," the best type of thinking is . . .*

8. List twenty words from the essay that you can't define. Look them up in a dictionary and recheck them in the context of the essay.

9. Does the essay become more *expository* than *personal narrative* as it progresses? Where do you think the expository approach is strongest?

10. What method of development does Golding use in paragraph eighteen?

11. In Chapter 6 you learned that there were many methods of definition, among them these: *defining, classifying, analyzing, providing synonyms, using examples or illustrations, describing a process, enumerating.* Find at least one example of each of these in the essay.

12. What kind of thinker are you? Can a person fit more than one of the three types? Write a five-hundred-word theme titled "My Kind of Thinking." If you wish, begin your theme with: *Although thinkers seem to fit several types, perhaps the most common is . . .*

ESSAYS FOR ANALYSIS AND DISCUSSION

The essays in this section provide ideas for discussion and possible subjects for themes. As you read, try to discover these basic elements:

1. The main *subject* of the essay
2. The *controlling attitude* toward the main subject
3. The information that *supports* or *illustrates* the controlling attitude
4. The paragraph breaks (topic sentences?)
5. The overall organization of the essay
6. The use of introductions and conclusions

When Jobs Clash[9]

1   Meet Kendall Crolius, 36, an account director at the J. Walter Thompson advertising agency in Manhattan. Every day, Monday through Friday, she awakens at 6:00 a.m., prepares for work and, if two-year-old Trevor stirs, snatches a few minutes of "quality time." At 7:10 she walks to the train station near her Connecticut home; by 8:30 she is in her Lexington Avenue office. During the next nine hours, she juggles the demands of clients and researchers, creative teams and media people. But no matter how hectic it gets, Crolius usually manages to catch the 5:18 train. When she reaches home, Trevor is waiting for her. By 10:30, she is asleep.

2   Meet Stephen Stout, 38, an actor currently understudying in the Broadway hit *The Heidi Chronicles*. Each day he gets up at 7:15 a.m. If it is not a matinee day, Stout spends the next ten hours with his two-year-old son, playing and running errands. At 5:15 he leaves his suburban home to catch a Manhattan-bound train, allowing ample time to meet his 7:30 call at the Plymouth Theater. On the nights that Stout does not appear onstage, he heads for home at 9:40, after the second act is safely under way. When he walks through his front door at 11:15, he is greeted by silence; both his wife and son are asleep.

3   Stout and Crolius are happily married, though they spend only a few minutes together on a standard workday. Both agree it is not an ideal arrangement. But this is the most compatible meshing of schedules in their eight-year marriage—and it beats the 18 months they spent on opposite coasts when Stout was pursuing television work in Los Angeles. "This is as good as it gets," says Crolius. "We're both working—and we're both living in the same city."

4   Welcome aboard Marriage Flight 1990, and fasten your seat belts: it's going to be a bumpy ride. Today's typical marriage is a dual-career affair. That means two sets of job demands, two paychecks, two egos—and a multitude of competing claims on both spouses' time, attention and energy. The two-job flight path is marked by demands for fairness and parity that require some mobility, a dose of originality and a high degree of flexibility.

5   Dual-income marriages are not unique to the '90s, of course. But as America heads into a decade that will see increasing numbers of women enter the labor force, career collisions promise to become more common and more acute. Among married couples, 57% of wives work, up from 39% two decades ago, and the number is expected to keep rising. If money is power, as family therapists warn, then some vexatious power struggles loom ahead: 18% of working wives earn more than their husbands. After two decades of toppling barriers, professional women are now reaping promising promotions.

6   But those new opportunities may mean longer hours or a relocation—demands that can conflict directly with a husband's needs and strain the fabric of a marriage. It is probably no coincidence that even as women make gains in the workplace, more than 50% of new marriages today end in divorce. The corporate restructurings of the 1980s have also contributed to a sense of instability as couples realize that no job is truly secure and long-term

[9]Jill Smolowe, "When Jobs Clash," *Time,* September 3, 1990: 82–84. Copyright 1990 Time Inc. Reprinted by permission.

planning may be all but impossible. The result is a feeling shared by many couples—that they are out there, all alone, with no precedents to guide them. "This is a transitional generation, in the middle of changing values and roles," says Betty Lehan Harragan, a career consultant and columnist. "Each couple is forced to make it up by themselves."

7   The upside of transition is that society's expectations no longer bar men or women from assuming any role they choose in either the home or the workplace. The downside is that those choices often prove costly. Many couples are discovering that the fierce careerism and materialism that drove the past decade are now exacting a steep toll in terms of personal satisfaction and relationships. If the 1980s were the Decade of Greed, the 1990s may well turn out to be the Age of Need—a time when quality-of-life issues triumphed over the quantity of material success. Already there are signs that people's priorities are shifting away from the workplace and back to home and community.

8   Yet couples are not having an easy time striking a healthier balance between the demands of home and workplace. "Everything has to be negotiated, and that's difficult for us," says family therapist Anne MacDowell. "We tend to want our way to be the right way and the other person's way to be wrong." Perhaps that is not so surprising, given the climate that spawned many of today's working couples. "We really *are* the Me Generation," says Karen Burnes, 34, an ABC-TV network correspondent, who admits that every day she must balance her job against her marriage to Rudy Rodrigues, 49, a consultant to the United Nations. "We were raised to do what we wanted to do."

9   In attempting to shift into the We mode, many couples find their biggest challenge is simply finding time together. Work hours conflict; travel demands interfere. Even relatively compatible schedules do not guarantee couples a daily hour of uninterrupted time together. Accommodation becomes all the harder when jobs land couples in different cities. Air Force Major Suzanne Randle, 44, was handed six weeks' notice to transfer from Nebraska to California, a move that will lengthen the commute to see her husband, a first officer for TWA who is based in St. Louis. "It comes down to, hey, it's tough making a living," Randle says. "You have to do what it takes."

10   Others are less sanguine. For almost two years, venture capitalist Ben, 35, and Elaine, 35, a marketing vice president, shuttled between Baltimore and Manhattan. "On weekends we were always trying to catch up," he says. "It was like a Slinky, underdoing, overdoing, underdoing, overdoing." When Elaine became pregnant a year ago, Ben quit his job to join her in New York. Ben, who has since found new work, says, "We discovered telephones are not like being there."

11   Maybe not, but fax machines and phones have become the lifeline of many a modern marriage. Burnes and Rodrigues speak by phone six or seven times daily. When Rodrigues recently traveled to the Afghanistan countryside, the lack of a telephone link-up threw the relationship off balance. "I felt like our whole foundation was shaken," says Burnes. "I had no feeling of control, no feeling of contact." Their new resolution: no more trips that place either one more than a phone call away.

12   Resilient couples have learned to find some advantages in their constant separations. Many speak of having more time for work, friends and hobbies; others point to their newfound self-sufficiency. Shelly London, 38, an AT&T district manager of public relations in Atlanta, and Larry Kanter, 38, a radio news anchor in the same city, find that incompatible hours help keep the romance in their relationship. "We're sort of always newlyweds," London says. "We're real jealous of our time on weekends."

13   Colliding agendas inevitably throw up questions of whose job is more important and who's in charge. Often the struggle for answers plays out in tussles over house chores. Women frequently—and justifiably—complain that most of the drudge work falls to them. The view from the male side, however, can be revealing. Ellen Galinsky, who as co-president

of Manhattan's Families and Work Institute often attends corporate seminars, says that when women complain that their mates don't help, the men seethe. "The men say, 'Every time I help, she tells me I'm doing it wrong. I quit. I'm not interested in being criticized all the time.'" Such conflicts often reflect deeper issues of power and expectation. "There's a lot of denial around the issues of envy and competition," says family psychotherapist Emily Marlin. "Who's doing better? And what does that mean?"

14   Therapists warn that often it means money. "In our culture," says therapist MacDowell, "power goes with money." Many women who earn less than their husbands admit to unease, citing the "dominance" enjoyed by the spouse. Those who make more typically wish that the breadwinning field was more level. Men, by contrast, tend to deny any feelings when they are outearned by their wives. They dismiss their wives' higher earnings with phrases like "I say more power to her" and "I don't feel threatened by it." Inevitably, such statements are followed by the words "I have a strong ego," a defensive refrain that seems to betray a discomfort not yet resolved.

15   That discomfort is certain to deepen as more working women find their career paths leading to a relocation. Women are still the "trailing spouse" in 94% of all job transfers that involve couples. But that is changing rapidly. By the end of the decade, almost a quarter of all transferees are expected to be women, up from 5% just 10 years ago. Feelings of resentment, helplessness and dependency that have long plagued displaced working women promise to be harsher for men. While potential employers rarely find it odd that a wife has given up a job to trail her husband, they often question the dedication of a candidate who puts his wife's career first. Friends betray their prejudices and heighten anxieties with questions like "But what are you going to do?" Moreover, most men are ill prepared to take a backseat role.

16   Men who have braved the trailing route know it can be rough. Last February, Ray Victurine, 35, left a job with an international agency in La Paz, Bolivia, to follow his wife to Seattle, where she had landed a job with a family and health organization. Four wageless months passed before Victurine found consulting work and settled on entering a Ph.D. program. "You begin to question your self-esteem," he admits.

17   As transfer options open for women, many couples are adopting a your-turn-my-turn strategy. Grace Flores-Hughes, 44, gave up a government job to follow the career of Lieut. General Harley Arnold Hughes, 54; she no sooner settled into an academic post in Omaha than her husband's career relocated them back to Washington. "I knew that one day if I needed something, he would support me," she says. That day came in 1987 when she was nominated by President Ronald Reagan to be director of community-relations service at the U.S. Justice Department. Harley Hughes, who faced yet another reassignment, possibly to Europe, decided that this time his three-star career would give. He retired five years ahead of schedule.

18   Given the emotional and economic toll, an increasing number of couples are simply choosing not to transfer. Confronted with the mounting resistance, companies are beginning to respond. Fully 75% of the 1,000 companies that belong to the Washington-based Employee Relocation Council offer services designed to make relocation more attractive to spouses, from writing basic résumés to pooling job listings with other companies to expedite a spouse's employment search.

19   The relocation backlash is just one symptom of the gradually changing attitude toward work. Employees are also beginning to balk at the long office hours that are the legacy of the '80s' corporate retrenchments that pared staffs and deepened the work loads of those who remained behind. Corporate loyalty is further strained by the growing realization that no matter how hard an employee works, no job is truly secure. "People feel 'the hell with it,'" says consultant Harragan. "They've had it with being overworked."

20   At the same time, people are growing disillusioned with the rewards of high-powered, high-profile careers. "People are asking,

'Where am I really going on the fast track?' " says psychotherapist Marlin. "They aren't dropping out, like in the '60s, but they are more introspective about the kinds of things they feel are ultimately going to be satisfying." Increasingly, couples speak of "quality-of-life" issues, as they weigh the demands of work against the desire for more family and leisure time. Worship at the career altar is becoming passé.

21   All this means a new array of choices for dual-income couples. As they sort their way through the maze of opportunities, therapists advise a high degree of communication and flexibility. Decisions that may bring careers into collision should be negotiated carefully, with both spouses voicing their feelings and misgivings. When exploring a job decision, worst-case scenarios should be addressed. Once a decision is reached, it should be reviewed periodically to make sure both partners are satisfied.

22   Discussion and sacrifice may not always alleviate conflict, but then the challenges of fitting two careers into one marriage never promised to be easy. "Each has got to pull some weight and make some compromises," says Johnnetta Cole, 53, who balances the demands of a marriage and five grown sons against her duties as president of Atlanta's Spelman College. "There's got to be an awful lot of dialogue because the rules are new." And they are always changing.

On Mending[10]

---

1   For some time now the torn pantyhose have lain across the towel bar. When I walk by I am startled to see the nylon legs, like those of the daddy longlegs spider, sway to and fro. I have deliberately left the stockings there to remind me to mend them.

2   Mend pantyhose? I must be mad! Who today mends stockings? What person sews up holes in stockings that cost less than a dollar? Who has the inclination? The time? If I were smart I'd throw them in the trash and buy pretty new ones. But the thing is: now and then I need to mend, to slip thread into needle, to make something serviceable again.

3   Mending is different from sewing. I grew up knowing that to mend was akin to saving an item from the "poorbox" sent to the church or Goodwill for the less fortunate.

4   As a kid I mended everything. I gave added life to favorite dresses, pinafores. I was chubby, my dresses often split under the arms and at the waist. I learned to have needle and thread handy. I hated mending socks. I had a tendency to pull the thread too tight. When worn the small lumps near the toes hurt awfully. I never minded having to sew a torn slip, though. The thought of torn underwear dangling from a starched dress was, to me, utterly repugnant.

5   I grew up mending. Once I restitched my tired Oxfords with extra-strong carpet thread, then smeared Shinola on the shoes. They looked almost new! I learned to "save" a torn

[10]From Mary Helen Ponce, "On Mending," *Frontiers*, 11.1 (1990):24–25. Reprinted with permission.

sweater by reweaving (from the inside) the ripped wool strands. Once I inherited them, I never minded mending my sister's hand-me-downs. It was with a certain amount of pride that I hiked or lowered hems, mended loose seams, secured buttons, or added rick-rack.

6   Mending was part of the immigrant experience. My parents, who immigrated from Mexico, both mended. My mother mended clothes, quilts, curtains. My father mended broken fences, rusty bedsprings, torn screen doors, and leaky faucets. Our adopted grandmother Doña Luisa mended broken hearts.

7   My older brothers, too, mended. They patched bike tubes, rewired old radios and bicycle spokes. Often they sewed the black punching bag that hung from the garage ceiling, busted from their daily workouts. Now and then they gave renewed life to an old jalopy.

8   My sisters were expert menders. They switched coat buttons with expertise so that the odd button, restitched near the bottom, was undetectable, and also mended torn slips and sofa covers. Often they mended my doll's clothes. In return for this I vowed not to snitch on them.

9   When my own children tore holes in jeans or dresses, I folded them into a sewing basket bought in Baja, sprayed a bright red, then lined with a tropical print. When the basket visibly bulged I picked a favorite television program, usually a documentary, then sat to watch and mend . . . and mend.

10   I liked to match thread to material. I never dared sew a red garment with pink or orange thread. No! The thread had to be the exact shade. And so it went. At times I used the sewing machine to repair damaged or "holy" jeans, as my kids called them. Mostly, though, I preferred to feel needle in hand, to weave in and out, to create magic (well, almost). Sewing Scout badges on my daughter's Brownie sash was not mending . . . but almost.

11   It's been a while since I mended clothes for my children, now grown. How they keep their clothes together I don't know. The boys probably use Krazy Glue, staple cuffs in place, and use paper clips as buttons. My daughter, though, mends. Not out of necessity (as I did) but out of habit or inherited tendencies. It is not cool to dance with dangling bra straps. Worse, at times an already short miniskirt needs to be hiked higher . . . higher!!

12   Once more I pass the dangling pantyhose. They invite me to take them down, mend, then put them away. Make them useful, wearable. I think I will. Mend them, that is. I'll wear them with boots, or underneath pants. Then I'll mend the tear in my robe, the loose sofa fringe, the lopsided drapes, the . . .

The Last Drops[11]

1 Swaminathan Asokan dreams of water. It gushes out of a giant tap and fills bucket after bucket. But then he wakes up—to a nightmare. For at Asokan's house in Madras, India's fourth largest city, there is no water. The tap has long been dry. So he must get up in the dark of night and, laden with plastic pails, take a five-minute walk down the street to a public tap. Since the water flows only between 4 a.m. and 6 a.m., Asokan, 34, a white-collar worker at a finance company, tries to be there by 3:30 a.m. to get a good place in line. His reward: five buckets that must last the entire day.

2 Compared with many of his countrymen, Asokan is fortunate. At least 8,000 Indian villages have no local water supply at all. Their residents must hike long distances to the nearest well or river. In many parts of the country, water is contaminated by sewage and industrial waste, exposing those who drink it to disease.

3 The sad state of India's water supply is just one sign of what could become a global disaster. From the slums of Mexico to the overburdened farms of China, human populations are outstripping the limited stock of fresh water. Mankind is poisoning and exhausting the precious fluid that sustains all life.

4 In the Soviet Union, the mismanagement of land around the Aral Sea has cut it off from its sources of water, causing the volume of the once giant lake to shrink by two-thirds in 30 years. Now storms of salt and pesticides swirl up from the receding shoreline, contaminating the land and afflicting millions of Uzbeks with gastritis, typhoid and throat cancer. In Beijing, one-third of the city's wells have gone dry, and the water table drops by as much as 2 meters

(2.2 yards) a year. In the Western U.S., four years of drought have left municipalities and agricultural interests tussling over diminishing water stocks. Says Ivan Restrepo, head of the Center for Ecodevelopment in Mexico, where as many as 30 million people do not have safe drinking water: "We've been enduring a crisis for several years now, but it is in this decade that it will explode."

5 Camouflaged by its very familiarity, the water problem has crept up on a world distracted by fears of global warming and other emergent environmental threats. Yet water could be the first resource that puts a limit on human population and economic growth. Shortfalls of water will mean shortfalls of food, since up to three-quarters of the fresh water that humanity uses goes for agriculture. Moreover, contaminated drinking water in heavily populated areas endangers the health of hundreds of millions of people. According to the United Nations, 40,000 children die every day, many of them the victims of the water crisis.

6 At the moment, countries are poised to go to war over oil, but in the near future, water could be the catalyst for armed conflict. Israel and Jordan, Egypt and Ethiopia, and India and Bangladesh are but a few of the neighboring nations at odds over rivers and lakes. Warns Arnon Sofer, professor of geography at Israel's Haifa University: "Wars over water might erupt in the Middle East in the '90s when states try to control each other's supplies."

7 Whatever the human consequences of the crisis, it has an even greater effect on many other living things. Fish, birds and countless creatures are crowded out, marooned or poi-

[11]Eugene Linden, "The Last Drops," *Time,* August 20, 1990:58–61. Copyright 1990 Time Inc. Reprinted by permission.

soned as industry, agriculture and municipalities reroute rivers, dry up wetlands, dump waste and otherwise disrupt the normal functioning of delicate ecosystems. The world is learning that there are limits to mankind's ability to move water from one place to another without seriously upsetting the balance of nature.

8   The idea of a global shortage seems incredible when 70% of the earth's surface is covered by H_2O. But 98% of that water is salty, making it unusable for drinking or agriculture. Desalinization is technically feasible, but it is far too expensive to use anywhere except in an ultra-rich, sparsely populated country like Saudi Arabia. Other options, like towing icebergs from the poles, are also beyond the means of poor nations.

9   The scarcity of fresh water for agriculture makes famines more likely every year. The world consumes more food than it produces, and yet there are few places to turn for additional cropland. Only by drawing on international stockpiles of grain have poorer countries averted widespread starvation. But those supplies are being depleted. From 1987 to 1989, the world's stock of grain fell from a 101-day surplus to a 54-day one. A drought in the U.S. breadbasket could rapidly lead to a global food calamity.

10   Even if rainfall stays at normal levels, current world food production will be difficult to maintain, much less increase. The food supply has kept pace with population growth only because the amount of land under irrigation has doubled in the past three decades. Now, however, agriculture is losing millions of hectares of this land to the effects of improper watering.

11   Without adequate drainage, continuous irrigation gradually destroys a piece of land— and any streams or rivers near it—through a process called salinization. As the heat of the sun evaporates irrigation water, salts are left behind. The water also flushes additional salts out of soils with high concentrations of minerals, leaving them to dry on the surface into a cakelike residue or to dissolve in groundwater and poison plant roots.

12   History shows that such environmental destruction can have far-reaching consequences.

The salinization of irrigated land led to the fall of Mesopotamia and Babylon, and perhaps even the Mayan civilization of Central America. Similar pressures are at work today. Sandra Postel of Worldwatch Institute estimates that 60 million hectares (nearly 150 million acres) of irrigated land worldwide have been damaged by salt buildup.

13   Human activities have also disrupted the delicate natural systems that maintain water supplies. To obtain wood and clear land for homes and farms, mankind is chopping down forests at an unprecedented rate. But vegetation traps water, reducing runoff and replenishing groundwater supplies. Throughout the world, tree cutting has led to floods, mud slides and soil erosion during rainy seasons and acute water shortages during dry periods.

14   Deforestation can set in motion forces that reduce the amount of rainfall in a given area. In a rain forest, for example, as much as half the moisture settles on trees and quickly evaporates into the sky, only to precipitate again in a continuous cycle. Thus when trees are cut down, rainfall may diminish.

15   Even in dryer regions sparse shrubs can help maintain rainfall. Some scientists argue that once ground cover is stripped, the land hardens and evaporates less moisture into the air. At the same time, the naked soil reflects more sunlight, triggering atmospheric processes that reduce rainfall by drawing dryer air into the area.

16   The result is desertification, a gradual conversion of marginal land into wasteland. This process is often driven by population pressures, which force people to work lands unsuitable for agriculture. In sub-Saharan Africa, for instance, settlers move into an area when it is wet and green, and then stay and remove the ground cover when the inevitable drought returns. Without a green barrier to stop them, sand dunes march inexorably forward.

17   While no place is safe from the effects of the water crisis, Egypt, in particular, faces hard times. The country's population of 55 million is growing by 1 million every nine months. Already the people must import 65% of their food, and the situation could grow far worse. The flow of the Nile, Egypt's only major water

supply, will be reduced in coming years as upstream neighbors Ethiopia and Sudan divert more of the river's waters. Egypt's only practical course is to brake population growth and reduce the enormous amount of water wasted through inefficient irrigation techniques.

18   Competition for water is especially fierce between Israel and Jordan, which must share the Jordan River basin. Many towns in Jordan receive water only two times a week, and the country must double its supply within 20 years just to keep up with population growth. "We are cornered," admits Munther Haddadin, a Jordanian development official. With time running out, Jordan hopes to draw additional reserves from the Yarmuk river. Israel, however, will fight any plans for use of the river that do not give guarantees of access to the Yarmuk waters that the country currently uses.

19   In the grip of a three-year drought, Israel too is far from secure, despite its formidable conservation technologies. An expected 750,000 Soviet émigrés will probably settle in the cities, where the use of pure water is the highest. At the same time, 750,000 Palestinians in the Gaza Strip face what Zemah Ishai, Israel's water commissioner, calls a "catastrophe" because of overpumping and contamination of groundwater.

20   A decade ago, a government study in China estimated that the nation's water resources might support only 700 million people. That was alarming, since the population had already reached 900 million. Unable to increase the supply, the Politburo took the simpler expedient of revising the study to conclude that there was enough water for 1.1 billion people. As the population continues to grow and now surpasses the 1.1 billion mark, China has gradually increased the numbers in the study.

21   Chinese leaders, aware of the true severity of the crisis, have at last begun to focus the nation's scientific talent on the water issue. The country has been working to develop salt-tolerant and drought-resistant crops, and it has begun to have some success in reclaiming salt-damaged land.

22   In the West the most troubled dry spot is Mexico, where a government report asserts that

"water will be a limiting factor for the country's future development." The demands of Mexico City's 20 million people are causing the level of their main aquifer to drop as much as 3.4 meters (11 ft.) annually. Water subsidies encourage the wealthy and middle classes to waste municipal supplies, while the poor are forced to buy from *piperos,* entrepreneurs who fix prices according to demand. Belatedly, the government has begun to establish a more sensible system of tariffs as well as promote water-saving devices like low-flush toilets.

23   Despite the global breadth of the water crisis, the situation is not completely hopeless. In industrial nations the revitalized environmental movement has spawned a fresh offensive against pollution. Jan Dogterom, who runs a consulting firm in the Netherlands, represents a new breed of detective hired by governments to track down the culprits who contaminate waterways. Faced with the knowledge that toxins can be traced back to their source, many companies comply readily in cleanup efforts. Says Dogterom: "It is my honest-to-God conviction that the West European rivers will be clean in 50 years, and the East European rivers will soon follow."

24   The water-supply picture may not be entirely bleak. Mohamed El-Ashry of the World Resources Institute estimates that around the world 65% to 70% of the water people use is lost to evaporation, leaks and other inefficiencies. The U.S. has a slightly better 50% efficiency, and El-Ashry believes it is economically feasible to reduce losses to 15%.

25   Government officials and businesses are looking for ways to reuse waste water. With the aid of advanced technology, even highly contaminated water can be made drinkable again. Alcoa has just begun to market a new claylike material called Sorbplus that helps clean water by adsorbing toxic materials.

26   Most tantalizing of all is the possibility that there are great, undiscovered reservoirs throughout the globe. Speaking in Cairo last June at a water summit organized by the Washington-based Global Strategy Council, Farouk El-Baz of Boston University raised hopes among African nations when he announced that an analysis of remote sensing data

has revealed unsuspected supplies of underground water in the dryest part of the Egyptian Sahara. El-Baz believes there may be twice as much water stored underground worldwide as previously assumed.

27   New supplies could take some pressure off rivers and lakes and would be a temporary godsend to millions of people. But if societies returned to business as usual, this bounty would only postpone the day of reckoning for humans and all other species. Humanity has long deluded itself into thinking that water shortages merely reflect temporary problems of distribution. Both industrial and developing nations are finally realizing that the world's fresh water is a finite and vulnerable resource, an irreplaceable commodity that must be respected and preserved.

It's a Small World After All[12]

---

1   The model gazes serenely at the magazine reader from the country-club cool of a Ralph Lauren ad. Dressed impeccably in a tweed jacket, silk scarf and elegant suede gloves, she projects all the dreamy remoteness that is typical of Lauren models, with one notable difference: she is black.

2   It was a long time coming, but an ethnic rainbow is finally sweeping across the fashion and advertising industries—and brightening them considerably. The blond, blue-eyed ideal is out, diversity is in, and the concept of beauty is growing as wide as the world. The new cast of faces is appearing not only in ads aimed at specific ethnic groups but in mainstream advertising as well. Revlon's Most Unforgettable Woman of 1989, chosen in a search across the U.S., is Mary Xinh Nguyen, a 20-year-old Vietnamese American from California. Such companies as Du Pont, Citibank and Delta Air Lines have populated current ads with a rich variety of blacks, Asians and Hispanics.

3   While many consumers still live in segregated neighborhoods, integrated ads have become the height of hipness. Reason: they have a sophisticated, global-village look. "Advertisers don't want to insult people's intelligence. They are reflecting how the world is," says James Patterson, chief executive of the ad agency J. Walter Thompson USA. If an ad features nothing but a herd of Caucasians, it can appear dated and stiff. The inclusion of a lone minority-group member has a similar effect. Says Ron Anderson, vice chairman of the Bozell ad agency: "Ten or 15 years ago, there was a sense of tokenism. Some advertisers would throw a black or Hispanic into an ad because they were sensitive to minorities. Now we use blacks and Hispanics to sell a product."

4   From supermodel Suzy Parker in the 1950s to Christie Brinkley in the early 1980s, fair-skinned models used to dominate advertising. Most ad experts trace the change to Europe, where couturiers, notably Givenchy, began employing black women as runway models. The French fashion magazine *Elle* helped pioneer the polyethnic look in its editorial pages,

then exported the philosophy to America when it launched a U.S. edition four years ago. (Catherine Alain-Bernard, fashion and beauty editor of the French *Elle,* says her magazine still gets a few letters from people complaining about black models and "giving jobs to immigrants.")

5   One of the first advertisers to embrace the rainbow look was Benetton, the Italian knitwear maker, which launched its "United Colors of Benetton" campaign in 1984. The ads picture handsome youths of diverse nationalities often standing arm in arm. The purpose of such ads is not just to appeal to ethnic customers who might identify with people in the ads but also to pitch an alluring sentiment of brotherhood. Esprit, a San Francisco-based sportswear company, went one step further by putting its employees in ads. Says Esprit spokeswoman Lisa DeNeff: "We sat up and said, 'Hey, why not us?' We had a lot of great-looking folks here. Many were ethnically different."

6   All over the globe, advertising is becoming more multiracial. Many ads in Japan, which often used to depict blonds because they represented the Western good life, are populated by blacks, Asians and Latins. "Japanese consumers now want to see somebody unique and somebody they can easily empathize with," says Hidehiko Sekizawa, senior research director for Hakuhodo, Japan's second largest ad agency. In France the two hottest commercials of the summer, for Schweppes and Orangina, featured Brazilian music and casts of brown-eyed, mixed-race beauties.

7   Modeling agencies are finding ways to meet the demand for fresher faces by scouting all over the world and staging more contests. "If you see a beauty, you don't worry about her color. The perfectly proportioned features are no longer so important," says Ann Veltri, a vice president at Elite Model Management.

8   Since consumers want to see real people rather than idols, advertisers expect the ethnic look to be around for years to come. "We don't want a colorless, odorless soup," says Guy Taboulay, the executive creative director in Paris for B.S.B., a U.S.-owned ad agency. "We want to see national identities and character. Tomorrow's culture will be made up of different cultures. That will be its strength."

Poets vs. Technology[13]

1   Is it preordained that poets deplore technology? Must creative artists, those people who celebrate blossoms and rainbows and explore recesses of the human heart, inevitably view engineers as adversaries? Regrettably, it sometimes appears that the answer is yes. Although public anxieties about technology have abated in recent years, the private misgivings of many writers have not. Engineers, like all citizens, are disturbed about environmental degradation, dangerous consumer products, and the arms race; they seek a cleaner, safer, more secure world. But still a fundamental mistrust of technology lies deep in the artistic psyche.

2   I pick up the *New York Times Book Review* and find an essayist lamenting that romance is

---

[13]Samuel C. Florman, "Poets vs. Technology," *Technology Review* (October 1990):73. Reprinted by permission.

not what it used to be, and that science and technology are largely to blame: "Technology is the knack of so arranging the world that you don't have to experience it." In the *New York Review of Books,* a writer appraising the papers of Thomas Edison speaks of engineering as "an alien power, crippling the sense of freedom that it was intended to serve." In his introduction to an anthology of contemporary American poetry, Andrei Codrescu writes that "the making of community against antisocial technology is the chief object of the poetry gathered here." He goes on to complain that "it's been our generational lot to sift through the debris of industreality [sic] to force reality through the cracks." In his book *The End of Nature* Bill McKibben voices an elegiac dread of technological change. McKibben tells of retreating to an Adirondack wilderness, where he finds sublime detachment swimming in a remote lake. But the roar of a motorboat rudely breaks the mood. When technology intrudes, McKibben writes, "you're forced to think, not feel."

3   One cannot quarrel with a person who values feeling, nor with the ideals of love or freedom. But why cast technology as the enemy? There have always been obstacles to achieving the euphoric states of being so celebrated in song and story. In earlier times, people faced with such harsh realities as failing crops, plagues, and marauding war parties must often have been distracted from ardent amours and blissful swimming sessions. Technology doubtless has changed the nature of life's diversions, in ways both pleasant and unpleasant, but I do not see why it has to be viewed as hostile to artistic fervor.

4   I do not expect contemporary poets to echo Rudyard Kipling's paeans to machinery, or to emulate the great yeasayer, Walt Whitman, "Singing the strong light works of engineers." I forgive them if they do not understand the passion inherent in engineering enterprise and ignore it in their work. I merely want them to stop treating technology as if it were the chief source of human discontent.

5   Little enough to ask, one might think, yet repeatedly I find reasons to feel discouraged.

Even as I write at my word processor, I am reminded of Wendell Berry's recent diatribe against this harmless tool in his book of essays *What Are People For?* Berry chooses to continue writing with a pencil, not merely out of personal preference, but as a statement of protest against high technology. His wife transcribes his work on a typewriter bought in 1956, a machine that is "as good now as it was then."

6   No engineer can speak to the concerns of creative artists as effectively as can one of their own, so I find comfort in referring to the wisdom of writer John Updike. "I use a word processor," writes Updike in a recent essay, "and the appearance on the screen of the letter I just tapped seems no more or less miraculous and sinister than its old-fashioned appearance, after a similar action, upon a sheet of white paper in my typewriter."

7   Machines simply do not bother Updike the way they do Berry. Having pondered the matter, he states the reason: "The capacity of human beings to absorb what they wish to and to ignore the rest," he writes, "seems to me almost illimitable." Updike fails to see how the human spirit is threatened by the computer, or by the carburetor, which responds "when I simplemindedly ask my automobile to go," or by the telephone, which has not fundamentally changed what people talk about. Perhaps Berry, McKibben, and similarly troubled souls could also cultivate the capacity to ignore those aspects of technology that do not answer to the cries of their heart.

8   Happily, Updike is not the only poetic creator who finds it possible to cope with technology. Let the last words be those of another luminary of the literary world, Saul Bellow:

9   "A million years passed before my soul was let out into the technological world. That world was filled with ultra-intelligent machines, but the soul after all was a soul, and it had waited a million years for its turn and did not intend to be cheated of its birthright by a lot of mere gimmicks. It had come from the far reaches of the universe, and it was interested but not overawed by these inventions."

Information Brokers Have All the Answers[14]

1   The call was from an Oregon Christmas tree grower. His question for Sue Rugge: What's the market for selling Christmas trees to Hawaiians?

2   Rugge hit the computer keyboard to search some of the hundreds of data bases at her disposal, then started dialing, not stopping until she had called most of the chambers of commerce from Kapaa to Hilo. Finally, she researched the cost of shipping the trees.

3   The answers: Hawaiians like Christmas trees as much as mainlanders, and they like 'em green and growing. By the time it was over, Rugge recalled, "we gave him statistics on how many Christmas tree stands there were on Oahu the previous year."

4   A cross between a research librarian and a hacker, Rugge is the prototype of a new kind of professional, an information broker. And while social scientists speak of people drowning in data in today's Information Society, brokers are people who blithely swim in it.

5   In the past five years, the number of information brokers has mushroomed from a handful to an estimated 800 to 1,000, and it's still growing fast. Their labors have broad implications for everything from how we do business to the way we make decisions in our personal lives. Simply put, the rise of these brokers means the amount of information easily available to anyone with the several-hundred-dollar fee has taken a quantum leap.

6   "Everybody thinks nothing has changed since the Dewey Decimal System," said Barbara Quint, a former Rand Corp. research librarian who has become something of a self-appointed theorist to the new profession. "Now all that's turned on its head. Librarians are on the cutting edge of society."

7   "Ask me anything," Quint is fond of saying. "I have the answer."

8   It's difficult to pinpoint when computerized information brokering was born, but some date it to the convergence of one of the earliest collections of data bases publicly available—a government-sponsored project called Dialog—and the energetic Rugge.

9   Rugge began brokering information in 1971, when a California recession threw her out of work as a corporate librarian and she began doing research for hire at local libraries. But in early 1979, when she combined her skills with the Dialog data bases and created a company called Information on Demand, the new profession started to take off.

10   Searching computer data bases "made the field much more efficient, able to do much more work in much less time and for much less money," Oakland, Calif.-based Rugge said.

11   There were no limits on the type of requests she fielded: What are the beer-drinking habits of East Asians? Get me the floor plans of the Vinohradska Hospital in Czechoslovakia. Find a location for filming in July that looks like Vermont in winter. And so on.

12   Rugge, 49, has long since sold Information on Demand—which grew to 50 employees—and started a new company, the Rugge Group. And Dialog—now owned by Knight-Ridder Inc., which also owns the San Jose Mercury News—is only one of a half-dozen major companies that together offer about 4,000 data bases containing everything from old issues of

---

[14]Jack Fischer, "Information Brokers Have All the Answers," *Houston Chronicle,* September 4, 1990:40. Reprinted by permission: Tribune Media Services.

416

the *Saturday Evening Post* to abstracts on infectious diseases and figures on Japanese tuna production.

13   There are perhaps a thousand businesses like Rugge's nationwide, estimates Linda Cooper, president of the Association of Independent Information Professionals, the brokers' fledgling professional group. Most are small operations, with one to five employees and gross revenues of about $50,000 to $500,000 a year, Cooper said. She said about three-quarters of those starting the businesses have backgrounds in library science, and the remainder come from a variety of disciplines.

14   "I began in 1982, and the field has exploded since then," said Cooper, who has been asked to research such arcane facts as the last dinner served at Alcatraz (fried chicken) and the effects of religious deprogramming on a high school student's grades. "I don't even have to explain to people what I do anymore."

15   Cooper said the majority of her colleagues made their money not from individuals, but from companies in need of market research. Other typical customers are public relations writers, people preparing executive summaries for CEOs, and legal and scientific researchers.

But more exotic types, like private investigators, are also common.

16   This article itself in some ways reflects the brokers' work. When a reporter told Cooper he was working on a feature story about her and her colleagues, she quickly conducted a search on the topic and faxed the resulting three-page bibliography to him.

17   "You can have your librarians at the newspaper retrieve the full texts for you," she said. And they did.

18   The full implications of the world of information brokering are still anyone's guess, but some things are already clear. One is that the amount of information a person needs to be well-informed is increasing.

19   The field is already seeing the emergence of specialists. There is an information broker in Philadelphia who specializes in researching only information related to oceans, from trade routes to marine biology. Another searches only for facts about Alaska.

20   "It used to be that time and space were obstacles to getting information, but that's not the case anymore," Cooper said. "Now just about anything can be found, if you have the budget."

Convicted of Relying on a Prayer[15]

1   The jury forewoman was trembling. After she announced the verdict, several of the jurors began to sob loudly. The defendants held hands but showed no emotion upon hearing the guilty pronouncement. Climaxing a dramatic and closely watched trial that pitted church against state, David and Ginger Twitchell were convicted of involuntary manslaughter in a Boston courtroom last week. Their crime: letting their sick 2½-year-old son Robyn die because they chose to follow their religion and rely on prayers rather than call a doctor. "This has been a prosecution against our faith," lamented David Twitchell, a lifelong Christian Scientist. No, countered prosecutor John Kiernan, it was a "victory for children."

2   The conviction was the fifth in two years against Christian Scientist parents who failed to seek medical treatment for their children—a record that the Boston-based church interprets as a crusade against its teachings. The Twitchells' sentence followed the pattern set in the previous cases. The parents were given ten years of probation, and they were ordered to submit their three other children to regular medical exams and take them to a doctor whenever signs of serious illness develop.

3   The two-month trial turned on the question of whether the Twitchells were guilty of "wanton and reckless conduct" in not seeking medical help for Robyn, who died in April 1986 of a bowel obstruction, after five days of illness. The parents, who had summoned a "spiritual healing" practitioner, maintained that their son had shown only intermittent flulike symptoms and seemed to be recovering just before taking a fatal turn. But medical experts testified that the child would probably have been fever-

ish, vomiting and in obvious pain before his death. Had he been taken to a doctor, they asserted, the boy would still be alive. In one poignant moment at the trial, David Twitchell sadly voiced his misgivings: "If medicine could have saved him, I wish I had turned to it."

4   The eight-woman, four-man jury deliberated for 14 hours before delivering its verdict. The Twitchells' attorney, Rikki Klieman, promptly announced plans to appeal. Her primary argument, she says, will be that Judge Sandra Hamlin misinterpreted a 1971 Massachusetts statute on child abuse and neglect, which creates a legal exemption for those who believe in spiritual healing. Some 44 states provide some sort of religious exemption. In the Twitchell case, the first to test the Massachusetts law, Hamlin ruled that "a subjective belief in healing by prayer" is no excuse for not obtaining medical help when a child is seriously ill.

5   Defense attorney Klieman also questioned the judge's rejection of her request to poll the jury members, a practice sometimes used to ensure that a verdict correctly reflects the views of the jurors. "The fact that the jurors were weeping," she said, "shows every single reason they should have been polled."

6   Several Massachusetts legal experts believe the Twitchells' claim of a statutory exemption will prevail on appeal. Says Harvey Silverglate of the Massachusetts Association of Criminal Defense Lawyers: "It's virtually impossible to convict the parents in the face of that exemption." Silverglate and others think the Twitchell conviction—particularly if it is overturned—could ultimately prompt nationwide efforts to

[15]From Alain L. Sanders, "Convicted of Relying on a Prayer," *Time,* July 16, 1990:52. Copyright 1990 Time Inc. Reprinted by permission.

repeal legal exemptions for spiritual healing. While that would be a tremendous blow to the Christian Scientists and other religious groups, it would, say child-advocacy groups, be an important step toward granting the nation's children a fundamental human right. Says Jetta Bernier of the Massachusetts Committee for Children and Youth: "No individual should have to suffer and die because of the religious beliefs of another."

We Can Pay Young Women Not to Get Pregnant[16]

---

1   A lot of people talk about overpopulation; a comparative handful does anything about it. And that handful has not as yet accomplished much. Despite the best efforts of numerous international organizations and various government initiatives, world population still continues to surge at the rate of about 2 million a week.

2   How do you slow down, let alone stop, the relentless increase of humanity? The best idea I've heard in a long time is to do it with money. To be precise, bank accounts. One for every woman in the world.

3   In America, the plan would work like this: When a girl reached puberty, she could—if she freely chose to do so—notify a local public-health office. At that point, a financial clock would start ticking. If she went a year without getting pregnant, the government would put a check for $500 in her account. No strings: She could take it out the next day and spend the whole thing, start a personal scholarship fund for college, or whatever she liked.

4   If she then went a second year without getting pregnant, the government would in-crease her annual payment to $600. The third year would be $700, and so on, reaching around $1,200 at age 20. Participation would be totally voluntary, and the payment non-discriminatory. A millionaire's daughter and a welfare kid would be treated exactly alike.

5   Suppose a young woman who has joined the plan decides that she wants a baby? There is nothing to stop her. Of course, she wouldn't get a check in the year she becomes pregnant. But payment would resume the year after, starting back at $500 and again slowly building.

6   What would this all cost? Less than you might think. Suppose that the plan went into operation next year and that 90 percent of American girls who reached puberty in 1991 chose to join. Suppose further that not one of those 2 million 12- and 13-year-olds got pregnant. In that case, the total cost in payments would be approximately $1 billion, plus another $2 billion or $3 billion to set up and staff the public-health centers.

7   Assume that in 1992 we again enrolled 90 percent, and so forth for five years; and that in all that time, not one of those participating had

---

[16]Noel Perrin, "We Can Pay Young Women Not to Get Pregnant," *Houston Chronicle,* July 30, 1990:11A. Reprinted with permission of the author. Perrin teaches environmental studies at Dartmouth College in Hanover, N.H.

a baby. That would mean a maximum possible payment in the fifth year of about $10 billion. That may seem like an enormous sum. But it's less than the state of California alone will spend on Aid to Families with Dependent Children in one year.

8   In the District of Columbia, it costs $30,000 to $40,000 per year to raise one disturbed child in a group home. Most of such children now in care were born to teen-age girls who should never have had the burden of motherhood thrust on them so soon. By contrast, $900 (the amount that the plan would pay a D.C. 17-year-old who had never gotten pregnant) seems pretty small.

9   In my own small state of Vermont, a 19-year-old mother with two children will get about $10,800 in cash and food stamps from the state this year. The $1,100 she would have received under the plan if she had never been pregnant begins to look like a real bargain.

10   A few months ago I published an outline of this plan in a national magazine. I received hundreds of letters in response. Some agreed. Some hated the idea—chiefly, it seemed, those who don't yet believe that overpopulation is threatening the health of the planet. A few called it a proposal for "genocide." Their argument: Since the black and Hispanic birth rates in the United States are much higher than the white birth rate, the plan might produce a disproportionate reduction of minority population. But even if each ethnic group's birth rate wound up the same, this completely voluntary program would hardly be genocide. It would be gen-equality.

11   But could such a project ever get started— here or anywhere else? Or is it just one of those ivory-tower ideas that looks good on paper but would never happen in the real world?

12   As it turns out, the plan is already working in at least one American city. It costs even less than the ivory-tower version. And it provides additional benefits.

13   In 1986, Planned Parenthood of the Rocky Mountains began a pilot program of paying young women not to get pregnant. It has since become known as the Dollar-a-Day Teen-age

Pregnancy Prevention Program. Twelve young women in Denver formed the original group. Their average age was 15. Four were already mothers; four others had had abortions.

14   These young women were invited to come to a weekly meeting. Each got $7 if she came and was not pregnant. (The group uses the honor system. There are no pregnancy tests.) They also got soft drinks and cookies. Some of the young women came from homes so poor that they said they would have attended just for the food.

15   But a third motive soon developed: The young women rapidly formed a support group. The doctor who ran the program never lectured; she listened. In the end, the group had 18 members, of whom 15 finished the two-year program without getting pregnant. And without having any more abortions, which some might well have had.

16   In January 1988, Rocky Mountain Planned Parenthood started a second group in the same neighborhood. Ten young women joined and so far none has become pregnant. Meanwhile, two more groups have been organized. Some of the young women in these programs have clearly had their expectations of life raised. "I wasn't expecting to have a baby so early," said Anna, a 16-year-old with a 9-month-old son. "I want to have more children, but not right now. Maybe when I'm 30." Anna used her $7 a week to buy diapers. Another girl in the group, asked about her plans, said simply: "Graduate from high school. Go to college."

17   The total cost of the program is $365 per year per young woman, and another $250 apiece for administration. By comparison, the average early-teen pregnancy costs Colorado taxpayers around $13,000.

18   Already there is a similar group in Rocky Ford, Colo., and one in San Mateo, Calif. Plans are afoot for several in Florida and one on the Eastern Shore of Maryland.

19   This plan decreases abortion, saves taxpayers money and plainly benefits the young women it serves—while at the same time making a start toward keeping the planet habitable. Is that ivory-tower stuff? Or plain common sense?

Telepower: The Emerging Global Brain[17]

1   The human use of communications contains the key to the future of our species. The linking of our optical and electronic technologies in new and different ways is not only the key to a new golden age, but a high-risk gamble as well. Our new telepower technologies can make us or break us.

2   The "global electronic machine" is where it all starts. This machine is far bigger than a nuclear aircraft carrier, a C5A cargo jetliner, or even a continuous-process automobile-manufacturing plant. It contains hundreds of millions of tons of coaxial cable buried underground and beneath the oceans. It includes electronic switches and exchange equipment with enough gold and silver to fully stock a large jewelry store. Parts of the machine are invisible because they are flying in space—orbiting in circles a tenth of the way to the moon. Over a hundred of these space communications devices are relaying billions of messages around the world every year. The parts of the global electronic machine are now so numerous that no one can count them. Billions of telephones, television sets, facsimile devices, telexes, computers, and radios are linked to this massive network. Each year, the colossal machine grows by leaps and bounds as fiber-optic cables, new electronic switches, and new "ports" are added to accommodate more users around the world.

3   The machine is making the global village a reality. Soon, people in remote Tuvalu and Niue in the South Pacific will be able to call Chicago, Toulouse, or Chiang Mai, Thailand. In the 20 years since the moon landing, the number of people able to see global events on television has expanded sixfold from 500 million to 3 billion people. Our ability to share information and knowledge is today creating global trade and culture. Tomorrow, it will begin to form a global brain—a global consciousness.

4   The power of the global electronic machine is already awesome. Just one satellite, the INTELSAT VI, can send 200 simultaneous television channels—enough to send all episodes of *Dallas* and *Dynasty* ever made all at once. It could also transmit about a thousand 300-page books in the span of one second. In short, the global electronic machine, this multitrillion-dollar universal linkage, is very fast and very smart.

5   The many dimensions of our growing telepower will bring us both good and bad changes. On the debit side, it will bring us telewar, technology-based terrorism, technological unemployment, and information overload. Yet, this telepower will also bring hope for high-quality schooling, nutritional advice, and medical services through tele-education and telehealth techniques.

6   Well into the twenty-first century, there can even be hope for the building of a true global consciousness and ultimately for the emergence of a "global brain." Eventually, we may even see the evolution of a new human species.

The New Globalism

7   Increasingly, there will be a global economy and a global market, where remoteness largely disappears. Everyone, even in Burkina Faso and Borneo, will "plug in" to the global electronic machine.

8   Examples of the electronic global village

[17]Joseph N. Pelton, "Telepower: The Emerging Global Brain," *The Futurist,* September–October 1989:9–13. Reprinted with permission by the World Future Society, 7910 Woodmount Ave., Suite 450, Bethesda, MD 20814

today are everywhere. Television coverage of the 1988 Summer and Winter Olympics reached an estimated global audience of 3 billion, or 60% of the world. Close to $100 trillion in electronic fund transfers occur globally via satellite or cable connection each year. Everything from weather forecasting and scientific data exchange to commodity trading, airline reservations, and global marketing are tied to the global electronic machine.

9   Most product-oriented industries are discovering that they can exist only in a global market. Their global competitors can outcompete them if they scale their production to local markets only. As the service industries become more and more predominant, the imperative to operate on a global scale becomes even more clear-cut, regardless of whether the business is retailing, banking, trading, transportation, or management consulting. Low-cost communications systems, economies of scale, global marketing systems, deregulation, and corporate consolidation and merger all serve to create the age of globalism.

Jobs in the Telepower Economy

10   Both labor and patterns of work face a period of great turmoil in the age of telepower. Changes to be faced include perennial and lifelong job retraining, technological unemployment, the 168-hour workweek, telecommuting to work, and "electronic immigrants" competing for local service jobs.

11   The global electronic machine cannot help but redefine work and reshape the world's economies. One change already emerging is the 168-hour workweek. With a global society, the movement of the sun and of the economy never stops. Airline booking systems, global electronic-fund-transfer systems, satellite-system controls, and hundreds of computer systems, robotic manufacturing units, and power and telecommunications networks run day and night, seven days a week, 365 days a year. Our electronic servants do not need to eat or sleep and usually are most productive if they work every hour of the week— 168 hours. This means more shift work, more automation, and even more telerobotics so that many plants and

facilities can be monitored and controlled from remote locations.

12   The extent to which work of all types can be automated will undoubtedly lead to a reduction in jobs. Between now and the twenty-first century, the biggest impact will clearly be in manufacturing, and laid-off workers will be largely retrained for new jobs in the service industries.

13   However, many of these new service jobs will not be challenging, high-tech occupations, but low-paying activities such as fast-food work, retail clerking, or aiding teachers or nurses. More significantly, artificial intelligence and expert systems will be replacing highly skilled service jobs by around 2005, according to MIT economist Charles Jonescher. Beyond examining the effects of automating assembly-line jobs in manufacturing, we will soon be talking more about replacing medical diagnosticians, educators, market researchers, design engineers, and a host of occupations that a decade ago seemed irreplaceable by "machine skills." It is clear that both unemployment and underemployment due to technological advances are likely to be very big problems in the future.

14   Retraining workers and creating new and meaningful jobs are the key. Unfortunately, today's educational and training systems are not geared to the coming change. In most industrialized countries, educational and training systems are now designed for about 3% to 4% of the total population, but it is likely that in coming years some 10% to 20% of the population will need some degree of mid-career educational assistance.

Converging Technologies

15   The new telepower technologies will affect more than just jobs. The scope, structure, and marketing strategies of high-technology corporations will also be greatly affected. It seems likely, based on current trends, that we will see the consolidation of many key technologies, particularly computers, robotics, artificial intelligence, telecommunications, advanced transportation, aerospace, and advanced energy systems. This combination of converging technol-

ogies is called, for lack of a better name, "telecomputer-energetics." The parallels in technology that result from computer chips, solar cells, digital telecommunications, artificial intelligence, and advanced software development create a powerful incentive to create economies of scale, density, technology, and scope in these increasingly interrelated fields.

16   Such diverse corporations as Mitsubishi, Toyota, TRW, General Motors, IBM, and ARCO show clear signs of tele-computer-energetics in the making. GM, with the acquisition of EDS, Hughes Aircraft, and several smaller robotics and software firms, is now in a strong technology position with regard to computers, telecommunications, aerospace, robotics, and advanced energy and transportation systems. Although the silicon chip is the clearest connecting link in the move toward tele-computer-energetics, it is likely that artificial intelligence will become the true "brain" from which all the other activities will derive in the twenty-first century. For tele-computer-energetics firms, they need not be the biggest, but the brightest. In fact, most very large firms such as GM seem to have problems managing the most-advanced new technologies.

"Electronic Immigrants"

17   The key element in charting corporate and economic activity in the age of the global brain is that no important trend can or will be "local." Tele-computer-energetics, technological unemployment, and the 168-hour workweek will be experienced around the world. The global electronic machine will serve to make these changes happen more quickly as the constraints of time are overcome. One trend will happen as a direct result of the global machine: the creation of a new type of global worker, called the "electronic immigrant."

18   This new worker will telecommute to work over great distances, perhaps even many thousands of miles. People in the relatively cheaper labor markets—such as Jamaica, Barbados, the Philippines, India, and China—will be recruited and trained to perform a variety of services that can be performed remotely, such as computer programming, word processing, in-

ventory control and management, or telephone sales.

19   The ability to recruit and electronically import cheap professional services into the United States, Japan, and Europe could become the top international trade issue of the twenty-first century. Beyond the trade and job impacts of electronic immigrants, there will also be political impacts. If more and more jobs in a developing country are those held by electronic immigrants working for a wealthier country, there could come a time when the economic ties begin to dictate political relationships. This is to suggest that if the electronic-immigrant trend continues unchecked, we could see the creation of "telecolonies," whose local finances and politics are largely controlled from an overseas capital.

The Dark Side of the Machine

20   The age of telepower relates to a breakthrough in knowledge and capability for humanity, but the journey to this new frontier will be difficult, challenging, and often dangerous. For instance, telepower backlash aimed at women and minorities becomes a possibility: Where technological unemployment is occurring, there is often particular pressure applied to women and minorities to surrender their jobs first.

21   The abuse of the global electronic machine's power is perhaps the greatest of dangers to be faced. The challenges posed by the dark side of telepower include invasion of privacy, information overload and super-speed living, technology-based terrorism, telewar, and electronic totalitarianism.

22   Averting these misuses of telepower must be a top priority if we are to achieve an enlightened and productive future.

Teleservices

23   One might start to conclude that advanced telepower technology produces only negative or hazardous results. This is certainly not the case. Without new advanced electronic services, our lives could in fact be far worse, and many important social problems would only deterio-

rate. Most people, given a thoughtful choice, would not go back to serfdom, the plague, starvation, and worse. One of the areas where telepower is helping to create a more beneficial future world is that of tele-education, as well as that of the closely related fields of telehealth and telemedicine.

24   Many educational systems around the world are extremely dependent on advanced electronic technologies. In China, for instance, over a million students receive more than 150 hours of educational programming per month live via satellite from Beijing. This programming is locally produced by the Ministry of Education and by Central China TV. Eventually, all 10 million Chinese teachers will be trained through expansion of their tele-education system started under INTELSAT's Project Share only three years ago. One might speculate about whether Chinese satellite education was a partial stimulus to new calls for political cybernetics and game theory. When we eventually invent such a Von Neumann machine, it will mark the start of an artificial and rapidly accelerating evolutionary path. Some believe that the greatest challenge of the twenty-first century for humanity will be to keep up with machine-based evolution. It seems a remote issue today, but then the dinosaurs did not foresee their ultimate obsolescence either.

25   One thing is clear: Telepower technologies are doing more than creating a global economy or generating new telecolonies to facilitate the electronic flow of work and labor into new markets. Telepower means more than just speeded-up living and work patterns and phenomena like the 168-hour workweek. Certainly, telepower implies good and bad, strength and weakness. Positive patterns such as electronic education, telehealth, and telecommuting to convenient neighborhood work centers are likely to be offset by negatives, such as loss of privacy, technological unemployment,

information overload, and technoterrorism. In short, it is of some importance to recognize and differentiate the positive from the negative and to build on the desirable aspects and reduce or eliminate the undesirable.

26   With telepower, one should maintain a long-term view, since we are ultimately creating not just a new technology, but in effect designing a new fate for our species. We humans are beginning to evolve in new ways. Each time we extend our global electronic machine so that everyone is more linked to everyone else, we become different. Each time we invent a higher level of artificial intelligence, our own intelligence is challenged in new and different ways. As we create new and more-intricate "smart" environments, we are altering our future.

27   Biological evolution will no longer be in command as the forces of telepower reign supreme. As radical as it may seem, *Homo sapiens* may be replaced as the superior thinking being on Planet Earth during the course of the twenty-first century. What characteristics or skills the new species will possess is hard to say. The most likely key difference will be a brain of higher memory capacity, faster thinking skills, and improved communications skills. The new species will be more intelligent, more civilized, and perhaps even wiser—a species with a more-global consciousness and more-emphatic links to the rest of the species. The true mystery is whether this new "species" will be derived from humans, from bioengineering, from machines, or from another telepower source. Perhaps it will be dubbed *Homo electronicus*. Another century or so must pass before we know for sure.

28   The evolution of this interlinked species that communicates directly with all other beings will indeed mark the beginning of an interlocked consciousness that can be called, quite simply, the Global Brain.

About the Author

Joseph N. Pelton, former director of strategic policy for INTELSAT, is now director of the interdisciplinary Telecommunications Program and director of the Advanced Telecommunications Research Center at the University of Colorado—Boulder, Boulder, Colorado 80309. He is author of more than 100 articles and reviews as well as six books, including *Global Talk* (Astro Associates, 1981), a 1982 Pulitzer Prize nominee.

Women, Minorities—Bright Hope for Business[18]

1   Business leaders are fascinated with the wealth of statistical data generated in this information age in which we live. As we face daily operating decisions, we rely on measures of everything one can imagine from how the cost of our products reflects how much we spend on health benefits to how an acquisition will affect the value of our stock. We must know, is it more cost-effective to renovate a facility than to replace it? What will downtime cost us? We pay a great deal of attention to these numbers, converting them to charts and graphs, cross-tabulating and analyzing them ad infinitum. All of this to arrive at the absolute best decision.

2   Why, then, is the business community, with its heavy diet of data, so slow to respond to perhaps the most significant demographic shift of this century?

3   Why are businesses so blind to the demographics which forecast a dramatically different work force for the coming millennium— demographic data which asserts that:

- Two-thirds of the new entrants into the work force between now and the year 2000 will be women.

- Sixty-one percent of all women of working age are expected to be employed outside the home by the year 2000.

- Minorities will account for 29 percent of the new entrants into the work force between now and the year 2000, twice their current share.

4   Already, women and minorities are occupying greater numbers of jobs, especially in managerial and professional fields. Yet those numbers are not being fully reflected in the executive ranks. Another thing the demographics illustrate is that any organization that continues to depend on white males as its primary source of high-level employees is going to have a very limited field to choose from.

5   Clearly, any company that excludes women and minorities from opportunities shoots itself in the foot. The primary consideration should always be getting the right person for the job. So, why would businesses limit their own choices?

6   Yet, *Fortune* magazine (July 30) recently found that 799 public companies it surveyed did just that. Of the 4,012 people listed as the highest-paid officers and directors at these companies, only 19, or less than one-half of a percent of them, were women. No minority figures were noted.

7   I believe that the leaders of corporate America must regard this data as seriously as they do other business information and act decisively to change these numbers. And if we want to attract the best women and minorities into our businesses, we must establish a track record that shows we offer solid opportunities for them to move up. How can we do that?

8   I don't claim to have all the answers on this issue. In fact, we are far from where we want to be at Tenneco. But, first let me say how I think we should *not* proceed. I do not believe in taking the "quick fix" approach. Companies should not respond by sticking women and minorities all over the organizational chart with Post-it notes. What we need is a planned, reasonable approach—one which develops candidates internally, providing them the opportunities along the way which will be the stepping stones to the top.

---

[18]From James L. Ketelsen, "Women, Minorities—Bright Hope for Business," *Houston Chronicle*, August 27, 1990:11A. Reprinted with permission.

9   This approach to upward mobility might include the following five strategies:

■ Assure that there is a commitment to creating advancement opportunities by selecting and promoting managers who embody the belief in a major role for women and minorities.

■ Broaden the involvement of women and minorities in the policy and program-making process through the use of active advisory councils. Empower them and listen to them. Along these lines, our own women's advisory council convened 170 of my company's top women for a leadership conference this summer.

■ Link executive bonuses to the successful hiring and promoting of females and minorities to fill key positions. Money motivates.

■ Design family-friendly benefits to meet the needs of the new work force. If they are not forced to choose between family obligations and career opportunities, all employees will be better able to meet company goals as well as their own ambitions.

■ Expand the capacities of women and minorities by providing training and development and, most importantly, meaningful op-portunities—line positions with profit and loss responsibility. We can't pigeonhole these workers in traditional staff areas and then declare them unprepared for greater responsibility.

10   My firm's pursuit of these strategies and goals is partly a response to the demographics—we want to be ahead of the curve, not overwhelmed by it down the road. It is also part of our overall commitment to leadership in our products, our communities and our workplaces—we want the best employees from all backgrounds in order to ensure we maintain and build on our leadership position for the future.

11   At Tenneco, we are by no means where we want to be, and some of our divisions are making better progress than others. But we will stay the course, and we will succeed.

12   I believe companies that come to recognize the aptitude and competence available to them in the emerging crop of women and minorities are sure to prosper. Their female and minority employees will move ahead and broaden opportunities for all who follow their lead. These businesses will greet the challenges of the coming century with a strong and capable work force equipped to meet its challenges.

About the Author

Ketelsen is chairman and chief executive officer of Tenneco, a Houston-based diversified industrial company which is the city's largest public corporation.

Index

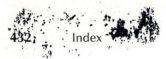